An African American Dilemma

An African American Dilemma

A History of School Integration and
Civil Rights in the North

ZOË BURKHOLDER

OXFORD
UNIVERSITY PRESS

OXFORD
UNIVERSITY PRESS

Oxford University Press is a department of the University of Oxford. It furthers the University's objective of excellence in research, scholarship, and education by publishing worldwide. Oxford is a registered trade mark of Oxford University Press in the UK and certain other countries.

Published in the United States of America by Oxford University Press 198 Madison Avenue, New York, NY 10016, United States of America.

© Oxford University Press 2021

Library of Congress Cataloging-in-Publication Data
Names: Burkholder, Zoë, author.
Title: An African American dilemma : a history of school integration and civil rights in the North / Zoë Burkholder.
Description: New York, NY : Oxford University Press, 2021. |
Includes index. |
Identifiers: LCCN 2020049213 (print) | LCCN 2020049214 (ebook) |
ISBN 9780190605131 (hardback) | ISBN 9780190605155 (epub) |
ISBN 9780190605162
Subjects: LCSH: School integration—Northeastern States—History. |
African American schools—Northeastern States—History. |
Public schools—Northeastern States—History. |
Segregation in education—Northeastern States—History. |
African Americans—Education—Northeastern States—History. |
African Americans—Civil rights—Northeastern States—History.
Classification: LCC LC214.22.N67 B87 2021 (print) |
LCC LC214.22.N67 (ebook) | DDC 379.2/630974—dc23
LC record available at https://lccn.loc.gov/2020049213
LC ebook record available at https://lccn.loc.gov/2020049214

DOI: 10.1093/oso/9780190605131.001.0001

1 3 5 7 9 8 6 4 2

Printed by Sheridan Books, Inc., United States of America

To
Christopher N. Matthews

The tripartite—discrimination, prejudice, and segregation—is embedded in the matrix of American customs and mores on one hand, and is in conflict with the democratic ideals of our society on the other hand, resulting in what Gunnar Myrdal describes as the "American Dilemma."
—Urban League of Philadelphia, 1963

CONTENTS

ACKNOWLEDGMENTS

Researching and writing this book was a long and collaborative project supported by a research grant on education from the Spencer Foundation and a sabbatical from Montclair State University. Susan Ferber at Oxford University Press is the most brilliant and gifted editor on the planet and I would like to thank her for her patience, understanding, and help over the past few years as this book came together. It is my honor to acknowledge the generous encouragement, constructive criticism, and unfailing support of friends, family, and colleagues who have helped me along the way.

I owe debts of gratitude to many of my colleagues in history and education. Jon Zimmerman was an early fan of this project, and he offered guidance on every aspect of this book, from writing grant applications to revising chapters. Thank you, Jon, for pushing me to think more carefully about how African American debates over school integration diverged from larger discourses on integration versus separation. Jim Fraser is a longtime supporter of my work. He was kind enough to invite me to be a visiting scholar at New York University's Department of Applied Statistics, Social Science, and Humanities, where I had access to the wonders of the Bobst Library, including spectacular online databases and the rich collections of the Tamiment Library and Robert F. Wagner Labor Archives. Natalia Mehlman Petrzela co-hosted the history of education writing group with me at NYU, where I benefited from robust intellectual exchange on a wide range of topics relating to racial justice and public education with her and some of the best scholars in the world. Diana D'Amico Pawlewicz, Jonna Perrillo, Victoria Cain, Leah Gordon, Michelle Purdy, Barbara Beatty, Nancy Beadie, Michael Glass, Ansley Erickson, Lauren Lefty, Jack Dougherty, James Anderson, Judith Kafka, David García, Hilary Moss, Crystal Sanders, Joan Malczewski, Lisa Stulberg, Jon Hale, Alex Hyres, Ethan Hutt, John Rury, Robert Cotto, Jr., and Derrick Alridge were among the many fantastic colleagues in the history of education who pushed me to think more critically about school integration and Black educational activism in the North, and I am grateful for their critical engagement with different aspects of my research. A special thanks to Patrick Jones, Zebulon Miletsky, Walter Greason, and Constance Diggs for meaningful discussions at the Association for the Study of African American Life and History conference in Charleston. Michelle Purdy and Rachel Devlin will forever have my gratitude for their critical feedback on drafts. A special acknowledgment goes to the anonymous reviewers who read drafts of this manuscript very carefully and provided excellent suggestions for how to improve it.

My education in race-making and law-making in the long civil rights movement came directly out of a fellowship at the Charles Warren Center for Studies in American History at Harvard University, led by the indefatigable Evelyn Brooks Higginbotham and Kenneth Mack. Conversations with Rachel Devlin, Peniel Joseph, Tom Guglielmo, Matthew Countryman, Kevin Mumford, Scott Kurashige, and Clarissa Atkinson helped me begin to understand the complexity and nuances of the long Black freedom struggle.

Colleagues at Montclair State University have provided enthusiastic support for my teaching and scholarship in the history of education. Particular thanks to Dean Tamara Lucas of the College of Education and Human Services who insists that critical educational scholarship can help Americans address racial inequalities in public education today, as well as Jaime Grinberg, Helenrose Fives, Liz Rivera Rodas, Pablo Tinio, Nicole Barnes, Jamaal Matthews, Maughn Gregory, Alina Reznitskaya, Monica Taylor, Eric Weiner, Kathryn Herr, David Kennedy, Mark Weinstein, and Maria Cioè Peña for their collegiality in the Department of Educational Foundations. Brenda Godbolt ensures that we all get to work in a beautifully functioning and well-organized office. Colleagues in other departments have indulged me in long conversations on the subject of school desegregation and racial justice in the North including Leslie Wilson, Jennifer Robinson, Danné Davis, Rachel Garver, and Kate Temoney. Graduate assistants in the Department of Educational Foundations including Ryan Herrmann, Dror Nawrocki, Chae Yoon Kim (Amy), Molly Kosch, Grady Eric Anderson, Joe DiGiacomo, David Herren, and Arthur Schmidt offered invaluable assistance tracking down references in the library, locating sources online, and preparing notes and annotated bibliographies that were essential to this research.

This book would not have happened without the eager assistance provided by librarians and archivists who helped me uncover crucial sources. At Montclair State University, Denise O'Shea, Eduardo Gil, Darren Sweeper, and Kevin Prendergast truly went above and beyond to make sure I had access to every single book, journal article, and government report that I needed. I visited a great number of archives and special collections, and still others worked with me remotely to provide resources. I'd like to acknowledge the extraordinary contributions of archivists at these institutions, including the Schomburg Center for Research in Black Culture at the New York Public Library, the Moorland-Spingarn Research Center at Howard University, the Manuscript Division of the Library of Congress, Charles L. Blockson Afro-American Collection at Temple University, Urban Archives at Temple University, Tamiment Library and Robert F. Wagner Labor Archives at New York University, Charles F. Cummings New Jersey Information Center at the Newark Public Library, Newark Public Schools Archive, New York City Municipal Archives, New Jersey State Archives, the William H. Smith Memorial Library at the Indiana Historical Society, Massachusetts Historical Society, Historical Society of Pennsylvania, Boston Public Library, Chicago Public Library, Philadelphia Public Library, the Local History Collection at the Montclair Public Library, Northeastern University Archives and Special Collections, Archives of Labor and Urban Affairs at Walter P. Reuther Library at Wayne State University, Rare and Manuscript Collections at Cornell University, Beinecke Rare Book and Manuscript Library at Yale University, and Special Collections Research Center at George Washington University.

Christina Miesowitz Burkholder, Ervin Burkholder, and Tai Burkholder have provided moral and material support as well as hot meals, childcare, and unwavering faith in my scholarship. A special thanks to Dex Matthews and Hollis Matthews for their unconditional love, constant support, and generous encouragement.

Christopher N. Matthews is an anthropologist and historical archaeologist whose research investigates the lived experiences of African Americans and Native Americans in the Northeast. He believes scholarship on the past can help remedy racial injustice today, and I am inspired by his impressive record as an anti-racist scholar and activist. He helped me puzzle through some of the most challenging aspects in the research, analysis, and writing of this book, while also performing the herculean tasks of everyday life it takes to raise a family. This book is dedicated to Chris Matthews, with love.

An African American Dilemma

Introduction

Above the Delaware River in New Jersey sits a red brick mansion cloaked in verdant ivy. For the first half of the twentieth century it sat as the centerpiece of a sprawling 300-hundred-acre boarding school that included boys' and girls' dormitories, an amphitheater, a gymnasium with hardwood floors, an auditorium, a chapel, athletic fields, tennis courts, and a vocational trades building. Those lucky enough to visit the school would have seen dozens of well-groomed students strolling paths shaded by sprawling oak, maple, and sycamore trees. Faculty and school administrators would have been there too, dressed in the fashions of the day, perhaps even playing croquet with the students on the lawn. Luminaries such as Booker T. Washington, W. E. B. Du Bois, Mary McLeod Bethune, Paul Robeson, and Albert Einstein dropped in to observe the school's unique blend of academic and vocational learning. Following a trip there in the summer of 1942, First Lady Eleanor Roosevelt described it as "a really beautiful site. The big trees shade the lawns and buildings as you look straight down the Delaware River."[1]

Founded in 1886, the Bordentown Manual and Industrial Training School for Colored Youth was a public boarding school led by Black faculty and administrators and serving an all-Black student body. Designed on the model of "manual training and industrial" education for Black students in the post-Reconstruction South, the Bordentown School developed a more progressive approach under the leadership of Harvard-educated Dr. William Valentine. Black families throughout New Jersey and nearby Pennsylvania lauded the school's strong academics, sensible vocational training, commitment to racial uplift, and appealing extracurricular options.[2]

And yet, the Bordentown School's reputation as the "Tuskegee of the North" was not enough to save it after *Brown v. Board of Education* prohibited racial segregation in public schools in 1954. Declaring "the institution is a segregated school in its practical operation," New Jersey Governor Robert B. Meyner insisted the Bordentown School had to be closed.[3]

Figure I.1. The Administration Building at the Bordentown Manual Training and Industrial School for Colored Youth, c. 1950. Courtesy of the New Jersey State Archives, Department of State, Trenton, NJ.

Home economics teacher Eleanor Smythwick was one of dozens of Black educational activists who begged the state to keep the school open on a non-racial basis, writing, "The Manual Training School has offered shelter, activity, and opportunity to many a youth . . . that makes real the meaning of a democratic society. Has such a program outgrown its usefulness in and to the State of New Jersey?" Black students, parents, alumni, and teachers viewed the Bordentown School as a sanctuary dedicated to Black education and racial uplift. They could not fathom how a decision meant to outlaw segregation in the Jim Crow South required the shuttering of a cherished institution in the North.[4]

Not all Black northerners, as it turns out, agreed that the Bordentown School should be saved. Civil rights activists associated with the National Association for the Advancement of Colored People (NAACP) and the National Urban League quietly agreed it should be closed. They had fought to integrate the school and modernize the curriculum since World War II; but little had changed, and they believed the school's manual training and industrial approach was anachronistic.

Figure I.2. Students playing croquet at the Bordentown Manual Training and Industrial School for Colored Youth, c. 1930. Courtesy of the New Jersey State Archives, Department of State, Trenton, NJ.

More important, they vehemently objected to the existence of a "colored" school in the North. Civil rights activists insisted it was better for Bordentown students to go home and attend local public schools on an integrated basis. The closure was worth it, they reasoned, to advance school integration and the broader civil rights movement in the North. Following a two-day public hearing, the New Jersey State legislature voted to withhold funding for the school's operation, which effectively led to its closure.[5]

The bitter controversy over the closing of Bordentown School illustrates the central theme of this book: debates in northern Black communities over which would better serve the larger freedom struggle—school integration or separate, Black-controlled schools. Black support for separate schools was not new in 1955 when Black citizens opposed the closing of the Bordentown School, nor in 1935 when W. E. B. Du Bois stunned the civil rights community by answering the question, "Does the Negro need separate schools?" in the affirmative. As this book details, the question of which would better serve the northern civil rights movement—racially integrated or separate, Black-controlled schools—stretches back to school integration battles in Boston in the 1840s and forward to arguments over Afrocentric charter schools today.

An African American Dilemma offers a social history of northern Black debates over school integration from the 1840s to the present. While African Americans have experimented with myriad strategies to equalize public education, perennial debates over school integration versus separation merit special scholarly attention. School integration seeks to break down the insidious effects of residential segregation created by decades of redlining, housing discrimination, white flight, gentrification, and discriminatory zoning by deliberately engineering diverse schools, typically by busing students out of their racially homogenous neighborhoods. Separation requires these very plans to be dismantled so that Black parents can have control over local, majority-Black schools in their immediate neighborhoods. Although it is not impossible, it is very difficult to pursue both strategies at the same time. To date, neither has been entirely successful, yet both ideals—integration and separation—reappear with each new generation of students, parents, educators, and leaders who insist that quality public schools will improve Black students' life chances, empower Black communities, and begin to redress larger racial inequalities in American society. By chronicling the long history of these debates including when and where they occurred, who was on each side and why, and how they were resolved, this book seeks to shed light on the complex relationship between Black educational activism, school integration, and the larger civil rights movement.

This sweeping geographical and temporal framework reveals new patterns in Black educational activism that revise our understanding of the history of school integration in the North. Much of the scholarship on the history of African American education has focused on the South, where the vast majority of African Americans lived before the first and second Great Migrations of the twentieth century. This important work explores how and why whites tried to prohibit people of African descent from gaining an education and how they intended school segregation to be a potent tool of racial oppression. It also details how Black educational activists fought tirelessly to educate themselves, build and support schools for Black youth, ensure jobs for Black teachers and principals, and secure adequate public funding and support for racially restricted schools. In the mid-twentieth century, southern Black educational activism centered on school desegregation as a way to dislodge Jim Crow discrimination and advocate sweeping civil rights reform. Historians have explored how school desegregation unfolded in different southern towns and cities, the role of Black women and teachers in the long struggle for educational equality, and the tangible improvements that school desegregation brought in terms of access to resources, educational opportunities, and Black academic achievement. Scholars also acknowledge the substantial burdens that school desegregation placed on southern Black communities, especially the loss of beloved Black-controlled schools and thousands of teaching and administrative jobs for Black educators, and the harmful dismantling of school desegregation plans since the late-1980s.[6]

Other scholars have turned north, where the history of African American education looks very different given the earlier creation of public schools, the initially smaller population of Black citizens, state laws prohibiting school segregation, and the exponential growth of northern Black communities in the twentieth century. The majority of this scholarship focuses on a specific community, typically a large city where civil rights activists organized petitions, boycotts, marches, and lawsuits as early as the 1840s. Thanks to this excellent work we know more about how Black communities organized to challenge school segregation and inequality; the ways that educational activism informed Black political protest; Black experiences in independent schools; Black struggles for community control and self-determination; how whites used restrictive real estate practices and gerrymandered school assignments to increase school segregation; northern white resistance to school integration; the gradual reversal of court-ordered desegregation plans; and the role of white women, the media, and conservative political associations in discrediting school integration as a viable reform.[7]

One central message from scholarship in both the South and the North is that meaningful school integration has rarely been achieved in the United States due to institutionalized educational racism and persistent white resistance. As such, claims that the United States tried school integration and that it did not work are both inaccurate and misleading. This finding serves as an essential corrective, yet scholars still struggle to explain the relationship between the history of Black struggles for school integration and the long civil rights movement.[8]

An African American Dilemma amplifies the existing scholarship on the history of African American education and uses it to construct a new analytical framework that looks for patterns of Black educational activism across the North from the beginning of public education to the present day. The North is an imagined landscape as much as a physical one; a place that has long been associated with freedom and opportunity for African Americans. This study focuses specifically on communities north of the Mason-Dixon line and east of the Mississippi River where the largest Black communities developed over the course of the first and second Great Migrations. The states of New Jersey, New York, Pennsylvania, Ohio, Indiana, Illinois, Michigan, Connecticut, and Massachusetts feature prominently because these states had large, diverse, and politically active Black communities. Occasionally, examples from farther West appear when these communities featured major school desegregation lawsuits with regional implications. Most northern states outlawed school segregation in the late nineteenth century, which created more time and space for Black educational activists to experiment with school integration strategies than in the South, where school desegregation did not begin in earnest until 1964. The North offers the opportunity to analyze how Black educational activists have conceived of and used school integration since the founding of free, tax-supported public schools and how and why others have rejected this approach in favor of separate, Black-controlled schools.

An African American Dilemma considers not only large cities with famously bitter school desegregation battles but also suburbs and rural towns where smaller Black communities—or occasionally a single Black family—made a valiant stand against educational racism. It places dozens of small, medium, and large battles for Black educational equality into a larger context, in the process uncovering previously unknown connections between them, or sometimes, the stark differences and inconsistencies that defined them. For example, it was not uncommon for one Black community to launch a highly publicized campaign for school integration in the early twentieth century while a neighboring town quietly supported separate, Black-controlled schools. In other cases, Black men and women would support school integration one year and separation the next in response to rapidly evolving social and political contexts. This study acknowledges the hard and important work of Black northerners who fought for school integration and the equally challenging and essential work of those who supported separate, Black-controlled institutions. Both forms of activism transformed educational history for the better by rejecting white supremacy and insisting on the inherent dignity and worth of Black children and the central role of public education in the Black freedom struggle.

The central finding of this book is that either school integration or separation dominated the political discourse of northern Black educational activists during particular historical eras. During each period, a chorus of dissent, debate, and counter-narratives pushed Black communities to consider a fuller range of educational reform. The dynamic contours of these debates, as well as how they fit into the larger political and intellectual projects of racial justice, reveal new insights into how African Americans have viewed public education as central to the struggle for freedom and how school integration has played a distinct, but malleable, role in this effort. [9]

Telling this history requires a clarification of key terms. The Black educational activists featured in this book include not only professionals who worked for major civil rights organizations like the NAACP and the Urban League but also Black parents, teachers, school principals, scholars, ministers, adolescents, and children who chose to speak out or take action in support of either racially integrated or separate schools. Many of these Black educational activists did not see themselves as civil rights activists; in fact, some rejected the strategies and goals of the NAACP and Urban League. Their work had real meaning and lasting influence, however, and collectively, Black students, parents, and community members participated in political activism when they advocated for either school integration or separation. Black educational activists were united in their belief that schools offered a powerful tool for racial uplift, liberation, economic advancement, and social justice, but they were divided over whether school integration was the best strategy to achieve these goals.

The terms "integration" and "desegregation" also require elaboration, as even scholars and civil rights activists do not agree on their precise meanings. This book employs historian Kevin K. Gaines's distinction between desegregation as the dismantling of state-sponsored racial segregation and integration as deliberate racial mixing. Gaines defines "integration" as "the demise of separate Black institutions" and "desegregation" as "the overthrow of the regime of racial subjugation defined by the exclusion of Black people 'from access to power, wealth, education, status and dignity.' " This framing recognizes that autonomous Black institutions, such as all-Black schools, did not necessarily represent a rejection of integration but rather employed separateness to overcome its effects in order to pursue the ultimate goal of desegregation.[10]

Based on these definitions, northern Black support for school desegregation, or the removal of racial classifications in school assignments, was unwavering and universal. However, this does not mean that Black northerners always embraced school integration—which required breaking apart majority or all-Black schools in order to create racially mixed ones. Many Black northerners preferred the option of separate schools with Black faculty. As such, separation is a distinct concept from segregation. Swedish economist Gunnar Myrdal wrote that "one deep idea behind segregation is that of quarantining what is evil, shameful, and feared in society." Segregation is a form of violence against Black Americans, while separation represents a voluntary project of Black institution-building intended to promote racial uplift and the affirmation of Black identities.[11]

While the Black civil rights movement achieved so many righteous victories in the twentieth century, it also suffered terrible defeats. The failure to equalize public education for Black students is among the most troubling of these losses. According to the Civil Rights Project at the University of California, Los Angeles, racial segregation in American public schools has been increasing nationwide since the late 1980s. Multiple studies have documented that "majority minority" schools tend to have fewer resources and significantly lower levels of academic achievement as measured by student test scores, dropout rates, graduation rates, and numbers of advanced and AP classes. American public schools are becoming more segregated by race and socioeconomic class each year, which correlates directly with unequal educational opportunities and outcomes. Many of the nation's most segregated schools today can be found not in the South but in the supposedly progressive North.[12]

Unlike public transportation, parks, restaurants, movie theaters, and even hospitals, which were successfully desegregated, schools are intended to offer a route out of poverty and to serve as an equalizing mechanism in a deeply unequal social order. In the United States, access to a quality public school provides every child, no matter the status of his or her birth, with a shot at achieving the American Dream. Thus, equalizing access to public education represents one of the most pressing, unfinished agendas of the Black civil rights movement and a crucial site of analysis for scholars.[13]

The title of this book offers a deliberate nod to one of the most renowned studies of the twentieth century. In 1944 Gunnar Myrdal published his groundbreaking analysis of American race relations, *An American Dilemma: The Negro Problem and Modern Democracy*, in which he famously argued that the so-called Negro Problem was really a problem of white racism. Myrdal claimed that Americans faced a gripping dilemma caused by the inherent tension between widespread faith in democracy and equal opportunity, on one hand, and explicit racial discrimination against African Americans, on the other. He was among the first white scholars to treat anti-Black racism as a moral conundrum and a profound political crisis.[14]

Just as Myrdal identified white racism as the source of the "Negro Problem" and the American Dilemma it created, this book emphasizes white racism as the cause of the African American dilemma, or the question of whether school integration or separation provides the best route to equality and justice. The resulting debates remain unresolved precisely because northern whites continue to discriminate against students of color in public schools.

School integration can help equalize educational opportunity and advance the civic function of public education in a democracy. But it is not a simple undertaking, and as the following chapters demonstrate, Black educational activists have long disagreed over whether integration is the best strategy to achieve a structural vision of educational equality and redistributive justice. Meaningful school integration requires a frank reckoning with how institutionalized racism has long discriminated against Black students and parents in ways that harm Black students and create vastly unequal educational opportunities. To that end, Black students benefit from many of the features historically associated with separate schools, including working with a cohort of Black students, studying with Black teachers, and learning about African American history, art, literature, culture, human rights, and social justice in an encouraging environment. Black students must learn in classrooms free of stereotyping and racial bias that are governed by fair administrative procedures including class placement and student discipline. Parent Teacher Associations, fundraising, school clubs, field trips, and extracurricular activities must be open to all on equal terms in ways that recognize and limit the corrosive effects of white and middle-class privilege. If computers and high-speed internet in every home are essential to student success, then administrators are responsible for ensuring that all public-school students have access to the technology they need to succeed. School integration that falls short of these goals cannot equalize educational opportunities or advance the larger goals of the Black civil rights movement.[15]

In other words, mixing Black and white students inside of formerly white schools is not a viable model for meaningful school integration. Generations of Black educational activists have supported separate schools as institutions that nurture the intellectual and emotional growth of Black youth while empowering Black communities. The argument for separate schools has always contained within it a vital critique of majority white schools as hegemonic institutions that fail to meet the needs of Black students and, consequently, fail to meet the larger purpose of public education in a democracy. This history of northern Black debates over school integration versus separation offers powerful lessons on the insidious nature of institutionalized racism, the potent agency of Black educational activists, and the liberatory potential of public education.

Chapter 1, "Caste Abolished: Integration for Freedom, 1840–1900," examines the earliest debates over school integration versus separation in Boston, Rochester, Cincinnati, Jamaica, New York, and a number of smaller towns. It argues that Black northerners viewed integrated public schools as essential to abolishing slavery, securing Black citizenship, and eliminating racial prejudice. For abolitionists and Black leaders, as well as many families, the symbolic ideal of school integration took precedence over concerns about the quality of education available to Black youth. In contrast, many Black families and teachers prioritized access to high-quality education over symbolic political objectives. Faced with outspoken and even violent white opposition to Black education, these activists supported separate schools where they believed Black youth would thrive. The ensuing debates between Black integrationists and separatists were intimately tied to the abolitionist movement, Civil War, Reconstruction, and the rise of Jim Crow. By the turn of the twentieth century, Black northerners had won the right to attend public school on an equal and integrated basis, yet they struggled against a rising tide of bigotry and residential segregation.

Chapter 2, "The Education that Is Their Due: Separation for Racial Uplift, 1900–1940," identifies a distinct uptick in northern Black support for separate schools. The rise of scientific racism fueled anti-Black discrimination that accelerated alongside the first Great Migration and the Great Depression. Hostile whites segregated classrooms and buildings in open defiance of state law as Black populations increased. At the same time, there is compelling evidence from Pennsylvania, New Jersey, New York, Ohio, Indiana, Illinois, and Michigan that Black families either passively accepted or actively requested separate classrooms and schools in order to access Black teachers. Faced with intense discrimination, many Black northerners, like those in Philadelphia, believed separate schools would offer a higher quality education and more of the teaching and administrative jobs that sustained the Black middle class. Still, this position was far from universal, and many northern Black communities energetically resisted school segregation. A growing number of Black intellectuals and civil rights activists vehemently objected to any form of state-sponsored segregation and campaigned actively for school integration.

Chapter 3, "A Powerful Weapon: Integration for Equality, 1940–1965," highlights an enormous resurgence of northern Black support for school integration alongside the expanding civil rights movement. The outbreak of World War II created economic opportunities that drew Black migrants North in a second wave and sparked more militant civil rights activism. African Americans in the North interpreted separate schools as symptomatic of an older generation's tendency to accommodate, rather than confront, racial inequality. NAACP leaders persuaded northern Black communities to reject school segregation. By citing anti-discrimination legislation and organizing petitions and boycotts, these activists won the formal desegregation of public schools in the North between 1940 and 1954. A new generation of social scientists overturned the science of white supremacy, and cutting-edge research in psychology insisted that interracial contact between young people was the most effective way to reduce prejudice. This potent combination of political organizing, civil rights activism, the decline of scientific racism, and the emergence of the Cold War pushed school integration to the forefront of national politics. When the US Supreme Court ruled separate educational facilities were inherently unequal in 1954, northern Blacks pressed schools to integrate. The process was contentious, especially when school districts closed Black schools and fired Black teachers in the name of integration, as they did at the Bordentown School in 1955. Many Black families, like those in Chicago, were frustrated by the shortcomings of school desegregation plans that were unable to overcome state-sponsored residential segregation. By 1965, many Black northerners expressed frustration with the politics of school integration and what they viewed as its failure to improve the quality of education for Black youth.

Chapter 4, "A Conflict in the Community: Separation for Black Power, 1966–1974," charts the most contested phase of Black educational activism in the North as support for Black-controlled schools expanded alongside the Black Power movement, even as court-ordered school desegregation expanded across the urban North. "Community control" activists, like those in New York City and Newark, New Jersey, saw a revitalized form of school separation as a rational response to what they viewed as the dismal failure of integration. They called for community control over administration, curriculum, pedagogy, student discipline, and teacher hiring in majority Black schools and called for desegregation plans to be halted. Student activists demanded Black history courses, fairer discipline and dress code policies, more respect for Black culture, and even the option of all-Black facilities and extracurricular activities. Not everyone agreed with this renewed vision of autonomous Black institution-building, especially an older generation of civil rights warriors and those in communities working to expand existing school desegregation plans. Although briefly appealing, community control and Afrocentric curricula did not successfully equalize public education and receded in the early 1970s.

Chapter 5, "An Armageddon of Righteousness: Integration for Justice, 1975–Present," documents how northern Black educational activists created a new and transformative vision of school integration that blended Black nationalist ideals of self-determination with the goal of racially diverse and inclusive schools. This was a delicate endeavor, as integrationists had to navigate a political context that included an increasingly conservative US Supreme Court and vocal white resistance to what was inaccurately portrayed as "forced busing." Black educational activists maintained that for all of its challenges, integration was the single most effective way to guarantee equal school financing, qualified teachers, advanced courses, adequate facilities, and a robust set of curricular choices including academic and vocational options for Black students. Social scientists claimed that school integration created more socioeconomic diversity by giving Black students greater access to social networks that fostered college and career opportunities. This chapter considers two districts where Black educational activists successfully fought for and won integrated schools: the suburban town of Montclair, New Jersey, and the city of Hartford, Connecticut. It also locates strong support for separatism in the form of Afrocentric public schools, which became popular again in the early 1990s and survive as charter schools in select cities into the twenty-first century. Meanwhile, the 2007 US Supreme Court ruling in *Parents Involved in Community Schools v. Seattle* sharply curtailed, but did not prohibit, school desegregation plans. The struggle for northern school integration remains in flux and unresolved—but many Black educational activists continue to advocate for schools that are racially diverse and committed to nurturing and affirming Black identities in institutions with explicit restorative justice frameworks.

The book concludes with a consideration of how northern Black debates over school integration versus separation transformed the Black civil rights movement. Black northerners who participated in acts of educational protest challenged institutionalized racism in American schools and enacted lasting, substantial improvements. They organized grassroots movements that demanded specific reforms in local public institutions, in the process mobilizing Black northerners to become involved in local, state, and national politics. The inherent tensions between school integrationists and separatists created a dynamic, evolving grassroots movement for Black educational reform that insists on racial justice in public education and moves Americans closer to the meaningful reforms that will create equitable and high-quality public schools for all.

In the popular imagination, school integrationists and separatists stood on opposite sides of an intellectual chasm that could not be breached through moral persuasion or political compromise. On one side stood traditional civil rights warriors who believed school integration offered the best way to secure equality and civil rights, and on the other stood black nationalists who insisted that only separate, Black-controlled institutions could fortify Black youth for the coming revolution. This framing, however, is overly simplistic and ignores the ways that Black educational activists on either side overlapped and intersected with one another, ultimately transforming Black educational reform and mobilizing tens of thousands of African Americans to fight for more democratic public schools. The stories in this book offer the opportunity to consider not only the extraordinary range of Black educational activism in the North stretching back to the common school movement and forward to the present, but also how this work—much of it carried out by women and children—inspired the larger civil rights movement and created substantially more equal and equitable public schools.

Caste Abolished

Integration for Freedom, 1840–1900

In March 1859, abolitionist Frederick Douglass dared to ask which was more important to the Black freedom struggle: the ballot or the book. His answer was the book, in the form of equal access to the newly formed system of tax-supported common schools. "There are 13,675 colored men above 21 years of age in the State of New York, while there are 15,778 colored children of school-going age. Contact on equal terms is the best means to abolish caste: *it is caste abolished*," Douglass emphasized in his newspaper, *Douglass' Monthly*. He was especially interested in the socializing aspect of schools, noting, "With Equal Suffrage, 13,675 Black men come in contact on equal terms, for ten minutes once a year, at the polls; with equal school rights, 15,778 colored children and youth come in contact on equal terms with white children and youth, three hundred days in the year, and from six to ten hours each day. And these children, in a few years, become the people of the State." Douglass reasoned that integrated schooling was an effective antidote to racial prejudice. If the goal was to end the arbitrary and unjust discrimination against African Americans, Douglass concluded, "The nature of the contact, as a caste abolisher, is altogether in favor of the school contact." For educational activists like Douglass, equal school rights created the necessary conditions for universal suffrage and full civil rights by establishing Black racial equality, which could only be accomplished if caste, and separate "caste schools," were abolished.[1]

Between 1840 and 1900, the struggle for "equal school rights," or access to racially integrated schools, became a defining feature of northern Black political protest. At the same time, many Black students, parents, ministers, and teachers held fast to the idea that separate schools offered unique benefits unlikely to be found in mixed schools. Northern Black communities struggled to determine which of these two strategies—school integration or separate, Black-controlled schools—offered the best way to secure freedom and equal civil rights.

This quandary was further complicated by the fact that Americans viewed early common schools as citizenship training institutions, while the question of Black citizenship was unresolved until 1868. Many African Americans believed attending public schools on an equal and integrated basis would fortify their citizenship claims. The same idea occurred to white northerners, which is precisely why so many fought to keep Black students out of the public schools. Separate schools offered a potential compromise, but over time they drew criticism from Black educational activists who viewed separate schools as discriminatory. Northern Black debates over school integration were not static through this long period, nor were they fully resolved. Instead these debates evolved in response to local and national politics and flared up through Emancipation and again as Jim Crow inched inexorably North.

This chapter contextualizes African American debates over school integration within the larger effort to create a system of free public schools in the North. It then analyzes some of the most spectacular confrontations between Black integrationists and separatists in Boston, Massachusetts; Cincinnati, Ohio; and Rochester and Jamaica, New York, recorded in local school board records, the white and nascent Black presses, and occasionally in court documents as Black families sued for the right to attend integrated schools. Both integrationists and separatists, who advocated diametrically opposed strategies, viewed public education as vital to the Black freedom struggle and made contributions to the early Black civil rights movement in the North. In the process, they transformed the landscape of public education in the North and affected the ability of Black families to access equal educational opportunities in the new public schools.

The Struggle for Equal School Rights

From the 1820s through the end of the Civil War in 1865, elite white reformers advocated tax-supported "common schools" to prepare an increasingly diverse population for democratic citizenship. Black students, however, faced stark discrimination at the hands of local school boards. "We are naturally led to suppose that the farther north we travel, the less prejudice we have to encounter. Mistaken idea!" proclaimed one disappointed Black writer in 1827. Noting that African American children were either segregated in inferior facilities or excluded from the public schools throughout the North, he concluded, "From this want of education has arisen the idea of 'African inferiority,' among many, who will not take the trouble to enquire into the cause." Like other Black educational activists of his era, this writer insisted that only proper education could raise the social and economic prospects of free Blacks, elevating them to full citizenship.

Throughout the North, abolitionists pursued twin goals of abolishing slavery and establishing schools for free Blacks.[2]

As a body of Black protest thought about public education evolved during the antebellum, Civil War, and Reconstruction eras, integrated schools came to represent access to deeply cherished political objectives associated with freedom, including full citizenship, equal civil rights, cultural assimilation, economic opportunities, and social equality. School integration, or the struggle for equal school rights, was a profoundly patriotic movement, as northern Blacks sought to take their rightful place as American citizens.[3]

The same period witnessed the rise of scientific racism that insisted humans could be divided by innate, biological differences. According to the scientific theory of polygenism, human races represented distinct species that did not share a common ancestor. Individuals of each race supposedly possessed innate capacities for intelligence, character, and temperament that were unchangeable. Since race and heredity were fixed traits, an individual could not be improved through education or any change in social environment. As such, race scientists cautioned that "miscegenation," or racial mixing, posed a dire threat to "white" civilization. These scientific theories emerged alongside the growing abolitionist movement and, later, Emancipation. While free Blacks and some white allies argued that freedpeople should be integrated as equals into the body politic,

Figure 1.1. "Turned Away from School," *Anti-Slavery Almanac*, 1839. Division of Rare and Manuscript Collections, Cornell University Library, Ithaca, NY.

many whites cited racialist science to argue that Blacks were innately inferior, could not be improved through education or assimilation, and as a result must be excluded from social and political institutions.[4]

In this anxious political climate, many white Americans forcefully objected to Black efforts to secure equal educational opportunities, especially in integrated schools. To exclude Black students, they argued that innate differences would make integrated schools illogical and unfeasible. For instance, when the Boston School Committee rejected a Black petition for school integration in 1846, it insisted, "Now, in the opinion of the School Committee, here is a race not only distinct in respect to color, hair, and general physiognomy, but possessing physical, mental, and moral peculiarities, which render a promiscuous intermingling in the public schools disadvantageous, both to them, and to the whites." A white newspaper in Boston concurred, fretting that Black parents were not interested in the "leveling principles" of mixed schools, as petitioners claimed, but instead hoped to attain "mixed marriages." Fears about racial mixing and "amalgamation" were not limited to the slaveholding South and created an explosive political climate for the school integration movement. Black activists who fought for abolition, equal rights, and school integration risked violent retribution from white opponents.[5]

French nobleman Alexis de Tocqueville expressed astonishment at the degree of racism he witnessed in free northern states in 1831. "In that part of the Union where the Negroes are no longer slaves, have they come closer to the whites?" he queried. "Everyone who has lived in the United States will have noticed just the opposite," he answered. "Race prejudice," he opined, "seems stronger in those states that have abolished slavery than in those where it still exists, and nowhere is it more intolerant than in those states where slavery was never known." Similarly, in his study of the Black community in Philadelphia, W. E. B. Du Bois observed, "The whole period from 1820 to 1840 became a time of retrogression for the mass of the race, and of discountenance and repression from the whites."[6]

Northern whites took dramatic steps to bar or discourage Black students from attending the public schools, even as the common school movement gained traction in the 1820s and 1830s. An abolitionist newspaper in New Jersey editorialized that Black children "are almost universally made to feel like outcasts when they enter our school houses by a coarse treatment by teacher and pupils which not only degrades them, but deprives them of the ordinary facilities of learning, and hence are unwilling to go." Some states, like Ohio, passed legislation that excluded any child "with a visible taint of African blood" from its public schools, even if segregated alternatives were unavailable. Small towns regularly declined to admit Black students to local public schools, leaving these children without any education. When Black parents tried to subvert these exclusionary laws by sending their children to private academies, northern whites responded with vigilante justice.[7]

White citizens in Canterbury, Connecticut, waged a war against Quaker teacher Prudence Crandall in 1833 because she ran a school for free girls of color. Local whites refused to sell her goods, and when that failed to stop her, they poisoned her well, arrested her, and finally set fire to her school. Crandall refused to give up. A gang of masked men armed with clubs and iron bars attacked the school in the dead of night, shattered ninety panes of glass, and battered down the door. The students fled for their lives and Crandall absconded to Illinois. Two years later, white citizens in Canaan, New Hampshire, celebrated the fourth of July by marching on the racially integrated Noyes Academy and threatening to demolish it unless its Black students left town. When they refused, a mob of 100 white citizens hitched up ninety yoke of oxen to the schoolhouse and dragged it from its foundation and dumped it in a nearby swamp.[8]

The more viciously whites protested the education of Black children, the more intrepidly northern Black parents, students, and community leaders fought for full and equal access to tax-supported public schools. Writing in 1857, Black educational activist William C. Nell reported widespread efforts to gain "equal school rights" in Rhode Island, New York, Pennsylvania, and Connecticut. He recounted the story of a young white woman in Bucks County, Pennsylvania, who "conquered the prejudices which opposed the ingress of colored pupils into her school, and she is now dispensing the dew drops of knowledge to all who seek, irrespective of accidental differences [of birth]." Wherever possible, Black educational activists worked with white allies to garner support for integrated schools. Quakers and abolitionists frequently agreed to help. "We owe it to them, as children of an oppressed race," reflected one white supporter in New York. Arguing that "free school instruction for colored children" was a moral and religious obligation, he elaborated that it was also sound public policy that would save local children from a life of ignorance and poverty.[9]

By the end of the Civil War, Black educational activists had won legal access to public schools throughout the North. Initially, most northern school districts agreed to admit Black students on the condition that they attend separate classrooms or schools. Over time, Black educational activists made more assertive demands for integration by signing petitions, attending protest meetings, delivering speeches, publishing critiques, and filing desegregation lawsuits. They boycotted public schools, sometimes for years, and educated their children at home or in protest schools until white school boards and state legislatures capitulated to their demands. What started as a trickle in antebellum New England accelerated in the 1870s and 1880s as Black northerners used their newly acquired political power to advocate equal school rights. They despised "monuments of their own degradation" and called for existing Black schools to be torn down. More than one Black school burned to the ground in a mysterious fire, set not by white citizens opposed to Black education, but by Black citizens opposed to separate schools.[10]

Perhaps it was the burning schoolhouses that gave pause to some African Americans. Writing in "defense of those who have not favored the abolition of colored schools," Thomas Paul Smith tried to persuade Blacks in Boston to pursue school desegregation, so that Black children could attend any school in the city, while also supporting separate Black schools staffed by Black teachers. He wrote, "We believe colored schools to be institutions, when properly conducted, of great advantage to the colored people. We believe society imperatively requires their existence among us." Black teacher Katie D. Chapman, among others, agreed. "I know that the stand I take upon this subject is bitterly opposed by many, but I have not yet been convinced of the fact that mixed schools are as a rule more beneficial to the Afro-American pupil than are the separate ones of the same grade and excellence," she wrote in 1888. "In the first place," asked Chapman, "is it not true that a teacher must understand his or her pupils in order to be thoroughly successful?" Even as school integration movements were achieving victories throughout the region, strong support remained for the option of separate, Black-controlled schools.[11]

The Shot Heard Round the World

Boston was the site of an early and especially spectacular battle between Black school integrationists and separatists. The struggle for equal school rights here stretched from 1840, when the Black community first petitioned for school integration, through 1855, when the state legislature outlawed racial segregation in the public schools. Although movements in Nantucket and Salem preceded it, Boston's action served as a catalyst for a powerful movement for school integration throughout the North.[12]

Like most northern cities, Boston had a tradition of separate Black schools dating back to the late eighteenth century. In 1787, Black Bostonians petitioned the state legislature for schools of their own, as they received "no benefit from the free schools." The request is notable because legally Blacks could attend the city's fledgling public schools alongside whites, although the fact that only two or three Black children did so hints at high levels of exclusion. The state legislature denied their petition, so Black activists petitioned the City of Boston in 1798 and 1800, again to no avail. Black leaders subsequently established a school with the support of white benefactors, and in 1808 they moved it into the new African Baptist Meetinghouse in the Belknap Street Church, founded and ministered by prominent Black Bostonian Thomas Paul. By 1812 the city provided modest financial support, and in 1815 a wealthy white merchant named Abiel Smith left a bequest that funded the school's expansion. As the "Smith School" grew, it was incorporated into the Boston Public Schools as the only grammar school open to Black children, and in 1835 administrators moved it into a dedicated school-house. By this time Boston had constructed three separate primary schools for Black children and taken complete control of the Smith School, firing the Black teachers and replacing them with white ones.[13]

What had begun as an attempt by Black Bostonians to gain access to public schools had morphed into a state-sponsored system of racially segregated and unequal education by 1840. Similar histories unfolded in Trenton, Philadelphia, New York, Newark, Hartford, Portland, Providence, New Haven, and Detroit as Black activists first requested separate schools and then ceded control of them to public school administrators. By this time a new generation of Black educational activists in Boston was grappling with how to address blatant inequalities amid a time of intensifying racism. School integrationists, however, imagined that racially mixed schools could accomplish far more than simply equalizing educational opportunities.[14]

Black abolitionists launched Boston's school integration movement in 1840 as part of a sweeping campaign to assert racial equality, civil rights, and full citizenship. The demise of Black voting rights was especially troubling, as several northern states began to delineate voting privileges along racial lines. Excluded from or mistreated in white social organizations and churches, Black northerners created their own. The increased visibility of Black social development and political protest, in turn, fueled white suspicion and hostility. Schools were intertwined in these anxieties as Black elites viewed education as the most effective way to cultivate Black respectability and uplift in the face of determined white oppression. Whites seethed about the fictive ignorance and supposed vice of Blacks but, paradoxically, violently opposed Black education. By 1841, towns including Providence, Portsmouth, Portland, Nantucket, and Salem sustained at least one racially segregated "African" school, while Boston, New Haven, New York, and Philadelphia supported multiple schools for "colored" students. These segregated schools reflected the increasing significance of racialist science and a growing white preference for racial apartheid. Faced with either total exclusion from the public schools or separate schools, many northern Blacks chose the latter.[15]

Boston was a hotbed of the nation's most militant form of immediate abolitionism, associated with white activist William Lloyd Garrison and his newspaper the *Liberator*, founded in Boston in 1831. Garrison and his allies rejected any plans for gradual emancipation, demanding instead immediate emancipation and full citizenship for all Blacks. Garrisonians stood in stark opposition to more moderate abolitionists who advocated gradual emancipation followed by the deportation of Black Americans to "colonize" Africa. According to colonizationists, it was better to deport freedpeople to Africa, where they could develop their own society and enlighten the native populations, than to allow them to remain in the United States where they would either live as a reviled underclass or, worse, foment revolution.[16]

Radical abolitionists working with Garrison and his friend and colleague, Frederick Douglass, refuted claims that Black racial inferiority and white prejudice stood as permanent obstacles to equal citizenship. Black abolitionists overwhelmingly supported anti-colonization efforts by organizing protest meetings and conventions such as one in New York City in 1839, where they passed numerous resolutions opposing the American Colonization Society. The nascent Black press kept up a regular harangue of the American Colonization Society, contending it fostered "vulgar, unnatural, malevolent, ferocious prejudice against the free colored population."[17]

Radical abolitionists viewed school integration as an integral component of the movement to abolish slavery, eliminate racial barriers to citizenship, and integrate freedpeople into American society. The fight against school segregation fit neatly into concurrent campaigns to remove racial restrictions on the franchise, public transportation, marriage laws, and jury service. Equal participation in schools would prove Black intellectual equality and capacity for democratic citizenship while also reducing white prejudice. According to this logic, the primary objective of school integration was not to equalize educational opportunities but instead to help secure freedom and equality for African Americans.[18]

William C. Nell was the acknowledged leader of the school integration movement in Boston, along with John T. Hilton, a dynamic member of the Massachusetts Antislavery Society. The son of a founding member of the Massachusetts General Colored Association, Nell attended Boston's separate Smith School as a youth where he suffered the insult of racial segregation firsthand. As a student, he earned one of the highest scores on a citywide examination. Nell's initial delight hardened into bitter resentment when he realized that Black students would not be honored in the same manner as whites for their academic achievement. Whereas white students received a Benjamin Franklin silver medal during a formal award dinner at Faneuil Hall, Black students received only a book and were barred from the banquet. Seething with indignation, young Nell swapped places with a friend working as a waiter at the award dinner. The chairman of the Boston School Committee, Samuel T. Armstrong, recognized Nell and called him over. "You ought to be here with the other boys," Armstrong whispered. Later that night Nell vowed, "God helping me, I would do my best to hasten the day when the color of the skin would be no barrier to equal school rights."[19]

Figure 1.2. Portrait of abolitionist William C. Nell. Collection of the Massachusetts Historical Society, Boston, MA.

In 1840 Nell submitted the first of many petitions to the Boston School Committee demanding the elimination of racial distinctions in school assignments. The School Committee ignored his request, and Nell withdrew from educational politics for a time and focused on desegregating railcars. Three years later, Nell turned again to school segregation in Boston. Once a blessing, but now considered an abomination, separate schools riled militant abolitionists and their white allies in the Massachusetts Antislavery Society, including Garrison and the orator Wendell Phillips. These white abolitionists lauded Black efforts to close separate schools in Nantucket and Salem between 1842 and 1844, encouraging Black Bostonians to protest separate schools. Black educational activists submitted new petitions in 1844 and 1845, demanding school integration in Boston and charging that the Smith Grammar School's white principal, Abner Forbes, was a cruel and ineffective teacher.[20]

At first the majority of Boston's Black community of roughly 2,000 took little notice of the abolitionist-led school integration movement. To cultivate support, Nell and Hilton emphasized the mistreatment that Black students suffered. As political pressure mounted, the Boston School Committee agreed to look into the accusations against Principal Forbes, including "cruel, unusual, severe, and unjustifiable punishment; neglect of duties of the school; loss of the confidence both of parents and pupils; and improper treatment of both." Following nearly a week of hearings, white school administrators cleared Forbes of all charges. Expressing "indignation" at the "atrocious report," Nell and Hilton organized a protest meeting and launched a school boycott.[21]

Charges that a white teacher abused Black students created titillating headlines. An angry letter to the *Boston Courier* declared that the charges against Principal Forbes represented a thinly veiled attempt to compel the School Committee to integrate the schools. As the author insisted, "the opposers of Mr. Forbes have been heard to confess that their plan, AMALGAMATION, can only be effected by abolishing the Smith school, and this can only be done by the removal of Forbes. I think there is no mistake in this matter, and all the citizens have to do is say whether they are ready for the main question, *amalgamation*." An article published in the *Olive Branch* observed, "There is as much propriety in negroes marrying with the orang outang, as in the matrimonial amalgamation of the Saxon and Negro races, and the motely schools proposed are the forerunners and producers of such amalgamation. Let, then, such mixing be avoided in our cities, where it can easily be done. Give the negro liberty, but keep him in his place."[22]

Such venomous attacks raised the stakes of the school integration campaign for Black Bostonians, as did an 1845 Boston School Committee report that labeled the Smith School "unsatisfactory" and "in deplorable condition." Observers visiting the school noted, "The attainment of the scholars are of the lowest grade; a few can read aloud from the class reader, but cannot understand any other than the simplest passages." The report confirmed that a number of Black families had withdrawn their children from the school over the past year, and others had moved to nearby towns with integrated public schools.[23]

With renewed vigor and mounting popular support Black educational activists submitted another petition on February 6, 1846, to the Boston School Committee signed by eighty-six parents and guardians of children in the "colored" schools. Noting that "the establishment of exclusive schools for our children is a great injury to us, and deprives us of those equal privileges and advantages in the public schools to which we are entitled as citizens," the petitioners asked "that such exclusive schools be abolished, and that our children be allowed to attend the Primary Schools established in the respective Districts in which we live." Observing that the racial segregation of children was "unlawful," the petition added that separate schools cost more and accomplished less than integrated ones. It added, "All experience teaches that where a small and despised class are shut out from the common benefit of any public institutions of learning and confined to separate schools, few or none interest themselves about the schools, — neglect ensues, abuses creep in, the standard of scholarship degenerates, and the teachers and the scholars are soon considered and of course become an inferior class."[24]

The 1846 petition also emphasized Black abolitionists' moral objection to racial categorization and state-sponsored discrimination. Men like Nell and Hilton viewed distinctions based on skin "complexion" to be arbitrary, dangerous, un-Christian, and anti-democratic. They rejected scientific claims that skin color indicated inherent difference.[25]

The Boston School Committee picked up on this radical critique of racial theory and responded to it directly. "We have become familiar with the taunt, that it might be difficult to decide on the requisite degree of ebony which a child's pigment might possess, in order to entitle him to the distinction of a colored child." Insisting that it was not a question of "*complexion*, merely" as the petitioners contended, it retorted, "But, this is *not* the ground of distinction. It is one of *races*, not of colors, merely. The distinction is one which the All-wise Creator has seen fit to establish; and it is founded deep in the physical, mental, and moral natures of the two races. No legislation, no social customs, can efface this distinction."[26]

In addition, a separately published Minority Report revealed evidence of a crucial rift among the Boston School Committee. Penned by two white Garrisonians, Edmund Jackson and H. I. Bowditch, the 1846 Minority Report offered a scathing dissent. The authors asserted the Majority Report reflected racial prejudice of a "crushing severity" and urged the immediate elimination of separate "caste schools." Jackson and Bowditch granted that separate schools were not necessarily inferior, but nevertheless advised the School Committee to end "exclusive schools" as an act of social justice:

> One of the great merits of our system of public instruction, is, the fusion of all classes which it produces. From a childhood which shares the same bench and sports, there can hardly arise a manhood of aristocratic prejudice, or separate castes and classes. Our common school system suits our institutions, promotes the feeling of brotherhood and the habits of republican equality. To debar the colored race from these advantages, even if we still secured to them equal educational results, is a sore injustice and wrong, and is taking the surest means of perpetuating a prejudice, that should be deprecated and discountenanced by all intelligent and christian men.[27]

Black Bostonians responded to the two School Committee reports with protest meetings, resolutions, and rousing speeches. The *Liberator* published an excerpt from the Majority Report critiquing the report as filled with "flimsy yet venomous sophistries" that revealed "what weak and deluded creatures still exist in our very midst." Garrisonians dismissed the Majority Report's claim that "the distinction is one of races not colors," asking if this was so, why the "Celtic Irish," widely understood to be racially distinct from "Anglo-Saxons" were not assigned to separate schools.[28]

Although the School Committee refused to integrate the schools in 1846, every year the School Committee voted on the question, there were more votes in favor of school integration. In 1844 the vote of the Grammar School Committee was 24 to 2, in 1845 the vote of the Primary School Committee was 55 to 12; and in 1846 it was 59 to 16.[29] Despite the reassignment of Principal Forbes to a different school and the placement of a new white headmaster at the Smith School, integrationists escalated the school boycott. Average attendance at the Smith Grammar School dropped from more than 100 pupils before the boycott began in 1844, to 66 in 1848, to a low of 53 in the spring of 1849.[30]

As school integration became a defining feature of Black political protest in Boston, it spawned new questions and criticisms within the Black community. By 1849, a small but vocal group of Black separatists emerged to challenge the integrationists. Thomas Paul Smith, the nephew of a Black minister who helped establish one of the first schools for Blacks in Boston, collected 120 signatures on a petition requesting a Black teacher for the Smith School, a move designed to establish Black support for separate schools. Drawing on a venerable tradition of Black institution-building and racial uplift, Smith spoke eloquently in defense of separate schools. Outraged, the integrationists condemned Smith as a "young ambitious bigot" and accused him of fraud.[31]

In the summer of 1849, Black integrationists and separationists each submitted petitions to the Boston School Committee asking for opposing educational reforms. The integrationists collected signatures from 202 people who wanted to "ABOLISH THE SMITH SCHOOL" and assign Black children to the schools closest to their residences. They insisted they would not be satisfied with a Black teacher at the helm of the separate school, chiding, "We hail the circumstance an attempt to quiet our efforts against its dissolution." Meanwhile, the separatists submitted three counter-petitions, signed by sixty "colored clergymen and parents," twenty-three "colored citizens of Boston," and forty-two "colored boys and girls," all urging the appointment of a Black teacher for the separate Smith School. [32]

To review the matter, the School Committee convened a special subcommittee composed of Andrew Bigelow, Unitarian minister; Edward Beecher, Congregational minister; Sampson Reed, druggist; Horace Duppe, physician; and Theodore Russell, attorney. These white men granted Hilton's request for a public hearing, which resulted in more than five hours of heated debate as Black integrationists and separatists tried to persuade the special subcommittee to institute their preferred reform.[33]

Speaking on behalf of the integrationists, Hilton, Robert Morris, Charles Roberts, and Benjamin F. Roberts argued that Black Bostonians were opposed to separate schools given the "scattered state of our residences" throughout the city, which made the commute inconvenient for many families. More important, integrationists contended that "exclusive schools" were an obstacle to their "common rights" as American citizens, and that such schools created "the odious distinction of caste." Hilton observed that Boston was the only Massachusetts town to run a dual school system and flatly rejected the idea that Black families would accept separate schools under any conditions, even if they had Black teachers.[34]

In response, Smith, John H. Roberts, and Robert Wood contended that given the "existing state of public sentiment" toward Blacks, it would be "suicidal in its nature and consequences" to abandon separate schools. They further "affirmed that their abandonment would be contrary to the wishes, as well as injurious to the interests, of a large body of their own people deeply concerned (for such there are) in the cause of education, the improvement of their race, and the best welfare of their young." Smith insisted that if the colored schools were abolished, "I am confident that out of more than four hundred children in this city, between the ages of four and sixteen, who ought to attend school, and of whom a large portion would, if they had a competent teacher to their liking, not fifty would be found in all the white schools, and such is the opinion of a large majority of parents who have children to send to school." Smith added that Black Bostonians' preference for separate institutions was visible in their preference for separate churches, noting, "They do not, and will not, attend the white churches, although there is none closed against them."[35]

The special committee acknowledged the competing factions within the Black community. Bigelow, Reed, Dupree, and Beecher signed off on the Majority Report, which called for the continuation of the Smith School under a Black teacher and chided integrationists for overstating their case. "They denounce the Smith School as an insufferable grievance; calling it 'a great public nuisance;' an institution that only does evil, and evil continually. Its existence, they cry, is an 'insult' to the colored people; it creates or fosters the most odious distinctions of caste; and so vehement and concentrated is the hostility leveled against it, that it would seem to be regarded as the only bulwark of oppression left among us;— whose fall would instantly restore the enslaved to freedom, the down-trodden to independence, the blind to fullness of understanding, the weak and outcast and despised to perfect fellowship with the wise, and a position at once of dignity, an elevation, and power." The rebuke continued, belittling integrationists for daring to hope that integrated schools would break down barriers to the jury boxes, legislative halls, business opportunities, and military service. The report concluded by pointing to the existence of separate Black churches, asking, "Now, it is respectfully submitted, if there be no degradation in the worshipping together, can there be aught in a schooling together? If there be no prejudice to the colored parent on the score of caste, in the one case, should there be fear of it to the child in the other?"[36]

Russell authored a lone dissent, published as a Minority Report, suggesting the Smith School remain open as one option in an otherwise desegregated school system. The School Committee rejected Russell's compromise and authorized more than $2,000 worth of upgrades to the Smith School. It hired Black Bostonian Thomas Paul as principal in August of 1849, explaining, "It appears both natural and proper that one of their own race, of intelligence and education, will be more likely to be successful than any other."[37]

Immediately following this action, the integrationists organized a protest meeting at which Smith and Roberts asked to speak for the minority position in defense of separate schools. Hilton shot back that Smith was mistaken when he said he spoke for the minority, as white supremacists "John C. Calhoun, Henry Clay, the American Colonization Society, and the native pro-slavery community, were with him."[38] The integrationists renewed their commitment to equal school rights, promising "never to countenance one moment an exclusive school." They asked parents and students to expand the Smith School boycott while castigating Smith and "the white wire-pullers and the colored wire-pulled" and denouncing Black separatists as "evil."[39]

Calls for Smith to speak rang out in the church. Shouts of "yes, yes!" and "no, no!" and cheers echoed through the building as Roberts rose to speak on behalf of the separatists. Roberts acknowledged, "There is considerable excitement on the question among the people of color, and a difference of opinion does exist on the subject." He attempted to elucidate how separate schools, run by a Black teacher, would represent "liberty" on "her march of triumph through the world." He continued, "The position of Mr. T. P. Smith, myself, and many others is this; We are now and have been in favor of removing all legal disabilities from our oppressed people; we are in favor of the doors of all the world's schools being thrown open to such colored children as may desire to go." The separatists expressed support for Russell's Minority Report, which called for desegregating the city's schools, but preserving the option of separate colored schools run by Black teachers.[40]

This compromise was unacceptable to integrationists, who viewed separate Black institutions, especially public ones, as barriers to full participation in American social and political life. By insisting not only that the schools must be integrated but also that Black schools must be abolished, the integrationists framed the debate in terms that angered supporters of separate Black institutions and their mission of racial uplift. According to integrationists, it was impossible to have both.

On September 17, 1849, the battle for equal school rights in Boston erupted into righteous fury. That morning a group of "rude boys" affiliated with the integrationists had stood in front of the Smith School and energetically discouraged Black students from entering. The police dispersed the protestors, who promptly organized a community meeting that evening.

Inside the Belknap Street Church that evening were the city's most prominent Black abolitionists including William C. Nell, John T. Hilton, Benjamin F. Roberts, Henry L. S. Thacker, and Robert Morris Jr. They were particularly incensed that the School Committee had hired one of Boston's most respected Black citizens, Thomas Paul, as the new Smith School principal, a move they interpreted as a devious strategy to trick Black parents into supporting separate schools. Their interpretation had merit, as the appointment of Paul and a new Black assistant teacher, Chloe A. Lee, generated serious interest among Black parents, as did the School Committee's recent renovations of the Smith School.

Paul's supporters gathered outside the Belknap Street Church as the integrationists massed inside. They hoped to engage in "free discussion" on the "vexed" question of school integration, but the integrationists refused to allow the separatists to speak, although they were permitted inside to listen. Integrationists castigated Paul for "having accepted a post so wholly repugnant to their repeatedly expressed wishes and their legal rights" that they deemed him "unworthy of their confidence or respect." Nell stepped to the podium as the "increased zeal and determination" of the audience of school integrationists rose to a crescendo and proposed a set of resolutions designed to humiliate Black supporters of what he termed "exclusive schools."[41]

"Resolved," charged Nell, "that in our present struggle for equal school privileges, we shall not be frowned down by the opposition of the enemies of human progress nor shall our zeal be in any degree abated by the insidious efforts of those identified with us in complexion, but who, alas! to their shame be it recorded, are reverting, by their *animus*, the hand upon the dial-plate to our liberties."[42]

This was too much for Smith and his allies, who hissed and stomped their feet. Although instructed to ignore the interlopers, a few integrationists took the initiative to "secure order" by hustling Smith and his friends outside. At this point the separatists began to pelt the church with "a volley of stones and other missiles" which broke windows and rained down debris on the integrationists inside. The police were called to break up the violence for a second time that day.[43]

The tensions on display the night of September 17, 1849, culminated on May 7, 1851, when Nell and his friends beat Smith severely and tarred and feathered him. Nell was found guilty of the crime and thrown in a "solitary dungeon" for resisting arrest after he refused to pay a $25.00 fine. In a city where revolutionary activism was held in the highest regard, Nell and his conspirators hoped to establish their own credentials as true patriots while casting doubt on their separatist opponents.[44]

Meanwhile, the remainder of the school year saw an expansion of the Smith School boycott as enrollment continued to drop despite the new presence of Black teachers. Black activists on both sides eagerly awaited the ruling of the Massachusetts Supreme Court in the nation's first school desegregation lawsuit, filed by integrationists fed up with the School Committee's intransigence.[45]

A Growing Integrationist Movement

Benjamin F. Roberts, a member of Boston's Black elite and an ardent school integrationist, sued the Boston School Committee in 1848 on behalf of his five-year-old daughter, Sarah. He sought her admission to the city's "white" public schools, the abolition of the grossly inferior facility reserved exclusively for "colored" children, and $600.00 in damages. Reflecting on his decision to bring the lawsuit against the city, Roberts wrote, "Colorphobia deprived us of common schools and many other privileges: we were assailed and hooted at in the streets."[46]

Years of protest, petitions, meetings, and boycotts had been unable to persuade the Boston School Committee to integrate the schools. Black abolitionists and their white allies hoped that legal action would achieve what political protest could not. Charles Sumner, one of the most eloquent white abolitionists of the era, and Robert Morris, one of Boston's few Black attorneys, represented Roberts. Citing the "great principle" of equality enshrined in the Constitution of Massachusetts, they argued "that all men, without distinction of race or color, are equal before the law." Sumner insisted that racially segregated schools could never be equal.

> It is easy to see that the exclusion of colored children from the Public Schools is a constant inconvenience to them and their parents, which white children and white parents are not obliged to bear. There the facts are plain and unanswerable, showing a palpable violation of Equality. *The Black and white are not equal before the law.* I am at a loss to explain how anybody can assert that they are.[47]

Nonetheless, the court ruled in March 1850 that the Boston School Committee had the legal power "to make provision for the instruction of colored children, in separate schools established exclusively for them, and to prohibit their attendance at the other schools." Chief Justice Lemuel Shaw explained that school boards possessed the right to divide children into separate schools whenever expedient. For instance, some schools were set aside for boys and others for girls, some were restricted to children of a particular age, and still others were established for poor children who were too old for primary school but not yet capable of academic work in the grammar schools. He concluded, "The committee, apparently upon great deliberation, have come to the conclusion, that the good of both classes of schools will be best promoted, by maintaining the separate primary schools for colored and for white children."[48]

While the Court's ruling in *Roberts* was a crushing blow to Black integrationists, its legacy would prove even more devastating. Responding directly to Sumner's argument that racially segregated schools were inherently unequal, Chief Justice Shaw articulated the "separate but equal" doctrine that would come to haunt Black Americans' quest for equal rights. In 1896 the US Supreme Court would cite *Roberts* as its leading precedent in *Plessy v. Ferguson*.[49]

Boston's Black integrationists refused to concede defeat in the wake of *Roberts* and escalated the battle with petitions, boycotts, protest meetings, speeches, and publications. Meanwhile, the school integration movement spread throughout the northeast. In early 1848, Black educational activists in Rochester, New York, organized and demanded an end to separate "colored" schools. Frederick Douglass moved to Rochester late in 1847, accompanied by Nell, who spent two years working at Douglass's newspaper, the *North Star*. Douglass and Nell brought with them a sense of righteous indignation at school segregation coupled with years of experience campaigning for integration. As in Boston, Black integrationists in Rochester had to contend with a segment of the Black community that valued separate schools, especially those staffed by Black teachers. After learning that Black separatists planned to circulate a petition asking for the continuation of Rochester's "colored" school, Douglass fumed, "We should feel the most intense mortification if, while many of the most respectable white people of this city should be in favor of admitting our children to equal privileges in the use of our common schools, a single colored man should be found opposed to the measure." He elaborated:

> It is very clear to us that the only way to remove prejudice, and to command the respect of our white fellow citizens, is to repudiate in every form, the idea of our inferiority by maintaining our right to civil, social and political equality with them. If we are in doubt on this point, our despisers may well be resolved. If they can only say that the colored man himself is impressed with a sense of his unfitness for equal privileges, their own prejudices may be plausibly justified.[50]

A Report of the Committee on Colored Schools recommended that Rochester abolish its separate schools, as it cost the city $15.62 to educate each student in the separate "colored" school, compared to the cost of less than $5.00 to educate all other students. Noting that Rochester's separate school "was first conceived and has been maintained solely in consequence of the 'prejudice against color,'" the Committee stated, "we trust that the enlightened, generous, and philanthropic portion of the citizens of Rochester are as willing to open the doors of their Free Schools to those whose only impediment is their color." Despite this strongly worded recommendation, the Rochester School Board decided to open a second "colored" school in 1849. Black parents pushed back with requests to enroll their children in nearby white schools and a boycott of the "colored" schools. In response, school leaders adopted a de facto integration policy in 1850, which permitted Black children who lived far from a "colored" school to enroll in a neighborhood school for the sake of convenience. Inspired by Douglass's lofty rhetoric and frustrated with inadequate separate schools, a majority of Black families in Rochester enrolled their children in the formerly all-white schools. On July 7, 1856, the Rochester School Committee closed the last "colored" school due to under-enrollment, in effect integrating the school system.[51]

Encouraged by the success of integrationists in Rochester, Boston's Black activists escalated their attack in the wake of the disappointing *Roberts* ruling. Back home in Boston, Nell petitioned the state legislature to take action against racial discrimination in Boston, collecting 1,469 signatures in favor of school integration. This petition, combined with an unrelenting school boycott, additional litigation, and the rise of the nativist Know-Nothing Party, motivated state legislators to take action. In 1855 the Massachusetts legislature passed a bill stating "no distinction shall be made on the account of the race, color, or religious opinions, of the applicant or scholar," and the new governor signed it into law. The School Committee decided to keep the Smith School open to Black students, but as in Rochester, so many Black families chose to enroll their children in integrated schools that it was closed due to low enrollment.[52]

Boston's Black integrationists feted Nell on the evening of December 17, 1855, in honor of his long and victorious struggle for "equal school rights." Nell acknowledged a segment of the school integration movement that remains largely invisible in nineteenth-century archival records. As he explained, "While I would not in the smallest degree detract from the credit justly due the *men* for their conspicuous exertions in this reform, truth enjoins upon me the pleasing duty of acknowledging that to the *women*, and the *children* also, in the cause especially indebted for success."

In the dark hours of our struggle, when betrayed by traitors within and beset by foes without, while some men would become lukewarm and indifferent, despairing of victory; then did the women keep the flame alive, and as their hopes would weave bright visions for the future, their husbands and brothers would rally for a new attack upon the fortress of color-phobia. Yes, Sir, it was the mothers (God bless them!) of these little bright eyed-boys and girls, who, through every step of our progress, were executive and vigilant, even to that memorable Monday morning (September 3, 1855) the trial hour, when the colored children of Boston went up to occupy the long-promised land.[53]

Nell explained that Black mothers accompanied him to persuade school administrators that Black families wanted to attend "white" schools. Black women visited the homes of white teachers and school committee members where they pledged to have their children "punctually at school, and neat in their dress," and to aid their instructors in all other ways.[54] What is more, Nell described how Black mothers "labored at home to instill into the minds of their children the necessity of striving to obtain and also to appreciate these rights." As these examples suggest, Black women played an active, yet underappreciated role, in the early school integration movement.[55]

Emancipation and the Question of Citizenship

Even as Nell and Douglass, among others, celebrated the end of separate "colored" schools in northeastern cities, nationally abolitionists were embroiled with the implications of the Fugitive Slave Act of 1850, the Kansas-Nebraska Act of 1854, and the 1857 US Supreme Court decision in *Dred Scott v. Sanford*.[56]

Although radical abolitionists remained committed to eliminating racial discrimination and segregation, the struggle for equal school rights paled in comparison to protecting free Blacks from capture, helping enslaved people escape North, and campaigning to end chattel slavery. Nevertheless, even in these trying times, Black northerners continued to campaign for school integration. Black activists in Providence, Rhode Island, submitted multiple petitions to end separate "caste schools" in 1858, 1861, and 1864, suggesting that school integration remained a vital concern at the local level through the Civil War. Black parents in Chicago balked at legislation passed in 1863 that removed any child with more than "one-eighth Negro blood" from the regular public schools and assigned him or her to a designated "colored school." By organizing school boycotts, enrolling those who could pass for white in the neighborhood schools, and encouraging flagrant disobedience in the separate "colored" school, Black Chicagoans pressured the board of education to rescind the order.[57]

In pointed contrast, Black educational activists first in Troy, New York, in 1855 and then in Albany in 1859 organized boycotts to pressure administrators to hire Black teachers for separate "colored" schools. Similarly, Blacks in Philadelphia won their battle to hire a Black teacher for a separate school in 1862, when John Quincy Allen was hired at the separate Banneker School. The leading Black civil rights organization in Pennsylvania, the State Equal Rights League, issued a statement supporting the hiring of Black teachers in 1865. Since school administrators restricted Black teachers to all-Black classrooms or schools, these campaigns represented support for separate schools. As these varied examples demonstrate, Black northerners remained active in their efforts to improve public education in the Civil War era but divided on whether school integration or separation offered the better avenue of reform.[58]

While a majority of Black students in New England and the Mid-Atlantic states of New York, Pennsylvania, and New Jersey had access to common schools by the mid-1850s, although typically on a segregated basis, thousands more remained excluded from the common schools because of their racial identity. In regions that bordered slave states, especially in the Midwest, whites feared an influx of free or runaway slaves from the South and took steps to discourage African Americans from moving to or settling in their communities, including barring Black children from the public schools. In the 1850s, Illinois, Indiana, and Iowa passed legislation prohibiting Black immigration while Ohio narrowly defeated a similar proposal. These same states either required or permitted racially segregated schools. In many communities, Black families struggled to access public education over the strenuous objections of whites, who feared that admitting Blacks to the public schools would draw more freedpeople to their communities. At the outbreak of the Civil War, a substantial majority of Black children living in the lower Midwest were excluded from public schools. Those who did attend public schools in cities like Cincinnati and Indianapolis did so on a racially segregated and unequal basis.[59]

In the fall of 1864, Black civil rights leaders called for a National Negro Convention in Syracuse. Delegates included prominent Black activists from New York, Boston, Philadelphia, Detroit, Rochester, Hartford, Portland, Albany, Buffalo, Newark, Pittsburgh, Cincinnati, and Cleveland, among other major cities. As president of the convention, Frederick Douglass reminded delegates of the discrepancy between America's democratic claims and her debased abuse of Black civil rights. He asserted, "We are here to promote the freedom, progress, elevation, and perfect enfranchisement, of the entire colored people of the United States; to show that, though slaves, we are not contented slaves; but that, like all other progressive races of men, we are resolved to advance in the scale of knowledge, worth, and civilization, and claim our rights as men among men."[60]

Following the Union victory in spring 1865, Black northerners launched their plan to advance "in the scale of knowledge" and claim their rights as men among men, with voting rights and school integration at the forefront of their agenda. It proved a fertile time for Black educational activists, who won access to public schools throughout the North. White Republicans worked alongside Black northerners to revoke discriminatory statutory restrictions and pass laws to protect Black civil rights. For instance, Indiana, Illinois, Iowa, California, and Oregon repealed their Black Laws between 1863 and 1867. Even more important, Congress proposed and the states ratified the Thirteenth, Fourteenth, and Fifteenth Amendments to the US Constitution that outlawed slavery, guaranteed equal citizenship to Blacks, and secured the franchise for Black men.[61]

Although some Blacks still questioned whether integrated schools provided the most supportive learning environment for Black youth, the glaring inequalities between Black and white schools and the fact that Black students were often barred from public high schools convinced most Blacks that equal educational opportunities required integrated schools. For example, Black students in Detroit could only attend public school for six years in separate schools, whereas white children could attend school for twelve years. Black activists used boycotts and litigation to pressure school boards to admit students on a non-racial basis. However, school administrators and the courts resisted these demands by claiming that racially segregated schools were not illegal or by simply ignoring state laws and court rulings that required school integration. Cognizant that their votes could provide a crucial margin in local and state elections, Black northerners pledged allegiance to candidates who condemned separate schools. As a result, between 1866 and 1877, every northern state except for Indiana that had previously required or permitted school segregation passed legislation prohibiting it.[62]

This legislation represented a remarkable victory for Black educational activists. It compelled white school administrators to admit Black children to previously restricted school districts and symbolized equal citizenship. Equal access to public schools generated new opportunities for Black northerners to prepare for skilled jobs and professional work, and demonstrated the Black community's commitment to self-improvement, assimilation, and democratic citizenship.

The laws did not, however, end the practice of racially segregated and inferior public schools. White school administrators and politicians conspired to gerrymander school district assignments and create schools that were predominantly or entirely Black in spite of state laws. According to historian Nell Irvin Painter, by the late 1870s, segregated schools were the rule throughout the South and in the border states, despite efforts to create integrated public schools during Reconstruction. In most northern states, "segregated schools were normal, if not the rule." In his summary of Black education in the nineteenth century, W. E. B. Du Bois notes, "Then there grew up later in the century distinct Negro public school systems, supported by the state, usually with colored principals but not as well equipped as the white schools. These systems spread in northern cities like New York, Philadelphia, and Cincinnati."[63]

With the end of Reconstruction, Black educational activists in the South fought to preserve existing Black schools and ensure that Black teachers were hired to teach in the separate schools. A successful campaign to replace white teachers with Blacks in St. Louis, Missouri, in 1877 demonstrated that this approach could be successful, even as anti-Black discrimination increased. Black northerners followed southern educational politics with keen interest, and some activists were convinced that advocating for Black teachers in separate schools could represent a smart strategy in certain northern communities. For example, a group of Black families in Detroit submitted a petition to the school board in 1872 requesting a Black teacher for their children. The petition asked "that their children may not be confined to an education from text books alone, but that they may be trained . . . in such deportment and principles as may best fit them for usefulness in the natural positions that they may be called upon to fill in life." This is especially notable since Blacks in Detroit had finally compelled school authorities to assign Black children to the formerly "white" schools just the year before.[64]

At the National Convention of Colored Men in Nashville in 1879, prominent Chicago attorney Ferdinand L. Barnett emphasized the many benefits of having Black teachers in separate Black schools, explaining:

> White teachers in colored schools are nearly always mentally, morally, or financially bankrupt, and no colored community should tolerate the imposition. High schools and colleges are sending learned colored teachers in the field constantly, and it is manifestly unjust to make them stand idle and see their people taught by those whose only interest lies in securing their monthly compensation in dollars and cents. Again, colored schools thrive better under colored teachers. The St. Louis schools furnish an excellent example.[65]

This strategy was especially appealing to northern Black educational activists who lived in places that operated segregated Black schools in open defiance of state law. For instance, even after Ohio outlawed racial segregation in the public schools in 1887, small towns like Felicity, Oxford, Chillicothe, and Yellow Springs refused to allow Black children to enroll in schools understood to be "white." When Black children arrived to enroll at the "white" school in Felicity on September 10, 1887, a crowd of white boys and men gathered outside and refused to permit the Black families to enter "their" school. Violence raged there for two years as Blacks sued for the right to send their children to school on an integrated basis, at one point running out of town a Black Oberlin graduate hired to entice Black families to attend the separate school. "So hot was the race feud," observed the *Atlanta Constitution*, "that the Blacks were forced to accept separate schools."[66]

Similarly, Black parents in Philadelphia reported tremendous obstacles to enrolling their children in neighborhood schools, even after racial segregation was outlawed in 1881. Merle Nichols reported that when he attempted to enroll his children in a nearby majority white elementary school, it "raised a great excitement among the children and teachers." Some of the students threatened to withdraw, others called out racial epithets, and a white teacher instructed Nichols to enroll his children at a "colored" school. Like other Black families in Philadelphia, Nichols found the separate school run by Black principal Jacob C. White Jr. to be welcoming, while the predominantly white schools always seemed to be full.[67]

An incident from Fair Haven, New Jersey, reveals how Black support for school integration could waver in the face of adamant white resistance. Trouble began in 1881 when Zumella Johnson, the town's only Black teacher, resigned from the one-room "colored" schoolhouse, forcing the district to temporarily close the school. With no other option, Black parents attempted to enroll their children in the town's functioning public school, which served white students. County Superintendent of Public Schools instructed the Fair Haven authorities not to admit the Black students, writing, "When in a district there are distinct schools, intended to keep the races, apart, the pupils of one school have no right to demand admission to the others." Within days the "colored school" burned to the ground in a mysterious fire, most likely set by Black educational activists. Dubbed a "race war" in the press, the episode inspired New Jersey lawmakers to outlaw racial segregation in the public schools. Shortly thereafter, Fair Haven leaders organized a general meeting, where Black citizens were asked to vote on whether to accept a brand-new modern schoolhouse to serve the Black community. Pastor Williams implored Fair Haven Blacks "not to accept anything except full permission to associate with the whites and to attend their school." Prominent white leader General Clinton B. Fisk urged the Black community "to accept whatever was offered by the whites" and not to send their children where they were not wanted. It is unclear whether Black parents were motivated by the lure of a high-quality separate school or the threat of white retaliation, but Fair Haven's Black community voted to accept the separate school.[68]

A few years later, the nearby town of Long Branch, New Jersey, built a sep-arate school for Black pupils. The school board reported, "At first some of the colored people, who are ever sensitively jealous of their rights as 'American citizens of African descent,' insisted on sending their children to the white school." But within months this opposition faded as Black parents discovered that they were not barred from the white school and that their children preferred to study with Black teachers. The school board concluded, "The opposition gradually and quietly gave way, and the later months of the year were marked with some success." As these examples reveal, even though de jure racial segregation in the public schools was outlawed, de facto school segregation persisted and, after 1877, started to expand.[69]

The Failure of School Integration in Cincinnati

School segregation in the North blossomed despite the growing size and polit-ical power of northern Black communities and Black northerners' preference for integrated schools. How and why this happened is demonstrated in school integration debates in late nineteenth-century Cincinnati, where Blacks fought for and won school integration, only to see separate schools spike in the early twentieth century.

Like many midwestern cities, Cincinnati initially excluded Black students from public schools. Black abolitionist Peter H. Clark organized the Black com-munity and convinced the city to build separate schools for Black students. Under Clark's leadership, from 1849 to 1874, Cincinnati's Black community elected its own school trustees with the power to hire faculty, approve curricula, maintain school facilities, and contract for repairs in the "colored" schools. In the wake of the Civil War, Black school trustees established Gaines High School, the city's first public high school open to Black students. Clark served as principal, hiring outstanding Black faculty and developing academic programs including a normal school to prepare teachers. Thanks to Clark's efforts, the number of Black teachers increased from three in 1850 to thirty-six in 1880, establishing a crucial segment of Cincinnati's Black middle class.[70]

These educational developments were undercut by changes in the city's political economy in the late nineteenth century that resulted in deteriorating conditions for Black citizens. Cities like Cincinnati grew into industrial powerhouses after the Civil War as a result of new forms of mass production, technology, and transportation, especially railroads. Industrialization and ur-banization had adverse consequences for northern Blacks, as opportunities for skilled artisans declined and heavy industries relegated Black workers to the lowest paying menial jobs. Meanwhile, the size of northern Black communities swelled after the Civil War as tens of thousands of freedpeople moved north. The Black community in Cincinnati grew from 3,237 in 1850 to 5,444 in 1870, and 8,179 in 1880. An economic depression from 1873 through 1879 heightened competition between Black and white laborers, further decimated Black employment opportunities, and strained race relations. As the material circumstances of northern Blacks declined in the 1870s, whites responded with hostility, policing the color line with renewed vigor. Blacks in Cincinnati faced increasing residential segregation and growing exclusion from public venues as white officials refused to enforce the Civil Rights Act of 1866. In 1873 the Black community lost control over the system of separate schools when the Ohio legislature passed laws that placed the state's Black schools under white school trustees. Black schools remained, but they were administered by white people.[71]

At the national level, the Republican Party began to withdraw its support for Black civil rights in 1875. Southern Reconstruction was drawing to an end as the white planter elite reasserted its power, increasingly by force. Courts and legislatures were retreating from visionary promises of "equality before the law" and Jim Crow segregation and discrimination were on the rise. In response, a small but vocal number of Black leaders began to advocate independence from the Republican Party.

In 1875, Peter H. Clark suggested that Ohio Blacks support whichever party promised to advance Black political objectives. He reasoned that Republicans would ignore civil rights issues if they believed Blacks had no viable alternatives at the polls, and he used his power and influence to split the Black vote in Ohio. In 1876, he briefly joined the Workingmen's Party, a socialist organization, and then returned to the Republican Party again before switching to the Democratic Party in 1882.[72]

In August 1883, Clark endorsed Democratic gubernatorial candidate George B. Hoadly, who vowed to support Black civil rights in Ohio. As the Republican gubernatorial candidate Joseph Foraker had a shoddy record on Black civil rights, many Ohio Blacks followed Clark's lead. Hoadly won, thanks to a thin margin delivered by Black citizens. When asked about his strategy of splitting the Black vote, Clark reasoned, "I never thought it wise to be concentrated in one party, thus antagonizing the other great party and tempting it to do against us as Republicans what they would hesitate to do against us as Negroes. Whenever colored men find themselves in accord with Democrats in local or National issues they should vote with them and thus disarm much of the malevolence that is born of political rather than racial antagonisms." Ohio Blacks had demonstrated that their vote could be decisive. Hoadly ushered a bill through the Ohio legislature that prohibited racial discrimination in restaurants, saloons, barbershops, and other places of public resort and threatened violators with a $100.00 fine. Encouraged, Black activists pressed for the repeal of the remaining

Black Laws, which included laws that permitted, but did not require, racially segregated public schools. This pushed the question of school integration to the forefront of Black political protest in Ohio.[73]

By 1884, most Black citizens in Ohio preferred integrated schools. From Cleveland and other communities in the northern part of the state that no longer operated racially segregated schools, African Americans objected to separate public schools as wretched vestiges of de jure segregation. From the middle regions of the state including Columbus, Springfield, and Xenia, Blacks viewed anti-discrimination legislation as an effective tool to require integration in those communities that still ran dual school systems. In the southernmost regions of the state, including Cincinnati, the Black community was more divided. Black parents, teachers, and ministers wondered what would happen to Black teachers and students if Cincinnati's schools were integrated. Clark emerged as an outspoken critic of the proposed legislation to outlaw school segregation, arguing that while the remaining Black Laws must be repealed, Blacks should fight to retain the option of separate schools. He organized Cincinnati's Black teaching force and lobbied legislators to retain some Black schools in a desegregated system.[74]

Black integrationists were outraged by Clark's position, insisting the majority of Black citizens disagreed. "The sensible people of Ohio almost to a man who are not directly connected with the colored schools as is Peter H. Clark, have cried out against this disgrace being heaped upon them, for the sole purpose of benefitting a few. Should thousands be losers that a *few* be gainers?" asked a Black newspaper, the *Christian Recorder*. "No! Peter H. Clark is fighting for his personal benefit and we are contending for equal rights for our people, with their able assistance, and will not be satisfied until our people are allowed to attend whatever school they wish, and not be compelled to huddle themselves in separate apartments."[75]

Clark retorted that he did not object to mixed schools but to the version of school integration practiced in most northern school districts. "I do not advocate schools in which colored pupils are tolerated and colored teachers shut out," he retorted. "I have now on my school benches a class of young men and women who are looking forward to the honorable career of teachers. When they graduate, I can find them such employment and in their native state." He cautioned that teaching jobs would evaporate in an integrated system, just as they had in cities like New York. "Close the colored schools, put these girls and boys into the mixed schools, if they persevere to graduation, which but few of them will do, the occupations open to them will be those of coachmen and laundry maids to their white schoolmates." Far better, he reasoned, to maintain separate schools where Black students could thrive and Black teachers could find employment.[76]

Editors of the *Christian Recorder* were willing to print Clark's arguments for separate schools, but not without a caustic rejoinder. "As it relates to Mr. Clark's position, we have to say, first, that he is wrong in his *theory*, and second, that he is wrong in his *practice*." School integrationists in Cincinnati in 1884 echoed the sentiments of abolitionists in the 1840s, contending that mixed schools would facilitate assimilation and integration into mainstream society, while separate schools were undemocratic and inherently dangerous. Rarely did integrationists address the pressing question of discrimination against Black students or teachers in mixed schools. This left space for Black separatists to propose an alternative vision of separate, Black-controlled schools with equal resources and facilities, staffed by caring Black teachers and administrators committed to racial uplift. Many Black families were drawn to the idea of a more supportive and nurturing school for their children.[77]

The debate over school integration burned brightly in Cincinnati for three more years, as Black educational activists struggled to figure out whether integration or separation provided greater resources to the Black community. Many people expressed disappointment that integrated schools created such hostile environments for Black children. "In the North we are struggling for mixed schools. The mixture, so far as it has gone, has been a miserable farce," observed Reverend Benjamin F. Lee, writing in support of separate schools. "With Peter H. Clark I say mixed schools, yes; but mock mixed schools, no." Some Black educators, ministers, and parents were skeptical that integrated schools would treat Black children with love and compassion and were deeply concerned that without separate schools, Black teachers would struggle to secure jobs. Examples from the region supported these fears. For example, when New York City opened its white public schools to Black children in 1873, attendance at the all-Black schools fell off considerably and the number of Black teachers in the city declined sharply. School leaders in Pittsburgh hired only a few Black teachers before 1937, when the Black community there agreed to the creation of separate schools. In the early 1880s, Cincinnati had the highest number of Black students and teachers of any school district in the state, and except for a few ministers and entrepreneurs, Black teachers comprised nearly all of the city's Black middle class. The end of separate schools, some feared, was a serious threat to the economic, social, and political health of the Black community at large.[78]

Integrationists, in contrast, viewed integrated schools as state-sponsored recognition of equal citizenship and the best way to equalize educational opportunities. The Black *Cleveland Gazette* and the white Republican *Cincinnati Commercial* both supported school integration, arguing that separate schools offered an inferior education due to limited curricula, overcrowding, and substandard facilities, and furthermore, that it was brutally inconvenient for many Black families to travel long distances to attend separate schools. Integrationists also emphasized the financial burden of operating a dual system. This was true, and the high costs of operating separate schools compelled many communities to integrate their schools, so that by 1885 approximately 90 percent of Ohio's separate schools had already been abolished. By this late date, the only large towns or cities with dual systems were Springfield, Dayton, and Cincinnati, and by the end of the year, Springfield integrated its schools. The school integration movement had the moral high ground and the more compelling logic, resulting in widespread support among the Black masses. Having learned from his mistake in the previous election, Republican gubernatorial candidate Joseph Foraker promised Black voters that he would outlaw school segregation if elected.[79]

Black voters in Ohio threw their weight behind the Republican candidate, and Governor Foraker followed through on his campaign promise. Speaking before the Ohio House of Representatives on March 10, 1886, Representative Benjamin W. Arnett, a Black legislator and former teacher, decried the continued existence of state-sponsored racial injustice. "One would think that at this time of our civilization, that character, and not color, would form the line of distinction in society, but such is not the case," intoned Arnett. "It matters not what may be the standing or intelligence of a colored man or woman, they have to submit to the wicked laws and the more wicked prejudice of the people." Arnett argued that Black citizens viewed separate schools as the most detestable form of racial discrimination, continuing, "The foe of my race stands at the school house door and separates the children, by reason of 'color,' and then denies to those who have a visible admixture of African blood in them the blessing of a graded school and equal privileges." On February 16, 1887, the "Arnett Law" was signed into law, officially outlawing racial segregation in Ohio public schools. To punish Clark for supporting Democrats, the Republican-dominated Cincinnati School Board forced him to resign as principal of Gaines High School in the spring of 1886.[80]

Separate Black schools in Ohio did not disappear in the wake of the 1887 Arnett Law. In the southern, farming regions of the state, white school boards violated the law. When Black families sued and the courts ordered the district to integrate, newspapers reported that white farmers pushed Black families out of the region, with the objective of keeping Black children out of the public schools. "Whenever his lease runs out, he is now quietly informed by his white landlord that the latter has another man for his place. Upon applying to other farmers in the same district, he is certain to be refused. In this manner white farmers gradually, without violent or harsh means, have removed colored people from among them, until there is not one left in some entire school districts."[81]

A number of Black parents in Cincinnati requested the continued operation of separate Black schools as "branch" schools, an entreaty the white school board was delighted to grant. Over the next decade, however, Black families in

Cincinnati slowly abandoned separate schools. As enrollment in these schools declined, Black teachers and administrators lost their jobs, much as Clark had feared. Gaines High School was closed in 1890 due to low enrollment and deteriorating facilities. By 1900, when nearly all of the "branch" schools had been phased out, there were only twelve Black teachers left in the Cincinnati Public Schools. Although Black students could now enroll in white high schools, few did so. Gaines High School had graduated 112 students during its twenty-one years of existence, including 74 who became teachers. Only 36 Black students graduated from high school in the decade after Gaines was closed, and by 1910 Cincinnati had graduated only 56 Black students despite a large increase in the Black population.[82]

In 1896, Black state representative William H. Parham presented the Cincinnati Board of Education with a petition signed by more than 700 Black citizens alleging that "Black pupils were subject to indignities and insults and were not given an equal opportunity with white students in mixed schools." The School Board ignored the petition. As southern Blacks moved into Cincinnati, they became concentrated in the West End and Walnut Hills neighborhoods, where school administrators gerrymandered school boundary lines to concentrate Black students in certain schools. In 1902 the school in Walnut Hills was renamed the Frederick Douglass School and was opened to Black students in the city regardless of residence. In 1914, the Cincinnati School Board hired Black educator Jennie Porter Smith to run a separate school for Black students in the West End, the Harriet Beecher Stowe School. By the late 1920s Cincinnati's separate schools had developed into prominent institutions with substantial support from the Black community. De facto racial segregation was increasing in northern school districts like Cincinnati, but the development of high-quality schools like Douglass and Stowe, staffed by Black teachers and administrators, made these schools appealing to some Black parents.[83]

A Last Stand against Jim Crow Schools

One of the last great battles for school integration in the nineteenth century erupted in Jamaica, New York, at the time a small, semi-rural suburb of New York City whose Black community dated back to the colonial era. As was common for the region, a separate school for Black children was first started in 1854 in the local African Methodist Episcopal (AME) church and then moved into a dedicated building in the early 1880s. By 1892, Black parents were not satisfied with the dilapidated, one-room "colored" schoolhouse, staffed by a single Black teacher who taught an ungraded class of more than seventy-five students. When the school board refused Black families' modest requests to add another room and hire a second teacher for the "colored" school, Black parents switched strategies and demanded school integration.

In 1892, Reverend Langford of the Jamaica AME church filed a lawsuit stating that his two children were denied admission to the town's white schools and forced to attend a segregated and inferior "colored" school. School superintendent Willian J. Ballard stood firm, citing a state law that permitted separate but equal schools for "colored" children. He informed Black families that they could not enroll their children in the newly constructed public schools "on account of color" and if they wished to challenge the board's policy they would have to resort to the courts. Black parents rose to the challenge. They launched a boycott of the public schools, decimating the attendance at the "colored" school and filed a series of legal actions against the school district. Outraged by this protest, town leaders dispatched truancy officers to arrest parents for violating school attendance laws.[84]

Following his arrest for withholding his three children from the "colored" school in the spring of 1896, Samuel B. Cisco told reporters that he had refused to pay the court fine in order to raise awareness about the Black struggle for school integration. "I have never paid any fine and do not intend to pay any," he told the Brooklyn Daily Eagle. "I and my father and mother have paid taxes in Jamaica for eighty years, yet I am denied a place in the school near my house, while Irishmen, Italians, and Dutchmen who have been here only three months, can go in these, although covered with dirt." He elaborated, "I am a man of means in business here and yet on September 3, when my three children were sent to school where my neighbors' children attend, they were put out and sent home crying. The colored school is three-fourths of a mile further away than the white School No. 3, and it is in the low swampy portion of the village and they are not taught as well as the children of the white schools." Cisco's goal was equal educational opportunities, but it is also clear he prioritized the basic right of Black Americans to attend public institutions on an equal basis. Anything else, he made clear, would be unacceptable.[85]

Jamaica's lengthy and contested school integration battle was closely followed in the local and national press. Writing in the summer of 1896, the Washington Post castigated the Jamaica Board of Education for offering such blatantly inferior facilities to Black students, contending, "[Cisco's] children are entitled to as good an education and to as comfortable surrounding as the children of any white person in Jamaica." What first appeared to be sympathy for Black students, however, quickly turned into a defense of the "separate but equal" doctrine established by the US Supreme Court in Plessy v. Ferguson just one month earlier.

The Washington Post editorialized, "It is not to be supposed that Cisco or any other colored father of a family would have dreamed of thrusting his children into a white school, to be made unhappy by the slights and snubs of the rest of the pupils, if he could have had for them proper advantages at the colored school. Persons of self-respect never insist on going where they are not wanted, and where their presence is regarded as an intrusion. Only very common and vulgar persons, white or Black, ever do such things." Depicting Black school integration efforts as appropriate, given the poor quality of the separate schools, this argument suggested that Black efforts to integrate schools "where they are not wanted" would be "vulgar" if the schools were equal.

The *Washington Post* added that school integration was a pointless objective in the North, given the rancorous degree of anti-Black sentiment. "We do not believe the negro will ever be liked or treated any better in the North than he is at this moment. The antipathy is constitutional and ineradicable." The article concluded, "We are quite sure, however, that the school authorities of Jamaica, L. I., are exactly like the school authorities in nine out of ten cities, towns, and villages at the North. The negro is personally disliked by the white people of that section, and the sooner he recognizes that fact and regulates himself accordingly, the easier will be his path through life." This argument, which was gaining traction throughout the North, pressured northern Blacks to accept de facto school segregation as long as facilities were approximately equal. It suggested that Black citizens who insisted on school integration were violating an unspoken, but apparently unmistakable, tenet of American social etiquette.[86]

Although the *Washington Post* might have been correct about northern antipathy to Black civil rights, it misjudged Black families in Jamaica. Faced with mounting political pressure over what the press dubbed "Jamaica's School War," in 1896 the board of education hired a second Black teacher, and in 1899 a third, while a Black student was admitted to the local high school for the first time in 1898. Then in June of 1899 the Jamaica School Board closed the "colored" school, sent the Black children to white classrooms on a temporary basis, and completely renovated the "colored" school.

The *Brooklyn Daily Eagle* reported in 1900, "The building has been thoroughly overhauled, modernized and enlarged since it was closed in June, and is said to be so much more attractive than the other schools of the place that the white children are envious of the Blacks in the matter of their school accommodations." Nevertheless, roughly half of the Black families in town, including the Ciscos, refused to send their children there and continued to press for school integration. In 1899 and early 1900 New York's higher courts ruled against the Ciscos, refusing to compel Jamaica school officials to enroll Black children in the "white" public schools.[87]

As Black families prepared another appeal, Republican lawmakers introduced a bill that Governor Theodore Roosevelt signed into law in April of 1900 stating, "No person shall be refused admission into or be excluded from any public

school in the state of New York on account of race or color." Assemblyman
George Wallace, the white attorney who represented the Cisco family, helped
guide the bill through the state legislature. "I am well satisfied with the result,"
he told reporters. "The passage of this act is a good thing for the colored children
of the state. Experience has shown that they do not make as good progress in a
separate colored school as when attending one of the common schools. In the
latter they have competition with the children of other races, which arouses their
ambition, quickens their perceptions and is great aid to their progress." Historian
Carleton Mabee notes that while there was a dangerous loophole in the new
law that permitted rural school districts in the state to continue to operate separate schools, Jamaica's successful integration effort seems to have inspired Black
communities in Roslyn and Hempstead, both on Long Island, to challenge
school segregation.[88]

Following passage of the law, Queens school officials opened the public
schools in Jamaica and nearby Flushing to children of all races and closed the
separate Black schools. While Black families in Jamaica celebrated this historic
victory, their neighbors in Flushing were far more ambivalent. For five years
while Jamaica fought a tenacious battle for integrated schools, Black families
in Flushing quietly declined to take action against their town's separate school.
Mabee argues that Flushing's Black community preferred separate, high-quality
Black schools to integrated ones. Thanks to effective Black leadership and sympathetic white Quaker allies, Flushing's "colored" school grew into an excellent
institution led by a dynamic Black principal, Mary Shaw. Principal Shaw offered
a rigorous academic curriculum taught by Black teachers that prepared students
for entry into some of the nation's best colleges including Columbia, Cornell,
and Yale. By the end of the nineteenth century, Black northerners expressed a
pragmatic view of school integration, prioritizing it in communities where blatantly inferior separate facilities existed and continuing to support high-quality
separate schools.[89]

Conclusion

By the turn of the twentieth century, Black educational activists in the North
had won a series of hard-fought and transformative victories against racial segregation and discrimination in the public schools. Legal school segregation
had been dismantled and growing numbers of white Americans accepted that
Blacks wanted and deserved equal educational opportunities. However, most
white northerners preferred the idea of separate, but equal, public schools to
racially integrated ones. The sharp escalation of southern Jim Crow stimulated
white resistance to integrated facilities in many parts of the North, which in

turn complicated the Black struggle for school integration. Faced with intransigent white racism, some Black northerners made a conscious decision to reject
school integration as a strategy in favor of separate, Black-controlled schools,
funded at equal rates to white schools, which they believed would benefit Black
students and the economic and political development of Black communities.

2

The Education That Is Their Due

Separation for Racial Uplift, 1900–1940

As editor of the *Crisis*, the popular magazine of the National Association for the Advancement of Colored People (NAACP), scholar and activist W. E. B. Du Bois received dozens of plaintive letters documenting racial injustice. In 1932 one such letter crossed his desk from Dayton, Ohio. Recounting a common trend in the region, the letter explained that Dayton's white leaders proposed to create the city's first "all-Negro school." The author elaborated, "Up to the present time we have had no all-colored schools, though Negro children have been restricted in the use of swimming pools, and segregated in gymnasium classes. One grade school has a main building with both white and Negro children under white teachers, and a temporary building for colored children under colored teachers."

While Dayton's Black community reluctantly accommodated these slights, some feared the proposed separate high school represented an escalation of state-sponsored discrimination. On the other hand, as "there seems to be an un-written law that white children should not be placed under Negro teachers," the new school would create valuable teaching positions for Black college graduates. What is more, the school would be named in honor of one of Dayton's most famous native sons, Black poet and writer Paul Lawrence Dunbar. African Americans in Dayton faced a terrible dilemma: should they accept the new separate high school in service to the race or reject the creeping advance of Jim Crow? The letter concluded with a humble plea, "May I ask what you yourself would consider wise in such a situation, and what you would think the main trends of Negro thinking would be?"[1]

Du Bois responded, "It is always unfortunate and against the fundamental idea of free popular education to separate the pupils on any artificial basis." The problem was, he conceded, "this ideal cannot always be reached." Du Bois was apprehensive that prejudiced teachers would limit Black students' poten-tial, resulting in lower levels of academic achievement. He concluded, "It would be most unfortunate if the new Dunbar High School were made exclusively a Negro school. On the other hand, if Negro children in the mixed schools are not receiving proper attention and training, if they do not enlist the interest and friendliness of the teachers, if the teachers must inevitably and always be white, then colored children cannot receive in such schools the education that is their due and some separation is almost inevitable." Du Bois conceded that Blacks might have to accept "some separation" in order to ensure that their children receive "the education that is their due." The following September, the separate Paul Lawrence Dunbar High School enrolled its first class.[2]

From the turn of the twentieth century to the start of World War II, school segregation in the North increased, sometimes in the form of separate schools with Black teachers like Dunbar High School and sometimes in the form of majority Black schools with white teachers created through residential segregation and discriminatory school assignment policies. Widespread Black support for school integration faded as northern Black communities, now home to hundreds of thousands of southern migrants, struggled to mitigate increased racial hostility and limited economic and educational opportunities. For many of these Black parents, students, teachers, ministers, and community leaders, the option of separate schools with Black teachers was far preferable to abuse at the hands of white teachers.

This chapter looks at Black educational activism in communities throughout the North but focuses on Philadelphia, the northern city with the largest Black population. It was home to the first major social scientific study of an African American community, conducted by W. E. B. Du Bois. Importantly, Philadelphia school administrators made explicit and deliberate efforts to expand school segregation as part of a coordinated campaign of progressive reform. As whites increased school segregation, Black citizens split between those who supported the option of separate schools with Black teachers and those who staunchly insisted that only integrated schools could advance the social and economic well-being of the Black community.

The Color Line Moves North

Although northern school segregation increased between 1900 and 1940 as northern Black populations grew, its most troubling manifestation was along those northern regions that bordered the South. These northern borderlands, including southern portions of New Jersey, Pennsylvania, Ohio, Indiana, Illinois, and parts of New York, adopted patterns of race relations that looked more like the Jim Crow South than the supposedly progressive North. School districts here were more likely to operate separate Black schools with Black faculty in open defiance of state law. Many Black families and teachers came to support these separate, Black-controlled schools even as civil rights leaders, the Black elite, and Black scholars objected.[3]

Farther north, school administrators concentrated Black students into schools that may have contained some degree of racial mixing. These majority Black schools did not necessarily have any Black faculty, although if the district did employ Black teachers or principals, they were likely to be found here. As the size of northern Black populations grew exponentially over the first four decades of the twentieth century, so too did residential segregation. White northerners promoted high levels of residential segregation through restrictive real estate covenants, discriminatory real estate practices, discriminatory banking practices, blockbusting, and violent white resistance to Black families who did manage to secure a home in a "white" neighborhood. High rates of residential segregation made it easier for school authorities to concentrate Black students in certain schools through optional attendance zones, gerrymandered attendance lines, racialized school feeder patters, and discriminatory decisions about school transportation and construction. Both separate Black schools and majority Black schools increased throughout the North between 1900 and 1940. School administrators tried to deny or obfuscate the increase in northern school segregation, as it violated state law and drew the ire of civil rights activists. In response, Black social scientists and civil rights organizations worked to document northern school segregation and its consequences on the quality of public education for Black students.[4]

Much of the evidence for school segregation from this era comes from the work of black scholars. As determined by Howard University's Charles H. Thompson, "In several states such as Illinois, New Jersey, and Pennsylvania separate schools exist despite the law against them." Civil rights leader Lester Granger reported in 1935, "From the University town of Princeton, including the capital city of Trenton, southward to Cape May, every city or town with a considerable Negro population supports the dual education system with a building for its white and a building for its Negro pupils of the grammar grades." By segregating the students by race, white administrators were able to dole out more resources to the schools that served white students, while limiting funding and support for majority Black schools. Educator Horace Mann Bond testified, "In Ohio, and Indiana, and Kansas, and Illinois, Philadelphia, and southern New Jersey, wherever the schools are separated, you will find after ten or fifteen years, the colored school is going into decline." A rapidly increasing Black population, residential segregation, and potent anti-Black racism created segregated schools in Chicago by 1925 and Detroit by the early 1930s.[5]

When sociologist Charles S. Johnson surveyed American race relations in 1938 as part of Gunnar Myrdal's renowned study, he concluded, "In spite of the presence of legislation prohibiting segregation in the schools of some states with southern exposures, such as New Jersey and Illinois, in practice segregation is accomplished in some localities through administrative measures." He also found evidence of explicit segregation in cities throughout the North. Johnson concluded, "Unofficially, a dual system exists in the Chicago schools. The restricted covenant laws, keeping the masses of the Negro population in limited residential areas, results in almost solid Negro enrollment in schools in these areas." Sociologist Ira De A. Reid documented increasing racial segregation every year in Pittsburgh, where numerous schools had more than 90 percent Black students. The Black press condemned these northern "Jim Crow schools" as the antithesis of American democracy.[6]

Scholars found there was shockingly little consensus over the question of school separation within Black communities. In 1923, principal of the all-Black Cheyney Training School for Teachers in Pennsylvania, Leslie Pinckney Hill, wrote, "There is a wide-spread and heated discussion current at present along the border states and in some of the northern states on the relation of the public schools to the Negro population. This discussion, notably in Ohio, Pennsylvania, and New Jersey, is dividing colored people into bitter camps and factions."[7]

White scholar Louis A. Pechstein elucidated, "By way of general statement, rival points of view maintain with reference to the education of negro youth in northern cities. The so-called radicals clamor for mixed schools, the conservatives advocate separate schools as superior." As Thompson concluded, "Negroes have not made up their minds whether they should fight this illegal extension of the separate school, because they are still confused on the issue whether separate schools with approximately equal facilities are more or less advantageous than mixed schools 'with prejudice.'"[8]

Even though many northern Blacks supported the option of separate, Black-controlled schools, northern school segregation expanded as result of white racism, not Black preference. White school administrators implemented new ways to isolate Black students such as creating a separate class for "backwards" students and then assigning every Black student to that class. They manipulated school catchment zones and transfer policies, allowing white students to transfer out of majority Black schools while refusing the same privilege to Blacks. This created schools with very large Black majorities, sometimes located just blocks away from schools with virtually no Black students. Scholars and the Black press condemned this as akin to Jim Crow schools in the South. Such practices were common throughout the North, especially in large cities like Philadelphia, New York, Detroit, Pittsburgh, Cleveland, and Chicago. Picking up on Black quarrels over whether to demand school integration, school administrators in some northern communities added another weapon to their arsenal—the offer of a separate but "equal" school for Blacks, to be staffed and administered by the local Black community.[9]

That is what happened in Dayton, Ohio, in 1932. Given the political dominance of whites and escalating racism, Black residents had to decide whether to accept a separate school, which promised a safe haven for their youth and coveted teaching jobs for Black teachers, or to place their children on the front line in the battle against Jim Crow. Faced with this grim choice, most northern Black families were ambivalent about school integration. As the *Crisis* observed in 1923, "The question is this: when colored children go to mixed northern public schools do they receive the proper education, encouragement and attention; and if they do not, what is the remedy?"[10]

Staking Out Competing Positions

College-educated Black elites, including college professors, newspaper editors, doctors, and members of fledgling civil rights organizations like the NAACP and the National Urban League maintained that mixed schools would safeguard educational equality. Echoing an earlier generation of Black abolitionists, they argued, "Separate schools for colored people benefit only whites," by allowing whites to "hog" the best resources. What is more, integrationists believed that separate schools increased prejudice and exacerbated racial tensions, ultimately harming the larger struggle for Black equality. As the Black *Philadelphia Tribune* insisted, "The intelligent colored citizen travels and observes, that in every city where the separate school system is in vogue, race hatred has grown apace."[11]

The Black elite was also apprehensive about the escalation of state-sponsored segregation in the North. Civil rights leaders such as the NAACP's William Pickens rejected separate schools under any circumstances. "It is a monster that grows by that which it feeds upon, and whose appetite is not appeased but magnified by what is thrust into its mouth." Pickens continued, "Consider the schools: segregation in kindergarten stimulates a desire for segregation in the grades; when it is established in the grades, there is sure to be a call for segregation in the high schools; then the atmosphere around the universities becomes less tolerant toward any group which has already been cast out by the rest of the school system."[12]

Following this logic, separate schools, even if they served the purpose of improving Black student achievement, undermined the freedom struggle by fueling racial prejudice, expanding Jim Crow, and eviscerating equal citizenship. Integrated schools, by contrast, would assimilate Blacks into mainstream society. As José Clarana hypothesized, "The Negro's best hope for a place in the new America lies in learning to understand the new Americans. He can best do this by going to school with them, using the same books they use, thinking the same thoughts they think."[13]

Academics like Dwight O. W. Holmes concluded that segregated schools violated America's democratic creed. He charged, "First, segregation always implies inequality of status and that one group is dangerous to the other; second, segregation always means inferior accommodations for those segregated, and third, segregation prevents the races from knowing each other though the usual means of communication." From this perspective, school integration was a non-negotiable tenet of Black civil rights. Integrationists vilified Black supporters of separate schools as "traitors" who "betrayed the race" or, as civil rights leader A. Philip Randolph put it, fools who "sold the race to the white man for a 'mess of pottage.'" By prioritizing the symbolic value of integrated schools and refusing to countenance separate schools, integrationists polarized the debate over school integration and left little room to acknowledge the urgent concerns of Black students, parents, and teachers.[14]

This sharp divide pitted Black families and middle-class Black teachers against the Black elite. Although the northern Black masses appreciated the ideal of school integration, they prioritized educational opportunities and academic achievement for Black youth. A high school diploma was a coveted objective. Many boycotted separate schools or sued school districts that segregated Black students in violation of state law. Although individual cases were won, these victories failed to halt the expansion of school segregation as the Great Migration continued. Black southerners evacuated the South at a remarkable rate, especially after World War I created new industrial job opportunities and cut off immigration from Europe. Between 1910 and 1940, approximately 1.8 million Blacks moved North. The northern Black masses—which included large numbers of southern-born migrants—were united in their efforts to access high-quality public education, but uncertain whether school integration was the best way to accomplish this goal.[15]

As racial tensions in the North grew, they spilled over into public schools. Strange and disturbing stories circulated, such as a white teacher in Flushing, New York, who punished a twelve-year-old white girl by forcing her to dance with a Black classmate. A school in Asbury Park, New Jersey, seated white children on one side of every classroom and Black children on the other, with a wire fence in the middle of the playground to separate the children during recess. In Dayton, Ohio, a white school principal had the Black students put on a minstrel show. The Black students performed by "rattling bones, dancing 'coon jiggers,' cake walking, wearing red long-tailed, full dress suits and 'monkeying' in various ways." Whites in East St. Louis burned down not one but two different "colored" schools within a two-week period in an attempt to run Black families out of town. A Black school just outside of New York City was burned to the ground by angry whites, prompting the *Philadelphia Tribune* to speculate what would have happened if the "maniacal mob" had attacked while school was in session. "It would have laughed its hellish glee while the flames baked the tender bodies of those Black children to a crisp toast," the editor cautioned. When a Black student in Grove City, Ohio, dared to complain about segregated study hall, a white teacher beat him so severely the school nurse sent him directly to the hospital. In Philadelphia, a white teacher used book mending tape to glue shut the mouth of Black fourth-grader Jane Sebastian. "Oh Miss Rittenhouse know how to have some fun? Pull it off slow, so it will hurt," suggested Jane's white classmates. The teacher consented, and the white children gathered around Jane to peel the tape off her mouth as slowly and painfully as possible. Such bizarre and terrifying incidents forced Black parents to think carefully about how their sons and daughters would fare in schools run by whites.[16]

Physical violence and intimidation were not uncommon and occurred with the implicit sanction of school administrators and the police. Chicago documented "race wars" in its public schools in 1902, 1905, and 1907. In 1919, white students reported, "About thirty colored boys registered at Tilden last fall, but we cleaned up on them the first couple of days and they never showed up again. We didn't give them any peace in the locker room, basement, at noon hours, or between classes—told them to keep out of our way or we'd see they got out." When twenty-four Black students in Gary, Indiana, arrived at Emerson High School in 1927, 1,400 white students went on strike holding signs that read, "We want an all-white school" and "Emerson must be made white— niggers must get out of Emerson High School before we will return." In Indiana, Ohio, and New Jersey the Ku Klux Klan (KKK) demanded segregated schools. In Columbus, New Jersey, and Springfield, Ohio, high-ranking school officials openly acknowledged their KKK membership and promised to uphold the color line.[17]

These examples suggest why Black families sought out Black teachers, whom they believed would protect and inspire students. Although there is evidence that a handful of Black teachers taught racially mixed classrooms in Chicago, Cleveland, Detroit, New York, Hartford, Jersey City, and a number of smaller towns, the vast majority of northern school districts refused to place Black teachers in a position of authority over white students before World War II. Most Black teachers were restricted to elementary schools, so Black high school students had virtually no chance of studying with a Black teacher unless they attended a separate school. For example, in 1930 only one Black teacher taught in New Jersey's racially mixed high schools, although thirty-two Black teachers taught at the separate Bordentown Manual Training and Industrial School for Colored Youth. Black school principals, likewise, were restricted to separate schools or to supervising designated "colored" schools within the district, such as in Atlantic City, New Jersey. Many northern communities including Pittsburgh, Milwaukee, Akron, Des Moines, Evanston, Flint, Minneapolis, Omaha, and San Diego refused to hire Black educators. Noting that the number of Black college students was on the rise in the North, one scholar noted, "The only hope for this new army of the unemployed is separate schools."[18]

A Question of Black Teachers

Teaching was one of the best paying and most prestigious jobs available to educated Black men, and especially Black women, in the North through World War II. "About the only lines of endeavor open to the Negro boy [in Detroit] are that of the porter, waiter, bellboy, messenger or bootBlack," reported Ira W. Jayne of the Society for the Prevention of Cruelty to Children in Detroit in 1912. A year later, the *Crisis* confirmed, "Negro girls who graduate from a high school seem to feel that the only positions open to them which their dignity will allow them to accept are positions as teachers." Du Bois acknowledged that Black women faced an especially bleak job market, noting, "The education is the least difficult part. The great effort is to get the work after having prepared themselves for it."[19]

Black families in Pittsburgh in 1930 expressed frustration that local schools refused to hire Black teachers, given the fact that teaching was the top career choice for Black high school students. As one resident explained, "The Negro community would be much better off if some employment was provided for our girls after they finish high school that would keep them from working as domestics for rich white folk." Given that Black leaders emphasized education as the primary route to social and economic advancement, it was imperative to secure professional opportunities for Black graduates.[20]

Gunnar Myrdal attested, "The North is almost as strict as the South in excluding Negroes from middle class jobs in the white-dominated economy. The very lack of [legal] segregation in most Northern schools makes it more difficult for a Negro to get a teaching position." He noted that in 1944, 4 percent of professional workers in America were Black because of two factors: Black churches and separate schools. Teachers created the backbone of the Black middle class in the North as well as the South—they provided role models, community leadership, and economic support to those around them. "It appears to me that our position is not much unlike that of our professional brothers in Mississippi, Alabama, and Georgia," admitted C. R. Whyte, president of the Pennsylvania Association of Teachers of Colored Children in 1937. Black teaching jobs were more secure and far more numerous in the South. Whyte cautioned, "Ominous clouds are gathering about our professional horizon."[21]

Given the restricted job market, some activists believed the best way to capture more teaching jobs was to condone some degree of school segregation. Indeed, northern cities with separate schools had the highest percentages of Black teachers. For instance, Jack Dougherty shows that in 1930, 1.5 percent of New York City's teachers were Black (500 teachers), while 6.5 percent of Cincinnati's were Black (146 teachers) and 12.6 percent of Indianapolis's teachers were Black (238 teachers). In this case, New York City had a high number of Black teachers due to strong Black political power there, but cities that ran separate schools including Cincinnati and Indianapolis had even higher rates of Black teachers, even though Blacks in these communities had relatively less political power. This explains why Black educational activists in Milwaukee agreed not to challenge school segregation in exchange for more jobs for Black educators in 1939.[22]

The rapid expansion of northern public schools created relatively secure and high salary jobs that were especially attractive during the Great Depression. Writing from Detroit in 1934, Black citizens pondered, "Now, what will separate schools mean?" One resident answered, "As I see it, it will mean employment to several hundred Negro principals and teachers, the saving of homes for many who possibly will lose them otherwise, creation of jobs for colored truant officers, janitors, and several others with great possibilities of getting representation on the Board of Education." He concluded, "I may be wrong in my views but I think that the Negro leaders and educators of Detroit should advocate separate schools for colored."[23]

Beyond the fact that teaching jobs provided economic security and community leaders, some people believed Black teachers were kinder and more nurturing. Julia Clark, a Black teacher in New York City, warned, "If anyone thinks that the Negro child in the mixed schools of New York City receives as equal education with the white children, he is greatly mistaken." She detailed that her white colleagues viewed Black children as innately inferior and unable to learn. She concluded, "I truly believe that the boy who comes into contact with an inspiring faculty and a consecrated colored principal, such as Henry A. Hunt of the Fort Valley Normal and Industrial School in the heart of Georgia, will be better educated for manhood than the graduate of the mixed school in New York." Limited social science data from this period, such as a survey of Chicago teachers in the wake of the 1919 race riot, confirm that most white teachers believed in Black racial inferiority. In Pittsburgh in 1930, sociologist Ira De A. Reid found that vocational guidance was "an empty gesture so far as the Negro pupil in the public school," where the city's all-white teaching force encouraged Black boys to study automobile repair and Black girls to prepare for domestic work. Opportunities for Black students to participate in the extracurricular life of schools such as drama programs, sports, and clubs were

extremely limited in mixed schools, while separate schools offered far more robust opportunities.[24]

This kind of discriminatory treatment prompted many Black students and
their parents to consider the potential of separate schools. "In the northern
school where colored pupils attend mixed high schools there have arisen in the
past many difficult problems," conceded an editorial in the *Crisis*. "Often the colored pupils are not encouraged. In other cases they enter poorly prepared and
they feel the handicap of poverty and prejudice." When sociologist E. Franklin
Frazier interviewed Black youth, he discovered that a surprising number preferred separate schools. As one boy disclosed, "I attended a public school in
Long Island. I was one of about three colored children there. It was very nice
and we were treated like any of the other children. We could do everything the
other children did. It was kind of lonesome though and for that reason I'd rather
go to an all Negro school."[25]

While negative experiences with prejudiced white teachers compelled some
Black northerners to consider separate, Black-controlled schools, a rising Black
nationalist movement motivated others to embrace them as a positive way to uplift the race. Only separate, Black-controlled schools could deliver the kind of education that would cultivate racial pride and develop strong Black communities.
Samuel Scott of Minnesota complained, "Negroes ashamed of themselves make

Figure 2.1. An ensemble of Black students perform in the Philadelphia Public Schools.
Undated photograph by John W. Moseley, Ruth Wright Hayre Collection, Charles
L. Blockson Afro-American Collection, Temple University Libraries, Philadelphia, PA.

me tired. Why can't a nation be composed of people of different colors and different heights and different shaped noses?" He asserted, "We don't want amalgamation. We don't want to be white. We don't want to die out and disappear. What we want in America and throughout the world is the right to be Black and also to be men."[26]

In a similar vein, college student E. Frederick Morrow contended that "Nordic education" by white teachers was so harmful that it was practically fatal for a Black student. "First and foremost is the fact, that he unavoidably acquires a white perspective—a white sense of values as it were. The next step is that of seeing very little if anything in all thing things Negro—that is, always finding fault, always unpleased, always peeved or ungrateful for any enterprise undertaken by this race." Morrow cautioned that Black students who attended majority white schools changed for the worse. "The man rapidly deteriorates into a snob, and all race pride goes up in smoke. To what end then has all his education been? To no end!"[27]

Social scientists made important contributions to this debate, but it was not until the end of this period that a clear consensus in favor of school integration emerged. Through the 1930s, some scholars documented higher levels of Black academic achievement in separate schools. Lester Granger reported "that Negro students enter high school in larger proportion from separate schools, and graduate in greater numbers than those who attend mixed schools." Another study found that a separate Black high school in one northern border city produced more Black graduates in a single year than the city's five large integrated high schools combined. The author concluded, "Greater inspiration, greater racial solidarity, superior social activities, greater retention, and greater educational achievement are possible for negroes in separate public schools than in mixed schools." These data seemed to confirm what many Black students, parents, and teachers suspected—that Black students performed better in supportive all-Black environments than in hostile white-dominated ones.[28]

The *Crisis* conceded, "There is no doubt but that in some cities colored children in mixed schools are discriminated against. They do not get proper consideration or attention, they suffer veiled and open insult, they are systematically discouraged, and they leave school prematurely. Too many colored folk think the only remedy for this is a segregated school system in the North and they advocate this, not only because they think their children will be better treated, but also because such schools will furnish employment to numbers of educated and deserving Negroes who otherwise might not get employment." Black civil rights leaders were outraged that so many Black families supported separate schools in the North, as it fractured the ability of Black communities to resist the inexorable creep of Jim Crow.[29]

As the Urban League's magazine, *Opportunity*, lamented, "The issue of separate schools is moving northward with the rising tide of Negro migration. The color line in public education is vigorously asserting itself across the continent, from Atlantic City to Los Angeles." Northern Black educational activists responded with a mix of accommodation, appropriation, and resistance.[30]

The Limits of Black Educational Protest

Shortly after the 1896 US Supreme Court ruling in *Plessy v. Ferguson* legalized "separate but equal" facilities, Scott Bibb discovered that his fourth-grade son, Ambrose, and second-grade daughter, Minnie, would be reassigned to a new school for "colored" children in Alton, Illinois. Citing a state law that prohibited racial discrimination in the public schools, Bibb sued the school district. Seven times Bibb brought his case before the courts where twice the juries could not agree on a verdict and five times they ruled in favor of the school district. Finally, in 1908 the Illinois Supreme Court ruled in Bibb's favor and ordered the Alton Public Schools to admit his children to the "white" school. Displeased, school administrators declared the ruling applied only to Ambrose and Minnie Bibb and that other Black children would have to initiate their own lawsuits if they wished to attend school on an integrated basis. The superintendent added that twenty-one-year-old Ambrose had aged out of the public schools and that nineteen-year-old Minnie would be assigned to third grade due to her supposedly inadequate academic abilities. Alton's white community dispatched policemen to hold the color line at the schoolhouse door until Bibb conceded defeat and left town. Alton's Black community had fought the arrival of Jim Crow schools and lost.[31]

A similar story unfolded in the northern New Jersey town of East Orange, where in 1899 the superintendent hired the district's first Black teacher at racially mixed Eastern Elementary and then created a special classroom of "backwards colored pupils" for her to teach. Every Black student in the school was designated as "backwards" and placed in her classroom. In 1905 the school district created a second all-Black classroom with a Black teacher at racially mixed Ashland Elementary. More than 100 Black citizens boycotted this expansion of Jim Crow education but to little avail. Divisions within East Orange's Black community and a dearth of white allies undermined Black protest, and separate Black classrooms and schools expanded within the ostensibly integrated public schools of New Jersey for the next forty years.[32]

These examples from Illinois and New Jersey illustrate just two strategies that whites used to expand northern school segregation in blatant violation of state law. Late nineteenth-century anti-segregation legislation did not reflect a broad commitment to school integration in the North but instead a combination of Reconstruction era idealism and the desire to capture Black votes. This tepid commitment to racial justice eroded as hundreds of thousands of Blacks made the Great Migration. After 1900, non-compliance with anti-discrimination legislation increased sharply. Even when Blacks won school desegregation lawsuits, as they did in Alton, whites maintained segregated schools through narrow interpretations of court orders. Even when Blacks boycotted the creation of separate classrooms, as they did in East Orange, whites argued such classrooms represented pedagogical innovations, not racial discrimination.[33]

Progressive Education, Social Science, and Race

The rapid growth and modernization of public schools provided cover for whites to expand school segregation in the name of rational, scientific, progressive educational reform. Total school enrollment in northern cities skyrocketed between 1900 and 1940 due to European immigration and the mass migration of Blacks to the urban North. Progressive reformers insisted the public schools had a special role to play in assimilating these newcomers and preparing them for democratic citizenship. Between 1852 and 1918 every state passed a compulsory attendance law to ensure that the working poor received the ameliorative benefits of state-sponsored education. Urban school superintendents found themselves at the head of massive school systems that needed to be centralized, modernized, and made more efficient. New, modern techniques were devised to sort children as rapid, normal, or slow learners, most notably IQ tests. Eager to impose order on chaotic urban school systems, many administrators turned to the science of racial difference to make education more rational and efficient.[34]

American and European scientists insisted that human race determined a person's capacity for intelligence, morality, health, physical stamina, and "civilization," and that the distinct races could be placed on a hierarchy with people of Western European descent at the top and African ancestry at the bottom. The science of white supremacy was ascendant during this era and eugenicists viewed it as an objective way to solve intractable social problems like violent crime and generational poverty. They scoffed at the "widespread and fatuous belief in the power of environment, as well as of education and opportunity to alter heredity."[35]

Eugenicists insisted education could do little to improve the social or economic conditions of Black Americans. As Madison Grant wrote in 1916, "Speaking English, wearing good clothes, and going to school and to church does not transform a Negro into a white man." Medical doctors like Arthur MacDonald prepared reports for educators that detailed the racial differences between white and "colored" children by measuring head circumference, height, weight, sensitivity to heat, and intelligence. Inevitably, these reports found significant differences between white and Black children and then recommended segregated schools. Social scientists also perpetuated the myth of white supremacy. White educational psychologist Louis A. Pechstein argued that Black students in the North had much higher rates of "mental deficiency, overageness and retardation" than white students and that a survey of Black home conditions revealed a number of specific "problems" which could only be handled through "a carefully planned program of guidance" in separate schools.[36]

Black scholars including W. E. B. Du Bois, Horace Mann Bond, and Doxey A. Wilkerson, along with a handful of prominent white scholars, rejected the science of white supremacy and challenged eugenicists' claim that Black children required separate schooling. In Chicago, Black principal Maudelle Bousfield published a study, "A Study of the Intelligence and School Achievement of Negro Children," that proved the lower IQ and achievement scores of Black students were directly related to higher levels of poverty, previous educational opportunities, and home conditions such as lack of access to books. Antiracist scholarship by Black scholars and a handful of whites such as anthropologist Franz Boas had little effect on racialist science and educational policy until after World War II. The result was a toxic environment that placed white school administrators committed to modern scientific reforms at the heads of overburdened urban school districts desperate to economize and struggling to manage a sudden increase in the Black population.[37]

Segregation in the City of Brotherly Love

Home to the North's largest Black population of over 62,000 at the turn of the century, Philadelphia featured blatant efforts to segregate Black students and consign them to an inferior curriculum in the name of pedagogical reform. The resulting spike in school segregation and inequality, in turn, fueled a series of especially contentious debates over school integration in the urban North.

The City of Brotherly Love offered public education to Black students as early as 1822, albeit on a segregated basis. By 1850 there were eight "colored" schools in Philadelphia, and in 1862 the Black community successfully petitioned white school administrators to hire the first Black teacher for a separate school. Black supporters of "equal school rights" petitioned the Pennsylvania legislature to outlaw school segregation in 1881. The resulting legislation opened previously "white" schools to Black students in Philadelphia and many Black students moved into these schools, but it did not result in the abolition of the city's separate "colored" schools.[38]

W. E. B. Du Bois conducted the first comprehensive social science analysis of a Black community in the United States, which he published in 1899 as *The Philadelphia Negro*. The study paid special attention to educational opportunities, attainment, and discrimination against the city's Black population. He noted that Pennsylvania's 1881 law outlawing school segregation "was for some time evaded, and even now some discrimination is practiced quietly in the matter of admission and transfers." Du Bois found that the city's separate schools were supported "through a feeling of loyalty to Negro teachers," but that most Black students attended integrated schools staffed by white teachers. Although 85 percent of Black Philadelphians between six and thirteen years of age attended school, only about 11 percent were promoted from primary school to grammar school and less than 1 percent entered high school. Du Bois observed that Blacks in Philadelphia were making notable progress since the end of the Civil War, but that "the problem of education is still large and pressing." Even the "leading classes" among Blacks in Philadelphia had only a grammar school education. Du Bois concluded that "a college bred person is very exceptional" and that educational equality was a pressing civil rights issue for Black Philadelphians.[39]

Shortly after publication of *The Philadelphia Negro*, reformers abolished the old ward school boards and created a centralized Board of Public Education in 1905. From 1906 to 1914 Superintendent Martin G. Brumbaugh carried out a modernization campaign, and in 1907 he tackled "the problem of the colored child." Noting that Black students could choose between integrated or separate schools, Brumbaugh argued that separate schools were the better choice. He reasoned, "It has given to the colored child a better opportunity to move at his own rate of progress through the materials of the curriculum, which rate of progress is in some respects different from the rate of progress of other children." Brumbaugh cited the lower IQ scores of Black students to establish the claim that Black children had "somewhat different" academic abilities than whites. He continued, "It has enabled the Board of Education to give employment to a group of deserving members of the colored race, who by industry and capacity have won their certificates to teach in the public schools of the city."[40]

Brumbaugh encouraged Black parents to request separate schools, cautioning that when Blacks insisted on attending integrated schools in large numbers "a really difficult problem presents itself." He expounded, "The fact is that when the percentage of colored children reaches thirty or more the other children begin gradually to withdraw from the school. This fact, coupled with the additional fact that there are a number of qualified colored teachers in the city who are not at the present time in the employment of the Board of Education, leads me to suggest that wherever possible separate schools should be inaugurated for the colored children, and this possibility, so far as I can see, must be conditioned upon the parents of these children themselves."[41]

Brumbaugh claimed that school administrators had little control over whether schools had high percentages of Black students or whether white students opted to transfer out, but this was inaccurate. Du Bois documented discriminatory school assignment and transfer policies that artificially concentrated Black students in certain schools. Other northern cities did the same thing, like Chicago, where administrators used transfers to isolate Black students in certain schools and whites in others. New York City high schools limited the number of Black students accepted to each high school and then channeled students into segregated vocational courses. In Philadelphia, Brumbaugh needed Black families to request or at least support the expansion of separate schools, which were technically illegal according to state law. To sweeten the deal he promised to hire more Black teachers and principals for the new "colored" schools.[42]

Black Philadelphians were conflicted over Brumbaugh's scheme. By 1908, only 2,335 out of 7,559 Black students in the district attended separate schools. Reverend William A. Creditt, pastor of Philadelphia's First African Baptist Church and founder of the private Black Downingtown Industrial and Agricultural School, emerged as the city's outspoken advocate for expanding separate schools. He looked forward to the day when "there shall be no distinction in America on the count of race or color," but in the meantime, Creditt alleged separate schools offered a higher quality education and trained more Black leaders than integrated ones. He persuaded his congregation, fellow Black ministers, and neighborhood parents to petition for separate schools.[43]

In the fall of 1908 Brumbaugh added the Pollock School to the city's list of "colored" schools, noting, "We would not have thought of taking this step if the colored ministers of the Thirtieth School Section had not come to us in a body, asking that the Pollock School, which is in that section, be set apart for colored pupils in order that employment might be given to young women of the race who are graduates of the Normal School and otherwise could not obtain classes. So we have arranged the classes to provide places for eight colored teachers out of the twelve at this school." More than 400 Black parents signed Creditt's petition requesting a new separate school. Brumbaugh immediately moved Pollock's Black students into separate classrooms and made plans to transfer the remaining white students and teachers to majority white schools. To streamline these racial assignments, Brumbaugh created a dual list of teacher candidates—one "white" and one "colored"—that remained in effect until 1937. This hardened the informal practice of restricting Black teaching assignments into official policy, a fact that did not escape the attention of local civil rights activists.[44]

Black Philadelphians enraged by the expansion of separate schools and the creation of a segregated teacher candidate list organized a citizens' committee to investigate educational discrimination. Led by physician Dr. N. F. Mossell, the committee included a roster of elite Black male doctors, ministers, and newspaper editors. The group claimed that at least 2,000 Black students experienced severe racial segregation and discrimination in Philadelphia. Dr. Mossell noted that Black youth were often refused admittance to certain schools and that even in integrated schools Black children were seated apart from whites, denied the use of textbooks, or assigned to a "badly located, unsanitary and overcrowded" separate annex.

In 1912, the Black *Philadelphia Tribune* joined the fight. As editors Christopher J. Perry and John W. Harris charged, "Not withstanding the fact that quite a goodly number of tax payers of our city have made it known that they are opposed to the separate school system, the general public ought to know that Superintendent Brumbaugh, aided by a few sly colored men, is determined to make the colored people of our city endure the objectionable system." Issuing a call to arms, Perry and Harris insisted, "What will the citizens of Philadelphia do about the matter? Will they sit quietly while the manacles of race proscription are fastened around their limbs, or will they arouse their energies to and give battle to the devilish scheme?"[45]

World War I and the Great Migration

Battling the devilish scheme would have to wait, as the majority of Black Philadelphians failed to see the urgency in eliminating separate schools staffed by Black teachers, especially when most Black students attended integrated schools. This stance, however, would evolve as school segregation expanded and conditions deteriorated. As the start of World War I ignited the region's industrial economy, southern Black migrants rushed to Philadelphia, especially between the spring of 1916 and the spring of 1918, when over 40,000 migrants moved to the city. The arrival of tens of thousands of Black migrants sparked racial tensions and placed enormous pressures on Philadelphia's public schools.[46]

Black principal Daniel A. Brooks witnessed the changes that swept through Philadelphia firsthand. He wrote, "In 1916, thousands of Southern Negroes were rushing to Philadelphia to engage in war-work. Their numerous children were threatening to crowd into the elementary schools where few Negroes had previously entered. The usual 'solution' was proposed,—placing them in separate schools." The board of education selected old, derelict buildings to convert into new "colored" schools and crammed students of all ages into a single classroom. According to Daniels, "classes of 60 children were frequent, with ages from 8 to 16 in one class." Conditions in the separate schools were dramatically inferior to majority white schools. Daniels described, "Old, frame buildings, gas-lighted, with coal-stoves in many rooms, out-door water closets." Black Philadelphians were not pleased, but Daniels reflected, "In order to gain the advantage of having teaching positions opened to colored teachers, the situation was reluctantly accepted by the colored people."[47]

Meanwhile, Brumbaugh was amassing data so he could adjust public schools to the needs of the Black child. In 1910 white sociologist Howard W. Odum discovered that in Philadelphia, "the Negroes show 48.6 percent retardation and the whites 18.6 percent." Odum was unable to determine whether the higher levels of "retardation" were due to environmental or biological factors, but in the end it mattered little to Brumbaugh. The point was that Black and white children performed differently on IQ tests and thus required different kinds of education. A second study in 1913 discovered that "working age" Black students from the "colored" Durham School could only find work as domestic servants or errand boys while white boys at the nearby Potter School found more lucrative employment in factories and offices. A reform-minded man, Brumbaugh expanded industrial training and reduced academic coursework in the "colored" schools to better design schools to educate Black children for the jobs available to them, a strategy that was popular in other cities like Chicago. These progressive era educational reforms increased racial segregation and inequality in urban public schools.[48]

Figure 2.2. Sewing class in the Philadelphia Public Schools, 1929. Courtesy of the Special Collections Research Center, Temple University Libraries, Philadelphia, PA.

Black academics rejected Brumbaugh's plan to expand vocational training at the expense of academic education. Throughout the Jim Crow South, whites attempted to restrict Black students to a "manual training and industrial" curriculum that lacked the academic rigor of traditional public schools. "The latest attack on Negro education comes from Philadelphia," Du Bois seethed in the *Crisis* in 1915. "Very adroitly and cunningly the Negroes have been massed in segregated schools. Now 'industrial training' is to be introduced *in the Negro schools* and a representative of a leading southern industrial school is on hand to advise!" Du Bois added that Black parents would be pleased to have their children trained for skilled factory work, but protested, "They know that if their children are compelled to cook and sew when they ought to be learning to read and cipher, they will not be able to enter the high school or go to college as the white children are doing."[49]

A group of "prominent colored Philadelphians" mobilized to fight the expansion of separate, industrial schools, which they denounced as "un-Christian, un-American, and unjust." The *Philadelphia Tribune* noted that the strongest opposition to school segregation came from "those who were either born here or who have lived here for a long time," implying that Black support for separate schools came from recent southern arrivals.[50]

White school leaders ignored Black criticism and expanded vocational education in Philadelphia's fourteen "colored" elementary schools. Meanwhile school segregation was expanding throughout the state, including the nearby towns of Moton and Media. In 1915 the school board in Moton condemned its old, run-down schoolhouse and taxed all citizens to build a new one. When the new school was opened, school leaders lined up all the Black students and "marched them back to the old, condemned and dilapidated building and gave them all of the old school-books, while the white children were given the privilege of attending the new school fully equipped with the newest books and appliances."[51] Similarly, in January of 1917, the courts confirmed the legality of segregating Black children in Media after white school administrators testified under oath that "the separation of the pupils was not made because of color, but was a step toward efficiency." The white principal reflected, "I decided to put all the retarded students in classes by themselves, under specially trained teachers . . . and in going over the list of pupils I didn't look them up to find out what color they were. I sent all of those who were backward to the old school building." According to school officials it was a complete surprise to discover that they had classified every single Black student as retarded, and not a single white student.[52]

Civil rights leaders seethed that Black northerners were too complacent in the face of expanding school segregation. In July of 1919, Du Bois cautioned, "At present the tendency is to accept and even demand separate schools because our children so often are neglected, mistreated and humiliated in the public schools. This is a dangerous and inadvisable alternative and a wicked surrender of principle for which our descendants will pay dearly." Black parents such as Mrs. L. B. Smith in Des Moines, Iowa, organized "vigilance committees" to stop the insidious spread of school segregation. But not all Black parents agreed that school integration solved the problems related to educational discrimination.[53]

Black Nationalism

A surge in Black nationalism exacerbated the growing tensions between school internationalists and separatists throughout the North, especially in Philadelphia. In 1916, Marcus Garvey's Universal Negro Improvement Association (UNIA) mobilized a grassroots movement that emphasized separate institutions as the key to Black economic and political advancement. A bombastic and stirring orator, Garvey preached pride in Black racial identity and prophesized that Black Americans would achieve full equality only when they gave up their fight for integration and developed successful separate institutions, including schools. He promised that a better day was coming, and that by working together, 400 million people of African descent could liberate Africa—and Black Americans—from the yoke of white colonialism.

The Garvey movement was especially popular in Philadelphia, where Reverend James W. H. Eason of the People's Metropolitan African Methodist Episcopal Zion Church was its charismatic leader. By 1918 Philadelphia was a center of UNIA organizing, and between 1919 and 1920 more than 10,000 Black Philadelphians, mostly working class, joined the local chapter, making it the second largest chapter after New York City.[54]

Although it is difficult to uncover a direct link between the UNIA in Philadelphia and the debate over school integration, it seems likely that Garveyites in Philadelphia preferred separate, Black-controlled schools. A rash of vicious race riots in the summer and early fall of 1919 left Black northerners more skeptical than ever that integration was a viable solution. In the wake of these riots, a new racial militancy was born. The "New Negro" prized unflinching resistance to white supremacy and took a fierce pride in Black racial identity. "As a race we have decided already that we have fought the last battle for the white man. We have died for the last time for him," extolled Garvey in the *New Negro World*. "We shall now prepare to answer the call of Mother Africa when she demands of us our wealth, our strength and genius to deliver her from the grasp of the oppressor." The UNIA flourished under these circumstances, and Garvey's popularity grew to epic proportions in Philadelphia and New York."[55]

Speaking in Philadelphia on October 21, 1919, Garvey pointed out that American race relations were deteriorating and that efforts to integrate into white, mainstream society had failed. He warned, "Month by month they are lynching more Negroes than they ever did before; month by month more riots are going on in the industrial sections of this country than ever before. This is an indication of the spirit of the people that are living today." Garvey resolved, "If you think that the white man is going to be more liberal to Negroes than they are at present, you are making a big mistake. Every succeeding generation of the white race is getting more prejudiced against the Negro. It is time, therefore, for the Negro to look out for the future for himself." This message directly contradicted civil rights activists who insisted that school integration was the only way to equalize educational opportunities and improve race relations. Garvey warned that Blacks would be increasingly vulnerable in white-dominated institutions. Black Philadelphians only had to look at the local public schools to see evidence of these very trends. The best way to protect Black interests and advance the race, according to Garvey, was to develop separate, Black-controlled institutions.[56]

Garvey's faith in separatism and his celebration of African heritage resonated with the Black masses in ways that the NAACP's plans for integration and assimilation did not. "We have learned that Black is beautiful, Black is noble and that Black is the standard for the time," exclaimed Philadelphia's Reverend Eason. Speaking at a mass meeting in New York City, Eason placed a little boy named Lambert Tobias on a chair in front of a packed audience of over 6,000 people. "The Anglo-Saxon says to this little colored boy: 'You need not hope, you need not aspire, thus far shalt tho go and no farther.'" Eason continued, "The Universal Negro Improvement Association says to the colored youth: 'Rise, shine, for the light is coming. You can be anything under God's heaven you want to be.'" Such passionate rhetoric proposed that only separate, Black-controlled schools could offer the right kind of education. Black Garveyites in New Orleans were so convinced of the value of separate institutions that they declared to whites, "We like your Jim Crow laws," as they kept white people out of Black churches, schools, and social clubs. Of the 10,000 UNIA members in Philadelphia, it is hard to imagine many would join the campaign to abolish separate schools and compel city authorities to assign Black students to schools run by whites.[57]

Garvey's meteoric rise came to a screeching halt when he was convicted of mail fraud and sentenced to five years in prison in June 1923. Black leaders including Du Bois were relieved to see Garvey imprisoned and later deported to Jamaica. "This squat, energetic, gorilla-jawed Black man is one of the worst enemies of his own race," avowed the NAACP's William Pickens. With Garvey out of the picture and the local UNIA chapter defunct, Black integrationists in Philadelphia renewed their attack on school segregation.[58]

The Amazing Paradox of Black Teachers

Integrationists set their sights not on the local public schools of Philadelphia, but instead on Cheyney Training School for Teachers, located just outside of the city. Founded as the Philadelphia Institute for Colored Youth in 1834, the school relocated to a farm west of the city in 1902 as a secondary school dedicated to teacher training. Like the Bordentown School in New Jersey, it grew into a high-quality separate public school. The State of Pennsylvania agreed to provide state funding in 1920, establishing a public teacher training college that served Black students with a staff of Black faculty and administrators.

Just as Cheyney was about to receive its annual tax-funded appropriation in 1923, Philadelphia activists questioned the relationship between a "colored" state teachers' college and segregation in Pennsylvania's public schools. The Philadelphia chapter of the NAACP launched an investigation of Cheney that would develop into a campaign to integrate the city's public schools. According to NAACP leaders, the existence of Cheyney as a public institution for "colored" teacher education students fortified and reproduced racial segregation in the public schools of Pennsylvania. The NAACP wanted both Cheney and Philadelphia's public schools to operate as integrated institutions.[59]

While this school integration campaign drew the support of Philadelphia's Black elite, many Black students and parents remained undecided. Black teachers and principals, restricted to working in Philadelphia's "colored" schools, flatly opposed it. Cheyney's Black principal Leslie Pinckney Hill argued that the school did more to advance Black civil rights as a high-quality, separate college than it could as an integrated institution. He expounded, "I believe in no kind of enforced segregation, and in no kind of Jim-crowism. On the contrary, the whole weight of this school has always been exerted against these evils." He continued, "The very purpose of the Cheyney discipline is to develop a strong body of clear-minded leaders, who will consecrate their lives, if possible, to the stern task of helping to lift from the nation this incubus of Jim-crowism in all of it manifestations." Drawing on Black nationalism, Hill defended separate Black institutions. "The right to self-determination is the very essence of democracy. It is the Negro's surest weapon against Great Despair. When others will not help us, we will help ourselves. Any other attitude marks the craven or the poser." Hill implied that white-run schools could not offer the same quality of education, thus leaving the Black community bereft of leaders and unable to advance the struggle for social justice.[60]

Representing the Philadelphia NAACP, the Reverend William L. Imes and attorney G. Edward Dickerson penned an angry retort, contending that a separate teachers' college fortified state-sponsored racial discrimination. They fumed,

"The State having the bird, the cage, and the appendages, that is, the colored State Normal School, the colored school buildings throughout the state to give its graduates employment, and the children conveniently segregated out of line with the work of the established state authorities, the next step will be to again legalize what has been illegally done; and we shall have in law, as well as in fact, a complete segregated school system for the entire state." Imes and Dickerson predicted that segregation in the public colleges and schools would lead to Jim Crow cars, public conveyances, and loss of political status for Blacks throughout the North.[61]

Du Bois asked Black citizens to take a more measured and reasonable approach. He confirmed Imes and Dickerson's claim that state-sponsored school segregation "means the establishment of group hostility in those tender years of development when prejudices tend to become 'natural' and 'instinctive'" and called on "all true Americans" to oppose Jim Crow schools. However, he made a sharp distinction between evils of state-sponsored segregation and the potential benefits of separate, Black-controlled schools. The most valuable aspect of separate schools, according to Du Bois, was Black teachers.

Although Du Bois maintained that white teachers were perfectly capable of educating Black children, he recognized that anti-Black racism and high levels of racial segregation in American public schools meant that Black teachers played an absolutely essential role in the education of Black citizens. He insisted, "Without the self-sacrificing efficient colored teacher of colored youth to-day, we would face positive disaster." Since Cheyney promised to prepare more Black teachers in Pennsylvania, Du Bois believed it had tremendous value to Black citizens.

Du Bois explained, "Here we face the amazing paradox: we must oppose segregation in schools; we must honor and appreciate the colored teacher in the colored school. . . . Small wonder that Negro communities have been torn in sunder by deep and passionate differences of opinion arising from this pitiable dilemma."

Du Bois turned to the question of separate public schools in Philadelphia. "With the colored citizens largely asleep for a long time, the solution of separate colored schools has been accepted with only half-hearted protest." But now, Du Bois observed, Black Philadelphians were angry at Principal Hill for winning state funding for a teachers' college that served Black youth. He reasoned, "It does not follow that when a Black man makes a Black enterprise the best and most efficient for its purpose that he is necessarily a traitor or that he believes in segregation by race." He continued,

> It was the duty of Hill to make Cheyney a school. He did not found Cheyney. It was founded half a century before he was born. He did try

and is trying to raise it from the status of a second class High School without funds, equipment, or recognition, to one of the best normal schools of one of the greatest states of the union. Those folk, white or Black, who seek to saddle this programme with a permanent "Jim Crow" school policy in the commonwealth of William Penn deserve the damning of every decent American citizen.

Du Bois praised the motives and sincerity of Black educational activists in Philadelphia who were fighting against school segregation, noting that "in such a fight I am with them heart and soul. But when this fight becomes a fight against Negro school teachers I quit. I believe in Negro school teachers. I would to God white children as well as colored children could have more of them. With proper training they are the finest teachers in the world because they have suffered and endured and nothing human is beneath their sympathy."

In closing, Du Bois described seven steps that Black educational activists in Philadelphia should take to ensure educational equality, including halting the spread of segregated schools, desegregating teaching jobs, improving the quality of separate "colored" schools, and supporting Cheyney and working to open its doors to white students. Du Bois wanted Black northerners to move beyond a polemical debate that left no room for compromise. He encouraged Black citizens to support Black teachers and separate schools, even as activists worked toward the goal of school integration. Du Bois's erudition, however, appears to have fallen on deaf ears.[62]

A Revitalized Debate

The acrimonious dispute over Cheyney Training School for Teachers mobilized Black civil rights activists in Philadelphia and focused attention on the dire problem of educational inequality. A successful campaign in Springfield, Ohio, proved that northern Black communities could use school boycotts and litigation to combat school segregation. By 1920 there were over 134,000 Black citizens in Philadelphia, a 58.9 percent increase since 1910, and in the following decade the Black population would grow to over 200,000. In 1920 the "colored" schools started running on double shifts due to overcrowding, meaning that thousands of Black children only attended school for half a day in the city's oldest, most dilapidated buildings. In the integrated schools, Black students encountered disturbing examples of discrimination. One racist teacher insisted, "Biologists have decided that the Negro brain is yet undeveloped. They seem to be unable to progress beyond the Sixth Grade." Frustrated by deteriorating conditions, the Philadelphia NAACP issued a public statement to "disapprove of the present policy of progressively segregated public school in Philadelphia according to race and color." However, some Black students, parents, and teachers continued to question whether school integration was really a good idea.[63]

Fourteen-year-old Mary Isabelle Coleman wrote to the national office of the NAACP in 1923. She attended racially integrated Philadelphia High School for Girls, but based on her experiences there, she believed separate schools offered Black students the best chance for success. "I quite agree with the *Crisis* it is a fine idea to have colored teachers in all the schools. But I think it is also worthwhile to have more colored schools. I do not think it would mean a degradation in the system of teaching but a regeneration. It would be an incentive to the lower-grade pupils and also high-school pupils," she insisted. NAACP Executive Secretary James Weldon Johnson penned a kind response to Coleman, noting he was "very much interested in what you had to say." Nevertheless, the national and the local NAACP was unwilling to countenance an educational reform strategy that included support for separate schools. Its school integration campaign required the abolition of separate schools and the complete integration of public schools—and teaching jobs—in the North.[64]

Since the facilities for separate schools in Philadelphia were blatantly inferior to the mixed school, the lynchpin of the debate over school integration in the Black community was the question of Black teachers. Some Black families wanted to capture greater resources for the separate schools, not abolish them. This strategy was the surest way to support and expand jobs for Black teachers in Philadelphia, which Black families prioritized. Civil rights leaders did not. "Because certain people teach in them does not mean that they must support or promote the growth of a system that is ruinous to the great mass," reiterated the *Philadelphia Tribune*. "Those who must teach in these schools should accept it as an unavoidable hardship—In this spirit there is no quarrel—but to advocate a system which perpetuates Southern ideals is stupid, silly, and void of reason." Integrationists championed a colorblind teacher hiring and placement policy, but since most northern school districts, including Philadelphia, refused to allow Black teachers to teach white students, it was unclear how this policy was supposed to work.[65]

On May 23, 1925, the Pennsylvania Association of Teachers of Colored Children held its annual meeting at Cheyney Training School for Teachers. Members focused on the most pressing political question of the day—school integration—which they analyzed from all angles: Are colored schools necessary? When is a colored school improperly constituted? What are the dangers of colored schools? How may we keep our boys and girls in school? What is the effect of colored schools on attendance, retardation, physical equipment, and scholarship?

After vigorous discussion, Black educators concluded that separate schools were indispensable and that mixed schools duped parents into thinking they offered a higher quality education when in fact the opposite was true. "Mixed schools are an agent for our development only when they create a desire within us to remain in school and graduate," one member reasoned. On the other hand, separate schools offered nurturing environments designed to meet the needs of Black youth. "The reports from teachers revealing their work in teaching their pupils to respect racial achievement were inspiring. Poems are being learned, hero tales selected, special programs given, and our sorrow songs sung and understood. This is the dawning of a new day in which we give our children pride in our race instead of shame."[66]

Teachers concluded that Black students would be mistreated and poorly educated in integrated schools. It would be far better, they reasoned, to create supportive environments where Black youth could study Black history, music, and heroes in order to find inspiration. Black scholars like E. Franklin Frazier scoffed at these claims, complaining that Black teachers emphasized "too much inspiration and too little information." Frazier concluded, "Instead of filling the Negro's mind with knowledge and training him in the fundamental habits of civilization, his teachers have quite often led him from one emotional debauch to another. Surfeited with emotional appeals never resulting in action, the product of Negro education has become a spectator of civilization incapable of participation."[67]

By the spring of 1925 the debate over school integration versus separation in Philadelphia appeared to be at an impasse. There was universal agreement that Jim Crow schools were unconscionable, but there was also widespread faith that Black teachers inspired higher levels of academic achievement that led to better jobs, higher salaries, and more social prestige. Circumstantial evidence suggested that Black students did better in high-quality separate schools than hostile integrated ones. As Du Bois put it, "How else can we explain the astonishing fact that with practically the same kind of colored population in cities like Washington, Baltimore, Philadelphia, and New York, the 200,000 Negroes in Washington and Baltimore send out 400 colored high school graduates every year, while 250,000 Negroes in Philadelphia and New York send out only 50?"[68]

Throughout the region, school segregation got progressively worse and the number of separate Black schools increased. One report estimated the number of "colored" schools in New Jersey increased by 26 percent between 1919 and 1930, so that there were at least seventy "colored" schools in the state by 1935. School officials in Dayton, Ohio attempted to open a separate school in blatant violation of state law in 1924. It took a few years, but school segregation there expanded rapidly through the 1930s. Indianapolis was even more successful, and in 1927 the city opened a separate "colored" high school over the protests of the Black community. Similar trends unfolded in Philadelphia, which opened a new separate school in the fall of 1925 and forcibly transferred to it 300 Black students from mixed schools. A few months later school administrators designated majority Black Singerly School as "colored" and transferred out the white students and faculty. Blacks in Philadelphia were aware of the growing number of separate schools in the North but could not agree on the best response. White school administrators pressed their advantage.[69]

Superintendent Edwin C. Broome declared in 1926 that Philadelphia would no longer take parents' preferences into account when assigning students to separate schools. "No one wants segregated schools, but this in itself is no basis upon which we decide as to the advisability of the separate schools," he pontificated. Broome reiterated that white students refused to attend a school once "the colored was in predominance" and so the district believed it was "wise" to transfer out the white students and designate the school "colored." He declared that Black students were happier in separate schools and encouraged Black families to request equal resources for those schools. "If colored are more happy together, instructed by their own teachers, and ask for a hearing on an educational basis— they will be listened to. We will, I assure you, fight against poor school houses and poor equipment in South Philadelphia."[70]

Broome delivered this speech to the Pennsylvania Association of Teachers in Colored Schools. The growth of separate schools in the North meant more teaching jobs for Black teachers and principals. For example, when the number of separate schools in New Jersey increased from 52 in 1919 to 66 in 1930, the number of Black teachers in the state jumped from 187 to 418. Civil rights leaders stubbornly refused to acknowledge this point and focused instead on Philadelphia's callous new school assignment policies. The Philadelphia NAACP declared its undying commitment to school integration and the *Philadelphia Tribune* organized a Defense Fund to sponsor the coming legal battle against separate schools.[71]

Once again, Black civil rights leaders were disappointed when few Black Philadelphians joined the school integration movement. "Where are those who have been loud in their denunciation of segregated schools?" demanded the *Philadelphia Tribune*. "Have they decided segregated schools are good things?" Black parents like O. Z. Phillips justified their decision to support separate schools. "I know for a fact that the colored children in the minor grades will thrive and advance by far better under colored teachers than they will under white teachers," wrote Phillips, who had withdrawn his three children from integrated schools at various points, after which each child thrived in the "colored" schools of Camden, New Jersey, and Philadelphia. "I am opposed to mixed schools for two reasons: In the first place we as far as I can see and understand only have in Philadelphia segregated schools beçause wherever we have a mixed school of classes or students we only have white teachers." He continued, "Next thing

Figure 2.3. Black students and teachers in Philadelphia, where many prioritized the warm relationship between Black teachers and students over school integration. Undated photograph by John W. Mosley. Ruth Wright Hayre Collection, Charles L. Blockson Afro-American Collection, Temple University Libraries, Philadelphia, PA.

I know for a fact that the colored children in the minor grades will thrive and advance by far better under colored teachers than they will under white teachers." Such testimony infuriated integrationists, who penned angry rejoinders. "As you have so kindly given your readers the privilege of expressing their opinions of Segregated schools, I too have something to say," fumed H. Rush in the summer of 1929. "I think it one of the worst evils that could be thrust upon us. Still worse for any of us to welcome it."[72]

Civil rights leader A. Philip Randolph blamed Philadelphia's Black leaders for failing to inspire the masses and allowing whites to "force an inferiority complex down the throats of the Negro." Randolph could not understand why Black Philadelphians supported separate schools, imagining that only an "inferiority complex" could explain such defective reasoning. Civil rights organizations such as the NAACP, the Urban League, and the Brotherhood of Sleeping Car Porters refused to address Black families' concerns about the importance of Black teachers and the dangers of hostile learning environments. Meanwhile, the growing number of high-quality separate schools in the North offered an enticing alternative.[73]

High Quality, Separate Schools

By 1929, the number of separate "colored" schools in Philadelphia had grown to fifteen, and attendance at these schools was no longer necessarily voluntary. School segregation was escalating throughout the North in open defiance of state laws and over the objection of Black civil rights activists. The ability of Black northerners to resist segregation depended on the political and economic power of local Black communities. For example, Black citizens in New York City, Chicago, Detroit, and Cleveland successfully resisted blatant race-based school assignments because they threatened to withhold the Black vote from any candidate who supported school segregation. These cities offered mixed classrooms, schools, and, in New York City and Detroit, even teaching assignments, although the concentration of Black students into certain schools remained a major problem as it correlated with educational inequality. In communities where Blacks did not have significant political power, some Black leaders embraced separate schools as a way to negotiate for better facilities, control aspects of the curriculum, and secure jobs. When necessary, white politicians were willing to invest significant funds into separate schools to increase school segregation.[74]

This explains why the State of New Jersey allocated tens of thousands of dollars to the Bordentown Manual Training and Industrial School, which enabled Black principal William R. Valentine to build new facilities, attract more students, and dramatically increase enrollment. The Bordentown School drew hundreds of Black students out of their local school districts each year, especially in the southern part of New Jersey, leaving these districts distinctly whiter. Meanwhile, Black northerners adored the Bordentown School, as a Black-run institution dedicated to racial uplift. As Lester Granger noted in 1927, "Bordentown, therefore, means to New Jersey much more than a school. It is a successful, well-managed enterprise, if not owned, at least operated, by Negroes; and its steady growth and efficiency are matters of inspiration and pride to the race in that State."[75]

Similarly, school administrators in Cincinnati cheerfully allocated new funds to separate Black schools in the 1920s, even though policymakers had outlawed school segregation there in 1887. In 1924 they moved the "colored" Harriet Beecher Stowe School into a brand-new schoolhouse equipped with twenty-eight classrooms, a catering department, laundry, sewing room, print shop, house construction room, cabinet making and woodworking shops, power machine laboratory, swimming pool, cafeteria, and gymnasium. The school's Black principal, Jennie D. Porter, boasted that students studied Black history and learned to appreciate spirituals sung by the Teachers' Glee Club. She rationalized, "Our children are no longer ashamed of their own people." In 1928 Porter completed her doctoral dissertation, which investigated the question, "Shall the Negro in the North be educated in separate Negro schools or mixed schools?" Based on her work at the Harriet Beecher Stowe School, Porter recommend separate schools.[76]

Racist northern whites were willing to invest in the expansion of school segregation. A revitalized Ku Klux Klan rose to power in the 1920s, including in Indianapolis, where KKK leaders insisted the city remove Black students from the public high schools. In September 1927, Indianapolis school officials reassigned every Black high school student to a brand-new "colored" high school, leaving the others exclusively white. Blacks had no say in this process, but many decided to embrace the opportunity presented by a separate, Black-controlled high school. "Segregation is not desirable, my God no!" decried the Black *Indianapolis Recorder*. "But forced upon us, many degrees of happiness may accrue to us as a result of it."[77]

Indianapolis's Crispus Attucks High School opened with forty-eight Black teachers and a Black principal, all with excellent academic credentials and some with advanced degrees. The school board appointed Matthias Nolcox, a Black graduate of Indiana University with a doctorate in education from Harvard University, as principal. The school's athletics teams, drama clubs, debate clubs, and school newspaper became the pride of the Black community, and Black students relished participating in extracurricular activities that had been denied to Black students in Indianapolis's mixed schools. As in other northern communities, this separate Black high school grew into a cherished institution.[78]

In Chicago, where the Black population increased dramatically during the Great Migration, the South Side's Wendell Phillips High School developed a reputation as an outstanding Black high school, even though it was not officially a separate school. As late as 1912, there were only four Black students in Wendell Phillips's graduating class, but between 1910 and 1920, Chicago's Black population grew from just over 40,000 to nearly 110,000. Between 1920 and 1930 it more than doubled again, and many of these new arrivals crowded into Chicago's South Side. In 1921, school authorities assigned Black math teacher Maudelle Bousfield to Wendell Phillips. By this time, the student population was more than 75 percent Black, and the percentage of white students continued to decline precipitously each year as school administrators granted transfers for white students. Bousfield became dean of girls in 1926, the first African American dean in the city, and then principal of Wendell Phillips in 1939, the first African American high school principal in Chicago. Although majority Black, the high school was racially mixed, as was the teaching staff. "Phillips had a low-down name when I took it," Bousfield admitted. She bolstered the public's view of the school through student performances in music, arts, and athletics, and cultivated school pride by developing strong academics, vocational training, and citizenship education. Wendell Phillips High School became so popular in the Black community under Bousfield's leadership that students started using fake addresses to get into the school.[79]

While school segregation was plainly undesirable, there was a huge difference between the overcrowded and dilapidated "colored" schools of Philadelphia and the high quality, Black-led schools in cities like Bordentown, Cincinnati, and Indianapolis, or even racially mixed, Black-led schools like Wendell Phillips in Chicago. These outstanding Black schools, rare as they were, provided a glimmer of hope that separate schools could be equal. What is more, these schools proved that majority Black schools could nurture Black academic excellence. Crispus Attucks High School's 1933 yearbook listed ninety-two graduates and stated that they would be attending prestigious colleges including Fisk, Tuskegee, Purdue, Howard, Lincoln, DePauw, Dartmouth, Wilberforce, Indiana University, and Oberlin.[80]

The Great Depression Sparks Protest

The start of the 1929 school year coincided with the beginning of the longest and most severe economic downturn in American history. Northern Black communities were hit hard as Black workers were the last hired and first fired, and public schools entered a period of stark retrenchment as funding evaporated. In northern communities like Cairo, Illinois, tensions between whites and Blacks intensified as jobs and resources grew scarce. Whites in Cairo not only vigorously policed the color line at the schoolhouse door during the Depression years, but they also refused to allow Black citizens to use the public parks or library. When northern communities were forced to make difficult decisions about cuts to school funding, majority Black schools were vulnerable targets.[81]

Black Americans had more faith than ever that a quality education meant better prospects for Black youth. The Department of Interior reported that literacy rates of Black Americans had increased from 2 percent in 1850 to 84 percent in 1930. More than 19,000 Black students were enrolled in college in 1930 and more than 2,000 earned bachelor's degrees that year. This means that nearly as many Black students earned college degrees in just the year 1930 as the total number of Black college graduates in the United States before 1900.[82]

Johns Hopkins professor E. A. Schaal noted, "The rate at which the Negro has been receiving higher education in this country has been greatly accelerated during the last three decades. The giving of higher education to a submerged race with such rapidly increasing speed spells change for that race in relation to the dominant race." Schaal was right. More Black Americans than ever worked as university professors, doctors, nurses, social workers, dentists, social scientists, teachers, journalists, politicians, and small business owners. Increased educational opportunities fueled the expanding Black middle class and proved that education functioned as a powerful tool for racial uplift. Formal education was increasingly important to job prospects in a modern industrial economy. As educational retrenchment hit Black families especially hard, many began to reconsider the dangers of separate schools.[83]

Sociologist Charles S. Johnson conceded, "Some Negroes view the [school] segregation as an unmitigated evil, dangerous to the status of the Negro in northern sections, while others see many benefits to the race in the form of closer racial solidarity, greater inspiration to Negro youth, and more positions for Negro teachers." Writing in the *Crisis*, George F. McCray confirmed, "The most heated intellectual battles among us have been fought over the education of our children."[84]

As the debate over school integration was hashed out against the backdrop of the Great Depression, support for school integration grew throughout the North. This was because in many communities, including Philadelphia, Black citizens noticed that educational retrenchment devastated majority Black schools. Already located in dilapidated buildings with overcrowded classrooms and a dearth of supplies, most separate schools sank to new lows as school funding was decimated. Even racially mixed schools with a majority of Black students seemed to suffer disproportionately. "There is a constantly growing narrowness here that smacks of Dixie," complained reporter J. Max Barber after surveying race relations in Philadelphia. "Nowhere is this more evident than in our public schools."[85]

To take one example, in 1931 the Philadelphia Board of Education announced that, as a cost-cutting measure, all elementary schools would be limited to grades one through six and that all seventh and eighth graders would be moved into existing junior high schools. Black Philadelphians interpreted this decision as racially motivated, as the "colored" elementary schools included grades one through eight, whereas the racially mixed elementary schools—staffed by white teachers—were already limited to grades one through six. When the administration removed seventh and eighth graders from the "colored" schools and sent them to existing junior high schools, it eliminated numerous Black teaching positions, but none for whites.[86]

School segregation made it easier for whites to hoard scarce resources, but these actions were so blatant that Black citizens objected. Black Philadelphians responded with protest meetings and symposiums on "Segregation in Our Public Schools." Civil rights leaders asked Black citizens to rally around three goals: electing a Black representative to the school board, abolishing the dual Black and white teacher candidate lists, and getting Black teachers hired in the secondary schools. Notably, these requests did not include the abolition of the separate schools, allowing Black integrationists and separatists to work together toward shared goals.

In the summer of 1934, the Pennsylvania Association of Teachers of Colored Children petitioned the Philadelphia Board of Education for the right to work in integrated junior and senior high schools. Thanks to active support by local and national civil rights leaders and strong backing from local Black families, the Black teachers won. Although this modest reform neither ended school segregation nor substantially improved the quality of education available to Black students, it demonstrated the ability of Black educational activists to organize and challenge explicit school segregation.[87]

Throughout the North, Black communities began to take action against educational discrimination. The extraordinary variety of educational discrimination throughout the region meant that acts of resistance took many different forms. Johnson reported, "The general facts of Negro segregation and discrimination are well known to everyone in the United States but there is little realization of the great variations in customary interracial practices from one locality to another." In other words, throughout the North patterns of race relations, including educational discrimination, varied tremendously. This made it challenging for Black educational activists to unite in campaigns that extended beyond a single school district, as neighboring school districts had their own unique policies and practices. This fact was complicated by the very small size of northern school districts, which typically encompassed a single town or city.

Wynetta Devore's ethnographic study in New Jersey documented a wide variety of Black educational experiences in that state. She discovered some students attended dilapidated one-room, all-Black elementary schools while others attended more modern, yet still segregated, facilities. Many attended integrated schools, but integration did not necessarily mean Black students experienced educational equality. For example, in 1927 James Moore moved from the rural town of Sharptown, where he attended an integrated school, to the slightly larger town of Woodstown, which operated a separate school. He recalled in Sharptown, "I heard the term 'Nigger' constantly and we fought." When he moved to Woodstown, he was surprised to find his all-Black school located in a fine, four-room, brick schoolhouse with better books and supplies than the integrated school. "I didn't see it as different from any other school except that it was all Black," he recalled. Other students described being terribly mistreated in integrated schools where white teachers forced Black students to sit together on one side of the room, discouraged Black students from attending high school, and refused to allow Black students to take specific vocational courses such as carpentry or typing. Still others recall attending integrated schools and feeling perfectly at ease. "I never had any problem," reported Arnetta Barron, who graduated from Atlantic City High School in 1938. "You had as many white friends as you had Black friends." Such a rich variety of experiences informed a broad range of student and parent perspectives on the debate over school integration. In some cases, it was clear that educational inequality was tied to racial segregation and that integrated schools would provide relief, but in other cases, white teachers and students were the problem.[88]

White school authorities deliberately expanded school segregation during the Great Depression in New Rochelle and Rockville, New York; Paulsburo, Toms River, Lawnside, East Orange, and Montclair, New Jersey; Berwyn, Chester, and Brentwood, Pennsylvania; Cleveland and Wilmington, Ohio; Detroit and Port Huron, Michigan; Boston and Springfield, Massachusetts; and Monrovia, California. In each of these cases, Black parents protested as school districts created discriminatory school assignment policies, transfer policies, or exclusively "colored" schools. These Black communities perceived increasing segregation and racial discrimination as an act of hostility designed to exacerbate educational inequality.[89]

The science of white supremacy continued to have a visible impact on educational administration through the 1930s. An attorney for the Trenton public schools told reporters, "Each race has certain inherited characteristics and it has been abundantly established that races prosper in their own groups and rise to higher heights under the emulation impulses than they would otherwise." A principal in Atlantic City was more direct. "I believe in segregation. They need a certain teaching that white children don't. They are like little animals. There is no civilization in their homes. They shouldn't hold up white children who have had these things for centuries. They are not as clean. They are careless about their bodies. Why should we contaminate our race?" The superintendent in Trenton agreed, "The problem of retardation is more serious among colored children than among any other racial group. I am inclined to believe that the further extension of segregation and a real social welfare program is the only real practical solution when we consider the present economic and social burdens which are placed on the colored group."[90]

Evidence of blatant racism and deteriorating educational conditions compelled Black northerners to reevaluate school integration. An emerging Black civil rights movement created interracial labor movements and helped shape President Franklin D. Roosevelt's New Deal. Organized campaigns against lynching, job discrimination, and the poll tax inspired Black northerners to protest educational inequality.[91]

Small but numerous examples of Black resistance percolated up from the grassroots. In Berwyn, Pennsylvania, Black parents organized a school boycott after district leaders built a new and modern elementary school, but told Black families they would be restricted to the old ramshackle one. The *Philadelphia Tribune* scoffed, "After a great effort, sufficient funds were raised to have the school erected but the Negro children were to be forced to jeopardize their little lives by attending a school which was too dangerously located for white children to attend and which lacks all modern facilities, such as recreation grounds or parks for the youngsters to play in." Parents in the historically Black town of Lawnside, New Jersey, demanded transportation to the nearest "white" school so their children could benefit from mixed schools. In Pittsburgh, John Burnett sued the school district when it refused to admit his two children to the high school on the grounds that no Black child had ever attended it. Parents in Montclair rallied when the superintendent proposed separate elementary and middle schools for Black children in 1933. The superintendent told Black parents they "ought to be satisfied with arrangements for separating Negro school children" and reminded them that "colored people in the South had to take the crumbs and were glad to get them."[92]

The NAACP provided support to northern Black communities and established a track record of combating northern school discrimination. When New Rochelle, New York, redrew school catchment zones in a way that assigned all Black students to the Lincoln School, the local NAACP protested, "It is our belief that this is a long step in the direction of Jim Crow schools in New Rochelle. Jim Crow schools, wherever found, do not get the consideration that white schools do. Less money is spent on them. They are not so well kept up; and the least efficient teachers are assigned to these schools."[93]

Black parents decided to stem the rising tide of school segregation in Cleveland, where residential segregation and school transfer policies were creating "dismal, uninviting, cheerless" majority Black schools. As the Crisis reported, "Central High School on Fifty-Fifth Street, is the dirtiest, most dismal looking school in Cleveland. Rubbish lines the street on both sides and to the front of the building. Ladies of easy virtue ply their trade, weaving in and out of groups of students going and coming from school. Central High has become a 'colored' school." Even New York City public schools, typically celebrated for their equal treatment, came up short. Following a race riot in 1935, observers noted, "The Negro in Harlem has made serious complaints against the schools of his community on the grounds that they are old, poorly equipped and overcrowded and constitute fire hazards, in addition to the fact that, in the administration of these schools, the welfare of the children is neglected and racial discrimination is practiced."[94] Sometimes these complaints were made in a far more dramatic fashion, such as when Black activists in East Orange, New Jersey, burned a fiery cross in front of Ashland School with a sign that read, "Stop Jim Crowism in this school."[95]

Charles S. Johnson concluded that by 1940, laws outlawing school segregation were effectively meaningless in northern cities with large Black populations. The Black press condemned these northern "Jim Crow schools" as the antithesis of American democracy, setting the stage for the coming revolt against school segregation.[96]

As debates over school integration versus separation escalated, Black scholars in education, psychology, sociology, and philosophy brought their disciplinary expertise to bear on the question. Instead of illuminating the best strategy, however, they laid bare the extent of the problem of racial discrimination in northern Black schools in ways that complicated arguments on both sides.

New Scholarship on School Integration

Established in 1932, Howard University's *Journal of Negro Education* curated the nation's most prominent scholarship on questions relating to Black educational equality. Although journal editor Charles H. Thompson was a fervent believer in school integration, he published a range of scholarly perspectives. In the inaugural issue, Black psychologist Mary R. Crowley argued that school integration did not necessarily result in higher levels of Black academic achievement. She analyzed two groups of fifty-five Black students, one from separate schools and the other from integrated schools in Cincinnati. The students were of similar age, IQ scores, physical health, family history, and social status. Crowley discovered that Black students in the separate schools scored higher than their counterparts in integrated schools on tests in history-civics, arithmetic, and language usage. She concluded, "The segregated schools of Cincinnati are as effective, on the whole, as are the mixed schools, in their academic training of Negro children." She added that further studies should consider extracurricular opportunities at mixed and separate schools, as well as the emotional support and vocational guidance offered in each.[97]

Crowley's article reignited a scholarly controversy dating to 1929, when her white advisor at the University of Cincinnati, Louis A. Pechstein, published "The Problem of Negro Education in the Northern and Border Cities." Pechstein claimed that separate schools led to higher levels of Black academic achievement than integrated ones. As evidence, he cited the fact that Black students graduated at higher rates from separate schools than integrated ones and that more than 80 percent of America's Black leaders had attended separate schools. Pechstein confirmed that northern school districts were becoming more racially segregated as a result of the Great Migration and tracking policies based on IQ scores. He admitted northern whites were becoming more prejudiced against Blacks with each passing year and blamed the white press for stoking the flames of racial resentment. He asked, "Can the negro be better trained to cope with this heavy newspaper anti-social propaganda in a mixed school, where evidences of racial prejudice and academic failure are not far to seek, or in a segregated school, where he is taught to have some racial pride, self-esteem, and confidence in the capacity of his race to progress through its own best efforts?"[98]

Integrationists feared that Pechstein, a prominent educational psychologist and dean of the College of Education at the University of Cincinnati, would validate northern school segregation. He presented his work at major conferences and spoke to reporters about his findings. The *Cincinnati Enquirer* reported, "Data presented by Dean Pechstein pointed definitely to the general opinion held by school authorities in Northern cities that segregation of negro and white children in separate schools accomplished far more than can be gained in mixed classes." In response, W. E. B. Du Bois invited Pechstein to publicly debate the statement—that separate schools are best for American Negroes in northern cities. The debate never took place, but Du Bois published an angry retort to Pechstein's article in the *Crisis*.[99]

Du Bois acknowledged that Black students, just like the first generation of Irish and Italian immigrants, struggled to do well in school. "In a thousand different communities Negro pupils have proven their ability to profit by the public schools; they have made high records and graduated with honor." Du Bois explained that limited social and educational backgrounds hampered Black students, not innate racial difference. "Their poverty is part of a universal problem; their retardation is due to wretched Southern school systems; their dullness comes from poor food and poor homes and there is absolutely no scientific proof that it is Negroid." He resolved, "Every one of these problems has a well-known and adequately tested solution."[100]

Du Bois came to believe that separate schools could be effective educational institutions as long as the separation was voluntary. In January 1934 he wrote that Black Americans "must stop being stampeded by the word segregation." He explained that separate Black neighborhoods and schools were only objectionable if they were accompanied by discrimination. He continued, "There is no objection to schools attended by colored pupils and taught by colored teachers. On the contrary, colored pupils can by our own contention be as fine human beings as any other sort of children, and we certainly know that there are no teachers better trained than colored teachers. But if the existence of such a school is made reason and cause for giving it worse housing, poorer facilities, poorer equipment and poorer teachers, then we do object, and the objection is not against the color of the pupils' or the teachers' skins but against the discrimination." Du Bois preferred integrated schools, but felt that Black Americans should voluntarily form groups to protect their interests during times of crisis.[101]

In April 1934, Du Bois expanded his argument, insisting that even in the North, Black Americans lived in a world that was separate and apart from whites. Black northerners were excluded from hotels and restaurants, had difficulty

finding residences outside of the meanest neighborhoods, and faced humiliating discrimination on trains and public conveyances. He continued, "Their
children either go to colored schools or schools nominally for both races, but
actually attended almost exclusively by colored children. In other words, they
are confined by unyielding public opinion to a Negro world." Noting that racial
discrimination had been growing worse for twenty-five years, Du Bois suggested
that Black citizens reassess whether integration could improve the social and economic conditions of the Black masses. This question had special salience in
the public schools. Du Bois determined, "If he cannot educate his children in
decent schools with other children, he must, nevertheless, educate his children
in decent Negro schools and arrange and conduct and oversee such schools."
Du Bois's critique of integration confounded and angered NAACP leaders,
who insisted that integration was the key to racial equality. Citing irreconcil-
able differences, Du Bois resigned as editor of the *Crisis* and from the board of
directors of the NAACP in June.[102]

The following year, the *Journal of Negro Education* invited prominent scholars
to contribute an article on "the courts and the Negro separate school." The goal
was to critically analyze whether Blacks could use litigation to achieve integrated
and equal public schools. Most of the contributors concluded that only integrated schools would allow Black Americans to achieve their rightful place as
equal citizens. "The basic dilemma of educational segregation arises from the inevitable conflict between the short-term and the long-term point of view on this
question," observed Black philosopher Alain Locke. He asked Blacks to focus
on long-term objectives and fight through minor inconveniences to secure integrated and equal public schools. Black historian and educator Horace Mann
Bond pointed out that separate schools were a result of white racial prejudice,
and that such schools were nearly always unequal. He warned of the "consequent
effect upon the minds of the segregated Negro children, who are separated from
white children as one would take from a school those with measles, or chicken-
pox, or diphtheria." These schools not only reinforced racial prejudice and
created unequal opportunities, according to Bond, but caused damage to the
minds of Black children. Black educational psychologist Howard Hale Long
maintained that separate schools could cause psychological trauma to Black
children.[103]

Du Bois dissented in a pointed article entitled, "Does the Negro Need
Separate Schools?" He began, "Race prejudice in the United States today is
such that most Negroes cannot receive proper education in white institutions."
Du Bois elaborated, "There are many public school systems in the North
where Negroes are admitted and tolerated, but they are not educated; they are
crucified." According to Du Bois, there was little the Black community could
do if white citizens demanded separate schools. He believed it was "futile" to

compel "by law a group to do what it is determined not to do," noting such efforts were a "silly waste of money, time, and temper." He cautioned that Black families were too often duped into believing that integrated schools were better than separate ones. Du Bois added, "I have long been convinced, for instance, that the Negroes in the public schools of Harlem are not getting an education that is in any sense comparable in efficiency, discipline, and human development with that which Negroes are getting in the separate public schools of Washington, D.C."[104]

Du Bois proposed a compromise to the enduring debate between school integrationists and separatists. He agreed that mixed public schools of white and Black, rich and poor children represented the democratic ideal and emphasized his own preference for such schools. Then he insisted that the real question was not whether schools were integrated, but instead which school could offer the best education to Black youth from their tender elementary years through professional training. A meaningful education required not only loving teachers but also opportunities for Black students to study Black history, the social science of racial equality, and Black art and literature. He continued, "A separate Negro school, where children are treated like human beings, trained by teachers of their own race, who know what it means to be Black in the year of salvation 1935, is infinitely better than making our boys and girls doormats to be spit and trampled upon and lied to by ignorant social climbers, whose sole claim to superiority is ability to kick 'niggers' when they are down." A black does not need either segregated or mixed schools, concluded Du Bois, "What he needs is Education."[105]

Du Bois's suggestion that Blacks should focus on the quality of education for Black students, while thoughtful and reasonable, failed to satisfy either integrationists or separatists. An emerging body of social science scholarship provided hard evidence for activists on both sides of the debate. It also challenged scientific claims of white racial superiority, documented the relationship between school segregation and racial prejudice, and revealed the many factors that influenced student academic achievement including aspects of home life that were out of reach of educational reformers. As this body of social science scholarship grew and evolved, it became clearer that racial segregation in public schools had potentially harmful effects on Black children's social development, white children's racial prejudice, and the ability of both to get along with one another. It also became evident that broad patterns of school segregation tended to correlate with mistreatment of majority Black schools. Just as popular support was building for school integration in the North, so too was social science evidence that demonstrated the egalitarian function of integrated schools.

Figure 2.4. Black teachers worked to improve education for Black youth through professional associations like the Organization of Teachers of Colored Children in the State of New Jersey. May 14, 1932. Courtesy of the New Jersey State Archives, Department of State, Trenton, NJ.

Conclusion

In 1935, the NAACP announced a major campaign to equalize public education for Black students. Black attorney Charles Hamilton Houston designed and oversaw this ambitious, long-term legal strategy. Writing in the *Crisis*, he claimed that northern Blacks erroneously believed separate schools were better for Black students. Even if some Black children experienced racism in majority white schools, Houston countered, that was no reason to round up all the Black children and isolate them in separate institutions. "If this logic is followed, then all the Jews, Italians, Greeks, barbarians, blondes, brunettes, the ugly, and the beautiful should have separate schools established for them, because some of their group are discriminated against."

Like most civil rights leaders of the time, Houston glossed over the question of Black teachers in the North, saying only that "schools are not employment bureaus." Moreover, he claimed that in cities like New York and Chicago where Black teachers taught in mixed schools, "Such discrimination may be reduced to a tolerable minimum." Houston reminded readers that, even in the North, separate but equal schools were a "fiction" and that separation of schoolchildren fanned the flames of racial prejudice and eviscerated Black civil rights. He concluded, "Finally, the Negro separate school is more than an educational institution; it is an instrument of social policy and a symbol of social status. There is no denying the fact that to segregate is to stigmatize, however much we may try to rationalize it."[106]

Thanks to Houston's brilliant legal strategy, the NAACP won a series of decisive victories in the years leading up to World War II including a school desegregation case in Maryland that compelled school authorities to either equalize or integrate high schools in 1937. School officials elected to retain separate schools and invest money in improving the Black high school, but the fact that courts would compel a Jim Crow school district to equalize a "colored" school was a triumph. The US Supreme Court ruling in *Gaines v. Canada* confirmed that if the State of Missouri offered graduate legal training to white students, it must offer equal opportunities to Black students in a state-sponsored college. In June of 1940, the Fourth Circuit Court of Appeals ruled that Norfolk, Virginia, could not pay Black teachers lower salaries than white teachers.[107]

None of these court rulings overturned the "separate, but equal" doctrine established by *Plessy v. Ferguson* in 1896, but they did demonstrate that the NAACP was capable of leading a successful legal assault on educational inequality. These legal victories were paving the way for a revolution in Black educational activism. As the United States hovered on the brink of war, Black northerners looked at racial inequality in their public schools with a new sense of outrage but also a distinct spark of optimism.

3

A Powerful Weapon

Integration for Equality, 1940–1965

Just across the Mississippi River from St. Louis, Missouri, stood the gritty industrial town of East St. Louis, Illinois, where Black students attended one of eleven separate schools, including the all-Black Lincoln High School. By the end of World War II it was evident that these schools were woefully inferior, an insult the Black community was no longer willing to suffer. In 1948, Black parents asked the board of education to build an auditorium at Lincoln High School and renovate the vocational workshops so the Black high school would have comparable facilities to the white schools. The school board dismissed these requests as "lacking in education, common sense, foresight, and judgment." East St. Louis resident David Owens appealed to NAACP executive secretary Walter White in New York City for help.[1]

Owens wrote, "Mr. White, here in East St. Louis, we do not even have equal educational facilities. The Lincoln High School does not offer courses in art, dramatics, or speech; and the workshop is deplorable. The situation is, indeed, desperate." White passed the letter along to attorney Thurgood Marshall, executive director of the NAACP Legal Defense and Educational Fund, who was spearheading a campaign to dismantle illegal school segregation in the North.[2]

Marshall determined that school segregation in East St. Louis and surrounding communities was clearly illegal and ripe for intervention. "There is neither justification, rhyme nor reason for the maintenance of these segregated schools." Marshall traveled to East St. Louis and persuaded the local NAACP to modify its strategy from requesting equalization to demanding school integration.[3]

As Black civil rights activists soon discovered, however, school integration was a contested strategy among Black citizens in postwar East St. Louis. "Most of the ministers, teachers, and community leaders are for segregated schools," conceded NAACP assistant field secretary Daniel E. Byrd. This point was driven home after East St. Louis's five Black principals canvassed Black neighborhoods, asking families to support the separate schools. NAACP representatives retraced the principals' route and implored the same families to demand school integration. "Some were reluctant, because the principals had told them that nonsegregated schools would cost the Negro principals and teachers their jobs," recounted one activist. Others feared violent white retaliation.[4]

The memory of racial violence was undimmed in East St. Louis, the site of one of the nation's worst race riots in 1917. According to W. E. B. Du Bois, "five thousand rioters arose and surged like a crested storm-wave, from noonday until midnight; they killed and beat and murdered; they dashed out the brains of children and stripped the clothes of women; they drove victims into flames and hanged the helpless to the lighting polls." Thirty years later, some community leaders feared a school integration campaign would ignite a new wave of violence. A local newspaper editorialized, "All of the ingredients for a recurrence of the 1917 race riot are simmering now, heated by the fire of race prejudice that has kept smoldering for these many years in the darkness of suspicion and fear. All that it takes is one overt act and the flames will envelop us." At mass meetings, Black ministers cautioned "now was not the time" for school integration, that such a strategy was "rash" and "a serious blunder."[5]

Overcoming these fears, the Black citizens of East St. Louis, like others in the North, agreed to fight to dismantle school segregation. As this chapter details, a rising tide of northern Black support for school integration swept the region for more than two decades following the outbreak of World War II. In the vast majority of communities, activists successfully compelled school authorities to end explicitly racial student placements and teaching assignments. For instance, after Illinois legislators threatened to withhold $667,989 in state funding, the school board agreed to desegregate the schools in the winter of 1949. Ignoring white student boycotts, threats of economic reprisals, and cross burnings, a small number of Black students in East St. Louis attended previously "white" schools for the first time in 1950.[6]

The NAACP regarded school integration as an opening wedge in the postwar struggle for racial justice and proposed to "draft" children for "active duty" in the war on Jim Crow. "Victory in the school matter should make it much easier to crack the theaters, hotels, and restaurants," enthused Byrd. He encouraged parents in East St. Louis: "The presence of the children in the schools is a powerful weapon and this time we must keep them there." This logic was widely appealing in the heady atmosphere of a surging civil rights movement. At the same time, some Black northerners questioned a political agenda that used children as "weapons" and contemplated the costs of closing separate schools. Black students, parents, and teachers raised their voices to question and critique school integration, even as it became a defining feature of the northern Black civil rights movement. This criticism, in turn, shaped Black educational activism

Figure 3.1. A flyer that reads, "We've been drafted for active duty by the NAACP!"
c. 1944. Visual Materials from the NAACP Records. Prints and Photographs Division,
Library of Congress, Washington, DC.

and influenced strategies and goals of northern Black educational activists as
they evolved from 1940 to 1965.[7]

School integration campaigns erupted throughout the North from World
War II through *Brown v. Board of Education* in 1954 to the height of the Black
civil rights movement in 1965. Black scholars not only documented the extent
of northern school segregation but also sought to understand its consequences
in terms of Black academic achievement and race relations with whites. Case
studies from rural Bainbridge, Ohio; small town Bordentown, New Jersey; suburban New Rochelle, New York; and urban Chicago, Illinois, reveal the evolution

of school integration battles as they progressed into the 1960s and why some Black educational activists were hesitant to support these campaigns.

Although Black northerners waged hundreds of successful school integration battles, school segregation increased between 1940 and 1965 due to government-sponsored residential segregation and discriminatory educational practices, fueled by white resistance to racial mixing in northern public schools. Increasing school segregation, in turn, led some Black educational activists to experiment with more aggressive integration strategies and others to consider radical new objectives. Among these goals by 1965 would be the revolutionary potential of separate, Black-controlled schools.

Wartime Black Educational Activism

Gunnar Myrdal's *An American Dilemma: The Negro Problem and Modern Democracy* (1944) maintained that the only way Americans could solve the "Negro problem" and achieve the democratic ideal was to abolish racial segregation and ensure equal treatment for Black citizens in education, housing, employment, voting, and law enforcement. Meanwhile, a majority of American scientists forcefully rejected Nazi claims of Aryan superiority and insisted that race was a "myth."[8]

During World War II, northern Black educational activists came to view segregated schools as abhorrent, anachronistic, and anathema to the Black freedom struggle. Integrated schools, by contrast, embodied democratic ideals including tolerance for diversity, equal citizenship, and fair play. For example, Black citizens in Oberlin, Ohio, insisted in 1940, "Men and women of this fair land of ours should encourage brotherhood and interracial school life for our children because in the days to come friendship and understanding will be invaluable assets to our national security." White allies, like those who supported school integration in New Rochelle, New York, in 1949, agreed it was not only undemocratic to "handicap" Black students by isolating them in segregated schools, but also harmful to white children. As one white parent testified, "The [white] pupils in such a school miss an important element of understanding in their education for democratic human relations and are themselves less able to adjust to their association with Negro children in high school. Integration therefore seems to be sound educational policy."[9]

The NAACP spearheaded the northern campaign for school integration between 1940 and 1965. Wartime civil rights activism pushed membership to nearly half a million people by 1945, and for the first time the NAACP included large numbers of working-class African Americans. Thurgood Marshall traveled throughout the North offering legal advice and organizational support to local branches in countless school integration battles. Between 1940 and 1954, the NAACP helped dozens of northern communities end racist school assignment policies that isolated Black students and teachers in segregated schools through petitions, school boycotts, and when necessary, lawsuits.[10]

World War II transformed everyday life for Black Americans as nearly 1 million men and women enlisted in the armed services, hundreds of thousands of Black southerners moved to the urban North, and civil rights activists launched the "Double V" campaign symbolizing victory over fascism abroad and racism at home. "Traditional patterns of behavior between Negroes and whites are being rather suddenly disturbed by the war," declared sociologist Charles S. Johnson. "Negro masses are becoming more articulate and their methods of protest more varied and intense, including, as they do, petitions and picketings, protest parades, mass meetings and mob violence."[11]

Writing in 1946, historian Herbert Aptheker observed that Black veterans were "fully determined to enjoy those democratic freedoms for which they fought." He elaborated, "It is they who are most prone to violate the humiliating Jim Crow customs and laws which seek to perpetuate the subordinate social status of the Negro people." White opposition to Black civil rights flared in the form of a revitalized Ku Klux Klan (KKK) and race riots in Detroit, Harlem, and Beaumont, Texas. Violent white resistance only inspired Black Americans to fight for their constitutionally guaranteed civil rights. A. Philip Randolph urged Black teachers to join the struggle, announcing, "To avoid race wars in America, colored people must retreat or fixtures and barriers must be torn down." Increasing numbers of Black citizens were ready to tear down the barriers to educational equality. Inside of separate, Black-controlled schools, Black teachers taught about African American contributions to the war effort, especially the role of Black servicemen and women.[12]

Black northerners emphasized wartime ideals of racial tolerance and fair play as they demanded equal treatment in the public schools. For instance, in Cairo, Illinois, Black teacher Hattie Kendrick sued the board of education for paying Black teachers less than whites. Activists in Philadelphia, Pittsburgh, Trenton, and Montclair, New Jersey, fought to desegregate teaching assignments that restricted Black teachers to teaching only Black children. Black parents in Abbington, Pennsylvania, successfully halted the school board's plan to exclude all Black children from the local junior high school, while Black mothers in Oxford, Ohio, spoke out against racially segregated parent-teacher associations, class plays, and high school graduation receptions. In Hartford, the Urban League protested the fact that only 5 teachers out of 800 were Black. In Hempstead, Long Island, Black parents objected when school officials assigned their children to majority Black schools across town, even though they lived in

Figure 3.2. Black teacher and Black students in Philadelphia during World War II. Note posters on the wall that include "Negroes in the War." Photograph by John W. Mosley. Ruth Wright Hayre Collection, Charles L. Blockson Afro-American Collection, Temple University Libraries, Philadelphia, PA.

a neighborhood served by majority white schools. These small, but successful, campaigns revealed that educational racism was vulnerable.[13]

The most celebrated wartime school integration campaign erupted in Hillburn, New York, in 1943 when a group of mothers launched a boycott against the separate Brook School. Thurgood Marshall toured Hillburn's elementary schools, noting that the modern eight-room Main School attended by white children had a library, gymnasium, music room, and large playground, while the nearby Brook School was a three-room, ramshackle building that lacked indoor plumbing. The local NAACP and the town's three Black educators voted unanimously to fight for integrated schools. Allies in New York City organized a rally to support the Hillburn school boycott at the Golden Gate Ballroom in Harlem. Flyers posted around New York made unflattering references to the Jim Crow South, asking, "Is Hillburn's Jim Crow School System in New York State or Mississippi?" The Hillburn student boycott, combined with the threat of litigation, compelled New York commissioner of education George C. Stoddard to close the all-Black Brook School and assign all children to the Main School.[14]

Figure 3.3. Thurgood Marshall with parents of African American students from Hillburn, New York, 1943. Visual Materials from the NAACP Records. Prints and Photographs Division, Library of Congress, Washington, DC.

The Black press welcomed Hillburn's successful school integration campaign as a dynamic contribution to the war effort and a sign that Black patriotism would be rewarded. "The rotten Hillburn school system shows up U.S. democracy in a bad light in New Delhi, Tokyo and Berlin," confirmed the *New York Amsterdam News.* "Therefore, it was more than worth the efforts of the NAACP and the courageous, race conscious parents of Hillburn to fight its Jim Crow school system." The *Afro-American* claimed white parents supported school integration as part of the war effort. "The colored boys and the white boys are all fighting together over there for the same damned things; it's funny we can't get along here," declared Albert Taylor, whose eleven-year-old son, Francis, attended the newly desegregated Main School.[15] Hillburn's school integration movement was successful thanks to unified support from the Black community, including the town's three Black female educators. Principal Kate Savery confirmed the Black educators were "very, very thankful for the Commissioner's decision" to integrate the schools, even though it put their jobs at risk.[16]

Black teachers and parents in Trenton, New Jersey, launched another wartime effort to end segregated schools and teaching assignments. Like many of their friends, Leon Williams and Janet Hedgepeth walked past their neighborhood school every day to attend the all-Black Lincoln Junior High School. The city's Black teachers affirmed, "When the capital city of our state joins the Deep South in its treatment of Negro students, it is time for all those who value democratic education to intervene." Leon and Janet's mothers sued the school board with the help of the NAACP. On January 31, 1944, the Supreme Court of New Jersey ruled, "It is unlawful for boards of education to exclude children from any public school on the grounds that they are of the Negro race" and ordered Trenton to integrate its public schools. The NAACP predicted that this case would set a precedent for school desegregation throughout New Jersey. However, the northern campaign for school integration remained largely muted until the end of the war as Black civil rights activists waited for the best opening to challenge racial injustice.[17]

The Quest for Integration in Postwar America

The end of World War II created the context that civil rights activists needed to articulate a more forceful demand for racial equality in the United States. In his 1947 book, *Jim Crow America*, white reporter Earl Conrad tried to capture why school integration was so vital to Black Americans at this moment. He recounted a story about his friend George, who happened to be the only Black student in his northern high school. A warm and funny young man, George was a champion athlete, class valedictorian, and beloved by teachers and classmates. Nevertheless, the day before the senior prom the principal summoned George into his office. He began, "George, you are the finest young man in the school. You have walked off with all the honors. You will go far." The principal paused, and then continued in a hushed voice, "That is why I know you will understand when I say that I don't think you should go to the senior prom. You will be a wallflower there, and you won't be happy. You know, George, it wouldn't be right for you to dance with our girls. You know that, now, don't you?" Tears of humiliation stinging his eyes, George sprinted down the street to Conrad's apartment, where he burst in and bellowed, "I tell you this white man will go down! This white man is not fit to live! This white man will yet learn that one-and-one half billions of people are of different skin colorings than he, and these may flood over and drown out the white civilization!"[18]

What is remarkable about this story is not the stark racial prejudice of a northern white school administrator but instead George's furious call for vengeance amplified for a national audience. Conrad explained, "This is the wrath and the anger of the unintegrated. This is the hate, a hate often made inevitable, of a people forced to reason in terms of color. This may well be the resolve of thousands of Negroes compelled to look with anger, mistrust, suspicion, and even loathing upon a mass of people domineering, indifferent, frequently vicious, rarely fully understanding. I tell the incident of my friend only because it illustrates the underlying principle of Negro American life—*the quest for integration*."[19]

The assistant commissioner of education in New Jersey confirmed that in terms of Black demands for school integration, 1947 marked a "brand new and forward-looking period, involving what might be termed drastic and major changes." If the quest for integration was defined as the underlying principle of "Negro American life" in postwar America, then separate schools were now oppositional to Black life.[20]

In a sign of the times, the New Jersey Organization of Teachers of Colored Children changed its name in 1945 to the New Jersey Organization of Teachers and pledged to fight for school integration. Five years later, the Pennsylvania Association of Teachers of Colored Children did the same thing and publicly supported the integration of teachers, students, and curricula in such a way "as to make all Pennsylvania schools the arsenals of the democratic way of life."[21]

Once reluctant to place their children in white-dominated schools, northern Black families rushed to enroll their children in previously "white" schools. University of Chicago law professor William R. Ming Jr. noted that "ministers, teachers, and the occasional medic" provided the leadership for school integration in the North, but that the strongest advocate for school integration was the Black working class—"farm laborers, domestics, and to a limited extent, industrial workers." Social scientist Bonita H. Valien confirmed the same trend in Cairo, Illinois, noting, "As is true in most communities where desegregation has been attempted, children who persisted in their right to transfer were, for the most part, from families of limited economic resources. None of the children from the higher economic level sought transfer of schools." The Black masses had the most to gain from higher quality, integrated public schools and they were less vulnerable to economic and social reprisals than middle-class Black families.[22]

Black educational activists adjusted their tactics to the varied local contexts found throughout the North. For example, in Indianapolis, the local NAACP asked the school board for a written statement detailing the district's policy on racial segregation, hoping to create an opening that could be used to demand school integration. Many activists worked to document segregation since northern districts did not officially keep track of students' racial identities and therefore were able to claim total ignorance about the possibility that schools were segregated by race. The New Jersey State Conference of the NAACP surveyed school segregation in fifty-two communities and used the findings to encourage local branches to challenge the most egregious forms of segregation.

In New York City and Philadelphia, parents and civil rights leaders collected data showing very high rates of school segregation and inequality, and they used these statistics to demand immediate relief. For instance, Philadelphia activists identified 26 elementary schools where the student body was over 90 percent Black and 114 elementary schools where the student body was more than 90 percent white. In South Jamaica, Queens, more than 200 Black parents showed up at a board of education meeting to protest deteriorating conditions in majority Black schools related to facilities, textbooks, supervision, and teachers. In Wayne, Pennsylvania, Black parents petitioned the school board to mix the Black students assigned to the separate Mt. Pleasant School with the white students at the all-white Strafford School. These varied forms of educational activism percolated up through the grassroots in communities throughout the North, putting school administrators on notice that Black communities would no longer tolerate segregated and unequal schools.[23]

Lingering Support for Separate Schools

A crucial factor in whether this activism was successful was the political and economic power of the local Black community. A school integration battle in the rural town of Bainbridge, Ohio, located about twenty-five miles southeast of Cleveland, illustrates why northern Black support for separate schools persisted in the postwar era. Founded as a farming village in 1817, Bainbridge was more or less all-white until a local foundry imported Black workers from Georgia during World War I. Some of these Black workers put down roots when a Jewish farmer agreed to subdivide his property and sell it to Black families in 1921. This small "allotment" was the only place whites permitted Black citizens to reside, and a small community of working-class Black families lived here into the postwar era. Most worked as either laborers or domestics for whites in the surrounding region.

Inspired by the global struggle for democracy, three Black residents decided to challenge Bainbridge's racially segregated schools in 1945. They traveled to Cleveland, home to the closest branch office of the NAACP, and asked executive secretary Charles P. Lucas for assistance.

Lucas promptly wrote to Thurgood Marshall explaining that Bainbridge maintained two elementary schools: a two-room shack that lacked indoor plumbing and electricity for the Black students and a modern, graded, twelve-room schoolhouse for the white students. Conditions in the Black school, the Chagrin Falls Park School, were bleak. As Lucas detailed, "Arithmetic is taught 15 minutes every other day. Other basic subjects are given a correspondingly short amount of time. There are no sanitary facilities. Water is pumped to one room, where there is a faucet about 18 inches from the floor and a bucket standing beneath it. No drinking cups are provided, and the children drink from their hands. There is an outdoor toilet. There are no screens at the windows. There have been 150 cases of impetigo in the last two years. This is a disease caused by filth." Despite repeated requests, Bainbridge officials refused to admit any Black children to the "white" school even though there were "several unoccupied and unused classrooms at the school."[24]

Bainbridge contained all the elements Marshall was looking for to advance the NAACP's legal campaign against northern school segregation, including clear-cut racial segregation and eager local supporters. He anticipated that an integration battle could be won swiftly in Bainbridge as it had in Hillburn. Marshall replied to Lucas, "The Chagrin Falls Park School situation is the type of situation which we must get to work on at once. The encroachment of segregation in the school system in Ohio and other states is challenging the entire program of our Association." He sat down with local activists in Cleveland to sketch out a school integration campaign not only in Bainbridge but also in other Ohio towns with separate "colored" schools including Hamilton, Xenia, Mansfield, Oxford, Hillsboro, Chillicothe, Dayton, and Middletown.[25]

Marshall soon discovered that Bainbridge's Black community was divided over the question of school integration. The NAACP's Mary E. Crawford toured the Black residences in the allotment, visited the local schools, talked to Black parents, and met with school leaders. She learned there was very little support for school integration among local Black residents. The separate Chagrin Falls Park School, although quite humble, was relatively new, erected in the summer of 1937 in response to a petition by the Black community. Up until that time students from the allotment had attended Bainbridge Elementary, but in 1937 Maranda Koggins, a former teacher in the Cleveland public schools, circulated a petition requesting a separate school. The school board granted the request and constructed a one-room schoolhouse inside the allotment, with Mrs. Koggins as the teacher.

The separate school was popular and enrollment increased, so the district added a second room and hired a second Black teacher in 1940. Although NAACP activists denigrated the two-room schoolhouse as "deplorable," others pointed out, "The school is about six years old and quite cheerful; it looks well from the outside. Compared with the houses that the people live in it stands out impressively." The Black students claimed to like their school, and parents insisted they only wanted their children to study the three Rs—reading, writing, and arithmetic—without the extravagant frills offered at the "white" school. The Black principal acknowledged that parents did not want to send their children to the Bainbridge school "because they would have to dress them better." Principal Thomas elaborated, "They could go to the allotment school dressed any way." Another investigator for the NAACP emphasized the severe poverty of Blacks in Bainbridge, noting children were "clothed very badly and were extremely dirty" and homes were "little more than shacks." Relatively pleased with their school, Black parents felt little desire to fight to send their children to the "white" school.[26]

The Bainbridge school integration campaign came to a head in November 1946 when community leaders proposed a $26,000 school bond to fund an expansion and renovation of the separate school. In case this subtle enticement failed, white leaders threatened to cancel Black citizens' relief checks if they dared to vote against the school bond or otherwise advocate school integration. Dismissing these threats as immaterial, Marshall instructed local activists to "work out a program to educate the community to the evils of segregated schools." The Cleveland NAACP organized a mass meeting in Bainbridge where it directed Black parents to vote against the school bond and demand integration. Local families were not so easily swayed. Principal Thomas attended the meeting and encouraged parents to ignore the NAACP and vote for the bond. The NAACP representative at the meeting, Alvin Lloyd, suggested that a delegation of Black parents should meet with the school board to demand integration, but nobody volunteered for the job.[27]

When it was time to vote on the bond, 115 Black adults from the allotment voted for it and only 16 against it. Faced with threats of economic reprisals and discomfort with sending Black children to the "white" school, an overwhelming majority of Black citizens voted to maintain a dual system. At the very least, Black citizens in Bainbridge were not prepared to fight for school integration at this time, although evidence suggests that many Black parents simply preferred a separate school with Black teachers. In the fall of 1946, the Cleveland NAACP wrote to Robert L. Carter in the national office explaining they were giving up on the integration campaign in Bainbridge.[28]

As this case illustrates, the NAACP sometimes struggled to convince Black northerners to fight for school integration when the local Black community lacked economic and political resources. When Marshall instructed the Cleveland NAACP to "educate the community to the evils of segregated schools," he not only presented a stark choice between school integration as good and separate schools as "evil," but also that anyone who disagreed with him simply lacked information. The solution, in Marshall's mind, was to "educate" separatists by presenting them with facts that demonstrated the superiority of school integration as a strategy. When Black parents questioned this logic, as they did in Bainbridge, NAACP activists struggled to articulate a convincing response. They were unwilling to address Black parents' concerns about how their children would fare in a white-controlled school, or what would happen to Black educators if the school was integrated. The result was a political impasse—Black civil rights leaders threw up their hands in disgust at the "selfishness" of Black separatists, while local Blacks remained suspicious of civil rights leaders' motives. In Bainbridge, it was not so much that Blacks preferred separate schools, it was that they did not want to join a movement that placed the Black community at risk in exchange for uncertain advantages.[29]

In contrast, other northern Black educational activists had significant political and economic power but nevertheless preferred to maintain the option of a separate, Black-controlled school because they believed a high-quality separate school was vital to Black families. This kind of activism is visible in towns like Indianapolis, Gary, Cincinnati, and Bordentown. Most of these schools were located just north of the Mason-Dixon line, where southern values had an especially potent influence.

This was the case in Dayton, Ohio, home of the Paul Lawrence Dunbar High School, erected in 1933 at the behest of the white community. At that time, W. E. B. Du Bois advised, "It would be most unfortunate if the new Dunbar High School were made exclusively a Negro school." Du Bois's support for school integration rested on the condition that mixed schools treat Black children fairly, and he was clear that nurturing separate schools were preferable to hostile integrated ones. Dayton's Black community had not requested separate schools, but it did not have the political power to prevent whites from expanding school segregation. Over time, many local Black families came to appreciate what they viewed as the benefits of separate schools, especially Black teachers, a curriculum that included Black history, full access to extracurricular programs, and high levels of academic achievement.

After being segregated in the locker room and forced to sit in the back of classrooms at majority white Roosevelt High School, Phyllis Blackburn Greer volunteered to transfer to Dayton's new "colored" high school in 1933. She explained, "I transferred to Dunbar because I felt that if there was going to be— if we were going to be separated by anything, we might as well be separated by an entire building as to be separated by practices." At Dunbar High School, the teachers told her, "We must be better than anybody else in terms of achievement because that was the only way we could ever get to be equal." She recalled Dunbar High School as her first positive experience as a student and one that inspired her to become a teacher.[30]

Dayton school leaders illegally confined Black elementary students to separate annexes or basements in "mixed" schools through the 1930s and 1940s. In 1936 the board of education created the first unofficial "colored" elementary school by removing the white teachers from Garfield Elementary, replacing them with Black teachers, and busing white students out of the neighborhood to other "white" schools. In the summer of 1945, Dayton school leaders did the same thing at Wogaman Elementary. "When school closed in June of 1945, there was an entire white staff at Wogaman," recalled Greer, by this time a teacher in Dayton. "When school opened in September, there was an entire Black staff under a Black principal . . . and at the same time white pupils who lived in the Wogaman area were transferred by bus out of the Wogaman School."[31]

By the summer of 1945, school integration campaigns were sweeping through northern Black communities. Black civil rights activists in Dayton decided to challenge overt and illegal school segregation, but they were hampered by lingering support for separate schools. Civil rights leaders were particularly incensed that Dunbar's Black principal, Frederic C. McFarlane, regularly cited W. E. B. Du Bois in his defense of separate schools. They believed McFarlane misrepresented Du Bois's views on school integration. Marian Smith Williams wrote Du Bois on behalf of the Dayton's Citizen Committee and the local NAACP to ask for his support in closing the separate schools.

She began, "As you perhaps know, we have in Dayton one segregated Negro high school, the Paul Lawrence Dunbar. . . . Despite the fact that Negroes are themselves partly to blame for its erection, there are those who now see their error and are anxious to atone for their sin." Williams described the ominous escalation of school segregation in Dayton, culminating with the most recent transformation of Wogaman Elementary into a separate school. The problem, according to Williams, was that Black leaders such as Principal McFarlane convinced parents that separate schools promoted racial uplift while integrated schools did not. She wrote, "He has indoctrinated the students attending Dunbar with his philosophy of racism and continually quotes you as favoring segregation as the only solution to the race problem in America." Williams concluded by asking Du Bois to publicly renounce his support for separate schools.[32]

For civil rights activists in Dayton, separate schools were a "sin" that reflected a "philosophy of racism," regardless of the quality of education available in these schools or the fate of Black teachers and students in integrated ones. In their minds, integrated schools would treat Black students with dignity and respect and Black teachers would be hired on their merits in a colorblind hiring process, a vision that school separatists doubted. Williams assumed Du Bois would agree and hoped his endorsement would galvanize Black support for school integration.

Du Bois received William's letter and penned a thoughtful response. "I do not believe in jim crow schools. They are undemocratic and discriminatory." He continued, "At the same time as I have said from time to time, the majority of Negroes in the United States depend today upon separate schools for their education and despite everything we can do that situation will continue longer than any of us now living will survive. We must, therefore, make the best of a bad situation and take every advantage of that situation." Du Bois emphasized that separate schools provided suitable jobs for Black teachers and that some are "very excellent schools." He cautioned Williams to consider each case of school integration on its own merits, as "there no single answer which will apply to all situations."[33]

Williams replied to Du Bois that she and her colleagues were "a bit shocked and sorely disappointed" by his letter. She continued, "Personally, I cannot agree with you that any segregated school system is more advantageous to Negro children. . . . I sincerely believe that in a northern city, such as Dayton, it is criminal to teach Negro children that segregation is the solution to the problem of race." Laying out the plan to dismantle segregated schools, she added, "This type of education we are opposing and shall leave no stone unturned to eliminate the dual system, which we consider most detrimental to the children, psychologically, educationally and materially. We regret, then, that you could not see your way to help us denounce it."[34]

When Du Bois responded to Williams's second letter, he did so publicly in the *Chicago Defender*. He wrote, "Of all the situations that confront us involving the problems of racial segregation, none is more difficult than that of education." Du Bois clarified that separation did not necessarily engender inequality and that educational inequality could not always be solved through integration. He continued, "I do not know which distresses me the most; the crowding and lack of discipline and poor organization in unsegregated schools of Harlem or the crowding and lack of discipline and lack of organization in the segregated schools of Atlanta. What I want is education for Negro children. I believe that in the long run this can be best accomplished by unsegregated schools but lack of segregation in itself is no guarantee of education and fine education has often been furnished by segregated schools." Although mild, Du Bois's rebuke offered a pointed critique of postwar school integration campaigns that focused on the narrow goal of mixed schools and refused to consider the well-being of Black students and teachers.[35]

After meeting with the Dayton Board of Education, Cincinnati NAACP president Theodore M. Berry concluded that there was not a clear legal path because it was difficult to prove deliberate school segregation due to the paucity of official school records. The school board "denied that Dayton followed a strict district system, or that Wogaman had been changed to a Negro school." He added, "It is apparent that Negro citizens of Dayton are divided as to their attitude on separate schools, with a large segment of the group indifferent on the question." In order for integrationists to win, Berry determined, "the opposition to segregation in schools must be sustained and vocal."[36]

Mobilizing the Black community to condemn Dayton's separate schools proved impossible at this time. Dunbar High School had a reputation for excellence in academics, sports, and music. In 1938, twenty-seven Dunbar students competed in a statewide academic competition at Miami University in Oxford, winning awards in biology, Latin I, and Latin II. Dunbar musicians played at the Oberlin Conservatory of Music and the choir performed at local theaters. The school's athletic teams were the pride of Dayton's Black community, and the local press followed the careers of outstanding Black student athletes recruited to play for prestigious colleges like Boston University. Dunbar High School offered a supportive academic environment and the opportunity to participate in extra-curricular activities that were racially restricted in many "mixed" northern high schools. Black citizens in Dayton did not necessarily object to school integra-tion, but they hesitated to join a movement that threatened an educational in-stitution they valued. As late as 1950, a Black educational activist reported, "We still haven't made up our minds about our schools. Roosevelt High School is bi-racial, while Dunbar High School is 100% segregated."[37]

Black families in small towns like Bainbridge and large ones like Dayton hesitated to support school integration, but between the end of World War II and the *Brown* ruling in 1954, the vast majority of Black northerners came to ad-vocate integration in all but a few towns in the northern borderlands where Black communities lacked the economic and political power to challenge overt white supremacy. Responding to growing Black political power, some northern states strengthened their anti-discrimination legislation. For example, New Jersey for-bade school segregation in its revised constitution in 1947, Indiana repealed its permissive school segregation law in 1949, and Illinois strengthened its existing anti-segregation law by adding an effective penalty provision. As a result, most race-based school assignment practices ceased and many separate Black schools were closed, because, as the *Chicago Defender* reported, "They were simply no longer needed."[38]

Pockets of entrenched school segregation remained, especially in northern communities that bordered the South. Evansville, Indiana, for instance, responded to the state's new anti-segregation mandate by offering all students a choice of where to attend school. By 1952, only fifty Black students attended previously "white" elementary schools in this city, while only one high school student dared to enroll in the "white" high school. Similarly, Roosevelt High School in Gary and Crispus Attucks High School in Indianapolis endured as separate schools into the early 1960s. "Not every parent wanted his child to be a pioneer," explained one scholar.[39]

Documenting School Segregation

The first step in challenging northern school segregation was to prove that it existed—an arduous proposition given that school leaders denied racial dis-crimination and did not keep official records of students' racial identities. For this reason, a number of scholars and activists traveled around the region in order to quantify the degree of northern school segregation. In Pennsylvania, scholars Hugh H. Smythe and Rufus Smith visited public schools in Washington, Aliquippa, Kennett Square, Avondale, West Grove, and Downingtown, where all the Black students were assigned to separate classrooms with Black teachers in racially mixed schools. They discovered the town of Chester operated separate "colored" elementary schools with Black teachers and an integrated high school with an all-white faculty, as did Johnstown, Carlisle, York, Morton, and West Chester. Smythe and Smith estimated that one-third of Pennsylvania school districts segregated students by race, and with the exception of Pittsburgh, the entire state prohibited Black teachers from instructing white students.[40]

White civil rights activist Norma Jensen of the NAACP conducted a similar survey of fifty-two communities in New Jersey, locating illegal "colored" schools in twenty-four towns. Jenson uncovered peculiar local variations, such as Wildwood, which divided an integrated elementary school into separate white and Black sections; Penns Grove, which housed a "colored" kindergarten in the basement of the "white" school; West Cape May, which assigned Black students to an annex located fifty feet behind the "white" school; Palmyra, where a Black teacher taught all the Black elementary school children in a single, un-graded classroom; and Haddonfield, which segregated Black students through fourth grade but then integrated them into classes with white students. In a larger survey, the New Jersey Division against Discrimination identified fifty-two school districts operating separate schools with Black teachers and noted that only nine of these districts could attribute segregation to "natural" geographic factors. The remaining forty-three districts created separate schools by blatantly gerrymandering school assignments. Similar practices were discernible in Illinois, where eleven counties maintained separate schools in defiance of state law. In the summer of 1953, Harry Ashmore, a moderate white southerner, commissioned a survey of twenty-five northern communities with populations ranging from 8,500 to 3,600,000 that were in the process of desegregating their school systems. He found "the experiences reported were as varied as the communities themselves."[41]

Even when faced with proof of explicit racial segregation in the public schools, administrators often denied any wrongdoing and refused to modify assignment policies. The Educational Equality League in Philadelphia published a report in 1953 that identified 10 out of 186 elementary schools as being completely racially segregated, with all-Black student bodies and faculties. It also noted that not a single Black school administrator could be found in the city's senior high schools and that Philadelphia did not employ any senior Black school secretaries or engineers. Superintendent Allen H. Whetter responded mildly, "We do not have segregation in Philadelphia's public schools. A child may go to any school he wants to, provided there is room for him. Our school boundaries are geographical and have no relationship to a pupil's race, color or creed."[42]

Commenting on these studies, the *Pittsburgh Courier* opined, "If segregation is bad in Mississippi and Texas, it cannot be good in New Jersey and Pennsylvania: and if we protest against its existence below the Mason-Dixon Line, why should we remain mum above it?" With these new data, civil rights activists believed they could launch more effective challenges to remaining northern school segregation. The Illinois State Conference of NAACP Branches promised the major objective of 1949 would be "the abolition of all discrimination and segregation in the school systems of the state."[43]

School integration battles erupted in dozens of northern communities between 1945 and 1954. Writing in the *Crisis*, educational scholar Virgil A. Clift explained that Black northerners "have come to the conclusion that the doctrine of 'separate but equal' works to his disadvantage in education. . . . In the North, we find much more concern and many more demands being made for integrated schools." These battles mostly skipped over the largest cities for the time being and emerged in suburban towns and small industrial centers with large enough Black populations to inspire whites to segregate the schools, but small enough school districts that segregation was obvious and the solution relatively simple. For example, integration battles erupted in the schools of Gary, Indianapolis, Evansville, and Elkhardt, Indiana; Long Branch, Fair Haven, Camden, and Mount Holly, New Jersey; Alton, Argo, Cairo, Ullin, Sparta, and Tamms, Illinois; Willow Run, Muskegon, and Albion, Michigan; Chester and Downingtown, Pennsylvania; New Rochelle and Hempstead, New York; and Dayton, Cincinnati, and Williamsport, Ohio.[44]

Black parents in Long Branch, New Jersey, complained that school leaders isolated Black students at Liberty Elementary, which had an all-Black student body and faculty. Franklin H. Williams explained, "This situation arises because of the failure of the School Board to assign a specific district to this school, thereby enabling white students living in the vicinity of the school to leave the area and attend other schools in the community. Negro students may also do this if they desire and some Negro children in the community do, in fact, attend other schools. As the result, however, of a long-continued custom, most Negro parents have continued to send their children to this school." In this example, Black educational activists in Long Branch could easily identify a segregated school, which they opposed on principle. This situation also presented a relatively easy solution, and activists petitioned the school board to end race-based school assignments and instead create a geographic attendance zone for Liberty Elementary.[45]

Needless to say, even when school leaders agreed to desegregation, as they did in Long Branch, it was rarely a painless process. The KKK circulated pro-segregation flyers in Long Branch extolling citizens to "Keep America Free from Niggers," and white parents balked at Liberty's inferior resources when it appeared their children might be assigned to the historically Black school. Long Branch was one of many northern communities that witnessed Black student protests, white student counter-protests, and passionate school board meetings. Often messy and sometimes even violent, postwar school integration campaigns dismantled the separate "colored" schools that dotted the landscape in defiance of state law. Legal historian Davison Douglas argues that white northerners agreed to school integration because they realized small changes to school assignment policy would have relatively little impact on school segregation due to the very high degree of residential segregation. Civil rights activists fought racist school assignment policies that funneled Black children into certain schools and permitted white students to transfer out of these schools. By 1954, they had largely achieved this objective throughout the North. Unfortunately, the racial isolation of Black students in northern public schools was increasing as the Great Migration continued to concentrate Black migrants into racially restricted, predominantly Black neighborhoods.[46]

Brown in the North

On May 17, 1954, the US Supreme Court ruled unanimously in *Brown v. Board of Education of Topeka, Kansas* that racial segregation in the public schools violated the equal protection clause of the Fourteenth Amendment. The case represented a historic victory for Thurgood Marshall and the NAACP and was a transformative event in the Black freedom struggle. Civil rights leaders and Black citizens were relieved, joyful, and emboldened by the ruling, which signaled that the federal government would enforce Black civil rights for the first time since the end of the Civil War. Ambrose Caliver, the nation's highest ranking Black educator in the federal government, was one of many who construed *Brown* as the beginning of a "Second Reconstruction" that would protect Black civil rights and improve race relations. Referencing Gunnar Myrdal's famous study, Caliver asserted, "The American dilemma has at long last been resolved."[47]

The NAACP's Walter White confirmed *Brown* restored Black citizens' trust in American democracy and the rule of law, exclaiming, "In overruling the 'separate but equal' doctrine laid down by *Plessy vs. Ferguson* in 1896, the court re-enforced the faith of all Americans in the basic justice of our system." The president of Lincoln University, Horace Mann Bond, concurred. "It is not for us alone. It is for Mankind, everywhere. It is an affirmation that these United States of America, conceived in Liberty, and dedicated to the proposition, that all men are created equal, has had a new birth, and sends this message throughout the

World in testimony thereof." Mordecai Johnson, president of Howard University, recognized the ruling as a triumph for democracy in the Cold War era. "If that decision had gone in the opposite direction," he divulged, "it would have been like tying up the world in a little package, putting a ribbon around it, and handing it to the Communists."[48]

There was near-unanimous Black approval of *Brown* in the North and South, as it confirmed that segregation on the basis of race was illegal, immoral, and reprehensible. Du Bois acknowledged that the US Supreme Court had ruled in favor of the Black plaintiffs to his "immense surprise." "Why did it do so?" he queried. "Because it realized that this nation was face to face not simply with a colored minority within its bounds, growing in efficiency, but with a world which contained an overwhelming majority of rising colored peoples; that if our fiction of democracy was to retain any validity whatsoever, it must at least give lip-service to the principle of an unsegregated system of public schools, not to mention discrimination in travel, housing, and civil rights." Even the most ardent supporters of separate schools stood firmly against state-sponsored racial apartheid. *Brown* was a remarkable accomplishment and a potent indicator of change to come.[49]

Like Frederick Douglass a century earlier, Doxey A. Wilkerson predicted that integrated schools would eradicate prejudice by bringing together Black and white children for a common purpose. "Think what full implementation of the Court's decision could mean," Wilkerson speculated.

> Some 9,000,000 white children and 2,600,000 Negro children now attending segregated elementary and secondary schools in the South would be brought together in the classroom and on the playground. This itself would be a telling blow against racism. Hundreds of thousands of white and Negro teachers would merge their professional associations for a common approach to common problems. White and Negro parents in thousands of communities would begin to work together in the PTA's. And this process of building Negro-white unity could be extended to scores of thousands of youths and their teachers in hundreds of southern colleges and universities. The impact of this development could do much to undermine the whole structure of Jim Crow laws and practices in all fields. [50]

Whether interpreted as a legal, political, or cultural victory, Black leaders believed *Brown* would be a formidable catalyst in the struggle for civil rights.

Brown prohibbited state-sponsored, de jure school segregation as it existed in the eleven states of the former Confederacy, six border states (Delaware, Kentucky, Maryland, Missouri, Oklahoma, and West Virginia), Washington,

DC, and part of three other states (Arizona, Kansas, and New Mexico). However, it was unclear how the ruling applied to segregated schools in the North. Chief Justice Earl Warren assumed the ruling would apply only to southern school districts that operated racially restricted "white" and "colored" schools.

But to many Black educational activists in the North, the logic that racially segregated schools harmed the "hearts and minds" of Black children suggested that segregated schools were inherently illegal, regardless of whether that segregation was legally sanctioned or created through residential segregation and gerrymandered school assignments. They insisted the ruling should apply in the North because they interpreted educational discrimination to be every bit as deliberate and insidious in the North as it was in the South. As Boston activist Ruth Batson explained, "The reading of this landmark decision by members of the [NAACP] Boston Branch Public School Subcommittee was that if legal segregation was illegal, it followed that the de facto segregation in practice in Boston would also be illegal. In our minds, segregation was segregation."[51]

The NAACP drafted an Action Program for Northern Branches which stated, "Racially restrictive practices in the North, although rarely dependent on law, do the same harm as the segregation which the Supreme Court outlawed. To the extent that these decisions will encourage NAACP Branches, invigorate our friends, fortify state statues prohibiting discrimination, and generally create a favorable climate of opinion in race relations, they will invaluably assist persons fighting bigotry in the North." The NAACP was confident that *Brown* augmented legal support for school integration in the North as well as the South. "In Philadelphia, as in Little Rock, there is no such thing as a 'separate but equal' school," insisted northern activists.[52]

In the wake of *Brown*, northern Black educational activists pressed local officials to make real the vision of integrated and equal schools. Parents in Englewood, New Jersey, were among the first to cite the *Brown* decision when they attacked illegal school segregation in the fall of 1954. The New Jersey commissioner of education reviewed the complaint and agreed that Englewood school administrators had illegally assigned Black students to the Lincoln School and white students to the Liberty School, regardless of where these children lived. The commissioner directed Englewood to create geographic-based school assignment zones and to either integrate or close the separate Lincoln Junior High School.

The fact that this New Jersey town successfully cited the *Brown* decision to win school desegregation inspired other northerners to do the same. Parents in New York City, Chicago, Boston, Detroit, and Philadelphia escalated their attacks on school segregation. Headlines like "Boston Integration Problem Serious," "Chicago Wants More School Integration," and "Would You Believe It, School Integration Trouble in New York?" broadcast multiple, emerging struggles for northern school integration over the next decade. "Undoubtedly one of the most significant developments in the realm of education was the sudden spread of the school integration front to several school districts in the 'liberal' North," reported *Ebony* magazine in January of 1962. [53]

It is no accident that northern school integration campaigns erupted during the period of "massive resistance" to school integration in the South. By 1956, the NAACP was deeply frustrated by the resistance of white southerners to the *Brown* ruling. Segregationists in the South used political power and extralegal pressure applied through white Citizens Councils and the KKK to undermine school integration, a fact that mobilized Black civil rights activists and inspired those in the North. The struggle for equal and integrated schools was not just morally righteous, but it was also backed by federal law. What is more, school segregation in the North was widespread, easily identifiable, and subject to direct action tactics like boycotts as well as lawsuits. This was an important civil rights battle that northern activists can and did win. "School segregation and inferior education are among the biggest problems facing northern Negroes today," Robert L. Carter, general counsel of the NAACP, wrote in 1959. Even the region's most racially fraught towns in the northern borderlands like Colp and Cairo, Illinois, witnessed school integration movements, much to the surprise of local officials. "While the South desegregates its schools slowly and with great reluctance, there is a growing storm in the North over school segregation," confirmed the *Los Angeles Times*.[54]

The metaphor was not misplaced. School segregation was increasing in the North, especially in the largest cities as a result of intense residential segregation and white and middle-class flight to the suburbs. In 1963, a detailed study of 200 northern and western school districts identified 738 schools where Black students were more than 90 percent of the population and another 403 that were between 60 percent and 90 percent Black. Noting that segregated schools were "the most explosive civil rights issue in the North," the Commission on School Integration of the National Association of Intergroup Relations Officials reported, "School segregation, of course, is not a new problem in the North; what is new is the unprecedented urgency with which the problem is now posed." It elaborated:

> The pressure for integration NOW probably stems from a complex of influences—the increasing importance of education for the life chance of every child during this period of declining employment opportunities for workers with little schooling, the flagrant inequalities usually associated with school segregation, the strong trend since World War II toward the extension of civil rights in many fields, and especially the vigorous and confident offensive which the Negro people

have recently mounted against all forms of racial discrimination, north and south. In any case, the segregated school has become one of the major battlegrounds in the North for the burgeoning civil rights movement which now so dramatically confronts the entire nation.[55]

The NAACP prioritized northern school integration, and in 1961 it promoted June Shagaloff to a newly created position as education director of the NAACP. Shagaloff, the daughter of Jewish Russian immigrants, coordinated with local NAACP chapters and offered guidance and resources to Black educational activists. She reported that NAACP branches supported school integration efforts in dozens of northern communities including Stamford and Norwalk, Connecticut; Chicago, Centerville, Fairmont Park, Joliet, Maywood, Mt. Vernon, Robbins, Danville, and Peoria, Illinois; Detroit, Michigan; New York City, Buffalo, Rochester, Syracuse, Westbury, Glen Cove, Malverne, Amityville, Hempstead, and Manhasset, New York; Newark, Paterson, Jersey City, Orange, Englewood, Montclair, Morristown, Plainfield, Bridgeton, and New Brunswick, New Jersey; Cleveland, Columbus, Portsmouth, Dayton, and Xenia, Ohio; Philadelphia, Ardmore, Chester, Coatesville, and Twin Oaks, Pennsylvania; Gary, Indiana; Waterloo, Iowa; Minneapolis and St. Paul, Minnesota; and Boston, Massachusetts.[56]

As the northern school integration movement expanded, so too did vocal white resistance to school integration. Leslie H. Fishel Jr., a historian at the Massachusetts Institute of Technology, found, "In the North, time and again a mild anarchy greeted a community's move for integration." In Colp, Illinois, the white teachers quit and parents removed every white child from the public schools following school integration in 1957. In nearby Cairo, white students stood and sang "Dixie" when faced with their first integrated basketball game. Segregationists in Chicago called in bomb threats to signal their hostility to Black demands for school integration. White parents in New York, Chicago, and San Francisco created organizations to protest school integration, citing educational concerns, real estate problems, tax fears, or a sudden passion for "neighborhood schools" in their fervent defense of the status quo. These actions inspired righteous indignation among Blacks and failed to halt or even slow demands for school integration.[57]

In this politically charged atmosphere, the debate over school integration versus separation receded but did not disappear. Instead, it morphed into something new as northern Blacks debated how integrated schools related to larger goals such as improved academic achievement, equal educational opportunities, reduced racial prejudice, and better race relations.

Between 1954 and 1965, the struggle for school integration in the North changed as integrationists found themselves battling against recalcitrant whites, increasing residential segregation, and urban public school populations that were becoming increasingly Black and Latino faster than integration plans could mix these students together. The decade following *Brown* traces a trajectory from glowing optimism to a hardened, more pragmatic realization that school integration would require significant sacrifice and lead to only partial gains. To understand this transformation, it is helpful to consider the experiences of Black educational activists in three different settings: rural Bordentown, suburban New Rochelle, and urban Chicago.

Closing the Bordentown School

By 1954 the remaining enthusiasts of separate schools were found in those few northern communities with high-quality separate schools like Bordentown, Dayton, Cincinnati, and Indianapolis. These schools either grew out of traditions of separate schools dating back to the nineteenth century, such as the Bordentown School, or they had a more recent lineage dating to the Jim Crow era, such as Cincinnati's Dunbar High School established in 1933. By 1954, these high-quality separate schools had become community fixtures by providing employment for Black educators and a supportive environment for students. The Bordentown School made a name for itself by blending the academic work required for a high school diploma with vocational training in fields like hair styling and automobile repair. The students, parents, alumni, and faculty who favored such schools were concerned about the implications of *Brown* for separate, Black-controlled schools in the North.

These fears were exacerbated in December 1954 when New Jersey governor Robert B. Meyner announced plans to close the Bordentown Manual Training and Industrial School as part of the state's effort to enforce the *Brown* ruling. Founded in 1886 by a Black minister, Bordentown School was a public boarding school built on the model of Booker T. Washington's famous Tuskegee Institute. The school reached its height of popularity during World War II before enrollment began to decline in the postwar era as more Black families sought out integrated schools.[58]

Governor Meyner reasoned that as a segregated school for Black students, the Bordentown School did not comply with the *Brown* ruling and therefore must be closed. The *New York Times* reported, "In what might be held as an example of desegregation in reverse, the state today ordered the closing next June of the all-Negro State Manual Training and Industrial School for Youths at Bordentown." Echoing the Supreme Court ruling, Meyner asserted that a separate school not only deprived students of the benefits of an integrated education, but it also retarded the development of Black children. He noted that because the school had

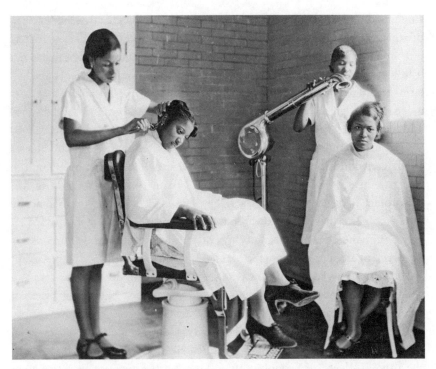

Figure 3.4. The Bordentown Manual Training and Industrial School for Colored Youth in New Jersey emphasized vocational training, such as this hair styling class, to ensure that students could find gainful employment after graduation. Courtesy of the New Jersey State Archives, Department of State, Trenton, NJ.

been "unable to induce white students to enroll at the institution" it was in "violation of the spirit of the constitutional provision against segregation."[59]

To students, families, and faculty associated with the Bordentown School, the governor's decision seemed punitive. Many found it impossible to fathom that separate schools harmed the "hearts and minds" of Black children or that they generated a feeling of inferiority. For Bordentown School supporters, it was precisely the separate and protected nature of the school that allowed Black youth to reach their highest potential.[60] In response to vehement protests from the Black community, Governor Meyner agreed to hold a public hearing on the school's fate on May 19, 1955.[61]

Those who spoke in favor of closing the Bordentown School claimed to be motivated by racial justice, although frequent references to the high per-pupil expenses at the school hinted at more material motives. James W. McGrew of the New Jersey State Chamber of Commerce proclaimed, "The taxpayers of New Jersey are spending the fantastic sum of $1,244 to educate each and every student enrolled in the Bordentown School," compared to $335.60 spent on

students in traditional vocational schools. McGrew demanded that the state jus-
tify this exorbitant expense or close the school. Politicians and business leaders
unanimously agreed that the best use of the school's campus would be to convert
it to a state institution for "mental deficients" where the industrial shops and
farms would provide job training for disabled children. Their proposal would remove the Bordentown School, its substantial campus and grounds, and the jobs
associated with it from local Black control.[62]

Supporters implored state leaders to keep the Bordentown School open as
an integrated institution. Many complained that there had been no attempt to
integrate the school. One teacher testified, "I haven't had any white boys sent
to my office to be enrolled. . . . In fact, they have made no real effort to integrate
the school. They have let it go without integration, even after it was passed on
in the Supreme Court."[63] Dean of Boys Major V. Daniels, agreed. "If there was
a movement afoot to integrate the Manual Training School, it was the best kept
secret I have ever known."[64] Supporters suspected white business leaders and
politicians were misconstruing the *Brown* ruling to deprive New Jersey Blacks of
a key educational institution, but they were unable to prove it. The New Jersey
legislature voted to withhold all funding and close the school.[65]

Black civil rights leaders either remained silent or encouraged the state to
close the Bordentown School in 1955. The Urban League of Eastern Union
County sent a telegram to the New Jersey State Legislature that supported
the immediate abolition of the school for being segregated and anachronistic.
The NAACP, similarly, felt that losing separate schools like Bordentown was a
fair price to pay for integration nationwide. When Philadelphia resident Mary
Winsor wrote to the national office that closing the Bordentown School was
"unjust and unkind," Henry Lee Moon, NAACP director of public relations,
responded with a strongly worded rebuke. "This decision is, we believe, entirely
justified inasmuch as the school has outlived its usefulness. Young Negroes may
now attend any of the state's training schools and do not require a separate institution for themselves. This is in accordance with the present trend which was
dramatized by the Supreme Court decision of May 17, 1954."[66]

Edward "Sonny" Murrain was one of many Black educational activists who
questioned the Bordentown School's abrupt end. He feared that a vital component of Black educational history and tradition was being thrown aside in the
rush to enforce *Brown*. Murrain wrote, "Most of us up North have been too smug
and flushed with victory to realize that desegregation, like bias, is a two-edged
sword. The imminent closing of Bordentown, long the subject of our pride
and praise, brings the problem of desegregation home where all may see." The
problem was that white leaders were not willing to assign white children to historically Black schools. This implied a threat to all schools that educated a majority of Black students with Black faculty, not just those high-quality ones like

the Bordentown School, Crispus Attucks High School, Dunbar High School, and the Harriet Beecher Stowe School.

The State of New Jersey made no effort to assist faculty and staff who were fired when Bordentown School was closed, and in many communities, such as Philadelphia, Black teachers were still largely restricted to majority Black classrooms or schools. For this reason, the abolition of the Bordentown School gave some people pause. What they wanted was not to retain a separate, all-Black school but instead to make a genuine effort to integrate the school by attracting white faculty and students, a strategy that government leaders refused to countenance. Black citizens were concerned that school integration not only seemed to unfold according to the terms and wishes of white officials but that it functioned as a "double-edged sword" that could harm northern Black communities.[67]

Suburban New Rochelle, New York

Known as a liberal outpost of New York City, New Rochelle gained a reputation as the "Little Rock of the North" based on the way white citizens responded to their Black neighbors' request for integrated schools. The town's two middle schools and one high school were well integrated, but the smaller elementary schools mirrored stark patterns of residential segregation. White residents assumed school segregation was a reflection of personal preferences, but Black residents viewed it as systemic racism and had been fighting New Rochelle's discriminatory school assignment policies since 1930. These efforts did not pan out until the *Brown* ruling created new possibilities for a legal attack on segregated schools.[68]

Black protest was ignited in 1956 when the New Rochelle Board of Education proposed a total renovation of Lincoln Elementary School, where more than 90 percent of the students were Black. Educational activists asked the school board to close Lincoln and disperse its students to the majority white elementary schools. After the school district refused to respond to four years of petitions, protests, meetings, rallies, and boycotts, a young Black attorney named Paul B. Zuber filed a lawsuit on behalf of Black families in the fall of 1960. One year later, federal judge Irving Kaufman found in *Taylor v. Board of Education of City School District of New Rochelle* that school leaders had repeatedly redrawn school boundary lines to concentrate Black students at Lincoln. Current patterns of school segregation in New Rochelle were no accident, concluded Kaufman, but the result of deliberate racial discrimination. Citing *Brown*, the judge determined that segregation in New Rochelle's public schools caused harm to Black students and that the district must take concrete steps to achieve integration.[69]

This case established *Brown* as an effective legal precedent for school integration outside of the Jim Crow South. It led Black educational activists and school district leaders to believe the courts would uphold *Brown* in the North, inspiring more aggressive school integration demands and concessions over the next decade. Black educational activists cited *Brown* to fight school segregation in Plainfield, New Jersey; Hempstead, New Rochelle, and Manhasset, New York; Springfield, Massachusetts; Gary, Indiana; Pontiac, Michigan; and Cincinnati, Ohio.[70]

New Rochelle previewed how both Black and white northerners would respond to school integration. While there were a handful of white supporters of school integration in New Rochelle, the more common response was frantic denial that school segregation existed, coupled with total resistance to modified school assignment policies. What is more, whites in New Rochelle resisted school integration plans while disingenuously claiming to be sympathetic to Black civil rights. To take just one example, School Board president Merryle Stanley Rikeyser called Judge Kaufman's decision "unjust" and stated that the board would appeal. In the same breath, he declared, "New Rochelle is proud of its wide diversity of racial and religious backgrounds and is eager to improve its status as a front-runner nationally in living up the ideals of a free society." He continued, "With the good faith of the community at stake, it is our obligation to ask a higher court to review the evidence concerning the realities."[71]

Such duplicitous claims fooled no one. As one southern journalist quipped, "When the good citizens of New Rochelle, New York, were accused last year of admitting Jim Crow to their schools, they denied it. When they were taken to court, they resisted. When the judge looked and saw old Jim sitting there plain as day and ordered his removal, a solid citizen of New Rochelle cried: 'Nobody understands our situation.'" The school board did not win its appeal of Judge Kaufman's integration order, but white residents continued to undermine school integration while expressing their undying support for racial equality. This subtle and supposedly colorblind white resistance proved especially elusive to legal and political challenges and destructive to school integration in the North.[72]

New Rochelle's arduous school integration battle sparked conflict among Black residents, especially after Black students started to attend majority white schools as part of a desegregation order. In the fall of 1961, 276 Black students applied for and received permission to transfer out of the majority-Black Lincoln School to attend one of the eleven majority-white elementary schools in New Rochelle. White classmates and teachers met the new arrivals cordially, but many of the former Lincoln students struggled academically and socially in their new schools. Meanwhile, the students left behind at Lincoln found themselves attending what many denigrated as a second-class school. "The school has become such a symbol of evil to integrationists that they would like to tear it apart with their hands the way the French destroyed the Bastille," admitted Superintendent David G. Salten.[73]

Further complicating matters, the only Black principal at that time in the state of New York worked at a majority white elementary school in New Rochelle, the Roosevelt School. Dr. Barbara T. Mason was a vocal critic of school integration plans, a fact that exacerbated divisions within the local Black community. Speaking to a *New York Times* reporter, she admitted that while she was disappointed that the Lincoln School had a student body that was 90.4 percent Black, she did not think that transfers on the basis of race were an appropriate remedy. "As a Negro," she said, "I don't want special treatment because I'm a Negro, whether preferential treatment or whether worse than other people." One year later, Mason lamented that when poor and working-class Black students from Lincoln transferred into predominantly white and middle-class schools, they did more harm than good to race relations.[74]

Mason elaborated that after Roosevelt School was integrated, teachers gave up their lunch hours and stayed after school to tutor the former Lincoln students and went through "great trouble" to meet with their parents. "Yet often this was not enough, and some of the transferees, instead of being stimulated by the educational aspirations of the Roosevelt children, seemed to give up trying at all," she continued. "In one grade, the average tested achievement of transferees did not rise during the school year, despite the essentially private tutoring many of them had received from their teachers." Mason concluded that Black students did not gain an educational advantage in integrated settings. She also suspected racial prejudice increased among white students after spending a year alongside poorly prepared Black classmates. All of this, she concluded, proved that removing children from their neighborhood school for the sole purpose of racial mixing was not only unproductive but potentially harmful.[75]

A report by the US Commission on Civil Rights found similar sentiments among New Rochelle's teaching staff, most of whom were white. "Dr. Mason's supporters say that the most unfortunate result of the poor showing of Lincoln transferees in Roosevelt is the creation of racial stereotypes in the minds of Roosevelt pupils. They claim that white children from a liberal background who had had no contact with Negroes before but whose home and school life taught ideals of brotherhood and the equality of man were thrown together with children of a far lower socioeconomic and cultural level who happened to be Negroes." As one white teacher summarized, "Some of the Roosevelt children actually understand that this is a cultural and not a racial difference, but all they see is that the Negro children are not as bright, clean, honest, or well behaved as they." According to George W. Foster Jr., the result was a "humiliating failure for the disadvantaged youngster and a hardening of attitudes against him among those who make the grade and see him fail."[76]

These claims that school integration caused racial animosity instead of promoting racial tolerance were potentially devastating to the school integration movement. Since the 1840s, Black civil rights activists and scholars advocated school integration not only as a way to equalize educational opportunities, but also as a strategy to cultivate greater interracial understanding. According to this view, school integration would have long-term, ameliorative benefits for American race relations. New Rochelle teachers and principals were not only denying that school integration could accomplish these ends, they were asserting that school integration spiked white animosity and negatively affected the self-esteem of Black students.

Black civil rights activists and parents in New Rochelle were having none of it. Zuber belittled Mason as "Aunt Jemima, Queen of Uncle Tom's Cabin." Black parents added that the reason their children did not fare well at Roosevelt School was "a subtle combination of slights and patronizing behavior, [and] Dr. Mason made them feel unwelcome." Meanwhile, the US Commission on Civil Rights reported that Black parents who chose to keep their children at Lincoln faced their own hardships, especially at the hands of Black integrationists who chided them for being "Uncle Toms and Aunt Jemimas for allowing their children to re-main at Lincoln." As the school year dragged on, Blacks in New Rochelle found themselves divided into two camps: integrationists, who claimed that Lincoln School was a symbol of segregation that provided an inferior education and must be abolished, and those Black parents who argued that children should not be denied the right to attend a neighborhood school because of their race. Moreover, there was no clear indication to Black parents that sending their children into majority white schools improved their academic achievement or boosted their self-esteem, and there was considerable evidence that the experi-ence was disappointing. Lived experiences on the ground, in other words, were varied and complicated.

As Black families struggled to make sense of these challenges, they adjusted their goals. They supported school integration but wanted to know more about how their children would be treated in newly integrated schools. Some stated plainly that if integrated schools were hostile places for Black youth, they would rather keep their children in a more familiar neighborhood school. Debates over school integration in New Rochelle drew attention to the fact that school inte-gration could proceed in ways that did not do enough to benefit Black children, while also emphasizing that there were aspects of majority Black neighborhood schools such as caring teachers and welcoming environments that were worth preserving.[77]

Integrating "Ghetto" Schools

"Success in New Rochelle has stimulated Negroes in other cities, coast to coast," cheered the US Commission on Civil Rights Commission in 1962. Investigators documented ongoing campaigns against northern school segregation in forty-three different cities in fourteen northern and western states. "The charges made against school officials in the cities of the North and West are various," the commission stated. "They include gerrymander of school zone lines, transfer policies and practices, discriminatory feeder pattern of elementary to secondary schools, overcrowding of predominantly Negro schools and underutilization of schools attended by whites; site selection to create or perpetuate segregation, discrimination in vocational and distributive education programs and in the employment and assignment of Negro teachers." The NAACP continued to uncompromisingly support northern school integration. As one report detailed, "Segregated schools do not—and cannot—provide the educational opportunities all parents have the right to expect for their children. Separate and unequal schools go hand-in-hand no less in the North than in the South. In city after city segregated schools are severely overcrowded, with a high proportion of temporary and substitute teachers, a rapid turnover of teachers, fewer classes for gifted children, an insufficient number of remedial reading and other special teachers, inadequate curriculum offerings and, frequently, biased educational and vocational counseling." As the report detailed, northern school segregation was not the result of accidental residential segregation—it was the consequence of deliberate efforts to isolate Black students in separate schools. Once segregated, discrimination in terms of facilities, resources, curriculum, and teachers followed.[78]

Despite growing support for school integration among northern Blacks, the racial isolation of Black children in northern public schools was getting worse through the early 1960s. The defining victories of the civil rights movement seemed to have dauntingly little effect on school segregation in the North. NAACP executive secretary Roy Wilkins cautioned, "Despite anti-segregation state statutes and the United States Supreme Court ruling of May 17, 1954, it is clear that segregated schools exist in many non-southern areas. Much of this is the result of patterns of residential segregation. However, a substantial part of it is the result of deliberate planning on the part of local school boards to contain Negro children in particular schools either by gerrymander of zone lines or by other devices."[79]

Massive population shifts that coincided with the Second Great Migration of southern Blacks to northern cities during and after World War II intensified the problem, as did postwar white suburban flight. Scores of racially restrictive laws, regulations, and government practices combined to create a nationwide system that concentrated poor and working-class Blacks in urban "ghettos." The term "ghetto" was used by social scientists and civil rights activists of the time to denote urban neighborhoods composed of poor and working-class people of color, created by discriminatory real estate practices, haunted by a lack of social services and with government-sponsored barriers to exit.[80]

Between 1940 and 1960, the nation's suburban population grew by about 30 million, which was more than twice the numerical increase in the population of central cities during the same era. The US Commission on Civil Rights further concluded that Black families living in the urban North tended to have more children than white families, and that Black families used the public schools at a higher rate than white families, many of whom sent their children to private or parochial schools. As a consequence, the percentage of Black children in urban schools tended to be higher than the percentage of Black residents in these cities. In Chicago, New York, Philadelphia, Buffalo, and Pittsburgh, the percentage of Black children in the elementary schools was at least twice that of the Black population in the city. Social scientists concluded that segregated schools in the North created undemocratic education for all children, personality damage to Black children, sub-standard school facilities and personnel, lower levels of academic achievement, early school dropouts, undeveloped human potential, and community strife.[81]

This increasing school segregation—unfolding against a backdrop of growing Black demands for school integration—made integration a defining goal of the northern Black civil rights movement. "One of the most dramatic correlates of northern school segregation today is the massive offensive which the Negro people are pressing to end it," determined Doxey A. Wilkerson in 1963. The battle for northern school integration moved into cities including New York, Chicago, Detroit, Milwaukee, Boston, Cleveland, and Philadelphia. In each of these places, Black educational activists struggled against not only recalcitrant white school boards and politicians, but also a high degree of residential segregation and a growing Black population. Women played a starring role in 1960s school integration movements. "Everywhere the parents of Negro school children, mainly the mothers, are in the center of the struggle—lobbying, organizing, demonstrating, getting arrested, and pressing their associates toward ever more militant action," Wilkerson confirmed.[82]

School Integration in Chicago

The Windy City provides an excellent case study of the seemingly paradoxical growth of school segregation during an era of coordinated Black educational activism. It also highlights key evolutions in integration strategies as activists encountered entrenched white resistance at the neighborhood, city, state, and federal levels.

Recognized by the US Commission on Civil Rights as "the most racially segregated city in the country" in 1959, Chicago was home to an assertive and well organized, yet largely unsuccessful, school integration movement. As in other northern cities, the percentage of white residents in Chicago declined in the 1940s, 1950s, and 1960s as the percentage of Black residents grew. In 1940, 90 percent of Chicago's total population of 3.4 million was white, a proportion that declined to 76 percent by 1960 as white Chicagoans decamped to the suburbs. Meanwhile, more than half a million Black migrants moved to Chicago between 1940 and 1960, where most were confined through force and real estate policies to a huge stretch of land on the South Side known as the Black Belt or Bronzeville.[83]

Accompanying these rapid population shifts were dizzying changes in public school demographics. In 1961, Superintendent Benjamin Willis pointed out that the Chicago public school population had grown by 146,000 in the past decade, with 22,000 entering in the past year alone. He added that many of the city's 450–500 schools had 100 to 150 percent turnover of students every year. Even massive school construction campaigns could not keep up with the pace of change, and as "Black" neighborhoods expanded block-by-block into new territory, the schools followed suit. Willis resorted to stop-gap measures including temporary classroom space—essentially corrugated steel trailers parked outside of schools—as well as double shifts. Dissatisfied middle-class parents began to leave the public schools by enrolling their children in private schools or moving to the suburbs, while those left behind found the number of majority Black schools growing every year. Meanwhile, some Chicago public schools served almost entirely white student bodies—and these schools seemed to have the best resources.[84]

By the spring of 1957, 91 percent of Chicago's elementary schools and 71 percent of high schools exhibited de facto segregation where 90 percent or more of a school's student body was either white or Black. The Chicago NAACP found that predominantly Black schools suffered in terms of overcrowding, school facilities, class size, teacher quality, and length of school day compared to white or mixed schools, an observation that was confirmed by the US Commission for Civil Rights. For instance, the average size of majority white elementary schools was 669 students, mixed schools 947 students, and majority Black schools 1,275 students. On a related note, only 2 percent of white elementary schools were on double shifts—where students attended only half a day—compared to nearly 20 percent of mixed schools. Over 80 percent of the students on double shift were Black. The Chicago NAACP concluded, "In the mixed schools the situation is less favorable than in the predominantly white schools, but more favorable than in the 73 predominantly Negro Schools. Negroes thus have a motive to move into the mixed schools, whites to move out."[85]

Superintendent Willis, the Chicago Board of Education, and Democratic mayor Richard J. Daley made a series of calculated decisions that exacerbated segregation and inequality. A progressive educator from Buffalo, who led the Chicago public schools from 1953 to 1966, Willis believed firmly in the "neighborhood school" as the best way to meet the social and emotional needs of children. Through the 1950s he oversaw reforms that reduced class size, improved teacher pay, and more than doubled the number of nurses and psychologists in the schools. Yet, Willis's defense of neighborhood schools stood at odds with Black educational activism after 1956. He refused to acknowledge any kind of racial inequality, including how his policy of adding temporary classroom space to overcrowded schools contributed to school segregation. In 1961, when asked how many all-Black schools existed in Chicago, Willis replied with customary indifference, "I have no idea." The superintendent believed his colorblind approach was admirable, but Black educational activists interpreted his stance as willful ignorance.[86]

In September of 1961, a coalition of Black educational activists in Chicago launched Operation Transfer. One hundred sixty Black families requested student transfers to nine all-white schools, but the board of education denied these requests. When ministers walked Black children to all-white schools to register them in person, white parents intervened. "A corner crowd swelled to nearly 100 on-lookers and a few catcalls greeted the group," reported *JET* magazine. "A dozen mothers, side by side with their backs to the newcomers, attempted to block the doorway." School officials and police officers disbanded the white protestors and sent the Black children home with a gentle reminder that they could not register for schools outside of their neighborhood. Black educational activists regrouped to consider their next move.[87]

It was at this point that discord broke out among Chicago's Black educational activists. The Chicago NAACP wanted to gather data, raise money, and build community support to pursue a long-term legal strategy, as did the local Urban League. However, a group of younger, more militant residents favored a more aggressive approach. They invited Paul B. Zuber, the same attorney who had filed the school integration case in New Rochelle, to file a lawsuit against Superintendent Willis and the Chicago Board of Education. The local NAACP was livid, but most Black families supported Zuber and discounted the NAACP's more cautious plan.

"The Chicago Branch [of the NAACP] is in a difficult position," conceded June Shagaloff. "The branch is being severely criticized in the Negro community for what appears to be an endless delay in instituting court action. . . . For the moment, at least, the NAACP has lost the leadership on the school issue." This is especially significant because NAACP leaders and the local and national level had become accustomed to leading northern school integration campaigns, particularly when it came time for litigation. But in Chicago, Black educational activists effectively bypassed the NAACP and initiated their own legal attack.[88]

In *Webb v. Board of Education of the City of Chicago*, Zuber asked the court to issue a declaratory judgment holding Chicago's neighborhood school policy illegal, as it engendered racial segregation in the public schools. He also asked for a court order to require the board of education to register students in schools outside their attendance zone where there were vacant seats. The case was dismissed on July 31, 1962, because the court ruled the plaintiffs had not exhausted the appropriate administrative remedies concerning complaints with local school policy.[89]

Black parents, impatient with the glacial pace of educational reform in Chicago, began to organize direct action campaigns that mirrored southern civil rights activism. On January 16,1962, eleven Black mothers staged a "study-in" protest with their children at the Burnside School. The adults were charged with trespassing and arrested by the Chicago police. The following day, seven more parents were arrested for a similar act of civil disobedience. The parents were protesting the scheduled transfer of their children from a racially mixed school to predominantly Black Gillespie School. The protestors insisted that the mostly white Perry School happened to be closer to their homes than Burnside and that Perry was "under-utilized."[90]

The parents lost their battle, but school integration lawsuits elsewhere inspired Chicagoans to escalate their attack. In June of 1962, the Illinois Division of the American Civil Liberties Union (ACLU) urged the Chicago Board of Education to begin a positive program of integration in the wake of a successful school desegregation case in Hempstead, New York. In *Branche v. Board of Education of Town of Hempstead*, the court ruled, "It is not enough to show that residence accounts for the fact of segregation," and that school boards must take positive steps to achieve integration in tax-supported, compulsory public schools. In late June, the Gary, Indiana, NAACP filed a lawsuit against school segregation, charging that arbitrary school assignment boundaries had created fifteen elementary schools that were "predominantly if not exclusively Negro" and eighteen that were "predominantly if not exclusively white." Edwin C. "Bill" Berry, executive director of the Chicago Urban League, announced in the summer of 1962 that like these other northern cities, Chicago was heading toward a segregated school system. Black educational activists founded a new organization, the Coordinating Council of Community Organizations (CCCO), in order to streamline educational activism of various civil rights groups fighting for school integration.[91]

Willis responded with a token integration plan, where Black students in overcrowded elementary schools could apply to transfer to open seats in nearby schools. Once the overcrowding in their "home" school had lessened, those students were expected to transfer back. The plan would affect at most 2,200 pupils, although critics noted it placed a burden on parents to identify whether they were eligible for transfer, apply, and then provide transportation to the new school. "The Board of Education has taken a small mincing step where a giant stride is required," chided Berry.[92]

The following year, sociologist Philip Hauser documented extraordinarily high rates of racial segregation and inequality in the Chicago public schools. He encouraged the board of education to expand school catchment zones to increase diversity. "We should get away from strict boundaries, but we will not get away from the problem," Hauser told the *Chicago Defender*. "The real problem is how to get desegregation in a school system that is 50 percent Negro." Faced with escalating white resistance, Mayor Daley, Superintendent Willis, and the Chicago Board of Education more or less ignored Hauser's findings and parried with another minuscule transfer plan that had little chance of desegregating the schools. The Chicago NAACP executive secretary intoned, "It is less than a precise commitment for integration and shows the board was reluctant to come up with any policy." Rosie Simpson, a local parent activist, castigated the plan as "a sugar-coated piece of nothing that may fool a few of the uninformed." She led community protests that included lying down in front of construction equipment to halt the building of a school campus made up of more than two dozen mobile classrooms, intended to serve Black students and prevent them from being assigned to empty seats in predominantly white schools.[93]

Chicago school integrationists participated in a series of boycotts, picket lines, sit-ins, mass marches, and meetings with political leaders. Tens of thousands of Chicago youth joined massive "Freedom Day" school boycotts in support of school integration in October 1963, February 1964, and June 1965 that were part of a coordinated series of school boycotts in northern cities including New York, Gary, Cleveland, Boston, Hartford, Indianapolis, Milwaukee, Detroit, and Chester. The struggle for school integration drew thousands of Black youths into direct action campaigns for northern civil rights. "The Negro Movement at this moment in American history is concentrating on equal education for Negro children—in northern cities as well as in the South," confirmed the *Chicago Defender*. Chicago protestors wanted to replace Superintendent Willis and develop an immediate, fully funded plan of school integration and capital improvement.[94]

As the school integration campaign gained momentum in Chicago, white resistance grew apace. Some feared that assigning Black children to majority white schools would imperil housing prices, thereby threatening white families' economic security. Many working-class whites in Chicago strongly opposed school integration, even though they tended to vote Democratic and espouse colorblind principles. One government report confirmed, "Segregated schools and housing had led to repeated picketing and marches by civil rights organizations. When marchers had gone into white neighborhoods, they had been met on several occasions by KKK signs and crowds throwing eggs and tomatoes."[95]

In the fall of 1963, students at all-white Bogan High School made headlines for staging an anti-integration rally on the front lawn of their school, where they chanted, "Two, four, six, eight, we don't want to integrate." The following spring, parents of sixty white children kept their children home from school after they were transferred from the racially mixed Altgeld School to a school that was nearly 100 percent Black. The white parents complained that the "Black" school had a "bad reputation," although it was unclear whether they meant the school's facilities or the students who attended it. Willis met with white parents and capitulated to their demands, thus appeasing white parents, but enraging Black ones. A survey of more than 1,000 white families found overwhelming support for Superintendent Willis and widespread condemnation of school integration in Chicago.[96]

Rifts among Black educational activists grew as the school integration movement wrestled with growing white intransigence and legal setbacks. Zuber promised to continue his legal attack on de facto school segregation, but the Chicago NAACP disagreed with his strategy and distrusted his motives. Meanwhile, membership in the Chicago NAACP plummeted. "Apparently there is a lot of petty bickering and rivalry and some of the [Chicago NAACP] local board doesn't want to do anything to help Zuber along, forgetting the children in ghetto schools who can't read, write, speak properly," chastised civil rights activist Lillian S. Calhoun. "So the NAACP is the great legal arm of the Negro's civil rights struggle. That dingblasted arm has just about atrophied here," she quipped.[97]

Relations between the Chicago NAACP and Zuber deteriorated so badly that Zuber wrote to Roy Wilkins, "As you might know I am handling the Chicago school case and it was set down for trial." He continued, "Some of the NAACP lawyers are still grumbling over the fact that an outside lawyer is heading up the case. They implied that we wouldn't get any help from them under those circumstances. I am sorry these fellows feel that way. I was asked to come to Chicago and I even offered to stay out of the matter if they would file. They refused so I filed." Zuber concluded, "All we are asking is that we are left alone to do the job." The more militant activists were asking the NAACP leaders to abdicate their leadership of school integration. The Chicago NAACP had no intention of doing so.[98]

In the early spring of 1964, the CCCO called for another massive school boycott. Leaders from the NAACP, the Urban League, and various elected

Black officials in Chicago, however, feared the strategy would backfire. The local NAACP and Urban League asked Black families to scale back direct action tactics in favor of political negotiations and legal strategies. Six of the city's elected Black alderman dispatched precinct workers to persuade Black parents not to participate in the school boycott. "We understand full well that they are serving their white masters and not the Negro people they claim to represent," scoffed CCCO leader Al Raby. The Black masses sided with the CCCO and supported the school boycott against the advice of mainstream civil rights leaders. "I think it shows again the impatience, and anger with the school administration for short-changing the children of Chicago," observed a sympathetic white alderman.[99]

"The boycott is strictly a move on the part of the Young Turks in the movement to wrest power away from the old leaders," one civil rights activist told *Chicago Daily News* reporter Georgie Anne Geyer in the spring of 1964. In an article entitled, "Negro Leaders Split over Rights Tactics," Geyer explained Chicago civil rights activists were divided into two camps. On one side stood the old guard, represented by the Chicago NAACP and the Chicago Urban League. They believed that direct action such as sit-ins and boycotts should be used judiciously to draw attention to political problems, but that they were not effective solutions to educational discrimination. The old guard was further concerned that direct action tactics were no longer the best way to convince Chicago school administrators to remedy school segregation. "Just as the body acquires resistance to antibodies, so the community acquires a resistance to sit-ins," assessed one old guard activist.[100]

On the other side stood the "young Turks," associated with SNCC and the Congress of Racial Equality (CORE). These activists supported direct action campaigns modeled on the southern civil rights movement, and they supported a more aggressive approach than the moderate NAACP and Urban League. "We've got to have so many people sitting in the street that there's no place to walk unless you walk over them," enthused one SNCC member. Geyer concluded, "If there is one basic difference between the two outlooks, it is that one skirts the status quo, kicking up dust, trying to influence and change things-as-they-are with protest. The other tries to involve itself in the dynamics of the society—political, social, economic—and to take the place of the powers that be."[101]

While Black Chicagoans overwhelmingly supported school integration, they disagreed over the best strategy to achieve it in such a vast, racially segregated, politically charged urban landscape. The NAACP, for decades the leading civil rights organization involved in northern school integration battles, struggled to assert its relevance as Black families grew frustrated with the intransigence of white officials. Northern Black educational activists who believed school integration would create better opportunities for Black children were ready and willing to adopt the more militant approach of activists in organizations like SNCC and CORE.

This more militant school integration activism was visible throughout the urban North. So too was a more vehement white resistance to northern school integration. In March 1964, 15,000 white New Yorkers marched on the board of education and City Hall to protest school integration. Virtually all of the city's principals agreed that further school integration would "hasten the flight of white, Negro and Puerto Rican middle-class children to private and parochial schools and to the suburbs." That summer saw both the signing of the Civil Rights Act of 1964 and the first of a series of northern urban rebellions in New York City, signaling both the growing success of the Black civil rights movement and also its limitations to improve the quality of life for millions of working-class and poor Blacks living in the urban North.[102]

The cheerful optimism that had greeted *Brown* in 1954 had transformed into a determined resolve to achieve school integration by any means necessary in Chicago and other northern cities. Moderates favored persuasion and litigation while more militant activists favored direct action and confrontation with school leaders and politicians. Surveys showed that northern school segregation was as bad or worse ten years after *Brown* as it was prior to World War II. In other words, there was little to show for the tremendous efforts, perilous risks, and occasional costs of the northern school integration movement. President Lyndon B. Johnson augmented federal support for school integration when he signed the Civil Rights Act of 1964 into law on July 2. Title VI of the new law stipulated that programs or activities receiving federal funding could not discriminate against individuals on the basis of race, color, or national origin.

In July 1965, the CCCO filed a Title VI complaint with the United States Office of Education in the Department of Health, Education, and Welfare (HEW) charging that the Chicago Board of Education willfully segregated students in the public schools. Hoping to compel city leaders to develop a more robust school integration plan, HEW officials withheld federal funds for the Chicago public schools. This action, however, only engendered more conflict over school integration among the Democratic representatives from Illinois who had supported President Johnson's civil rights agenda but who objected to federal intervention in local school affairs, especially if that federal intervention resulted in new school desegregation initiatives. Mayor Daley sat down with President Johnson to resolve the issue, and the federal funds were reinstated despite the fact that Daley refused to discuss a meaningful school integration plan. This episode marked the beginning of the federal government's involvement in school integration in Chicago, which would continue for the next twenty years. It also hinted at the limits of the federal government to compel school integration in northern cities.[103]

Conclusion

In 1965 the Black civil rights movement racked up sweeping victories including the Elementary and Secondary Education Act and the Voting Rights Act. The northern school integration movement, in contrast, did not have these kinds of clear-cut achievements. As sociologist Robert Dentler put it, "For every four or five schools in inner suburban communities that are desegregated, four or five new schools are opened in inner city ghettos. . . . [T]he actual net rate of Northern desegregation per year approximates zero." A court ruling in Gary, Indiana, in 1963 declared that northern school districts without a history of legal segregation were only prohibited from discriminating on the basis of race; they were not required to achieve racial balance. In 1964, the US Supreme Court declined to review the lower court's decision on this case, letting the ruling stand to create a precedent for other districts.[104]

One of the most notable developments of this era was the dramatic increase in vocal white resistance to school integration in the North. White mothers, in

Figure 3.5. African American children on the way to PS 204, 82nd Street and 15th Avenue in New York, pass mothers protesting the busing of children to achieve integration, September 13, 1965. Photograph by Dick DeMarsico. *New York World-Telegram and Sun* Newspaper Photograph Collection. Prints and Photographs Division, Library of Congress, Washington, DC.

particular, organized to halt all school desegregation efforts, and they physically intimidated Black students assigned to majority-white schools. Since school board members were either directly voted into office or nominated by elected officials such as mayors, it was easy for white majorities to pressure school leaders to resist voluntary school integration plans. Segregationists like Louisa Day Hicks in Boston chastised even modest desegregation proposals as "un-democratic, un-American, absurdly expensive, unworkable and diametrically opposed to the wishes of the parents of this city." School administrators, mean-while, feared that school integration plans would backfire. Kenneth L. Meinke, superintendent of Hartford public schools, warned that any attempt to assign children outside of their neighborhood schools "would almost certainly accel-erate the pace at which white families would leave the city." He concluded, "The result, inevitably, would be a predominantly nonwhite school system." Similar warnings—or threats—were issued throughout the North. Aware that white constituents preferred a high level of racial segregation in the public schools, administrators made choices about new school construction including site selec-tion and architecture that severely exacerbated racial segregation. As one scholar concluded, "With each new building, the landscape of education, premised upon the idea of neighborhood schools, became more entrenched."[105]

In the fall of 1965, Martin Luther King Jr. and the Southern Christian Leadership Conference (SCLC) joined the battle for school integration in Chicago, signifying that the struggle for northern school integration was now an official part of the national Black civil rights agenda. The New Jersey State Conference of the NAACP listed "an affirmative action program to end racial imbalance and de facto segregation in all schools in the State of New Jersey" as its top priority in the fall of 1965, followed by the need for fair housing and better employment opportunities.[106]

Black educational activists faced daunting evidence that school integra-tion was not working the way scholars had hoped to equalize educational opportunities, improve Black academic achievement, and reduce racial preju-dice. Irving Ankler, the white principal of Benjamin Franklin High School in New York City and a strong advocate for school integration, wrote, "The tragic fact is that during the very era when our nation is dedicating itself to a massive ef-fort at integration and racial justice, the public schools of our northern cities are almost inexorably marching toward greater de facto segregation." He continued, "In spite of the efforts of our boards of education, the hopeful pronouncements of our state commissioners of education, and the militancy of some civil rights leaders, the percentage of Negroes and Puerto Ricans attending de facto segregated schools in our northern cities has increased since the Supreme Court decision of 1954."[107]

It was at this crucial juncture that Black educational activists began to question whether school integration was the best strategy to improve educational opportunities for Black youth, given the geographic isolation of large numbers of Black students in urban areas and widespread white resistance in the North. "We want to integrate, but the white says 'NO.' Maybe we ought to forget it. Why should we integrate?" pondered Kenneth Guscott, a World War II veteran and president of the Boston NAACP. The *Boston Globe* confirmed, "This is a growing feeling among Boston Negroes a century after legal slavery, a decade after the Supreme Court decision, a year after its own racial crisis in the schools." The debate among northern Black educational activists over which would better serve the Black freedom struggle—racially integrated schools or separate, Black-controlled ones—was not resolved by the rise of the Black civil rights movement following World War II, the *Brown* decision, or the decade of successful educational activism that followed it.[108]

Conflict in the Community

Separation for Black Power, 1966–1974

Like many northern communities, the coastal town of Norwalk, Connecticut, had a long history of informal segregation that left an indelible mark on the educational landscape of the 1960s. Nevertheless, white school leaders were stunned when Waverly Yates, Black civil rights leader and chairman of the local Congress of Racial Equality (CORE), threatened a school boycott in the fall of 1968. What Yates objected to was not the existence of segregated schools—in fact, the town had instituted a voluntary school desegregation plan in 1963— but instead the "arbitrary, unreasonable, unlawful, and unconstitutional" de- struction of neighborhood schools. Yates was protesting the school integration plan, which bused children out of the predominantly Black and Puerto Rican Nathaniel Ely Elementary School into majority white ones. That fall, Ely Elementary was slated to be closed and its remaining students bused to schools up to nine miles away. Yates denounced this proposal and filed a legal complaint to halt it, explaining, "In the white neighborhood schools, the white parents have a lot to say about how things are run. But not the Black parents, because their power is diluted among many schools and because the schools the Black kids go to are often several miles from home." He believed Black parents could be better advocates for their children's educational needs through neighborhood schools like Ely Elementary—even if those schools had very few white students.[1]

"I walked the picket line five years ago to close that school because it was segregated," countered Norwalk parent Beatrice Brown. "To me, the sacrifice of busing my son is worth it for a decent education." Wilbur G. Smith, chairman of the Connecticut Conference of the NAACP, concurred and organized a community meeting to support school integration. Tellingly, Smith did not invite CORE rep- resentatives. Afterward, Yates complained that the NAACP "charged our people in Norwalk as being part of a 'cynical force in the community trying to bring back segregated schools.'" Yates rejected this characterization because he saw a crucial difference between the liberatory potential of separate, Black-controlled schools and the stigma of racially segregated ones. Furious, Yates declared that the working relationship between CORE and the NAACP in Norwalk was over. "The NAACP represents by and large middle-class Negroes," he chastised, "while CORE represents Blacks in the ghettos. Now this rift has been widened. There will be conflict within the community between Blacks and Negroes."[2]

As Yates's criticism suggests, between 1966 and 1974 the Black Power movement sparked renewed interest in separate, Black-controlled schools while other civil rights activists remained deeply committed to school integration. Motivated by Stokely Carmichael's 1966 rousing call for "Black Power," Black nationalists argued school integration had failed to achieve its primary objectives of improving educational opportunities and reducing prejudice. What is more, they believed Black students bore the brunt of the burden of school integration through long bus rides to hostile, majority white schools. In contrast, Black power activists insisted that community-controlled schools would build strong Black institutions, prepare children of color to thrive in a hostile society, and promote Black social and economic development. Importantly, as the example from Norwalk demonstrates, community-controlled schools worked only if Black children were not bused to distant majority white schools for the purpose of school integration.[3]

The fact that community-control activists voluntarily abandoned school integration was deeply troubling to Black academics and activists associated with more moderate civil rights organizations. They feared the rising separatist impulse would undermine recent gains of the civil rights movement. Economist Robert C. Weaver cautioned, "Separatism has had and continues to have a stifling impact upon the intellectual development and production of Blacks; it also inhibits their economic process." Prominent leaders including Martin Luther King Jr. of SCLC and Roy Wilkins of the NAACP urged Black northerners to fight for school integration not only to improve educational equality but also to fulfill larger mandates of the Black freedom struggle including integration and assimilation into American society. Mainstream civil rights activists continued to advocate school integration, only now they ran into confrontations with Black educational activists who renounced integration in favor of community control.[4]

This chapter investigates the era's most heated debates over school integration versus separation in the North during the height of the Black power era. It pays special attention to the evolving legal context of northern school integration, developments in how social scientists viewed the benefits of integration, and the steady growth of Black nationalism and white backlash that were hallmarks of the era. It analyzes the discordant "conflict in the community" over the question of school integration with passionate crusaders on both sides and a great deal of pragmatism by parents and students in the middle.

Interest in community-controlled schools built on a long tradition of separate schools dating back to the start of the common school era in the 1840s. But it also represented something entirely new, as community-control activists blended these older traditions of racial uplift with postcolonial, revolutionary, and Black nationalist ideologies. Supporters of community-controlled schools shared a sense of urgency and optimism—they were no longer waiting for the supposed benefits of school integration to materialize and were ready to take over a key public institution to improve life chances for Black youth. "It was generally concluded that the existing educational systems were not responsive to the wishes of the Black community," political scientist and Black power advocate Charles V. Hamilton explained. "Black people, having moved to the state of questioning the system's very legitimacy, are seeking ways to create a new system."[5]

This revitalized interest in separate, Black-controlled schools in the late 1960s had profound implications for the northern Black civil rights movement, which became much more diverse as activists clashed over strategies and goals. The community-control school movement destabilized long-standing political coalitions between civil rights activists and potential allies, especially teacher unions and white liberals. It also offered exhilarating possibilities for educational activism and reform.

This chapter aims to elucidate why interest in separate schools reappeared at this moment, who was on either side of these debates, how this influenced educational reform, and how support for community-controlled schools interacted with the larger Black freedom struggle in the North. Case studies from New York City, Newark, and Boston reveal how debates over school integration versus separate, Black-controlled schools evolved in this changing context. Frustrated by the limits of political reform, Black northerners wondered whether community-control of majority Black public schools could finally realize the goals of the Black freedom struggle.[6]

Black Power and White Resistance

Alongside the Civil Rights Act of 1964 and the Voting Rights Act of 1965, the Elementary and Secondary Education Act (ESEA) passed by President Lyndon B. Johnson in 1965 represented a monumental victory for Black civil rights activists. The overarching goal of this new legislation was not necessarily to create a more equal social order but instead to remove those barriers to equal opportunity that many Americans had come to regard as illogical, discriminatory, and unfair. By forbidding racial discrimination in public accommodations, education, and voting, as well as increasing federal oversight of compliance, these laws promised "fair play" for all. Compensatory education programs, funded by the ESEA, would make up for the supposed cultural deficiencies that afflicted the poor. In many ways, these civil rights laws seemed poised to finally resolve what Gunnar Myrdal had so poignantly described as the American Dilemma.[7]

While civil rights legislation removed some of the barriers to equal opportunity, it was not enough to overcome more than 200 years of deeply entrenched structural racism in housing, education, health care, and employment. It also ignited a white backlash that inspired vigilante violence, brought white supremacy into mainstream political discourse, and encouraged white southerners to abandon the Democratic Party in droves. Many white Americans interpreted civil rights legislation as evidence the nation had lived up to the American Creed by guaranteeing equal opportunity for Black citizens. In other words, white citizens believed that the valid complaints of Black civil rights activists had been addressed and that the problem of racial discrimination was solved. The reality was quite different, and as racism and inequality persisted, many Black activists were forced to recognize the limits of political reform. As historian Manning Marable acknowledges, "America's political economy was still profoundly racist, and Johnson's legislation had erased only the crudest manifestations of racial suppression." With white consciences salved, many were unreceptive to the next, more militant phase of the Black freedom struggle. This phase included a final, forceful push for school integration in the North, where by 1966, schools were every bit as racially segregated as they had been two decades earlier.[8]

Litigation, or the threat of litigation, remained the most effective tool to integrate northern schools and the NAACP continued to spearhead legal challenges. A series of judicial rulings calling for stronger, more aggressive school integration plans in northern cities including Pontiac, Michigan; San Francisco and Pasadena, California; and Ft. Wayne, Indiana, determined that "racially imbalanced" schools deprived Black children of equal educational opportunities, regardless of whether school officials had deliberately established segregated schools. Integrationists were further encouraged by a 1971 US Supreme Court ruling that found the Charlotte-Mecklenburg Board of Education failed to meet the mandates of *Brown* by relying on a neighborhood school assignment policy that happened to result in highly segregated public schools. This suggested that segregated schools resulting from residential segregation in the North would be subject to the same kind of judicial intervention. In 1973, the US Supreme Court heard its first case on the question of northern school integration and ruled in favor of the Black plaintiffs. *Keyes v. Denver School District No. 1* determined that "the Board, through its actions over a period of years, intentionally created and maintained the segregated character of the core city schools." The justices ruled that because deliberate racial segregation had occurred in one part of the school district with a goal of "segregative intent" against both Black and Mexican American students, the entire district would be held accountable and must initiate desegregation. This decision put northern school districts on notice that de facto school segregation would not be tolerated, that a violation in one part of a school district was enough to require a systemwide response, and that busing students to schools outside of their immediate neighborhood was an acceptable remedy. It provided a legal opening for Black educational activists to demand stronger and more ambitious school desegregation plans throughout the North, and as a result, many northern and western communities including Detroit, Dayton, Cleveland, Columbus, Boston, Indianapolis, Las Vegas, San Francisco, and Seattle instituted desegregation plans under court order (or the threat of court order).[9]

The visible expansion of new school integration plans in the North overlapped with a combustible mix of rising Black militancy and growing white resistance to Black civil rights. Deteriorating conditions combined with mounting expectations in northern "ghettos" pushed Black political unrest to the breaking point. Urban rebellions marked by rioting, looting, arson, and deadly clashes with the police spread through Harlem and Philadelphia in 1964, Watts in 1965, and Detroit and Newark in 1967, and 120 cities including Chicago and Washington, DC, following the assassination of Martin Luther King Jr. in 1968. Although many Black Americans viewed these rebellions as rational responses to intolerable conditions of police brutality, destitute conditions, and lack of opportunity in Black neighborhoods, many white Americans interpreted the unrest as irrational "riots" that revealed the pathology of Black culture—and the danger of Black people. White northerners began to openly question the validity of the Black civil rights movement just as the Black Power movement burst onto the national scene.[10]

A new generation of young, outspoken, Black Power leaders used sensationalist rhetoric to galvanize the Black masses and shock whites. "We stand on the eve of a Black revolution," Stokely Carmichael wrote in a typical jeremiad in 1967. "Masses of our people are on the move, fighting the enemy tit for tat, responding to counter revolutionary violence with revolutionary violence, an eye for an eye, a tooth for a tooth, and a life for a life. These rebellions are but a dress rehearsal for the real revolution." Black Power militants like Carmichael celebrated the idea of organized, armed Black response that would overthrow the white power structure and create a more egalitarian world with an equitable distribution of wealth and opportunity.[11]

Moderate civil rights leaders including King, Wilkins, and SNCC chairman John Lewis cautioned that threats of violence and urban rebellions would scare off white allies and turn the tide of public opinion against the civil rights movement. "Many whites sincerely in favor of integration will be silenced out of fear and confusion," admonished Bayard Rustin. "Riots do not strengthen the power of Black people; they weaken it and encourage racist power." Such concerns proved to be prescient. White opposition to school integration, always present but largely muted since World War II, burst forth vigorously and unapologetically.[12]

"We fought for what we have, over generations, and now it looks as if Big Brother, in Albany or Washington, is taking it away," seethed Robert V. Cimmino, a white critic of school integration in suburban Mount Vernon, New York. "We've gotten too many Negroes, too fast. Maybe one Negro in a class would be good—until everybody gets used to it," complained a white mother in Rochester. White northerners fumed over increased taxes, wasted school funds, or lower academic standards as they feverishly defended the need for everyone to stay in their neighborhood schools—an approach that guaranteed very high levels of racial segregation. "It'll be just like a military convoy—you can go on no faster than the slowest vehicle," grumbled a white father in Hartsdale, New York. "It doesn't help any when you bus children into a school who are two years behind their grade," echoed a white opponent of school integration in Queens. Even white teachers agreed. "They just don't belong here, not until they've had much, much more orientation, not until they're more like the rest of our children—and I guess that's how I feel," one teacher confessed, after working with Black children in a newly desegregated school.[13]

Social scientists fretted over growing evidence of massive resistance to school integration in the North. Roger A. Dentler, planning chairman for the Center for Urban Education at Columbia University, concluded, "The white taxpayer's image of a given public school is still affected by its percentage of Negro pupils. In a suburb that is 15 percent Negro, for example, a school that has 30 percent Negro pupils may be downgraded socially for that reason alone." He concluded that anti-Black prejudice "tremendously" slowed the process of school integration throughout the North. By 1968, whites in the North funneled their fear and loathing of school integration into an ostensibly colorblind rhetoric against "forced busing." As historian Joshua Zeitz concluded, "Many white northerners who supported civil rights when that commitment was confined to the desegregation of schools, public accommodations, and voting booths in the South instantly revolted against the Great Society when it came to *their* schools, workplaces, and neighborhoods."[14]

Northern white opposition to school integration mimicked the successful tactics of Black civil rights activists; whites staged mass protest marches and waved handmade signs demanding their civil right to "neighborhood schools." White students boycotted schools receiving Black students under desegregation plans, and their mothers taught alternative classes, much as Black mothers hosted "freedom schools" during school integration boycotts. White parents believed they had the moral high ground and used populist rhetoric to describe themselves as the beleaguered silent majority facing unjust persecution by irrational and distant government forces. The more state and federal agencies supported school integration in the North—which almost always required busing children out of their de facto segregated neighborhoods—the more white parents objected. By the late 1960s, white opposition to school integration was plainly a national problem, not just a southern one. "When the attack switched to de facto segregation, it turned out that the citizens of Chicago, Boston or Los Angeles are not all that more tolerant than the rednecks of Alabama and Georgia," quipped the *Los Angeles Times*.[15]

Elected officials fell in line behind their white constituents' objections to "forced busing." To take one example, local Democratic candidates in Long Island, New York, formalized their opposition to busing for the purposes of school integration in the fall of 1966. Busing was "the major issue, and had great effect" on the sweeping victory of local Republicans the year before, according to one observer. The only way for Democratic candidates to compete was to join Republican candidates in rejecting busing completely. "Oh busing, what campaigns have been run in thy name?" lamented Long Island CORE activist Lincoln O. Lynch. By the end of the year, white constituents throughout the North had pressured Democratic members of Congress into challenging the federal government's commitment to school integration. "There is uneasy talk about a so-called 'white backlash vote,' waiting in the wings to single out and dismiss summarily anyone trying to give special favor to Negroes, most particularly by encouraging them to live and go to school in white neighborhoods," determined Harvard psychiatrist Robert Coles. This pressure continued to increase into the early 1970s as white northerners revolted against school integration and became increasingly hostile to Black civil rights.[16]

In 1968 (and again in 1972), Richard M. Nixon was elected president on a staunch anti-busing platform that promised to restrict all children to their neighborhood schools and rescind liberal policy in education, housing, welfare, and the criminal justice system. Nixon orchestrated a massive rollback of federal enforcement of school integration. In a representative democracy like the United States, widespread opposition to school integration translated into eviscerated political support at a crucial moment. The emergence of the New Right in American politics made opposition to school integration and "forced busing" a central tenet of an ascendant conservative movement.[17]

Social Science and School Integration

Elected officials had to balance declining white support for school integration with mounting evidence that it offered the single most effective way to improve educational opportunities for minority children. The most compelling data came from white sociologist James S. Coleman's *Equality of Educational Opportunity*, known as the Coleman Report, published in 1966. Hailed by the *Washington Post* as "the nearest thing to an educational bombshell to come out of the Federal Government in a long time," the 737-page report represented the largest, most comprehensive, and most expensive social science investigation of racial equality in American public schools ever conducted.[18]

Coleman and his research team surveyed more than 570,000 students and 60,000 teachers and collected detailed information on the facilities available in more than 4,000 schools over a two-year period. Required by a provision of the 1964 Civil Rights Act, the purpose of the study was to ascertain whether racial minorities had equal opportunities in the public schools. While no one was surprised by Coleman's findings that Black, Puerto Rican, Mexican American, and Native American children suffered educational inequality and intense segregation, the report nevertheless stunned social scientists and the public with its finding that the key factor in students' academic success was the background of pupils and teachers—not the school and its material resources. "In effect, the report says that pupils do more to educate each other than does the school as such to educate the pupil," concluded the *Washington Post*. The *Boston Globe* was even more succinct, concluding "the Coleman Report means that better schools do no good."[19]

Black and white liberals focused on Coleman's discovery that a child from an impoverished home benefited from attending school with large numbers of middle-class peers and that middle-class children showed no decline in academic achievement in socioeconomically integrated settings. Racial liberals concluded that this meant school integration would solve racial inequality in education, a claim that conflated Coleman's finding about the value of socioeconomic school integration with racial mixing. It was also true that mixing poor Black youth with their middle-class peers would require racial mixing, since there were not enough Black middle-class students to ensure socioeconomic integration in separate schools.[20]

Writing in the *Journal of Negro Education*, Harrell Rodgers and Charles Bullock determined, "The importance of these findings is that many Black children can be placed in a middle income milieu only in an [racially] integrated environment." Other social scientists followed up on the basic premise of the Coleman Report and found that, in general, the study's basic conclusions held up to scrutiny, and that Black children attending integrated schools had higher levels of academic success than their peers in majority minority schools. This created a powerful incentive for liberal policymakers, educational leaders, and scholars to support more aggressive school integration plans nationwide.[21]

Ironically, the Coleman Report spurred political support for school integration at the very moment when many Black northerners were beginning to reevaluate it as both a strategy and a goal of the larger civil rights movement. Black nationalists rejected liberal claims that the Coleman Report warranted more aggressive school integration, instead pointing to other aspects of the report they believed illustrated the benefits of separate, Black-controlled schools. Of special interest was Coleman's finding that student attitudes had a potent effect on academic achievement, regardless of the quality of educational facilities. For instance, Coleman found that, overall, Black students felt in control of their fate "much less often" than whites. However, he also found that Black pupils who felt that they shaped their own lives had higher levels of academic achievement than white students who did not. Coleman concluded:

> Internal changes in the Negro, changes in his conception of himself in relation to his environment, may have more effect on Negro achievement than any other single factor. The determination to overcome relevant obstacles, and the belief that he will overcome them—attitudes that have appeared in an organized way among Negroes only in recent years in some civil rights groups—may be the most crucial elements in achieving equality of opportunity—not because of the changes they will create in the white community, but principally because of the changes they create in the Negro himself.[22]

Black power activists seized upon this finding to assert that only separate, Black-controlled schools cultivated Black students' resolve to overcome obstacles. CORE national chairman Floyd McKissick scoffed, "We are told that Negroes must be integrated into middle-class (and that means white) schools. . . . We are told that something called student culture really makes the difference. In other words, mix Negroes with Negroes and you get stupidity." Scholar and activist Nathan Wright Jr. agreed, noting, "The artificial moving of children about so that one group's presence in particular might benefit the other is both denigrating and manipulative."[23]

The Black power critique of school integration was fueled by the shortcomings of school integration to improve public education for most Black students in the North. Multiple studies documented increased levels of racial isolation in northern schools, despite years of school desegregation campaigns. Nevertheless, conditions in many majority Black inner city schools were genuinely bleak and parents were incredibly frustrated with the slow pace of change. Even ardent school integrationists like psychologist Kenneth B. Clark urged Black northerners to shift their focus from school desegregation to quality education, since he was forced to acknowledge "de facto school segregation was increasing in Northern cities despite Negro efforts to break it down." Black power scholar Charles V. Hamilton offered an enticing alternative to school integration he called the "comprehensive plan." Writing in *Harvard Educational Review*, Hamilton claimed that the Black masses had given up on school integration and were alienated from the school system. The solution, Hamilton insisted, required four key components: Black control of the decision-making process in local schools, parental involvement and alliances with (preferably Black) teachers, attention to Black children's self-esteem and psychological health, and improved curricula and instructional materials that featured Black people in positive and accurate ways. Hamilton's comprehensive plan did not require busing, was ostensibly flexible enough to work in any school, and promised to restore the vital link between Black families and the American Dream.[24]

Black northerners had to sift through these competing interpretations of social science data to determine which form of educational activism to support: integration or community-controlled schools. They measured the costs of school integration—financial, personal, and political—against the gains, especially better educational opportunities in majority white schools. Integrationists found the courts willing to support demands for an end to school segregation built through generations of explicit residential segregation and gerrymandered assignment policies. Nationwide, these desegregation plans resulted in the closing of separate and majority Black schools and the firing of Black teachers and principals as Black children were bused to formerly majority white schools. Even the NAACP was forced to admit that "many of our branches have been protesting against integration policies which placed the entire burden of integration on the Black community and children." In addition, most northern desegregation plans were the result of political compromise that did not do enough to secure equal educational opportunities for large numbers of Black students. Even where racial mixing was occurring, it was not clear that educational equality followed when whites retained control of administration, pedagogy, curriculum, parent teacher associations, and extracurricular activities.[25]

For instance, after a protracted battle established a "two-way" busing plan in Rochester, New York, in 1968, only 2,000 Black children were being bused out to majority white schools and only 150 white students were being bused into majority Black schools. This left more than 90 percent of Rochester's Black students behind in deteriorating, majority Black schools that lacked adequate resources or the political clout to secure these resources. Black parents wondered if the money spent on busing a tiny percentage of students would not be better spent on improving facilities and resources for all.

White parents in Rochester, meanwhile, grew increasingly frantic at the prospect that Black children would be bused into majority white schools. In one instance, white parents and children stood outside of a newly desegregated middle school shouting taunts and insults at Black students as they arrived. In this example, only about 10 percent of Rochester's Black students benefited from school integration, and it was not readily apparent whether these students were the lucky ones. Rochester school leaders and politicians were unable or unwilling to create a meaningful school integration plan that would improve the quality of education and equalize the schools for all Black students, and as a result, many Black families were disappointed and angry. "Integration is becoming phased out. We are not moving fast enough," admitted Rochester school administrator Norman N. Gross. "The Blacks already are beginning to say, 'We've had it. You've failed to produce. Why can't Black kids be educated by themselves?'"[26]

Even in successfully integrated schools, like Norwalk High School in Connecticut, Black students were not always satisfied in schools where the majority of students, teachers, and administrators were white. "If you're Black, you have to practically fight your way into an academic course. They think all we can do is wind up as waitresses of day workers—maybe get a typist's job if you're real smart," testified a young Black woman. A male classmate confirmed her grievance, "Maybe they don't know it, but they're always putting you down. Some English teachers won't even let you do a book report on 'Manchild' [*Manchild in the Promised Land* by Claude Brown] or 'The Autobiography of Malcolm X.'" Black students complained that white teachers and classmates did not treat them with respect, pointing to a lack of representation on student government. Their parents were equally frustrated by the refusal of Norwalk's all-white board of education to respond to serious concerns about transportation and school safety. Beatrice Brown, an outspoken advocate of school integration in Norwalk reconsidered her stance in the summer of 1969. She told a reporter that she only spoke up for the busing program because she feared the majority Black Ely Elementary School would offer an inferior education. But watching her children suffer slights in the integrated schools had changed her mind. "I've gone Black Power," she affirmed. She was not the only one.[27]

Community Control in New York City

In June of 1966, Stokely Carmichael captivated the nation with his demand for "Black Power" at a Mississippi rally. The phrase captured the anger and urgency among civil rights activists who were losing faith in nonviolent protest and civil disobedience. "What do you want?" Stokely called to the cheering crowd. "Black Power!" they shouted back. "What do you want?" he repeated. "Black Power!" they roared. Moderate leaders like Martin Luther King Jr. were troubled by the new slogan, which seemed controversial and potentially problematic, but they were unable to stop it.[28]

Three months later, the tall, handsome philosophy major from Howard University repeated his clarion call at Arthur A. Schomburg Intermediate School (I.S.) 201 in Harlem. Wearing a Black sweatshirt adorned with the bright yellow emblem of a roaring Black panther, Carmichael joined parents and civil rights activists protesting the board of education's refusal to dismiss I.S. 201's white principal and replace him with a Black one. "We have a right to run our school," Carmichael called out to a reporter. "Let's put a Negro principal [in a suburban school] and see how the white savages react."[29]

Carmichael's presence at the Harlem school protest was symbolic, but nevertheless poignant. The young firebrand drew attention to a relatively new strategy for Black educational activists in the North: community-controlled schools. New York City was the site of the North's most spectacular and successful confrontations over community-controlled schools, and as such what unfolded here had far reaching implications. Black New Yorkers were exasperated with the board of education's abysmal track record on school integration. Despite the fact that school officials claimed to have been working on school integration since the *Brown* ruling in 1954, school segregation had increased as more Black and Latino families moved into the city and whites absconded to the suburbs.[30]

Meanwhile, school administrators refused to enact policies that would result in more than token integration. In 1960, 15 percent of New York City schools had Black and Puerto Rican enrollments of over 85 percent. By 1968 the proportion had risen to 28 percent, despite open enrollment plans. Efforts to promote racial mixing of students and faculty had been met with obstinate resistance from white parents and teachers, and politicians proved reluctant to challenge these constituents. Although Black educational activists had fought long and hard for school integration in New York City, many were ready to consider alternative strategies to improve educational opportunities for Black youth. As Preston Wilcox explained, "The residents of that community decided once and for all that the educational problems of their children derived not from a *failure to integrate* but from the *success* of the New York City Board of Education in *failing to educate* their children."[31]

According to psychologist Kenneth B. Clark, the idea for community-controlled schools in New York City did not come from Black nationalists but rather from integrationists as they faced the blunt fact that racial mixing as a strategy had serious limitations imposed by demographics, geography, white resistance, and lack of political support. In 1965, Clark attended a meeting of educational activists who were trying to figure out how to respond to yet an-other setback in the city's school integration plan. One of the parents, Isaiah Robinson, rose to speak. According to an observer:

> Isaiah Robinson suggested, almost as a joke, that since white children would not be sent into Harlem schools and Black children were not being invited downtown in any meaningful numbers, maybe the Blacks had better accept segregation and run their own schools. A jolt of recog-nition stung all of us: Isaiah's joke was a prophecy. It is hard to get across the sudden sadness we all felt. We had worked together for a long time, Blacks and whites. We were close, loving friends. Now we had to agree to separate because the society would not recognize our marriage and, one way or another, the Black children had to be legitimized.[32]

As this example suggests, some Black educational activists embraced the idea of majority Black schools with community control not as an expression of Black nationalism, but instead as a pragmatic response to the failures of school integra-tion policy. Clark insisted this phenomenon was widespread, writing, "Most of those individuals in the minority communities who are now fighting for com-munity control have been consistent fighters for integration. Their support for decentralization is not, therefore, to be seen as a desire for separatism or a re-jection of integration, but . . . it is a strategy of despair, a strategy determined by the broken promises of the white communities." NAACP field secretary Sydney Finley agreed. "When school integration appears not to be forthcoming, a man stops thinking about integration and starts thinking about the quality of the schools in the Black ghetto," he reflected.[33]

Community-controlled schools garnered admiration from Black nationalists who explicitly valued separation for Black liberation. Activists like Carmichael and Hamilton believed that only by organizing into autonomous political and social units could Black citizens advocate for effective reform. "An awful lot of Black people have become alienated from the dominant educational system," Hamilton explained. "What we're trying to do with community control is to create relevant intermediary agencies." The growing popularity of the Black power movement revitalized northern Black educational activism. As a Black Illinois state senator from Chicago argued, "The Black community must tempo-rarily withdraw, organize, and then enter the mainstream with the power to move society." Hamilton insisted that Black communities must have the ability to hire and fire teachers and principals and to set the curriculum. He encouraged Black parents to establish their own boards of education and run their own schools.[34]

For varied reasons, diverse Black educational activists began to contemplate the possibilities of community-controlled education in New York City. The basic

idea was that the city would abandon controversial and expensive desegregation initiatives and instead endow parents and community leaders with jurisdiction over each school's curriculum, staffing, and expenditures. Black parents and
teachers could then do what white educators could not—see to the emotional,
social, and intellectual needs of Black students and communities.

Supporters insisted that community control offered a fair and reasonable response to decades of systematic educational racism. New York City Black educational activist Rhody A. McCoy maintained that since city, state, and federal
taxes paid by parents kept schools open, "Parents have the right to participate
in running these schools. This is part of their democratic American heritage."
This logic appealed to parents who believed schools were mismanaged by white
administrators and sabotaged by white teachers who did not believe in the potential of Black students to learn.[35]

Black educational activists wanted to improve dire conditions that had been
neglected for too long. "Action now, baby; right now!" urged parents in Boston,
where plans for school integration and improvement had stalled for years.
Similar demands ricocheted throughout the urban North, but were especially
audible in New York City. "We want a Black principal and Black teachers for our
Black children," said a parent picketing a board of education meeting in Harlem.
New York's new African American Teachers Association demanded "self-
control, self-determination, and self-defense" in predominantly Black schools.
As one leader explained, "All African-American teachers must seek teaching
positions in the Black community. Black teachers must protect Black children
against educational injustices and systematic genocide." Native American educational activists endorsed the Black community-control movement, comparing
it to the long struggle for cultural self-determination among indigenous peoples.
"Thus the integration-segregation controversy is entering a new and more complex stage brought on by the anti-integration stance of some Afro-Americans
coupled with the traditional attitude of Indians," concluded Native American
scholar Jack D. Forbes.[36]

Although potentially appealing to a range of Black educational activists and
their allies, community-controlled schools were met with surprise, outrage, and
indignation by many whites. Critics were uncomfortable with the idea that curriculum and teaching would be tailored to the needs of Black children and shocked
by the fact that Black educational activists were demanding—not asking—for
change. "Racist control of the schools—whether by Black Nationalists or White
Citizens Councils in Alabama—ought to be condemned," protested an editorial
in the *Washington Post*. Black power leaders were undeterred. "Everybody needs
to be shocked once in a while; it's often the only way to get attention," enthused
McKissick to an audience of 300 people at New York University. Black educational activist Merrill Martin agreed. "Any board of education that expects Black

people to respond without hatred to the daily humiliations inflicted by our racist society should stop pretending to educate and start becoming educated."[37]

New York City Teachers Strike of 1968

White administrators and teachers balked at proposals to remove authority from professional educators and place hiring, curriculum, and budget decisions in the hands of parents with little or no administrative experience. Community-controlled schools directly threatened the recently won gains teachers had achieved through robust union activism in the mid- to late 1960s. There were thirty documented teacher union strikes in 1966 and more than 100 in 1967, including major work stoppages in Newark, Detroit, Flint, and East St. Louis. Teachers were fighting for higher salaries, better working conditions, and more professional autonomy. In September 1967, nearly 50,000 New York City teachers walked out of their classrooms for two weeks. Eventually, the striking teachers negotiated a new contract that included a substantial increase in salary and benefits. The burgeoning community-control school movement directly threatened these gains, creating new and volatile tensions between teachers and Black civil rights activists, disrupting a fragile political alliance between majority white teacher unions and Black civil rights activists that had existed for many decades in cities including New York, Newark, Chicago, Philadelphia, and Detroit.[38]

New York City witnessed a particularly acrimonious clash between teachers and Black educational activists in 1968. A year earlier, the New York City Board of Education had granted experimental community control of the public schools to three majority Black and Latino neighborhoods including the Ocean Hill–Brownsville section of Brooklyn, where 95 percent of the students were non-white, and academic achievement was far below average. With funding from the Ford Foundation, activists established a local school board of parents led by former Black principal Rhody McCoy, a graduate of Howard University with a master's degree in education from New York University. "The community has asked for control of schools here and the Board of Education's new project offers this," McCoy said. "We bring in programs that can be supported and interpreted by the parents with total community involvement. In this program parents determine what is needed in their schools." McCoy believed the key to community control was for parents to have a say in how money was spent in their schools and the ability to hire teachers and principals they admired and fire those they did not.[39]

On May 9, 1968, McCoy flexed his new authority by firing thirteen teachers and six administrators in Ocean Hill-Brownsville because he believed they were not fully supportive of community control. This abrupt termination, given without warning or due process, violated the terms of the teachers' employment contract as negotiated by the United Federation of Teachers (UFT). New York City school officials and UFT officials condemned McCoy's actions as illegal and unjust and ordered the teachers to return to work. But McCoy held his ground, insisting that community control of the schools meant jurisdiction over hiring and firing of personnel.[40]

Tensions escalated on May 14 when five of the fired teachers ignored their termination notices and showed up to work at Junior High School (J.H.S) 271. About forty protestors blocked the teachers from entering the building. "You've been ordered to report to Mr. McCoy's office. You can't come in," called out one protestor, Edith Rook, as she physically blocked the entrance to the school. At that point about 100 teachers at J.H.S. 271, all UFT members, walked across the street to protest what they viewed as the illegal removal of their colleagues. "All you good teachers come on in," the protestors called loudly as they ushered in the handful of teachers who were not participating in the boycott. Nearly 200 police officers hovered nearby, and at 8:25 A.M. they attempted to escort the five teachers who had been illegally terminated into the school to work, but protestors blocked their way and the teachers decided not to enter.[41]

Both sides—teachers and community-control activists—viewed their position as not only legal but morally righteous and fundamentally just. United Federation of Teachers (UFT) President Albert Shanker compared the teachers' experience in Brooklyn to school desegregation in Little Rock, Arkansas, in 1957, when National Guardsmen had blocked the entry of Black schoolchildren into a formerly "white" high school. McCoy decried the false promises that were made to the Ocean Hill-Brownsville community school board and called for Black and Puerto Rican parents to rally behind his decision to dismiss the unwanted teachers. He pressed, "This board has fought and taken on the whole power structure. But we haven't been given any power at all. We have been used as a buffer between the power structure and you, our brothers and sisters." The national media followed these developments with frank fascination, typically siding with the white educational establishment over Black community-control activists. While school officials and teacher unionists bandied about questions of due process, the press contemplated the racial tensions simmering just beneath the surface. To many people, it seemed that the main reason the teachers were fired was not because they did not properly appreciate a new form of school governance but instead because they were white or, in the case of one Black and one Puerto Rican educator, overtly sympathetic to whites. "Color should not be a test for teaching," editorialized the *Washington Post*. Acknowledging there were concerns on both sides, the editors concluded, "What has happened here is hardly a happy augury, however, for the future of local autonomy or decentralization in school administration."[42]

The conflict over McCoy's decision to fire teachers without due process had neither a satisfactory nor a quick resolution. McCoy refused to invite the fired educators back to work, so UFT teachers in Ocean Hill-Brownsville boycotted the remainder of the school year. When the issue remained unresolved at the start of the 1968 school year, Shanker called for a series of strikes that shut down public schools throughout New York City. Nearly 54,000 teachers struck for two days in September to demonstrate their sympathy for the fired teachers, but still McCoy would not be moved. The next strike lasted two weeks, and conditions were so tense that when the teachers returned to work, furious citizens pelted them with stones and eggs. Black New Yorkers could not fathom why so many white teachers seemed determined to undermine the community-control school experiment. "The teachers, who already have their educations, are more concerned with protecting tenure and jobs than they are in seeing that the kids in New York City can read and write," charged the *New York Amsterdam News*.[43]

Shanker called for the removal of McCoy and the dismantling of the community-controlled schools experiment. This time he organized a strike that lasted five weeks and was resolved only when state leaders negotiated an armistice in mid-November, coaxing the teachers back to work with the promise that thereafter, they would have a fair hearing before being fired or transferred. Black civil rights activists felt betrayed by this compromise and furious at the teachers' union and the New York City Board of Education. These sentiments erupted in heated confrontations throughout the city. In one, reporter Joseph Featherstone attended a panel discussion on community-controlled schools at the Ethical Culture Society where critics marched in and presented a bloody pig's head to a representative of the UFT. When the UFT representative declared this an act of violence, the audience erupted and chaos ensued. "People weren't arguing, they were screaming and spitting at each other," reported Featherstone.[44]

Following the strike, New York legislators negotiated a school decentralization bill that offered enough autonomy to satisfy Black civil rights activists and sufficient protections to placate the teachers' union. At the last minute, the bill gained the support of white conservatives who realized that decentralized schools placated demands for school integration. The bill quickly passed both houses of legislature and was signed into law less than an hour later by Governor Nelson A. Rockefeller on April 30, 1969.

This law did not represent a victory for Black educational activists who wanted community control of the schools. The *New York Times* editorial board concluded, "The basic weakness of the bill is not that it fails to provide community control; it is rather that the decentralized districts will be subjected to the supervision and judgement of a thoroughly political central authority, with the union power structure the dominating force." In the end, very little educational power or resources were redistributed to Black and Latino families in New York. Lawmakers successfully undercut the community-control school movement by offering token concessions that substituted decentralization for community control, elections for protest, and modest distribution of resources for mean-ingful redistribution.[45]

New York City's community-control school movement had seismic repercussions for how politicians, school administrators, and the public viewed the promise and pitfalls of this reform strategy in the North. Historians contend that it destabilized a long-standing liberal coalition of Blacks, Jews, and Catholics that believed in nondiscrimination, civil rights, and religious pluralism. Black New Yorkers came to view striking teachers with suspicion and then loathing. Whites, for their part, grew distrustful of Black activists demanding control of key institutions such as public education.[46]

Placing this episode into historical context shows that white northerners did not suddenly turn against Black educational activism in the late 1960s—large numbers of northern whites and their elected representatives in politics and on school boards had been committed to preserving white privilege in the public schools for decades. The same whites that stymied, opposed, deflected, and dodged Black demands for school integration after 1954 openly and force-fully objected to Black demands for community control after 1965. Black northerners, meanwhile, were left with the arduous task of discerning how best to improve the quality of education and the level of academic achievement in the urban North, especially as continued white flight and escalating white resistance to school integration complicated this effort.[47]

School Integration and Community Control after 1970

"What happened to community control of our schools?" asked New York Black educational activist and scholar Preston Wilcox. "Our casual response (though based in reality) would be that nothing happened—community control exists but only in white communities—FOR WHITES ONLY!" New Yorkers' disap-pointment with the nation's most ambitious experiment in Black community control of public schools served as a cautionary tale for educational activists in other northern cities, yet many remained intrigued by the possibilities of decen-tralization and local control, strategies that dovetailed nicely with Black nation-alist ideology. Further, Black opposition to northern school integration plans that privileged white students and placed inordinate burdens on Black families continued to escalate. According to the *Congressional Quarterly Researcher* in 1972, "Resistance to busing for integration is by no means limited to the white community. Many Black parents are opposed to seeing their children taken into strange, often unfriendly neighborhoods, and many Black leaders are concerned that court decisions requiring a racial balance will weaken the control of Black people over their schools."[48]

"We favor community control of all institutions in the Black community such as welfare centers, libraries, schools, hospitals, and police," explained political candidate Andrew Pulley. As New York City's experiment revealed, the struggle for self-determination in education generated intense competition with other vested interests such as teachers' unions. When seizing control of public schools proved too arduous or unappealing, some Black nationalists established their own schools. Historian Russell Rickford has traced the proliferation of independent Black schools that appeared in a few short years, so that by 1970 there were more than sixty Pan African Nationalist institutions nationwide, from preschools to postsecondary schools. Establishing an independent school allowed Black nationalists to have total control, but this tactic failed to reach the vast majority of African Americans, who relied on public schools. Community control of public schools remained a tempting possibility for this reason. In 1971, Carmichael reiterated that integration was inherently flawed and that most Black people remained mired in segregated and inferior housing, schools, and jobs. He concluded, "Such situations will not change until Black people have power—to control their own school boards, in this case."[49]

In sharp contrast, integrationists pointed to recent successful litigation and insisted the time was ripe to finally secure integrated and equal public schools nationwide. "Treading the paths of our fathers we as Black people have come to a place and point in time of history that we shall be free," sermonized Ewell W. Finley, a Black school board trustee in Malverne, New York. He continued, "This is our guarantee under the laws of this nation. Desegregating schools on Long Island is not a mistake, but indeed, is an investment in our democracy." As civil rights attorneys Michael B. Trister and P. Kent Spriggs explained, "The benefit perceived by the Black community is not that they can be schooled with the white children but that the presence of white children in the schools which they attend will insure that a racist schoolboard will take greater pains to provide a quality education which will of necessity accrue to the benefit of the Black children. It is a *realpolitik* position born of years of exposure to how the 'man's game' works." The NAACP continued to press for stronger and more comprehensive school integration plans. In January of 1970, the US attorney general's office promised the Department of Justice would put pressure on any northern school district whose teaching staff or student body were so "racially imbalanced" that there were identifiably "white schools" or "Negro schools," including communities with token school desegregation plans in place. Integrationists were delighted by this announcement, especially given President Nixon's promise to scale back busing for school integration nationwide.[50]

Many Black families, in contrast, were exasperated that increasing Black enrollment in public schools outpaced northern school desegregation efforts, while the academic achievement of Black students remained low. A terrible imbalance of power meant that in most cases, Black families experienced school desegregation very differently from whites. In 1970, the US Commission on Civil Rights acknowledged, "Racial integration in America has usually taken place on terms dictated by whites. Thus, since integration is nearly always a one-way street that Blacks travel to a white institution, then an implied inferiority of the Black man is inherent in the situation."[51]

Severe financial crises in American cities meant that urban public school buildings, many of which dated to the late nineteenth and early twentieth centuries, were literally falling apart. In nearly all-Black urban schools like the O. V. Catto School in Philadelphia, teachers admitted that high school students could barely read at a fourth-grade level and that the school was plagued by truancy, drugs, and violence. In Chicago, another study showed that 90 percent of Black students in the Woodlawn community either dropped out of school or received so little education they were classified as "in-school functional dropouts." In suburban areas with school desegregation plans under way, Black students were sometimes dissatisfied with the results. In suburban Plainfield, New Jersey, white students painted racial epithets on the school walls when a desegregation plan created more racial diversity. In response, Black students demanded the trappings of community control such as Black teachers and administrators, Black history courses, and less discriminatory disciplinary procedures.[52]

Northern school segregation continued to increase due to Black migration to northern cities, white and middle-class flight to the suburbs, and unrelenting white resistance to any plan to create more racially diverse classrooms or schools. In Chicago, a census by the Board of Education showed that school segregation had once again increased between 1970 and 1971, and that 94 percent of Black elementary students attended schools where more than 90 percent of the student body was Black. Robert Alpern, an attorney who oversaw an ambitious $2.8 million-dollar school integration pilot project in Detroit, reported that significant improvements in curriculum, teachers, materials, and textbooks in three neighborhoods was not enough to entice white families to attend school alongside Black students. "We should have recognized the extent of white resistance to integration," he lamented. According to Alpern, Blacks who had advocated for school integration in Detroit became first neutral, then openly hostile to the reform as whites abandoned integrated schools in droves. "In the face of such continued white antipathy, a Negro fighting for

integration looks 'silly,' " he conceded. Jeannette Bonen, a mother of eight and
a leader in Boston's "Operation Exodus" that sent Black children to white suburban schools, explained that school integration was only appealing to Black
families if it meant better schools. She added, "Most Black parents prefer [their
own] neighborhood schools if they are clean, airy, bright, and well-staffed, and
if their curriculum reflects the needs of the community." A Harvard sociologist
concurred that social science data supported this interpretation: "It appears that
integration increases racial identity and solidarity over the short run and, at least
in the case of Black students, leads to increasing desires for separation." The continued shortcomings of school integration, especially in large cities, compelled
many Black families to reconsider their support for integration as a tactic to improve public education.[53]

   Reports of violence further dampened Black support for school integration.
In one instance, when a Black high school girl refused to stand for the national
anthem in New Haven, Connecticut, a white male classmate punched her. This
prompted retaliation by Black students, and the fighting spread to another school.
In an unflattering article, the *New York Times* reported, "Bands of Negro students
roamed through a high school here today, overturning tables, breaking several
windows, and forcing the cancellation of classes at noon." Interviewed for the
story, a Black student explained he was also protesting "the attitude against us
that the white teachers have." A white English teacher confirmed his sentiments.
"You see it all the time, even though it's subtle. That fact is that subconsciously
or not, we just don't treat the Negroes the same as the whites and they know
it." White students, meanwhile, became alarmed and defensive by the militant
rhetoric of young Black nationalists. "It is kind of scary to have all this Black
power around and have no idea exactly what they are advocating," one white
student told the US Commission on Civil Rights. Another reported, "Power is
a very strong word and if you said, 'Black power' right away, if you don't know
what it means, you think that it's a force that is going to overpower you." Armed
police response to even minor altercations and Black student protests became
the norm. The mayor of New Haven, for instance, ordered "saturation patrols"
of uniformed officers inside the high schools following fights between white and
Black students. He insisted that the officers would be there until "anarchy and
lawlessness" had been driven out and promised the "troublemakers" would be
expelled. By the spring of 1970, Blacks in New Haven had formed armed security patrols designed to protect Black and Puerto Rican residents from white
vigilante justice and police harassment. Racial tensions were approaching a
breaking point, youth were at the epicenter of the disturbance, and school integration seemed to be one major source of the problem.[54]

   Charles V. Hamilton maintained that it was hardly surprising that Black
families nationwide embraced community control given white antipathy to

school integration and the failures of "ghetto schools." It was impossible to deny mounting interest in Black power and community control in the North, even for integrationists, as support for school integration wavered. Robert C. Weaver, secretary of Housing and Urban Development and the nation's first Black cabinet member, conceded, "Advocacy of Black separatism is inevitable. It has been and is a reaction to the frustrations of racism and the despair that follows. But it must be recognized also as a withdrawal or retreat; and paradoxically it achieves its greatest support at a time when the goal of integrationists—equal opportunity for competition—seems to be on the horizon."[55]

Beginning in 1969, psychologist Kenneth B. Clark hosted an annual retreat for Black intellectuals as part of a broader effort to shore up Black support for integration. He passionately defended the value of integrated schools, explaining, "This epidemic of separatist demands on the part of organized groups of Black students can be interpreted as symptomatic of the psychological stresses caused by the new challenges and threats of a nonsegregated society." He continued, "That many of these young people sought to explain their separatist ideology and demands under the guise of 'racial militance' merely betrayed their poignant and pathetic racial fears." According to Clark and the scholars working with him, including Ralph Ellison, Adelaide Cromwell Gulliver, William H. Hastie, Hylan Lewis, J. Saunders Redding, Bernard C. Watson, and Robert C. Weaver, the drive for separate schools was inherently dangerous, strategically flawed, and orchestrated by a tiny fraction of outspoken militants against the wishes of the Black majority.[56]

While Black intellectuals fretted over declining support for school integration, growing numbers of Black teachers and politicians embraced Black self-determination in public education. New Haven teacher Barbara Louis explained that the Connecticut Association of Afro-American Educators was dedicated to "developing the Black community economically, socially, and culturally." A gathering of more than fifty Black elected officials in Hartford stressed community control of the schools and participants bemoaned the dearth of Black history taught in majority white schools. "All we get is George Washington Carver and Martin Luther King when there are so many other fine Black people to admire and respect," insisted one teacher. In the Ferndale school district just outside of Detroit, Black educators were dismayed when the Department of Health, Education and Welfare charged the district with running a segregated system because of the existence of all-Black Grant Elementary school, established as a separate school with an all-Black faculty in 1926 and still going strong in 1970. A Grant teacher explained that their goal was to help Black children "think better of themselves" and noted that it would be far more difficult to inculcate Black pride if their students were dispersed throughout the district's majority white elementary schools.[57]

Holding fast to the promise of school integration, the NAACP continued to press northern school districts for more effective integration plans. In August of 1970, the Detroit Branch of the NAACP alleged that city leaders intentionally maintained a system of racially separate and unequal schools. The NAACP rejected the district's tepid student transfer plan and sought a new plan that would eliminate "the racial identity of every school in the [Detroit] system and . . . maintain now and hereafter a unitary, nonracial school system." The legal challenge worked its way through the courts for the next four years, just as similar lawsuits played out in the courts of Boston and other cities. In Detroit, when it was discovered that the only way to integrate the city's schools was to partner with nearby suburban districts, the NAACP did not hesitate to support this plan.

The court-ordered school desegregation plan for the 1972–73 school year encompassed Detroit and fifty-three surrounding school districts, amounting to the nation's most ambitious integration initiative to date. A local judge ordered Detroit school administrators to purchase at least 295 school buses in preparation. Suburban school officials immediately filed an appeal. Meanwhile, as NAACP leaders fought for school integration in Detroit, Black educational activists in Newark, New Jersey, pursued a revitalized vision of community-controlled schools in a city where the concept of "Black Power" had potent new meaning. [58]

Majority Control in Newark

From the ashes of urban rebellions rose a mass movement for Black liberation, and as scholars have shown, the Black Power movement after 1970 was rich, multifaceted, and energizing. According to historian Komozi Woodard, "The Black Arts movement, the ghetto uprisings, and an explosive African American sense of identity produced a new generation of Black Power organizations and leadership." One of the most crucial objectives of Black Power activists after 1970 was political power and the election of Black officials. [59]

These forces came to a head in Newark, New Jersey, in 1970. An industrial city located just across the Hudson River from New York City showcases what happened to the community-control school movement as it moved into cities with a Black majority. Perhaps the city, with its engaged Black citizenry, vibrant Black arts scene, and outspoken Black nationalists, could offer a new way forward for community control of public education. [60]

Hopes were raised in the spring of 1970 when Kenneth A. Gibson was elected as the first Black mayor of Newark, a first in a major northeastern city. "It's 'Nation Time' in Newark," cheered *JET* magazine, commending Gibson on overcoming "one of the most overt and blatantly racist political campaigns ever waged in big-city politics." NAACP's *Crisis* noted that his election "strengthens the position of those Americans, Black as well as white, who believe that substantial advances are possible through the political processes available within the American constitutional system."[61]

Gibson's historic election reflected rising Black political power in the urban North and hinted at political transformations to come. "Wherever the central cities are going, Newark is going to get there first," the new mayor was fond of saying as he struggled at the helm of a city recovering from a violent urban rebellion in 1967 and the myriad problems of a post-industrial city including corruption, financial crises, strained race relations, and massive white and middle-class flight to the suburbs. The mainstream press followed the rise of Black political power in Newark with fascination that bordered on dismay. "Newark has become an angry and anguished city as its Black community gradually takes over the city's politics, schools and cultural life from an ever-decreasing white minority," claimed the *New York Times*. "With a Black population that grew by nearly 25 percent during the last decade and is now 60 percent of the city's 380,000 people, Newark faces the possibility of becoming the first virtually all Black major city in the country."[62]

Newark was hardly "all Black," but the Black majority there nevertheless hoped that Black Power, in the form of elected Black officials, would finally bring meaningful reform to the city's troubled public schools. On the eve of the urban rebellion in 1967, administrators determined that 74 percent of public school students were either Black or Puerto Rican. A majority of Newark's teachers were white and commuted in from nearby suburbs. Schools with majority Black populations tended to be overcrowded and under-resourced, with very low levels of student achievement. The Education Committee of the Newark Branch of the NAACP documented high levels of racial segregation and discrimination in the schools, noting, "Teachers, primarily at the high school level, have complained to members of the Education Committee that students are being graduated from the elementary schools who are nearly illiterate. Leaders in the field of personnel and employment indicate a reluctance on the part of some employers to hire graduates of certain Newark schools because those graduates are not capable of performing properly. All the complaints have centered, primarily, about the schools with high-Negro enrollments." Eager to keep Black families politically engaged, Black Power activists and Mayor Gibson made a calculated decision to target educational reform.[63]

The most urgent problem was the new contract between the city and the Newark Teachers Union (NTU) crafted by the pervious mayoral administration following a teachers' strike in 1970. The contract promised salary increases, the right to binding arbitration, and a release from "nonprofessional chores" such as supervising children on the playground. Black parents were hurt and confused

Figure 4.1. Newark Mayor Ken Gibson posing with football players from Barringer High School, 1975. Photo by Roberta Pfeifer. Mayor Kenneth A. Gibson Collection & Photos from Mayor Gibson's Publicity Office. Charles F. Cummings New Jersey Information Center. Newark Public Library, Newark, NJ.

that the mostly white teachers' union had used an illegal strike—refusing to teach their children—to win concessions from the city that seemed to pay teachers more, give them more power, and yet require less work. As Newark scholar and activist Junius Williams recalled, "The Black community saw the strike as an attempt to do less and make more money, adding insult to injury to the perceived poor job teachers and principals were already doing for Black kids." These reforms did not represent the kinds of changes Black parents wanted to see in the school system, such as more Black teachers and administrators, a revised curriculum, and improved facilities.[64]

What Blacks and Puerto Ricans wanted was "to have some genuine say about what goes on in their schools, whether at the Board of Education level or the community level." Black residents were especially frustrated because they felt that white teachers, school administrators, and school board members were more interested in preserving good jobs for whites than in improving the quality of education for Black students.[65]

Forcefully articulating this vision was Black cultural nationalist and Newark folk hero Amiri Baraka. Born as LeRoi Jones in Newark, Baraka attended local public schools before going to college, enlisting in the Air Force, and finally embarking on a successful career as a poet and playwright. Following the assassination of Malcolm X in 1965, Jones stepped up his criticism of the pacifist and integrationist mainstream civil rights movement. He changed his name to Amiri Baraka and moved home to Newark, where he founded an artists' residence called Spirit House and a community organization called United Brothers of Newark. Baraka's blend of militant Black cultural nationalism and artistic passion drew followers. He published a newspaper called *Black Newark* designed to raise consciousness and mobilize Black voters. An article in the first issue was typical of Baraka's bombastic rhetoric. Describing how Newark responded to Martin Luther King Jr.'s assassination, Baraka wrote, "During the recent disturbances by the crackers, the United Brothers Security Unit was one of the main forces keeping our Black Youth from getting slaughtered on the streets by trigger-happy racist policemen." After helping to secure Gibson's election, Baraka turned his attention to overhauling the city's public schools according to the principles of Black self-determination. He recognized that this kind of visionary reform would require majority Black control over school governance and curriculum, which in turn would require seizing power from the board of education and the teachers' union.[66]

Baraka's growing popularity in Newark was matched by the political ascendancy of white nationalist Anthony "Tony" Imperiale from Newark's predominantly Italian North Ward. Following the rebellion in 1967, Imperiale formed the North Ward Citizens Committee, an organization that deployed vigilante gangs to secure "law and order." The ACLU of New Jersey condemned the organization as "a secret, uniformed, paramilitary organization composed solely of white persons dedicated to opposing by force and violence attempts on the part of the Negro American to achieve equality." Imperiale successfully channeled white resentment against Black gains in Newark. He traveled through the city with a retinue of bodyguards making inflammatory, anti-Black speeches wherever he went. "I didn't see any flags in the city of Newark lowered to half-mast when Gov. Lurleen Wallace died," he shouted at one rally in the fall of 1968. "Why not, when they could do it for that Martin Luther Coon?" Known affectionately as "The Big T" among Newark's Italian Americans, he recruited heavily among white youth and had thousands of enthusiastic followers. The North Ward Citizens Committee rejected Black civil rights, despised Black cultural nationalism, and set out to destroy the city's Black mayor and the man who got him elected, Amiri Baraka.[67]

Following Imperiale's rise to prominence, Baraka doubled down on his commitment to armed self-defense and blunt Black power rhetoric. Both Baraka and

Imperiale traveled through Newark with retinues of bodyguards, posturing and trying to drum up support among the masses. When Baraka turned his attention to the question of educational reform through community control of the schools, Imperiale was eager for a fight.[68]

Black educational activists in Newark were well aware of the long and bitter struggle for community control of schools in New York City. Although they were inspired by the Black nationalist rhetoric and confrontational tactics of educational activists there, they believed the political context in Newark required a subtler approach. Clarence Coggins, a Black community organizer, explained that activists in Newark "followed a pattern that had been set in another area, that did not have the same kind of political structure that we had." Newark had a majority Black population, a Black mayor, and thanks to the new mayor, representation on the board of education. What Newark needed was not decentralized, community control—instead, it needed to crush the last vestiges of white influence and power over the public schools and assert the right to majority rule.[69]

To do so, Black educational activists needed to wrest authority away from the white-dominated school board and the NTU. Gibson quickly appointed three new representatives to the board of education, shifting the balance of power to a nonwhite majority for the first time. Meanwhile, Baraka and other Black educational activists launched a campaign to vilify Newark public school teachers as white, middle-class, and more interested in their paychecks than the well-being of Black students. This was not entirely fair, especially since one-third of Newark's teachers were Black and the NTU president was a Black teacher named Carole Graves. Even so, it was an effective strategy that mobilized Black voters and moved the question of educational reform to the forefront of the city's political agenda in the fall of 1970.[70]

Jesse Jacob, one of Gibson's new Black appointees to the school board, was known for his hostility to Newark's unionized teachers. As the president of the Newark Board of Education, Jacob announced, "The board of education is going to run this school system now and they [the teachers] might as well get used to the idea. This board represents the community and the board is going to run the schools." Jacob elaborated that Black and Puerto Rican parents in Newark were fed up with the status quo in education. "The schools in this city are horrendous," he complained. "They're not teaching these youngsters anything. Most of the teachers don't know how to teach them, and they don't wish to teach them." He insisted that white teachers were unfit to educate children of color. "The teachers would like you to believe that it's all the fault of the family and community. That's not true. The teachers have to share their load of the responsibility and it's heavy."[71]

Black civil rights activist David Barrett confirmed Newark teachers were "beastly suburbanites . . . trying to avoid human interaction with our children."

Barrett described teaching for one year at Clinton Plaza Junior High School, where he said white teachers had virtually no respect for Black people. "I remember once we were in the teachers' room, and one teacher said: 'So-and-so's mother came in today. Why, you know, I didn't know she wasn't *married.*'" Barrett explained, "In the Negro community, we accept these things; we know they exist—but we don't stigmatize the child because of it." Felix G. Arnstein, a substitute teacher, agreed that white teachers in Newark exhibited appalling racism. He recounted the story of a school counselor describing young Black teenagers as "nothing but trash, getting pregnant all the time." Another teacher repeatedly stated that Black students were racially inferior, "saying that every one of them was good for nothing and inherently lazy—simply hopeless."[72]

Stories of racist teachers were amplified by the media and depicted on handmade flyers that circulated in Black neighborhoods, stoking anger and indignation. *JET* magazine reported that Newark's teachers lived in the suburbs and had little or no regard for the quality of education that Black youngsters received. It quoted a Black mother who elaborated, "No one is going to strike in those clean, well-equipped schools that their children attend, so they don't care." When forced to account for the fact that the NTU president Carole Graves was a Black woman, educational activists determined she had been "slightly misguided" by the American Federation of Teachers (AFT), which they pointed out was the same organization that "fought against and ruined the construction of a community-controlled educational structure in the Ocean Hill-Brownsville section of Brooklyn and was responsible for the firing of Rhody McCoy."[73]

Newark Teachers' Strike of 1971

When it was time for the board of education to sign a new contract with the NTU in January of 1971, Black community resentment was running high. Accordingly, the board of education refused to include the modest gains teachers had won in the last contract—including binding arbitration and release from nonprofessional chores—effectively stripping away the gains the teachers had won after going out on strike the year before. Predictably, the teachers were furious and called a new strike, their second in two years. On February 1, 1971, more than 1,880 teachers out of 4,400 walked out. Many believed they were acting in the defense of workers' rights and teachers' ability to effect meaningful change in the public schools. Imperiale championed the teachers' union, encouraging white families to support the strike. Black families were livid that the city's mostly white teachers were refusing to teach Black and Puerto Rican children in order to win more privileges for themselves, and they were outraged by Imperiale's support for striking teachers. Within hours, someone torched Carole

Graves's car and threw rocks through the front windows of her house. Graves complained that Gibson was employing strike-breaking strategies "unknown in Newark since the 1930s" and promised she would "kick, scream and do everything I can to resist them."[74]

Battle lines were drawn, and although there was a significant number of Black teachers on strike as well as a Black woman leading the teachers' union, the conflict was depicted as a race war between Black families and the majority white teachers' union. Baraka cultivated acrimony among Black families, while Imperiale rallied white families and the police force to support the NTU. The school board was split between whites who wanted to honor the previous administration's contract and Blacks and Puerto Ricans who wanted to write a new one with fewer provisions for teacher autonomy. With tensions and rhetoric mounting on both sides, a violent confrontation erupted over who would control the city's schools.[75]

Early in the morning on the second day of the strike cars screeched to a halt outside NTU headquarters where teachers were walking a picket line. About twenty young Black men throwing Black Power salutes with clenched fists jumped out of the cars and attacked the strikers, beating them to the ground.

Figure 4.2. Meeting of the Newark Teachers Union, 1971. United Federation of Teachers Photographs. Courtesy of the Tamiment Library, New York University, New York, NY.

According to a press release, "The bare facts are that a paramilitary band of young Black men, some 19, some older, some 25 years of age, surrounded and kicked, clubbed and struck 15 school teachers at about 7:30 a.m. on February 2. Sticks, brass knuckles and even a fire extinguisher were used before the slick hit ended and the attackers sped off on foot and in cars." Six white teachers, including two women, were rushed to the hospital where they were treated for broken bones and severe abrasions. Black teachers had also been walking the picket line and were physically assaulted, although not as badly as the white teachers. The brutal violence stunned the public and rallied support for the teachers. "You'll have the entire support of organized labor," promised AFL-CIO official Charles H. Marciante to a roaring crowd of 1,500 striking teachers. "The idea of goon squads roaming the city and attacking teachers is something that belongs in another century."[76]

Violence continued unabated throughout the eleven-week strike, one of the longest and most rancorous teacher strikes in American history. Some of the worst confrontations occurred between striking teachers and those crossing the picket lines. In the white neighborhoods where families supported the striking teachers, most schools were closed, but in the Black neighborhoods many Black teachers crossed the picket lines so that children would not go without schooling. Noting there was "no settlement in sight" on March 8, the *Christian Science Monitor* reported that community meetings designed to mediate the strike had ended in verbal, and sometimes physical, brawls. "It's been a very rough strike," conceded one striking teacher. "When we picket, we have to have our own guards around." Baraka and his supporters patrolled majority Black schools where they harassed picketing teachers, while Imperiale and his crew patrolled majority white schools and heckled teachers who crossed the picket line. Newark's overwhelmingly white business leaders pressured Gibson to resolve the strike by giving teachers what they wanted. Black school board president Jesse Jacobs publicly vowed never to give in and encouraged white teachers to quit so the board could replace them with caring teachers from the Black community. "If this is to be the year of attrition, then let it be. In the words of the old Negro spiritual, 'Free at last, praise God almighty, free at last.'"[77]

Attempting to mediate the escalating public relations disaster, Mayor Gibson called a community meeting in a suburban church to discuss a possible resolution to the strike. Two female reporters for the *Inner-City Voice*, published by the League of Revolutionary Black Voters, reported on the meeting, which was well attended by striking teachers. According to the reporters, "When Gibson walked into the church, the 75, mostly white teachers, charged inside, shouting insults at Gibson: 'You're nothing but a fat LeRoi Jones.'" The two women concluded, "It was infuriating for us to see Gibson humiliated by the white strikers before the audience. In this group of white suburbanites were probably people who have abandoned some of Newark's businesses and real estate, taking a lot of tax money with them."[78]

Black citizens felt betrayed not only by white flight that eviscerated Newark's tax base but also by white teachers and their allies who refused to respect a Black mayor or the wishes of Black school board members and Black parents. Building on the work of Black Power activists like Carmichael and Hamilton, activists in Newark believed that control of local public facilities would enable them to reverse institutional racism and develop an effective base of political power to challenge racism in the city as a whole. It was supposed to be a crucial next step in realizing the dream of Black Power in a city with a Black majority and a Black mayor. But white people—the teachers' union, organized labor, the media, the business community, Imperiale and his followers—seemed determined to oppose this strategy at every step. Black majority control of Newark's public schools was being thwarted by a white minority. NTU President Graves, in contrast, rejected the idea that race had anything to do with it and rebuked Black leaders for implying otherwise. As she saw it, "This is just a labor-management fight, Jesse Jacobs and LeRoi Jones interject this racial business because it's a good way to break the union and get control of the schools."[79]

The Newark teachers' strike dragged on for nearly three months. Gibson attempted to broker a settlement three times, but was undermined the first two times by the board of education, which refused to negotiate on the question of salaries, binding arbitration, or releasing teachers from nonprofessional chores. Finally, Gibson brought local Black community organizer and trade unionist Clarence Coggins in to help. Coggins was concerned about the potential for violence between Blacks and Italian Americans in Newark. Gibson appeared on television and implored residents to find a reasonable solution to the crisis. He published an essay called "A Call to Reason" that presented a compromise both sides could support. Black leaders including Graves and Baraka agreed the time to find a resolution had arrived, and Coggins helped build support from within the Black community for peace. Imperiale, in contrast, continued to stoke the flames of racial animosity. Jesse Jacobs held fast to his ideals but was finally overruled by a majority on the board of education. The new contract maintained a modified form of binding arbitration and removed the language excusing teachers from nonprofessional chores.

The Remnants of Community Control

The 1971 teachers' strike in Newark demonstrates that even with a Black majority and Black elected officials, it was very difficult for Black Power activists to have the kind of control they wanted over public education. Many of the objectives of the community control movement revived aspects of education that were found historically in separate, Black-controlled schools including an emphasis on Black faculty and tailoring pedagogy and curriculum to the needs of Black youth. These objectives did not appeal to other constituencies, and in fact, they did not appeal to all Black citizens.

Frustrated by the outcome in Newark, Jacobs insisted that striking teachers would be interviewed and assessed by community panels before they were permitted to return to work. In the screening process that followed, Jacobs removed dozens of white teachers from majority Black schools because they had supported the strike. Some Black parents approved—at South Tenth Street school, Black parents met returning striking teachers with baseball bats and would not let them through the front door. When a young Black teacher tried to intervene on behalf of her white colleagues, the parents forced her out as well. Many of these fired teachers were transferred to other schools, while others took this as an opportune time to retire. Hostilities between striking teachers—mostly white—and those who worked through the strike—mostly Black—continued for many years.[80]

Whites in Newark retained significant political power through the teachers' union, school administration, the board of education, and city council, not to mention the influence of business interests. Black residents, meanwhile, were not unified behind a single, clear political objective or strategy. A large number of teachers were Black, which undercut the claim that teachers were the enemy of Black families. Even Black civil rights activists were torn over who or what to support. Baraka was not universally loved; some Black parents found his dreams of Black Power unrealistic. One Black official chided, "Those things Imamu [Amiri Baraka] says about throwing out the whites are appealing, but impractical. We can't just shut Newark off from the rest of the country." Even some Black nationalists, including a local chapter of the Black Panthers, opposed Baraka.[81]

Following the defeat of community control in Newark, the board of education agreed to make a few modest concessions to Black educational activists. The most notable was the new Marcus Garvey School, housed in a school formerly known as Robert Treat. Baraka founded the school, which promised to educate Black youth and develop a strong Black community. Staffed by Black teachers and administrators, the Marcus Garvey School taught Black history, Swahili language, and Simba Wachanga—a youth-focused, pan-African nationalism designed to inculcate racial pride. In addition, two other Newark public schools were renamed for Black heroes: the Harriet Tubman School and the Martin Luther King Jr. School. In the fall of 1971, Lawrence Hamm, a seventeen-year-old Black member of the board of education who was recently appointed by Gibson, introduced a resolution requiring all public schools in Newark with a student body that was at least 50 percent Black to fly the Black liberation flag.

Eugene Campbell, the Black principal of the Marcus Garvey School, stated that displaying the flag was "an act of inspiration for students, a symbol of what Black people are." Interviewed by the *New York Times*, Baraka reflected on these educational reforms. "What the Black people, African people, are trying to achieve here is an old American concept—community control."[82]

This modest version of community control, however, did not do enough to address the larger problems that undermined the quality of education in the Newark public schools, especially the lack of adequate funding. This fact was driven home in the fall of 1972 when the ceiling of the Marcus Garvey School collapsed. A local newspaper editorialized, "Marcus Garvey, formerly Robert Treat, is an old school, a fact borne out in clear dimension by a preliminary engineering survey made after the classroom ceiling collapsed. The report disclosed at least 19 other similar structural defects in addition to ceilings in the gymnasium, hallway areas, and several offices." The article continued, "Nor does it stop with this school, either," and pointed to critical infrastructure problems districtwide. These problems did not go unnoticed by Black families in Newark, who remained exasperated with the public schools.[83]

In January of 1972, a group that called itself the "Ad Hoc Committee of 50 Black Clergymen" demonstrated outside of the West Kinney Junior High School in Newark and released an open letter to the public demanding new and better kinds of educational reform. Carrying signs that said, "We Need New Schools, Not Liberation Flags" and "LeRoi Does Not Speak for Us," the group insisted, "We will no longer allow the fanatic fringe of the Black community to sound as though it was speaking for the entire Black community." The clergymen pledged to attend future school board meetings to advocate for parents who were disinterested in Baraka's Black nationalism but hesitant to speak out for fear of retribution. The New Jersey State Department of Education noted that hundreds of Newark high school students appeared before the Newark Board of Education to voice "complaints regarding the conditions of their schools and education and to demand improvements in basic academic areas that are serving to impede their education and hinder their ability to go on to college." These Black educational activists, including students and clergy, were not asking for community control of the school. Nor were they asking for school integration. They were asking for reforms designed to improve the quality of education in Newark's highly segregated schools such as more funding, new school buildings, and better curricula and resources to prepare students for college.[84]

As scholar and activist Junius Williams concluded, after 1971 "the complexion of the board [of education] grew darker as Gibson continued to appoint his people, trying to find the right combination to turn the school district around. But there was a perception we were losing ground with our schools." Williams's perception was confirmed by historian Wilbur C. Rich, who analyzed whether Black mayors were able to usher in effective educational reforms in Gary, Newark, and Detroit in the early 1970s. Rich found that Black mayors were no more likely than white ones to improve the quality of education in urban schools. The problem was invariably battles for control of educational funding, hiring, curriculum, and governance between Black mayors and entrenched white power structures. Even in majority Black cities with Black elected officials, northern Black communities were unable to execute the kind of power and control over the public schools that Black Power activists believed would revolutionize education.[85]

Few citizens, of course, had the kind of power that Black educational activists in Newark and other northern cities wanted, such as the ability to hire and fire teachers and administrators or the power to dictate curriculum and pedagogy. Those kinds of decisions had been in the hands of professional school administrators for nearly a century. Whites in the North strongly resisted the suggestion that they should hand over control of the public schools—with their massive budgets, thousands of jobs, and political importance—to Black people. White parents, teachers, and school administrators in the North remained staunchly opposed to educational reforms proposed by Black citizens, whether these reforms focused on school integration or greater community control, and were largely successful in resisting any meaningful reforms designed to improve the quality of education for Black students.[86]

Detroit, Boston, and Massive White Resistance

By 1974, northern public schools had higher levels of racial segregation than southern ones. According to a study by the US Senate Select Committee on Equal Educational Opportunity, while school segregation in the South had been reduced, thanks to court-ordered school desegregation plans, school segregation in northern states such as New York, New Jersey, Michigan, and Ohio had increased so that the numbers of Black students who attended schools between 80 percent and 100 percent minority (Black and Latino) had jumped between 1 and 5 percentage points over the previous two years alone. What is more, about half of the nation's Black schoolchildren—3.4 million students—attended school in the country's 100 largest urban school districts, where 71.8 percent of them attended schools that were 80 percent to 100 percent minority, and 59 percent attended schools with student bodies that were between 95 percent and 100 percent minority. A report by the New York City Board of Education acknowledged the challenges of these demographics, writing, "While continuing to hold city school authorities responsible for creative programs to promote feasible integration in urban schools, state and national officials and law makers cannot ignore the fact that the correction of the growing isolation of our poor minority groups in urban schools is each year becoming less and less a condition which large city Boards of Education can deal with alone."[87]

"School Integration Resisted in Cities of the North," heralded the *New York Times* in the spring of 1974. Eugene Mornell, head of the US Commission on Civil Rights, acknowledged that political support for school integration in the North was by then nonexistent. He cited a contemporary example from Cincinnati, where the board of education approved a sweeping plan for school desegregation right before a newly elected slate of candidates took office. According to Mornell, "A month later, the new board members, who were elected on pledges to resist integration, decided 'not to implement' their predecessors' plans." Mornell documented similar problems in New York, Los Angeles, Chicago, Boston, and San Francisco, where school desegregation plans were thwarted by voters. Additionally, he observed that when white families could not use political power to stop school integration, they simply removed their children from the public schools. The combination of shifting demographics, white flight, political intransigence, and overwhelming white resistance sabotaged school integration in the North. The New York City Board of Education admitted that "exchange of city pupils with suburban school districts might be needed to carry out integration." It was evident that "metropolitan" school integration plans encompassing the mostly minority urban core and the mostly white suburbs would be required.[88]

This question came to a head in the northern city of Detroit, after state legislators passed a law in July 1970 that virtually enjoined the Detroit school board from implementing its modest school desegregation plan. The local branch of the NAACP contacted Nathaniel R. Jones, general counsel for the national NAACP in New York City. Working together, Jones and local Black educational activists crafted a legal strategy that proved the racial imbalance in Detroit's schools was a direct result of official actions by the state of Michigan and the Detroit Board of Education. Jones persuaded Judge Stephen Roth that discriminatory housing policies and school policies combined to create a nexus, and that policies of the real estate industry, the banking industry, and the Federal Housing Administration (FHA) worked together to create and maintain school segregation and inequality in Detroit.

Judge Roth agreed, and since state and city officials had conspired to segregate Detroit's schools, he required the state of Michigan to participate in the remedy. Specifically, Judge Roth ordered that desegregation should not be limited to the Detroit school district, but that it should and must include outlying suburban districts in a metropolitan desegregation plan. Whites in Detroit and the surrounding suburbs were furious. School officials immediately appealed and the Supreme Court agreed to hear the case.[89]

The Supreme Court had to decide whether a two-way school desegregation plan that encompassed an urban core and outlying suburban districts was legal, given evidence that city and state officials had deliberately promoted racial segregation. On July 25, 1974, the US Supreme Court ruled in *Milliken v. Bradley* that Detroit's metropolitan school desegregation plan was illegal, as it could not be determined that suburban districts were directly responsible for the racial isolation of Black children in Detroit. President Nixon's conservative, anti-busing appointees including Supreme Court Justice Warren E. Burger tipped the scales of justice in the favor of white suburbanites in the 5 to 4 ruling. The NAACP issued a strongly worded press release, "This is a most unfortunate decision, not only for the thousands of Black school children trapped in inner city schools, but also for the nation as a whole."[90]

In a scathing dissent, Justice Thurgood Marshall, appointed to the Supreme Court by President Johnson in 1967, criticized the Court for failing to live up to its democratic ideals. "The Court today takes a giant step backwards," he declared, "In the short run, it may seem to be the easier course to allow our great metropolitan areas to be divided up each into two cities—one white, the other Black—but it is a course, I predict, our people will ultimately regret." Mayor Coleman Young, the first Black mayor of Detroit, was more sanguine. "I don't think there's any magic in putting little white kids alongside little Black kids on a school bench," he told a reporter. The bigger problem, Young insisted, was a lack of adequate funding, resources, and political support for majority Black urban public schools.[91]

Because school district boundaries overlapped with township lines in the North, *Milliken v. Bradley* curtailed school integration as a strategy to secure equal educational opportunities for Black youth, promote racial tolerance, and symbolize the equality of Black citizens. Blacks were deeply disappointed but hardly surprised by the decision. Many whites were ecstatic. Janice Labon was a proud anti-buser from the Detroit suburb of Roseville, Michigan. As soon as she heard about the ruling, she picked up the phone and called her neighbor, shouting, "We won!" The *New York Times* editorial board declared the ruling "very reasonable" and "practical," while at the same time rebuking those Black civil rights leaders who criticized it.[92]

Any lingering doubts that northern whites were any more supportive of school integration than their southern counterparts were shattered later that fall when federal Judge W. Arthur Garrity Jr. ordered the Boston School Committee to implement a citywide school integration plan. This lawsuit was the culmination of two decades of dedicated Black civil rights activism to equalize Boston's highly segregated and unequal schools. Court-ordered desegregation in Boston offered the opportunity for northerners to engineer effective integration within a single urban school district, as it did not require partnering with outlying sub-urban districts.[93]

When school opened on September 12, 1974, television crews stood ready as buses carrying Black schoolchildren pulled into previously "white" schools in neighborhoods like Boston's working-class, predominantly Irish-American South End. Television viewers were not disappointed. White students and parents hurled rocks and insults at Black students and engaged in violent confrontations with police. White parents stood alongside their children, waving bananas at Black children in a deliberately vulgar racist gesture.[94]

By this time, Blacks in Boston were used to the racist antics of their white neighbors. "We laughed at them," recalled sixteen-year-old Black high school student Sandra Payne, who was on the front lines of the desegregation struggle as a junior assigned to Charlestown High School in Boston. What bothered Sandra and her classmates was not the insults or even the rock throwing—they had learned to hit the floor when they heard a brick coming through a school bus window. What hurt was the harassment by white students and teachers that transformed attending high school, once a pleasurable part of teenage life, into a dreaded chore. Sandra confessed she and her friends still felt like outsiders at Charlestown High School at the end of the year. White teachers treated them poorly and did petty things like refusing to give Black students a hall pass to use the bathroom while permitting white students to leave the classroom anytime without one. When white classmates were not throwing punches, they were dropping chalk and pencils instead of handing them to a Black classmate or spit-ting on Black students from the top of the stairs. White police officers, stationed inside of schools to keep the peace, made clear where their loyalties lay. "If a cop breaks up a fight between a Black student and a white student, the cop will pat the white kid on the back and say, 'Now run along, and give my regards to your brother,'" said Beverly Merrit, another Black student attending Charlestown High School. Given these experiences, it is hardly surprising that Black students like Sandra and Beverly began to critically reexamine the relationship between school integration and improved educational opportunities.[95]

Conclusion

Experiences in New York, Newark, Detroit, Boston, and other northern communities forced Black educational activists to reconsider school integration as a civil rights strategy. Former NAACP attorney Derrick A. Bell Jr., the first Black tenured professor at Harvard University Law School, reflected on Black Americans' growing skepticism. He explained, "The Boston school desegrega-tion experience provides dramatic proof that while the conclusion in *Brown* that state-mandated racial segregation 'generates a feeling of inferiority [in Black children] as to their status in the community that may affect their hearts and minds in a way unlikely ever to be undone,' court-ordered desegregation in a racially hostile environment may result in harm that is as bad or worse." Surveying the effects of *Brown* after two decades Bell concluded, "Today, opposition to desegregation is, if anything, greater than it was in 1954, and the pace of compliance in the major cities has slowed badly. Opponents have grown bold. Supporters have become weary."[96]

The key to understanding school integration in 1974, Bell argued, was not to focus on what had happened since 1954 but instead to view the evolution of Black educational equality stretching back to battles over school integration in Boston in the 1840s. In this context, it was clear that *Brown's* greatest contribution was that it established equal educational opportunity as a constitutionally guaranteed right that could not be satisfied by requiring Blacks to attend segregated schools. This did not mean, Bell cautioned, that *Brown* required school integration to secure educational equality. He elaborated, "Depending on local political, social and economic conditions, either integrated or separate public schools may best serve the educational interests of Black children." The goal was to create excellent schools for Black children, and such schools would require first-class leadership, responsive administrative structures, parental involvement, and accountability. Because so many Black children attended majority Black schools and the courts had limited school desegregation plans, Bell held out hope that the courts would be willing to enforce "orders requiring effective schools" to equalize educational opportunities for Black students. He concluded, "The truly integrated school is an educational and democratic ideal, but there is no reason to shun other alternatives when the ideal is not available."[97]

Both Bell's pragmatic approach to improving the quality of education for Black children, with or without school integration, and his belief that the courts could do more to ensure a quality education for children in urban schools, would come to be defining features of the next era of Black educational activism.

5

An Armageddon of Righteousness

Integration for Justice, 1975–Present

Although not as well known as the August 28, 1963, March on Washington, the May 17, 1975, March on Boston galvanized the northern school integration movement at a crucial juncture. Fifteen thousand citizens marched through the streets of Boston on the anniversary of *Brown* in a show of support for school integration. Black and white supporters held signs aloft proclaiming, "21 Years Is Too Long to Wait," "Quality Integration: Let's Do It Together," and "Save the Children." On the sidelines, Boston's infamous anti-busers jeered, "Eh, eh, what do you say, buses got to go today," but they were drowned out by jubilant voices chanting, "One, two, Freedom Now! Three, four, Freedom Now!"

As a large and diverse crowd of school integration supporters converged on the Boston Common, the Reverend Charles H. Smith stepped to the podium and announced, "We have come to tell America we will never turn back!" The crowd thundered its approval, waving arms and placards in the air. Thomas L. Atkins, president of the Boston NAACP took the stage and admitted with a wink, "I am glad to tell you that Boston is finally on C.P.T. Let me explain, Constitutional Protection Time!" The days of white supremacy were numbered, Atkins promised, and those on the front lines of school integration in Boston and other cities were the true heroes of the civil rights movement. Atkins reiterated that local and national NAACP leaders would support Black families and school integration struggles in northern cities including Boston, New York, Chicago, Detroit, Omaha, and Dayton.[1]

As the heady days of the Black Power movement receded, civil rights leaders like Smith and Atkins insisted that recent events proved that integration, rather than separation, was the best way forward. Roy Wilkins, NAACP executive director, maintained, "Truth to tell, integration is the only philosophy that goes anywhere under the present circumstances where there is a minority of 10 to 90. . . . Blackness is not enough." Vernon E. Jordan Jr., president of the National

Figure 5.1. Protestors demanding school integration at the NAACP March on Boston, 1975. Northeastern University Archives and Special Collections, Boston, MA.

Figure 5.2. Large and diverse crowd at the NAACP March on Boston, 1975. Northeastern University Archives and Special Collections, Boston, MA.

Urban League, proclaimed, "Rather than adopt a defensive position on busing, I believe that busing—and any other effective tool—should be used to breach that wall of segregation." As inspiring as it was, this rhetoric glossed over the fact that many Black northerners continued to have serious reservations about school integration and whether it was the best strategy to improve education for Black youth.[2]

Black educational activist Ellena Ross lived in a diverse neighborhood in Boston where her six children had thrived for years in the local public school. But now, her children were being reassigned to a distant school as part of the desegregation order—even though their neighborhood school was roughly half Black and half white. "I can't understand why they want to close down one school which is racially balanced to balance another school. It doesn't make sense. It's the children who will suffer," she said. Across town, Mrs. Russell P. Hale was distraught that her eight-year-old daughter, who had epilepsy, would be bused to a school far from home. It would be more racially diverse, but Hale would rather keep her daughter in a majority Black school close to home.[3]

Ross and Hale supported the idea of integrated schools, but found Boston's school integration plan inconvenient and unlikely to improve the quality of education for their children. They were not alone. "I don't think that school integration for the sake of integration is very important," stated local Black minister, Reverend Harold G. Ross Jr. "I advocate quality education at the neighborhood level." Quincy Allen, a Black father of six, made a similar point, "I believe in neighborhood schools—they should be able to get a good education anywhere." Such statements signaled ambivalence over school integration at the exact moment some activists believed it was finally within reach. Even the staunchest supporters of school integration viewed busing as a means to achieve quality public schools, not an end in itself. As Black mother, civil rights activist, and ardent integrationist Ruth Batson confirmed, "Busing is a tool that can be used for that goal."[4]

Black families wanted racially mixed schools, but they also wanted real power to influence their interests within those schools—a consideration that was often overlooked by the mostly white school administrators, attorneys, and judges who engineered school desegregation plans. Black educational activists were exasperated that whites denied Black families equal participation in integrated schools. Fears that school desegregation plans cost Black teachers and school administrators their jobs heightened these concerns.

Sociologist John H. Stanfield of Yale University argued that because so many people believed the purpose of school integration was to improve Black academic achievement, they seemed to think that "something magical occurs when Blacks and whites are placed in the same physical plant." They were unwilling, however, to consider that integrated schools represented a more ambitious democratic project to promote civic equality and social justice for all. Stanfield found that Black students were often marginalized with few Black teachers, a Euro-centric curriculum, and discriminatory policies in terms of tracking and student discipline, even in racially mixed northern schools. He concluded, "The refusal of society ruling groups to acknowledge that Blacks need decision-making authority in the educational system (and beyond) as well as equal opportunity to achieve, indicates that they are more concerned with making Blacks good workers in capitalistic America than with giving them control over their destiny."[5]

By 1975, Black educational activists asserted their right to control their destiny and the myriad factors that affected Black academic achievement and emotional well-being in integrated schools. For example, in Boston, parents and community leaders evaluated the merits and shortcomings of Phase II of the city's school desegregation plan. They concluded, "Since 1954 Black children have been legally entitled to an education that is free from discriminatory pupil placement. We thus support all actions necessary to deny the Boston School Committee the means by which it has historically abused Black children." They advocated integration as a way to right past wrongs, but they also questioned whether assigning students to new schools would be enough. They continued, "In and of itself, desegregation will not offer Black citizens that educational equality that must ultimately characterize just and lasting relief from the segregation practices by the Boston Public Schools. In the name of equity, we, therefore, seek dramatic improvement in the quality of education available to our children." As this chapter argues, Black northerners supported school integration, but only as part of a larger, broader, multifaceted reform initiative that prioritized providing a high-quality education for Black children that would support and enhance Black civil rights in America. School integration in the form of busing to create racially diverse student populations was simply not enough.[6]

The US Supreme Court shaped the backdrop against which northern Black debates over school integration versus separation played out after 1975. The court limited school integration as a strategy and forced Black educational activists to devise creative alternatives. At the same time, many Black northerners were frustrated by the slow pace and tepid results of northern school integration to date. Legal historian Davison Douglas determined, "By the 1990s many African Americans had rejected the integrationist paradigm that dominated earlier discussions of how best to insure equal educational opportunities for all children, favoring instead a return to neighborhood schools." Journalist Robert Anthony Watts interviewed hundreds of Black parents involved in school integration battles and concluded that "shattered dreams and nagging doubts" of Black families left most preferring neighborhood schools. He elaborated, "The prevailing view was that busing had been tried in the 1960s and the 1970s and had failed amid turmoil and massive resistance by white parents and white administrators. The view was that mixed-race schools may sound good in theory, but in reality Black children meet with harsh discrimination, suffer disproportionate punishment, are banned from leadership roles in clubs and activities, and in general have to live in an atmosphere that fails to respect their culture and history."[7]

The rise and fall of the Black Power movement offered sober lessons for Black educational activists in the North. The struggle for community control of schools in New York City and Newark revealed the stark limitations of attempting to control a major public institution in large, diverse metropolitan areas. Efforts to integrate public schools using boycotts and lawsuits, likewise, had mixed results in the North, where residential segregation and white flight outpaced school redistricting and busing so that racial segregation between districts grew more pronounced every year, even as school administrators claimed to be pursuing school desegregation.[8]

Despite this intense frustration, elements of both school integration and community control continued to offer enticing prospects for remedying educational inequality. Instead of being forced to pick between the two strategies, as they had in the past, Black educational activists began to weave together promising aspects of both to generate a more critical vision of school integration. What emerged in the mid-1970s was something new—an emphasis on school integration, but a conditional one that emphasized core components of separation that recognized and affirmed the identities of Black youth and insisted on an equitable share of power for Black students and families. At the same time, support for separate, Black controlled schools remained. A revitalized Afrocentric education movement in the early 1990s asserted that only schools with a distinct pedagogy and curriculum would have the power to overcome the "mis-education" of Black children in traditional public schools.[9]

Looking back on nearly a century and a half of Black campaigns for school integration in the North, former NAACP attorney and legal scholar Derrick A. Bell Jr. noted that while Black Americans have always had a resounding faith in school integration, experience had left them dispirited. He feared that many Black educational activists had become too fanatical in their support of either school integration or separation, and they failed to recognize that the way forward would require elements of both. Bell wrote, "In our time school desegregation has become an Armageddon of righteousness. In this passion play of the public schools the involved beliefs, like religion, touch on much that defies logic and confounds analysis. Yet growing racial tension portends a crisis in our country that justifies, and perhaps mandates, one more in the long line of attempts to understand."[10]

For the next thirty years, Bell dedicated his considerable talents to helping Americans understand how to improve public education, strengthen democracy, and advance the cause of racial justice through strategies that included both integration and high-quality, "model" all-Black schools. Bell was at the vanguard of a movement that wove together components of both integration and separation to fortify the nation's public schools and secure social justice. This effort required Black educational activists to continue the legal battle for school desegregation, especially as popular support for the program declined and an increasingly conservative Supreme Court continued to reduce the breadth and reach of school desegregation plans. This chapter follows the struggle for a more righteous school integration from 1975 to the present by considering declining popular and judicial support for school desegregation, a rising Afrocentric education movement, and examples of the region's most successful school integration efforts in both suburban and urban settings.

Declining Support for School Integration

Political pundits despaired that the 1974 US Supreme Court ruling in *Milliken v. Bradley* sounded the death knell for busing for the purpose of school integration. Norman Cousins, the liberal white editor of the *Saturday Review*, penned a heartfelt eulogy for busing in the winter of 1976. He lamented, "The evidence is substantial that busing is leading away from integration and not toward it; that it has not significantly improved the quality of education accessible to Blacks; that it has lowered the standard of education available to whites; that it has resulted in the exodus of white students to private schools inside the city or to public schools in the comparatively affluent suburbs beyond the economic means of Blacks; and finally, that it has not contributed to racial harmony but has produced deep fissures within American society." Cousins was a fervent believer in educational equality and the democratic purpose of public education, but he was forced to admit a point that many liberals conceded by this late date, "Busing hasn't desegregated the schools. It has resegregated them."[11]

Even sociologist James S. Coleman, whose 1968 report had boosted government support for school integration, retreated from earlier promises that integration would alleviate educational inequality. In 1975, Coleman made headlines with a new study that concluded school desegregation plans had caused more harm than good by fueling a vicious white backlash. He wrote, "The extremely strong reactions of individual whites in moving their children out of large districts engaged in rapid desegregation suggests that in the long run the policies that have been pursued will defeat the purpose of increasing overall contact among races in schools." Coleman concluded that white, middle-class families undermined school desegregation plans by either moving to school districts with fewer Black students, usually in the suburbs, or by enrolling their children in private schools.

This left behind white working-class families who could not afford to opt out of the public schools, so that in the end, Black students were being mixed together with poor and working-class white students, an approach that was unlikely to boost academic achievement for Black students. He concluded that courts could not always be effective levers of social change. Other prominent social scientists, including Thomas Pettigrew, Robert Green, and Christine H. Rossell, directly refuted Coleman's findings, but the damage was done. Public faith in school integration was declining, and those scholars whose research supported school integration after 1974 struggled to find a receptive audience.[12]

Figure 5.3. Anti-busing demonstration in front of Ford Auditorium, Detroit, 1976. Detroit News Photograph Collection. Walter P. Reuther Library, Archives of Labor and Urban Affairs, Wayne State University, MI.

White resistance to school integration in the North became more calcu-lated and better organized as activists tapped into a rising national conserva-tive movement. Opposition to integration took on a nativist tinge as detractors emphasized racially restricted, high-quality schools as a birthright, and one that white mothers were honor-bound to defend, even if this meant breaking the law. As a white mother in Chicago put it, "This is a traditional neighbor-hood. Our ancestors went to school here. Why should our children be uprooted and sent across the tracks?" In Boston, a 100-car motorcade of anti-busers sang "God Bless America" and waved American flags as they paraded through the city, claiming the mantle of patriotism for white families that resisted school integra-tion. In another event, white protestors carried a flag-draped coffin with a sign that proclaimed "Freedom Is Dead." In Detroit veterans dressed in uniform and carried American flags along with signs that read "Veterans opposed to forced busing anywhere." President Gerald R. Ford, followed by Presidents Jimmy Carter and Ronald Reagan, adamantly refused to support school integration. "I have consistently opposed forced busing to achieve racial balance as a solution to quality education," boasted President Gerald Ford, as he denounced court-ordered school integration in Boston.[13]

Black civil rights leaders fought valiantly to counter this avalanche of anti-busing, anti-school integration rhetoric. "As a citizen, Mr. Ford is entitled to his opinions, but he abdicates his role as the nation's leader when he articulates personal positions contrary to the ruling of the courts," wrote editors of the NAACP's *Crisis*. Others disputed the logic that busing children to school was in-herently problematic. "Busing is not the issue. We're here to see that our children get a better education by whatever means necessary," stressed Gloria Joyner of the Community Task Force on Education in Boston. Michael Meyers, director of Research, Policy, and Planning for the NAACP, was more explicit. "Busing as a 'problem' for many parents and politicians seems to dissipate if white children on the bus ride end up at lily-white schools. No, it's not the bus or the courts to which so many object. Stripped bare, the passionate objections to busing are thinly disguised arguments against the sensible mandates of justice."[14]

White northerners were not the only ones who objected to busing as a cen-tral feature of school integration plans. The Black Power movement mobilized Black educational activists throughout the North to interpret community con-trol of staffing, curriculum, and pedagogy as more important than racial mixing. Support for community-controlled schools waned over time, but the sense that integration did not automatically produce better opportunities for Black students lingered, as did reluctance to send Black children into hostile, white-dominated schools.

In Chicago, school administrators in 1977 were surprised when far fewer Black families signed up for a voluntary school desegregation program than

Figure 5.4. Black parents meet children getting off a school bus used for desegregation in Detroit, 1976. Detroit News Photograph Collection. Walter P. Reuther Library, Archives of Labor and Urban Affairs, Wayne State University, MI.

anticipated. Under Chicago's latest plan, 6,573 Black students were eligible to be bused to 51 underutilized schools in white neighborhoods, but as of the start of the school year, less than 1,000 Black students had signed up. Black parents and community leaders, including the Reverend Jesse L. Jackson, told the school district they feared for the safety of Black children in desegregated schools due to the frightening anti-busing rhetoric of white Chicagoans. In response, city officials promised to assign police officers and squad cars to protect the buses. Black families were given a choice: they could either send their children to a virtually all-Black neighborhood school known for low levels of academic achievement, or they could send their children to a majority white school across town known for higher levels of academic achievement and hope daily police presence was enough to deter violence against their children.[15]

"I don't think desegregation accomplished what it was designed to accomplish," admitted Denise Pruitt-Pope, a Black woman who integrated Boston public schools in the mid-1970s. "For the years I was there, the goal of quality education was just too high." Other Black students appreciated school integration because it gave them a chance to participate in the civil rights movement, but not necessarily because it provided access to better schools. "I'd probably do it again," stated Larry Turnbrow, who described his time at Boston's majority white Hyde Park High School as "pure hell" and had the scars to prove it. "I felt

I had really accomplished something. It reminds me of what kids went through down South." Derrick Bell Jr. found that even in integrated schools, Black students experienced lower levels of academic achievement and higher rates of disciplinary action than whites. In 1976 he wrote, "Civil rights groups refuse to recognize what courts in Boston, Detroit, and Atlanta have now made obvious: where racial balance is not feasible because of population concentrations, political boundaries, or even educational considerations, there is adequate legal precedent for court-ordered remedies that emphasize educational improvement rather than racial balance."[16]

The 1977 US Supreme Court ruling in *Milliken II* determined that compensatory educational programs were an appropriate remedy in a school district guilty of past acts of de jure segregation, such as Detroit. The district was ordered to consider remedies such as in-service teacher training, student reading and communication skills, vocational training, testing, students' rights and responsibilities, co-curricular activities, school community relations, counseling and career guidance, bilingual and ethnic studies, and citizen group monitoring. Importantly, the court ruled that the state governments found guilty of prior discrimination must help pay for these remedial programs. Bell, along with other Black scholars, viewed this list of compensatory programs as inadequate. He noted, "There was no concession that the educational components, as far as most of Detroit's Black children were concerned, were being ordered instead of rather than in addition to desegregation. But that, of course, was what was happening."[17]

Legal Retrenchment

Transformed by President Richard Nixon's four conservative appointments, the US Supreme Court began to limit school desegregation in the North as well as in the South beginning in 1974 with *Milliken I*. Two key cases out of Dayton, Ohio—*Dayton Board of Education v. Brinkman I* (1977) and *II* (1979)— demanded higher standards of evidence to prove the existence of deliberate, de jure racial segregation by school administrators and then limited the desegregation order for pupil assignments to seek only the racial mix in schools that would have existed without the constitutional violation. In other words, the Supreme Court created a new remedial standard that was far more rigorous, making it harder for Black citizens to prove intent to segregate while simultaneously reducing the demands for integration on school districts. Legal scholar Margo Evans explained, "The Constitution is now being constructed to require the elimination of deliberate segregation but not to require affirmative steps toward integration." The National Urban League's Vernon E. Jordan Jr. argued that these rulings were part of a growing national "counter-revolution" against Black civil rights, writing, "The Court, like the nation, also retreated in the 1970s."[18]

The Northeast was the only region in the United States where school segregation increased despite integration efforts, leading social scientists to determine it had the highest level of school segregation in the nation by 1980. Meanwhile, the courts deemphasized racial mixing in favor of providing greater resources to Black students in an effort to enhance educational opportunities in de facto segregated schools. This opened the door to litigation designed to capture greater resources for majority Black and Latino schools, just as it made it harder to achieve court orders for school desegregation. In 1980, Bell famously argued that white Americans would only support school integration when it converged with their interests, as it had, briefly, in 1954 during the height of the Cold War. Those interests then sharply diverged, especially as whites saw their privilege threatened by school integration in the 1960s and 1970s.

In the *Milliken* and *Dayton* rulings, Bell emphasized, the Supreme Court blithely handed local control of the public schools back to the same whites who had perpetuated generations of discrimination against Black students. He concluded that there were only two possible ways to improve educational equality at this point: anti-defiance strategy—essentially forced integration—or creating outstanding public schools to draw white families into majority Black settings. He preferred the second strategy, which he believed could be accomplished by improving existing integrated schools, where they existed, and developing model all-Black schools "where Black children, parents, and teachers can utilize the real cultural strengths of the Black community to overcome the many barriers to educational achievement." Bell's solution proposed a blended system of both high-quality integrated schools and high-quality all-Black schools designed to cultivate school integration through voluntary participation.[19]

Writing in 1975, educational scholar James A. Banks reflected, "The basic issue in this serious problem is not whether we should have racially integrated or segregated schools, but whether we are committed to creating schools in which the legitimacy of each ethnic culture is recognized and accepted, and where children, regardless of their ethnic identity, can attain the skills needed to survive in our racist and dehumanized society." He resolved, "I feel strongly that the learning conditions . . . which are essential for Black students to attain a quality education, can exist within all-Black as well as within integrated school settings. Each school environment must be evaluated in terms of whether it enables all children, including Black pupils, to attain a quality education, not whether it is racially mixed." Banks insisted that a high-quality education must offer all students—of all racial identities—an honest reckoning with Black history, new ways to recognize human intelligence in all its iterations, and teachers who respect the culture, language, and family traditions of all students.[20]

Robert L. Carter was part of the NAACP legal team that argued *Brown* before the US Supreme Court. In 1980, he wrote, "If I had to prepare for *Brown* today, instead of looking principally to the social scientists to demonstrate the adverse consequences of segregation, I would seek to recruit educators to formulate a concrete definition of the meaning of equality in education, and I would base my argument on that definition and seek to persuade the Court that equal education in its constitutional dimensions must, at the very least, conform to the contours of equal education as defined by the educators." Carter insisted that school integration was still a democratic ideal and one that had tremendous potential to equalize educational opportunities. But he conceded that it had not been an effective strategy to equalize public education to date, largely because of the fantastic power imbalance between white and Black citizens. He concluded, "Therefore, current civil rights strategy in education, it seems to me, ought to concern itself with many facets of educational policy—school financing, school districting, educational offerings, teaching methodology, and the delivery of services, among others." Integration was enormously important, according to Carter, but it could no longer be the preferred weapon in the civil rights arsenal. As Carter recognized, the debate over school integration versus separation was developing into something more critical, more malleable, and ultimately more potent as activists recognized the potential of school integration and separation, together, to advance the long Black freedom struggle.[21]

In the late 1980s and early 1990s, the Supreme Court erected new barriers to school integration nationwide. A series of decisions determined that once a school district met the minimum legal obligations of a court-ordered desegregation plan, it could return to local control. The Court then made it easier for school districts to fulfill their obligations under desegregation decrees. In 1995, the Court ruled in *Missouri v. Jenkins* that the state of Missouri could not be required to fund salary increases and remedial educational programs in the Kansas City public schools, as these constituted a kind of interdistrict remedy that exceeded the boundaries of *Milliken*. As legal scholar Bryant Douglass III concludes, "Twenty-one years after the landmark *Milliken* decision, the United States Supreme Court decided that it was finished with court-ordered desegregation, and its purpose had changed from 'eliminat[ing in] the public school all vestiges of state-imposed segregation . . . root and branch,' to restoring 'control of a school system' to 'state and local authorities.' "[22]

The results of these rulings, predictably, was that school districts everywhere scaled back desegregation efforts. Scholars estimate that the year 1988 represents the height of school integration in the United States, at which point almost 45 percent of Black students attended majority white schools nationwide. Since that time public schools have been resegregating by race and socioeconomic class, with northern states such as New York, New Jersey, and Michigan achieving the highest levels of school segregation in the nation. In 2007 the Supreme Court outlawed school desegregation plans in Louisville and Seattle, making it even harder for school administrators to create racially integrated schools.[23]

"The real challenge before us is not to enact *Brown* as a solution to segregated schools but rather to use *Brown* as a hypothesis for a new future," wrote educational scholar Gloria Ladson Billings in honor of the fiftieth anniversary of *Brown*. Indeed, Black educational activists have crafted bold new strategies to redress the long legacy of racial segregation and discrimination against Black students in the North by drawing on the lessons of the past to inspire hope for the future.[24]

Afrocentric Public Schools

"I am somebody. I look like somebody. I feel like somebody. I act like somebody. Nobody can make me feel like a nobody," seventh-grade Oumar Cole, wearing African kente cloth, shouted to his classmates at the Paul Robeson School in Detroit in the fall of 1998. An auditorium filled with hundreds of Black students bounced the words back to him, taking pleasure in the African affirmation ceremony, known as Harambee, that started every school day. "You are descendants of kings and queens and you must know that," bellowed fifth-grade teacher Mr. Murray. "Remember that you are somebody and not just anybody, but kings and queens!"[25]

Afrocentric public schools like the Paul Robeson School first appeared in the early 1990s and spread quickly to cities where most Black students attended majority Black neighborhood public schools. Taking the idea from the Black Power movement of the late 1960s, Black Power activists helped launch and support hundreds of small, independent Afrocentric schools nationwide in the 1970s and 1980s. These independent schools, however, educated only a tiny fraction of Black students. Hoping to reach a larger audience, some northern Black educational activists turned their attention to public school reform in the early 1990s. In cities including Portland, Denver, and Milwaukee, activists demanded that majority Black schools adopt an Afrocentric curriculum that emphasized Black contributions in history, literature, arts, math, and science. In Chicago, Detroit, Milwaukee, Minneapolis, Seattle, and Cincinnati, Black educational activists worked with local school administrators and politicians to create schools with a dedicated Afrocentric identity, while educators in Philadelphia advocated incorporating an Afrocentric curriculum throughout the district.[26]

Scholar and activist Molefi Kete Asante established a theoretical basis for Afrocentric education with the publication of his seminal work, *Afrocentricity: The Theory of Social Change* (1980). Asante built on the work of historian Carter

G. Woodson, who argued in 1933 that Black Americans were "mis-educated" by a white-dominated system of public education and that studying "Negro History" was an effective remedy. "Woodson's alert recognition, more than 50 years ago, that something is severely wrong with the way African Americans are educated provides the principal [sic] impetus for the Afrocentric approach to American education," Asante wrote in 1991. Academics like educational psychologist Asa Hilliard helped translate these ideas into practice through curriculum guides such as the African American Baseline Essays, which were adopted in the Portland public schools in 1989. The goal was to decolonize public education in America and create institutions dedicated to revolutionary Black liberation and political empowerment.[27]

Asante's central premise was that public schools were established by a white supremacist society for the purpose of subjugating minorities, including Black children. In their current form, American public schools could not be trusted to educate and emancipate Black youth. Asante believed that to counteract the racist foundation of public education, teachers needed to center the agency of Black students. He posited, "In education this means that teachers provide students the opportunity to study the world and its people, concepts, and history from an African world view. In most classrooms, whatever the subject, Whites are located in the center perspective position. How alien the African American child must feel, how like an outsider!" He continued. "The little African American child who sits in a classroom and is taught to accept as heroes and heroines individuals who defamed African people is being actively de-centered, dislocated, and made into a nonperson, one whose aim in life might be to one day shed that 'badge of inferiority': his or her Blackness."[28]

Asante's claim that white-dominated schools threatened the mental and emotional well-being of Black students not only tapped into a long tradition of separate, Black-controlled schools, but also appealed to families who found public schools to be callous, inhospitable, punitive institutions. Afrocentric education brought together the most compelling traditions of separate schools and refashioned them for the post-*Milliken* era. It promised to make schools welcoming places for Black children, where their history, identity, and culture would be affirmed and nurtured by a staff of teachers and administrators trained in Afrocentric pedagogy. Most of these educators were Black, unlike traditional public schools where whites dominated the teaching force and administration. Some Black northerners found this approach enormously appealing.

Writing in the *Philadelphia Inquirer*, Jennifer Franklyn argued that Afrocentric education drew on the same ideals as the nation's best historically Black colleges and universities. She said, "As a Howard University student in the '60s, I never took a course in 'Afro-American History' or 'Afro-American Literature' or anything with a similar title. But in each discipline within which I studied, my teachers made sure we knew about the contributions African Americans made to the discipline and the impact of the discipline on the lives of African Americans. This fit comfortably alongside our teachers' primary mission—to make sure we mastered the tools of the discipline, thus providing us with a solid foundation for further education and advancement." For activists like Franklyn, the appeal of Afrocentric education was that it would inspire children and boost chronically low levels of Black academic achievement.[29]

"The Afro-centric approach is something I could have benefited from," agreed Zandra Stewart as she enrolled her son in an Afrocentric public school in Chicago. Raushanah El Shabazz, a mother of two, concurred. "If we could get our children surrounded in our experience, to learn to love others and to love themselves, our children would succeed," she explained. Eugene Williams, another parent, added, "The present public education system gives you the impression that everything was created by white people. It simultaneously negates African American children." Black educational activists hoped an empowering curriculum would lead to higher self-esteem, which would improve academic achievement. "There is a direct correlation between low self-esteem and destructive behavior," confirmed educational activist J'Huti TaSeti. "If you give children the advantage of knowing themselves and who they are feeling positive about themselves, then that's instructing positive behavior. And so, if you grow up not thinking that you have people of purpose and a definite history, then you're going to have a low self-esteem, and you don't want to do anything that's positive. . . . It becomes a vicious cycle and we're about changing that cycle." Supporters believed a focused curriculum, as well as special features like African rites of passages, would help Black students thrive.[30]

While many Black educational activists imagined a connection between Afrocentric education, better self-esteem, and higher levels of academic achievement, some Black scholars proposed that Afrocentric schools could function as a legal remedy to the destructive effects of segregation. In 1954, *Brown* relied heavily on social science data that claimed segregated schools stigmatized Black students by creating "a feeling of inferiority as to their status in the community that may affect their hearts and minds in a way unlikely ever to be undone." In other words, even if schools, funding, teacher quality, and curriculum were the same, school segregation still violated the constitutional rights of Black children by generating a feeling of inferiority, which could impair academic achievement. The court's logic did not have lasting power, especially as a new body of social science research challenged the original psychological findings. More important, the courts no longer supported robust school integration plans. Northern public schools had the highest levels of school segregation nationwide and were trending toward ever higher levels of segregation and inequality.

Black scholars returned to the *Brown* ruling, which said that segregated schools caused low self-esteem which led to low academic achievement, and reframed this hypothesis to solve educational inequality by using Afrocentric schools to boost Black self-esteem. Sonia R. Jarvis, executive director of the National Coalition on Black Voter Participation, explained, "The implementation of an Afrocentric curriculum that seeks to enhance the self-esteem and academic performance of Black children is consistent with *Brown*." Writing in the *Yale Law Journal*, Jarvis noted that since legal challenges had failed to create more equitable and racially integrated schools, then a new approach was necessary to solve the crisis in Black education. One of the unanticipated consequences of the Black civil rights movement, noted Jarvis, was that middle-class Black families moved into suburban communities thanks to newly enforced nondiscrimination legislation. This meant that urban Black communities went from being economically diverse—as elite, middle-class, working-class, and poor Black families were all restricted to the same neighborhood—to being economically homogenous, as those with means fled the distressed urban core. Poor and working-class students of color were concentrated in under-funded urban public schools cut off from middle-class peers, families, political power, and social networks. Studies had found corresponding problems in these isolated, high-poverty urban schools including a limited curriculum, less qualified teachers, and far fewer educational support services like guidance counselors, social workers, school nurses, advanced course options, after school enrichment opportunities, and special education teachers.[31]

The benefits of creating Afrocentric schools in these neighborhoods were obvious, according to Jarvis. First, an Afrocentric approach promised to empower Black children by improving their self-confidence, self-esteem, and educational achievement. Second, higher levels of self-esteem among adolescents correlated with lower levels of drug use and teenage pregnancy, thus improving the quality of life in Black communities. Third, these more confident, more educated, more successful Black students would lead to reduced prejudice and improved race relations with whites. Fourth, and perhaps most notably, the Afrocentric solution cost virtually nothing and could be implemented without the political maelstrom of busing. Noting the appeal of this approach among Black families, legal scholar Eleanor Brown wrote, "The adoption of Afrocentric curricula arguably represents the most public and controversial departure by the Black community from the integrative ideal first delineated in the Supreme Court's 1954 decision in *Brown v. Board of Education*."[32]

Martell Teasley and Edgar Tyson were among the many Black scholars who agreed that an Afrocentric education would inspire students "to claim and regain control of their lives and future." Jarvis asserted, "Afrocentric curricula can help to meet the needs of Blacks in public schools that remain polarized despite thirty-eight years of desegregation. Such curricula promote *Brown*'s goal of improving the opportunities of Black schoolchildren. Such curricula need not be racially exclusive; they can provide educational benefits to non-Black students as well." Black educational activists nationwide found new meaning in the emancipatory promise of Afrocentric education.[33]

Howard University scholar Kmt G. Shockley agreed that an Afrocentric approach would help resolve the dilemma of Black education for the twenty-first century. He concurred with scholars like Asante who contended that public schools reproduced white supremacy, placing Black students in an impossible position—they could choose to refuse to participate in this mis-education by dropping out of harmful schools, or they could succeed in school, only to betray the needs and interests of Black communities. Shockley wondered, "Could it be that such a conundrum is felt by many of our students, so they exit the system or treat it like it is a joke?" The solution, according to Shockley, is to transform public schools into institutions that value the identity, history, culture, and community of Black students.

Shockley spent over a year observing a young Afrocentric teacher named Brother Ture in Boston. His vivid accounts of Brother Ture's pedagogy help explain the appeal of this curriculum to students and parents. For instance, Shockley describes talking to Brother Ture one morning before school, when the young teacher suddenly said, "Hold up brother, I gotta go get my warriors." He then ran outside to greet each student by name and welcome them to a day at school. "Who said, 'We can accomplish what he will?'" asked Brother Ture, as the students filed inside. "Marcus Garvey!" they shouted back. "What did Malcolm X say about chickens?" he pressed. "They come home to roost!" answered the students. "Okay, let's get our minds Black," extolled Brother Ture.[34]

Once the students were assembled, Brother Ture illustrated how an effective teacher established classroom discipline. Shockley observed, "When the bell finally rang, the students looked at Brother Ture. He held one finger up in the air and almost all of them got quiet. He put up a second finger and they straightened up in the line. He then put up a third finger and they turned to the left, then a fourth one and they turned to the right." Shockley reflected, "I thought about the Malcolm X story where he had such control and organization over members of the Nation of Islam."

Shockley concluded that Brother Ture's Afrocentric pedagogy offered a trenchant solution to the problems that plagued Black students in urban schools. These middle schoolers were well behaved, engaged, and inspired by their teacher, who obviously cared a great deal about them. Shockley argued that an Afrocentric approach was necessary in all settings where Black children were present, and he did not hesitate to prescribe a pedagogy that was quite different from the one used in majority white schools. Afrocentric scholars maintained that in order to create equality in educational opportunities for Black children, educators must develop pedagogies and curricula to meet the unique needs of Black children. He concluded, "Simply put, Afrocentric education is a type of education that forces teachers to exist inside the African reality during the time they are teaching Black students—it's a simple thing that for some reason keeps getting missed."[35]

Afrocentric curricula and schools had their impassioned defenders, but they were also a lightning rod for intellectual and political controversy. "They're based on the assumption that African-Americans are psychologically maimed and can only reconstitute themselves by developing very explicit race consciousness," critiqued Gerald Early, director of Afro-American Studies at Washington University in St. Louis. "I also get concerned about African-American people wanting to reconstruct segregation," he added. "We need to move forward, not backwards." Critic, poet, and activist Stanley Crouch agreed. "As a movement, Afrocentrism is another of the clever but essentially simple-minded hustles that have come about over the last 25 years, descending from what was once called 'the professional Negro,' a person whose 'identity' and whose 'struggle' constituted a commodity," Crouch wrote. In a biting criticism, Crouch wrote that Afrocentric education had little to offer of any intellectual substance and that it represented the tragic acceptance of defeat.[36]

Black school board member Leon Todd campaigned against an Afrocentric curriculum in the Milwaukee public schools in 1996. Denouncing the proposed curriculum as a "racist, ultra-conservative, nationalist, pseudo-science," Todd claimed that "Afrocentric education leads to the mis-education of children of color" by distorting history and distracting Black students from core academic content. Todd argued that poor, minority students would benefit more from a "back to basics" curriculum that emphasized the fundamentals than by teaching what he disparaged as "myths and lies." Other Black educational activists bristled at the rejection of integrated learning environments and were uneasy with the claim that Black children needed different curriculum and pedagogy. Harvard University sociologist Charles Willie opposed Afrocentric education in Detroit. "No school that is not integrated can provide a quality education," he insisted. "Diversity is one of the number one concepts of a good education," he added, pointing out that students at either all-white or all-Black schools suffered the harmful consequences of racial isolation.[37]

Afrocentric public schools peaked in the late 1990s, after which many were shuttered due to lack of political support, disappointing test scores, low enrollment, or controversies over management and funding. The growth of charter schools, however, kept the dream of Afrocentric schools alive into the twenty-first century. The tremendous surge in the number of charter schools nationwide, especially in urban areas, has proved to be a mixed blessing for Afrocentric public schools. On the one hand, it has allowed many Afrocentric schools to survive within the policy matrix of "school choice" as one charter school option among many. On the other hand, the expansion of charter schools has eviscerated the core appeal of Afrocentric schools as dozens of charter schools today promise to deliver "culturally affirming" and "ethnocentric" curricula and pedagogy. These schools do not reflect the anti-colonial, emancipatory Afrocentric theory and practice that grew out of the Black Power movement, but the distinction can be difficult to spot. "When you haven't had choices all your life and all of a sudden you have 85 different choices, you walk away from your culture and heritage," observed Bernida Thompson, principal of Roots Public Charter School, an Afrocentric charter school that was forced to close due to low enrollment in 2014. Asante agreed that large charter schools claiming to be "culturally affirming" were not Afrocentric and that they were guilty of "fooling the public with their rhetoric." Meira Levinson, a white political philosopher at Harvard University and former middle school teacher, added that there was a crucial difference between designing culturally relevant pedagogy for Black students and acquiescing to immense racial disparities in public education. She concluded, "The dilemma is if we celebrate segregated schools too much then we may forget that there is something better we can be striving for."[38]

The Promise of Suburban Integration

A major appeal of Afrocentric education was that it promised to address what *Brown* identified as a core problem of school segregation—feelings of inferiority and low academic achievement of Black students—without requiring controversial desegregation plans. Given high levels of residential segregation and the lack of political and judicial support for busing, many northern Black educational activists were willing to accept efforts to improve the quality of education for students trapped in "majority minority" schools as an alternative reform strategy, and some found Afrocentric schools alluring. This does not mean, however, that support for school integration was dead, only that it was most visible in those northern communities that had certain demographic and political conditions.

Located just fifteen miles west of New York City, suburban Montclair, New Jersey, had a racially mixed population, a strong local tax base, and the kind of cosmopolitan citizenry that valued both public education and racial progressivism. Lauded as "a modern mecca of racial and social harmony," Montclair proved that Black educational activists could force a predominantly white northern suburb to desegregate its schools. As the *New York Times* reported in 1994, "Montclair became integration Eden, a model for other districts and a haven for young families seeking a solid education in a multi-ethnic town." This integration Eden, however, was not the natural outcome of a progressive northern community but was in fact crafted over the strong objections of white families.[39]

Decades of struggle by Black parents, students, educators, community leaders, and a strong local NAACP chapter eventually forced the school district to break down entrenched patterns of racial segregation and inequality that were so clearly visible in the public schools. White families—even the supposedly "liberal" ones in Montclair—strongly resisted calls for school integration. Former Montclair Mayor William Farlie described the school integration battles of the 1960s and 1970s as "Armageddon arguments" as parents mobilized pro- and anti-integration organizations. When the dust settled, it was clear that while Montclair had engineered a school integration plan that created both racially diverse schools and happy parents, it had done so by prioritizing white families' concerns over educational equality for Black students.[40]

Fear that school integration would trigger white flight was so palpable that white school administrators did not bother to disguise it. As a result, blatant racial disparities were built into the new system from the beginning. Once an effective school integration plan was in place, however, Black educational activists found they could advocate for specific reforms, and so Montclair's public schools have continued to improve. The history of school integration in Montclair, although far from perfect, illustrates how northern Black educational activists used integration to improve educational opportunities for Black youth and create a school system with tremendous appeal to white and Black families.

Like other northern towns, Montclair had a long history of educational segregation and discrimination stretching back to the nineteenth century. Racist real estate and banking practices restricted Black families to a few clearly identifiable neighborhoods in the South End of town, where Black children attended schools alongside working-class Italian families for elementary and middle school, before moving onto the town's only high school.[41]

In the 1940s, Montclair civil rights activists challenged racial segregation and inequality in housing, schools, and recreation. A 1947 civil rights audit uncovered evidence of deliberate school segregation through discriminatory school assignment policies, specifically "optional attendance" zones that allowed white families to opt out of schools with Black majorities in racially mixed neighborhoods. It also noted that the district employed only one full-time Black teacher, Mabel Frazier-Hudson, who had been hired in 1946 following a dedicated campaign by Black families. Stirred by the postwar civil rights movement, Montclair's Black community boycotted for school integration in the fall of 1949. White school administrators balked, claiming they practiced "proper school administrative policies" in the "best interests of the town." White citizens were perplexed by this new Black educational activism. "Why not let sleeping dogs lie?" one resident wondered. Real estate brokers concurred, issuing dire warnings about property values and the looming threat of white flight. With limited economic and political power, Black families in Montclair were unable to make substantial changes to educational inequality during this period and school segregation continued unabated.[42]

The blatantly racist conditions of Montclair public schools remained intact in 1961, when a rising tide of civil rights activism inspired a renewed attack on segregated and unequal schools. Harris Davis spearheaded a new boycott after his daughter Lydia brought home her first report card from Montclair High School. Although Lydia had been an outstanding student with top grades at Glenfield Middle School, she could barely pass her high school classes. Harris discovered the coursework at majority Black Glenfield was well below grade level, leading to vast disparities in academic achievement in the high school for many Black students. He organized a Parents' Emergency Committee, which determined that school segregation was to blame. Black families in Montclair coordinated with local Black leaders to launch a major campaign for school integration.[43]

On the first day of school in September 1961, more than 60 percent of Black students boycotted Glenfield Middle School and the elementary school that fed into it, the Cedar Street School. Forty parents, mostly mothers, walked a picket line outside the school holding signs that read, "Discrimination Is Real at Glenfield," and "Our School Is Inferior, Our Children Are Not Inferior." Black parents and the local NAACP asked school leaders to close Glenfield Middle School so that its 185 students could be bused to one of the other three middle schools in town, which had larger student enrollments and more robust academic opportunities. Superintendent Clarence E. Hinchey feigned confusion, stating, "I don't understand at all why they should consider this a desirable thing to do." He was angered by the NAACP proposal to close Glenfield and reassign Black students to the majority white junior high schools in town. He complained that it would "completely disrupt the educational experience of some 1,700 junior high school students."[44]

Local activists amassed data detailing the stark inequalities between majority white and majority Black schools in Montclair and documented discriminatory school assignment policies. Schools in white neighborhoods had newer supplies, more rigorous academic curricula, better facilities, and more qualified teachers than majority Black schools. Yet modest attempts by the school board to address these inequalities were adamantly opposed by white parents and business leaders. A newly formed "Committee for Neighborhood Schools" disparaged Black demands as "hasty, radical departure from the neighborhood school program." When the Board of Education made plans to reassign Black students from Glenfield to Mt. Hebron, a nearly all white junior high school on the north side of town, white parents filed a lawsuit to block it, claiming the constitutional rights of white students had been violated since they had not been given the same kind of choice about which school to attend as the Black families. The New Jersey Supreme Court eventually ruled in favor of the white parents, but also instructed Montclair to desegregate its schools.[45]

A new superintendent took this court order to heart and planned a massive school reorganization that included busing fifth- and sixth-grade students from predominantly white Edgemont School to predominantly Black Nishuane School. The plan required local voters to approve a $4.3 million bond, which they did not—a vote that split sharply along racial lines. Frustrated but not defeated, Black parents and the local NAACP filed a complaint of racial discrimination with the New Jersey State Commissioner of Education on April 12, 1966. In August 1968, the state commissioner ruled in favor of the Black families, saying, "It is well established that [Montclair's school segregation] incontrovertibly constitutes a deprivation of equal educational opportunity for children of the minority race, that persistence of such circumstances in unlawful, and that the respondent has an affirmative duty to eliminate or alleviate such conditions to the extent that it is reasonable, practicable, and educationally sound to do so."[46]

The next nine years were tense ones in Montclair, as urban unrest in nearby Newark and throughout the North emphasized the growing militancy of the Black civil rights movement and the resistance of white northerners to open housing, school integration, and other civil rights reforms. Locally, small acts of rebellion including minor destruction of property and student-led boycotts underscored the Black community's commitment to racial justice. Many white citizens refused to countenance any school integration, especially proposals that included busing children out of neighborhood schools—no matter how disingenuously those "neighborhoods" had been defined by school administrators. Various attempts at modest busing plans were halted by white parents and their elected representatives on the Board of Education through 1975. Finally, the New Jersey Commissioner of Education issued a strongly worded order that Montclair must design a new assignment policy to integrate its racially imbalanced schools.[47]

This motivated Superintendent Walter Marks to design a desegregation plan that satisfied white parents and their anxiety over "forced busing." He met with various interest groups and crafted five possible school integration plans for town leaders. Local teacher Daniel Gill acknowledged Superintendent Marks's clever ploy. According to Gill, "Marks was a master politician. He arranged the plans so that most were really unappealing or unfeasible, and only a few were left that could work." The two most appealing plans relied on optional magnet schools to draw students out of their neighborhoods to participate in extraordinary educational opportunities. These students would be voluntarily bused to their new school, thus avoiding the specter of "forced busing" that was roiling large cities including Boston and Detroit. The Montclair Board of Education first voted for one of the unfeasible plans, even though it failed to meet the requirements of the commissioner of education and would likely cause the district to lose state and federal aid. Black parents responded with a sit-in at the board of education and demanded a better integration plan. Superintendent Marks supported the Black families, and eventually, facing negative press and the threat of losing more than $2 million in aid, the Montclair Board of Education agreed to integrate the schools.[48]

The school board approved limited freedom of choice for grades K–8, magnet schools, and some voluntary busing. The plan was to go into effect in the 1977–78 school year and sought low integration targets of only 25 percent minority students in each school. After speaking with Black families, Marks created a "fundamentals" magnet elementary school in the nearly all-white northern part of town at Bradford School, designed to draw Black families who wanted an emphasis on strong reading, writing, and arithmetic skills. In the Black neighborhood, Nishuane School was designated as a magnet school for "gifted and talented" education, where all students were considered gifted and talented and invited to take elective classes in topics like lizards, volcanoes, cooking, math magic, creative writing, art, foreign language, and music. The gifted and talented program was designed to appeal to affluent white families. Some of these elective classes were restricted by entrance tests, even for kindergarteners, in order to assuage white fears that Black children would drag down the quality of academic work. As a final sweetener, both Nishauane and Bradford would offer the district's only pre-kindergarten classes.[49]

The plan worked, and hundreds of families signed up for the new magnet schools and the buses that would carry their children across town. Building on this success, the district magnetized its middle schools in 1978. School administrators created a "controlled choice" plan that allowed parents to rank their preferences for school placement but also permitted school administrators to create racially balanced schools. Glenfield, in a Black part of town, was designated a gifted and talented, performing arts magnet to draw white families, and Mt. Hebron, in an overwhelmingly white neighborhood, was designated as an academic fundamentals magnet to attract Black families. An extensive renovation program at Glenfield created state of the art gymnasiums, dance studies, auditorium, and even a planetarium—renovations that had long been denied when the school served mostly Black families. To motivate white families, Superintendent Marks cancelled performing arts programs at Mt. Hebron. If white families wanted their middle schoolers to participate in music, theater, or dance, they would need to get on the bus to Glenfield. To make room for these white students, Black students would need to be bused to the previously "white" school.[50]

Mary Lee Fitzgerald assumed the role of superintendent in Montclair in 1981, and four years later she convinced the board to magnetize all of the elementary schools with a unique theme for each one, thus expanding the controlled choice program to the entire district. She tweaked each school so it would remain appealing to whites while she took no discernible steps to address the educational needs of Black students. For example, in 1987, Superintendent Fitzgerald designated Edgemont School as a Montessori school because the enrollment there was becoming "too Black," and she believed a Montessori theme would be especially appealing to white families. In another instance, when Black enrollment at Mt. Hebron inched above target goals, she implemented "ability grouping" to satisfy white parents' concerns that the presence of Black students lowered the academic rigor of the coursework.[51]

By the early 1990s, Montclair was celebrated as a national model of successfully integrated K–12 schools. There were no neighborhood schools, and all students could choose from the town's seven elementary and two middle schools—all of which had outstanding resources, high-quality teachers, and enticing special themes. By tweaking school assignments, administrators could ensure that demographics at each school reflected the demographics in the district—roughly 51 percent white and 49 percent Black, Asian American, or Latino. White and Black parents were generally pleased by the ability to select from a range of high-quality, well-funded schools with strong records of academic success and stimulating themes such as performing arts or Montessori. At the same time, it was evident that while each school was racially balanced, the classrooms within those schools were not. A direct legacy of the ability grouping programs designed to allay white parents' concerns over sending their children to school alongside Black children, internal tracking programs resulted in segregated classrooms districtwide. This segregation was especially glaring—and significant—at Montclair High School. In 1996, in a school with a Black population of 51 percent, the honors classes were typically 80 percent white, while remedial and non-academic classes were majority Black.[52]

Montclair had successfully integrated its schools, but test scores and graduation rates revealed that integration alone was not enough to equalize educational opportunities and academic achievement for Black students. Few Black families, however, countenanced a return to any kind of separate schools to address this problem. Instead, Black educational activists organized new support systems and intervention measures designed to help Black students achieve while holding the school district accountable. In 1989, local educational activists founded a non-profit organization called Improving Montclair Achievement Network Initiative (IMANI), designed to fortify the academic success of students of color so that all students graduated from Montclair High School prepared for college. The organization's name, IMANI, also refers to the seventh principle of the African American celebration of Kwanzaa. In the context of African spirituality, Imani means faith and a deep commitment to Black families, communities, people, and culture. It is notable that IMANI offers enrichment programs such as tutoring, book clubs, summer enrichment, and college counseling in majority Black settings with Black leaders. Supporters argue that these separate spaces designed to support and nurture Black students can boost Black student academic achievement within an integrated school system. In other words, IMANI strongly supports Montclair's integrated schools and also develops enrichment programs that draw on a long tradition of Black separation and self-determination.[53]

Twenty-first-century Black educational activism in Montclair has tackled the achievement gap between white and Black students. Between 2002 and 2012, almost half of the Black students in Montclair High School were in the bottom quarter of the GPA distribution, and about three-quarters were in the bottom 50 percent. The numbers for white students were almost exactly the opposite, and additional data revealed glaring inequalities in student suspensions, graduation rates, advanced class placement, and standardized test scores. In January 2014, a group of concerned parents, residents, and educators created the Achievement Gap Advisory Panel (AGAP). This group spent eighteen months collecting and analyzing data, as well as talking to parents, teachers, and school administrators about why there was a racial achievement gap and what could be done about it.

In its final report, the AGAP explained that it expected these racial disparities to be explained by socioeconomic class. Instead, it found that socioeconomic differences "could never account for all or even most of the racial achievement gap between white and Black students—of any background." The panel concluded, "Montclair students have vastly different experiences in our classrooms based on race, a gap that begins as early as third grade, a gap that has persisted for decades." The panel made specific recommendations to remediate the "opportunity gap" that led to this achievement gap and asked the district to hire a new assistant superintendent of equity and achievement. Dr. Kendra V. Johnson was hired to implement strategies to reduce the racial achievement gap in Montclair, which included removing distinctions between "high honors" and "honors" high school classes in 2016, instituting anti-racist training for all faculty and staff, and improving communication strategies between the school and traditionally marginalized families. In the spring of 2017, Montclair Board of Education member Joe Kavesh asked Johnson whether closing the achievement gap in the Montclair public schools would still be an issue twenty years from now. Johnson answered, "I would hope not, but the reality is that's going to depend on how committed you are to doing the work. This is hard work." It is also unrelenting, and Black families and community members remain committed to making integrated schools work in ways that result in true educational equality for Black youth.[54]

Controlled choice programs like the one in Montclair expanded in other northern communities, both suburban and urban, which permitted families to choose from among a limited number of local public schools with different themes, while also allowing school administrators to create racially and socioeconomically integrated schools by drawing on wider school catchment zones than traditional neighborhood schools. Notable versions in Cambridge, Massachusetts; Berkeley, California; and Seattle, Washington, helped cultivate racially and socioeconomically mixed schools in districts that would otherwise have high levels of segregation. While many families celebrated the opportunity to break down residential segregation and foster more diverse public schools, others became enraged if they did not receive their first-choice school placement. Some of these white families insisted that school integration plans violated the civil rights of white students. A handful sought redress in the courts that would eventually limit the ability of school administrators to create school assignment policies designed to overcome high levels of residential segregation in the North.[55]

The Battle for Integration in Seattle

Anthony Ray grew up in the housing projects of Seattle's predominantly Black Central District. Thanks to a new school desegregation plan, he was bused to predominantly white North Seattle for middle and high school. Ray appreciated the chance to attend schools with better resources, but he recognized that some people objected to the busing program that brought students like him into majority white schools. "I've heard things like, 'Forced integration is not good,' 'I want my kid to go to school in our community, that's why we moved here'—all those things I totally understand," Ray said. "But from my perspective, I didn't have the luxury of living in a neighborhood where a good school was. We didn't make that kind of money. My mom worked as an LPN at the King County Jail making six or seven bucks an hour. So, from my perspective, it was the best thing that could have happened to me." A teacher at Eckstein Middle School helped Ray discover his passion for music and pointed him toward a career in the arts. A decade later, Americans would know Anthony Ray as Sir Mix-A-Lot after his 1992 hip-hop song "Baby Got Back" skyrocketed him to international fame.[56]

Civil rights activists with local chapters of the NAACP and CORE forced the Seattle School Board to implement school integration in 1978. The "Seattle Plan" mandated busing for thousands of white and Black students to overcome residential segregation. The goal was racially balanced schools, or schools that did not exceed the percentage of Black students in the district by more than 20 percent. Within a few years, Seattle had virtually eliminated its segregated schools. Before the Seattle Plan, four of the city's eleven high schools were racially imbalanced. By 1980, only Cleveland High School remained out of balance, but only by a mere two students. Elementary and middle schools, likewise, were integrated by pairing majority Black schools with majority white ones.[57]

Although many residents believed the Seattle Plan revitalized the city's schools, others vehemently opposed it. An anti-integration group called Citizens for Voluntary Integration Committee (CIVIC) fought to put school desegregation on the local ballot so that city residents could vote on whether to end it. Sixty percent of Seattleites voted to outlaw busing for the purpose of school integration, but this ban was overturned in court. Black support for school integration in Seattle, initially very strong, began to waver as families realized that Black youth bore a disproportionate burden of integration including long bus rides and sometimes hostile learning environments in majority white schools. In 1985, Seattle's Black teachers and administrators reported that school integration was not boosting Black academic achievement and that test scores and graduation rates for Black students in Seattle remained far behind that of white students. The NAACP downplayed criticism of busing from both whites and Blacks, promising it would "not stand idly by and watch the Seattle desegregation plan be dismantled."[58]

By 1988, Seattle's public-school enrollment had fallen from about 100,000 to less than 50,000 due to shifting demographics, white and middle-class flight, and vocal white resistance to school integration. Superintendent William M. Kendrick proposed reducing the number of children being bused in an attempt to draw families back to the public schools. District leaders established magnet schools with exciting themes and developed a controlled choice plan to appeal to white and middle-class families. These changes did not address the educational needs of Seattle's poor and working-class Black students. Superintendent John H. Stanford, the first Black superintendent of Seattle Schools, presented evidence that claimed Black children who were bused out of their neighborhoods performed worse than their peers in majority Black neighborhood schools. Other scholars contested Stanford's claims, but the damage was done. Under Superintendent Stanford's leadership the Seattle School Board voted unanimously to end mandatory busing in 1996.

The only significant remaining component of school integration was a controlled high school choice plan that allowed incoming ninth graders to choose from any of the district's high schools, ranking their choices in order of preference. If too many students selected a particular high school as their first choice, then school administrators applied a series of "tiebreakers" to determine who would get the open seats. The first tiebreaker was whether the applicant currently had a sibling at the same school. The second tiebreaker considered the racial composition of the school and the racial identity of the individual student. If the school was more than 10 percentage points away from the district's overall white/nonwhite student balance, then administrators could give preference to students that would "bring the school into balance." This school assignment policy was similar to the one employed in other controlled choice districts, such as Montclair.[59]

When Seattle's rising ninth graders ranked their first-choice high school for the 2000–01 school year, 82 percent picked one of the five most popular schools: Ballard, Nathan Hale, Roosevelt, Garfield, and Franklin. Only one of these high schools, Garfield, had a student body population that was "within racial guidelines." Three of the remaining schools had too many white students, and one had too many "nonwhite" students, which is how the district classi-fied Black, Asian American, Latino, and Native American students. Therefore, a student's racial identity was a factor in school assignment at these four schools. A relatively small number of students, including Elizabeth Brose, who identified as white, were not assigned to their first-choice high school. Elizabeth's mother Kathleen insisted she felt "absolutely betrayed" that her daughter did not receive her first-choice school and furious that school administrators considered race when making school assignments.[60]

Kathleen Brose joined a local anti-integration group called Parents Involved in Community Schools, which sued the Seattle School District in the spring of 2001 for violating the civil rights of white students by considering race as a factor in school assignments. The case wound its way through the judicial system and landed on the docket of the Supreme Court in 2006 along with a companion case from Louisville, Kentucky. In *Parents Involved in Community Schools (PICS) v. Seattle School District No. 1* (2007) the majority, five justices, rejected the school assignment policy in Seattle and a similar one in Louisville, saying that both plans relied too heavily on individual students' racial identities. "The way to stop discrimination on the basis of race is to stop discriminating on the basis of race," declared Chief Justice John Roberts Jr. A minority opinion authored by Justice Stephen Breyer and co-signed by Justices John Stevens, Ruth Bader Ginsburg, and David Souter vehemently disagreed. "This is a decision that the Court and the Nation will come to regret," Breyer lamented.[61]

Importantly, neither the majority nor the minority opinion in *PICS* had the last word. That honor went to Justice Anthony Kennedy, who agreed with Roberts in certain respects and the dissenters in others. In the places where Kennedy agreed with Breyer, he represented the fifth vote, and it is those arguments that established the legal boundaries for school desegregation after 2007. Kennedy agreed with the majority that Seattle and Louisville's school assignment policies were problematic because they relied too heavily on students' racial identities, and they were insufficiently tailored to pass legal muster. However, he asserted the majority opinion went too far when it insisted on a rigid colorblind approach. "Fifty years of experience since *Brown v. Board of Education* should teach us that the problem before us defies so easy a solution," he elaborated. "If school authorities are concerned that the student-body compositions of certain schools interfere with the objective of offering an equal educational opportunity to all of their students, they are free to devise race-conscious measures to address the problem in a general way and without treating each student in a different fashion solely on the basis of a systematic, individual typing by race." Kennedy suggested that school boards could locate new schools in sites likely to attract diverse students, draw boundary lines with an eye to cultivating integration, allocate resources for special programs like magnet schools, and recruit students and faculty in a targeted fashion. Kennedy's ruling essentially meant that considering a student's racial identity in school assignment was illegal, but taking deliberate steps to create racially integrated schools in other ways was acceptable.[62]

Although Seattle essentially abandoned its controlled choice plan in the wake of the *PICS* ruling, other districts, including Montclair, made adjustments to school assignment policies and continued to create racially diverse schools through controlled choice. Elsewhere, Black educational activists decided to experiment with other integration strategies, including some of the ones Justice Kennedy listed as permissible. Ultimately, the *PICS* ruling generated new limitations, but it did not stop or impede Black educational activists who believed that integrated schools were an effective way to promote Black educational equality and the civic functions of public education in a diverse democracy.[63]

School Integration in Hartford

Like many northern cities by the late 1990s, Connecticut's capital city of Hartford was home to a high-poverty, majority Black and Latino school district surrounded by more affluent, predominantly white suburbs. Black educational activists here created one of the most successful models of school integration in the urban North, and one that reveals both the promise and the challenge of school integration in the twenty-first century.[64]

Black civil rights activists, like attorney and law professor John C. Brittain, filed *Sheff v. O'Neil* in 1989 to make educational opportunities available to those who could not afford to move out of the city to reap suburban educational advantages. "We believe the children of the state of Connecticut deserve much better than the education they are getting," asserted Elizabeth Horton Sheff, whose son, Milo, was the lead plaintiff. The case wound its way through the court system until finally, in 1996, the Connecticut Supreme Court agreed. The ruling held that the state constitution obligated officials to remedy conditions of racial and ethnic isolation of Black students in public schools. Acknowledging that state officials did not deliberately create segregated schools, the court nevertheless found that state government officials bore direct responsibility for highly segregated and unequal school districts. The ruling did not define a specific remedy, but instead ordered state legislators to "put the search for appropriate remedial measures at the top of their respective agendas."[65]

In *Sheff v. O'Neill* attorneys documented tremendous disparities between the Hartford Public Schools, where 91 percent of the students were Black or Latino and 47.6 percent were poor, and the majority white, middle-class, and affluent surrounding districts, ultimately concluding that students in Hartford had less rigorous coursework, lower test scores, less qualified teachers, and fewer educational resources. The lawsuit had the overwhelming support of Black families who were frustrated by years of inertia in the city's troubled schools. Comparing public education in Connecticut to apartheid schools in South Africa, supporters gathered to sing "We Shall Overcome" outside the courthouse on the opening day of the trial.[66]

Hartford educators testified that high levels of segregation created harmful learning environments for their students. Veteran teacher Gladys Hernandez explained that her first-grade students, many of whom lived in conditions of dire poverty, surprised her by finding joy in simple things like a walk along the Connecticut River. "It's like living in a dark valley—Hartford. Surrounded by these beautiful mountains, the suburbs," she told the court. Referencing the historic *Brown* ruling, she added, "What kind of self-worth can you derive when that is the way you have to live?" Principal Eddie Davis of Weaver High School, a virtually all-Black high school in the city's North End, added that race and socioeconomic class interacted in especially destructive ways in Harford's schools. "The high concentration of poverty has a major impact," Davis testified. "It requires support services, especially social workers, health care, school psychologists that we don't have. Poverty hurts. In this state and this country, wherever white children are, there are resources." Hernandez and Davis, among other witnesses, detailed the devastating consequences of school segregation. Their goal was a quality integrated education for all children, and attorneys insisted that segregated public schools harmed not only children of color in the city but also suburban white students. "Because of the racial, ethnic, and economic isolation of Hartford metropolitan school districts, these plaintiffs are deprived of the opportunity to associate with, and learn from, the minority children attending school with the Hartford school district."[67]

Faced with moving testimony and overwhelming evidence of educational segregation and inequality, the Connecticut Supreme Court ruled in favor of the plaintiffs. Governor John Rowland issued an executive order creating the Educational Improvement Panel and tasked it with developing a range of strategies to reduce racial isolation and improve the quality of education in Hartford. Eager to avoid a potential backlash against "forced busing," politicians investigated controlled choice plans that functioned so well in communities like Montclair and Cambridge, Massachusetts. From the beginning, it was clear that school integration in Hartford would have to include partnerships between Hartford and suburban districts. As the *Hartford Courant* observed, "The proposed policies encouraging students to cross school district lines are likely to generate the most debate. They would be dramatic steps in a state where school boundaries are considered sacred." Indeed, suburban school leaders lined up to protest the utter lack of space in their schools for children transferring from Hartford. "Hartford needs to clean up its own act first," grumbled one suburban school board chairman. Due to white resistance and delay tactics, as well as vague court orders and poor incentives for suburban school districts, very little desegregation took place between 1996 and 2003, until Black plaintiffs and their allies sought redress once again in the courts.[68]

Slowly, haltingly, and with tireless work by Black and Latino educational activists, Hartford school leaders crafted an interdistrict, controlled-choice plan designed to offer exciting new opportunities to both suburban and urban youth through specially themed magnet schools. For example, state and city leaders invested in new Montessori and environmental science elementary schools, and medical science, engineering, and performing arts middle and high schools in downtown Harford. As in other controlled choice districts, school authorities used school assignments to ensure a diverse student body at these magnet schools. The magnet schools with exceptional academic programs, like University High School, or new, multimillion-dollar facilities like Breakthrough Magnet School, grew to be especially popular. Eventually, magnet schools were built in suburbs including Avon, Bloomfield, East Hartford, Enfield, Glastonbury, Manchester, New Britain, Rocky Hill, South Windsor, West Hartfield, Wethersfield, and Windsor, drawing urban students out to suburban schools. In addition, Hartford's school integration plan permitted limited enrollment of Hartford students in more than thirty surrounding suburban districts through a program called Open Choice.[69]

By 2016, more than 45 percent of Hartford's Black and Latino students attended schools the state designed as "integrated." Scholars and policy experts commended Hartford's controlled school choice plan for creating diverse schools that pleased a wide range of constituents. President Barack Obama's education secretary John King traveled to Hartford and declared the city's desegregation plan could work as a model for the country. Media outlets acknowledged that, in this case, school integration seemed to be working well for everyone. Century Foundation scholar Kimberly Quick concluded, "This two-way desegregation plan has made Harford a model for effective school integration in a high-poverty, high-minority district."[70]

Scholarly appreciation for the model district, however, glossed over the disappointment of some Black and Latino educational activists in Hartford, as well as the frustrations of scholars who felt the voluntary desegregation plan was imperiled by weak policy tools and powerful disincentives for suburban districts. Black critics emphasized that while 45 percent of Hartford students attended integrated schools, 55 percent of students were left behind in racially isolated neighborhood schools that had not seen an influx of new resources. Many Black families wanted to send their children to the more integrated and better-resourced magnet schools, or alternatively, secure an open spot in a neighboring suburban school—but found themselves permanently waitlisted. The state's requirements that "integrated" schools have no more than 75 percent students of color meant that Hartford's magnet schools had to save places for white and Asian American students. This legal definition of "integrated" was especially difficult to maintain as more Black and Latino families moved to the suburbs. By 2019, many of the suburban students bused into Hartford's magnet schools happened to be Black and Latino. As a result, Hartford's school assignment policy made it easier for suburban white and Asian American families to attend the school of their choice, while Black and Latino families were more likely to be stuck on waiting lists and attending segregated neighborhood schools that lacked adequate resources.[71]

As frustrations mounted, some Black educational activists began to question the premise that integration was the best way to secure a high-quality education for all students. "I was a student in Hartford Public Schools when a prior lawsuit promised me a brighter future," LaShawn Robinson announced at a press conference in February of 2018. "But that promise has not been realized for my children." Robinson had five children enrolled in neighborhood, majority-Black schools in Hartford. Despite years of applying to the integrated magnet schools, none of her children had been accepted due to limited space and enrollment policies that favored white and Asian American applicants. Robinson sued to revise Hartford's school integration plan so that it could no longer reserve seats—sometimes empty ones—for white students at the expense of Black and Latino children. She appreciated Hartford's magnet schools, but unlike school administrators, she was not bothered by the idea that these schools could serve an entirely Black and Latino population. "This case is about my children's future, and my children's rights, but it's also important for all students of all races. Their race should not be a disadvantage to their ability to receive a quality education," she insisted.[72]

School administrators were sympathetic with parents like LaShawn Robinson, but they were also eager to preserve the controlled choice plan and the opportunities it created for thousands of Black and Latino students. Civil rights groups including the NAACP and the ACLU believed the problem could be solved by increasing the number of racially diverse magnet schools in Hartford, not reducing the number of white and Asian American children that attend these schools. "We believe the system needs to be expanded," contended NAACP Legal Defense Fund attorney Cara McClellan.[73]

Meanwhile, another crucial component of Hartford's integration plan faced new challenges from white suburbanites. Open Choice permitted Hartford students to enroll in available seats in suburban school districts and provided free busing for these students. Scholar Erica Frankenberg highlighted this strategy as Hartford's "most efficient means of placing students in integrated school placements." By 2017, more than 2,200 Black and Latino students woke early each morning to catch a bus to suburban schools. Many Open Choice participants credited the program for giving them access to better resourced schools, but some found majority white suburban schools to be unwelcoming to students of color. Anique Thomson, whose mother was a teacher in Hartford, enrolled in Open Choice for middle school. At her new suburban school, she was known as one of the "Hartford kids," a handful of Black and Latino students who attended Canton Public Schools through Open Choice. The commute was long, it was hard for Anique to make friends, and there were very few students of color. Tired of white students asking her about "the ghetto" and "food stamps," Anique persuaded her mother to let her return to a majority Black neighborhood school in Hartford for ninth grade. "Mom, I don't really think this is for me," she said.[74]

Mihammad Ansari, president of the Greater Hartford NAACP, confirmed that Open Choice made it challenging to support Black children scattered across multiple suburban school districts. "We get a lot of complaints from parents about how their kids are treated in those schools," he admitted. "So is that better for that student, that he or she is being bused out to a school to be integrated with whites, but they're met with hostility and a feeling of 'you're not wanted here'? Is that better for that student of color to be in that kind of situation?" This was the perennial dilemma facing Black educational activists—they wanted high-quality, integrated public schools, but not if children faced such intense anti-Black racism that they could not reach their highest potential.[75]

To further complicate school integration in Hartford, charter schools have been expanding rapidly in the city. Charter schools, which are privately operated with public funds, serve populations that are almost all students of color. While the state put significant resources behind integrating Hartford public schools, it permitted charter schools to operate and expand as highly segregated institutions, which in turn keeps rates of school segregation relatively high citywide. The rapid expansion of minority-serving charter schools nationwide garnered the critical attention of the NAACP, and in 2016 it called for a moratorium on charter school expansion until charter school administrators and policymakers addressed the concerns of Black citizens. Other civil rights groups including the Journey for Justice Alliance and the Black Lives Matter Movement agreed that charter schools needed to have more transparency and accountability, fairer disciplinary policies, fewer expulsions, and greater consideration to the implications of a public institution that exacerbates school segregation.[76]

"If we were operating in an ideal world, we would want diverse high-quality schools for every child," acknowledged Dacia Toll, president of Hartford's Achievement First charter schools. "The problem right now is there aren't enough great schools. So, in the effort to create more options, do we prioritize diversity? Or do we prioritize serving as many kids as possible who don't otherwise have good options and who, honestly, are more dependent on great public education to achieve success in life?" Educational scholar Julian Vasquez Heilig acknowledged there was something of a "civil war" among Black families, as those who prioritized integration clashed with those who prioritized charter schools. "You don't want the message to be that the only way our kids can learn is if they are sitting next to white kids in the classroom," confirmed Toll. "You want the belief to be in the potential of our kids of color."[77]

Educational reform in Hartford demonstrates that an interdistrict school integration plan based on magnet schools and voluntary busing faces challenges including political intransigence, white resistance, shifting student demographics, and the expansion of charter schools that exacerbate school segregation. The school assignment policy designed to create racially diverse magnet schools has been especially controversial. Racial quotas to ensure high-quality integrated schools in Hartford privilege white and Asian American students in the lottery-based admissions process over their Black and Latino neighbors. Yet, without explicit racial targets for student populations, Hartford's magnet schools would have very few white students. A majority of Black families and civil rights activists in the city are willing to work to expand existing integrated options for Black students, including magnet schools and Open Choice enrollment in suburban schools. A key part of this effort is to improve the way integrated schools work—by adjusting school assignment policies and by working with majority white schools to create more welcoming environments for students of color.

For example, Shabree Brown filed a complaint with the Commission on Human Rights and Opportunities when her son was treated unfairly by white students and administrators in suburban South Windsor High School alleging that the school system discriminated against students of color. But she did not want to remove him from the school, she wanted school leaders to take steps to eradicate racial prejudice among teachers, administrators, and students. "A school climate survey is what we'd like to see," she explained. "We'd like to see the commitment to make a change. South Windsor is a majority white environment and Hartford is different." Giovanna Shay of Greater Hartford Legal Aid represented the Brown family and agreed the point of the complaint was to force school authorities to substantially change educational theory and practice in order to educate all children fairly, including the Black and Latino students bused in from Hartford. "The whole purpose was the integrated education system," Shay affirmed. "We would like to see a commitment from the leadership in South Windsor to make the school climate more welcoming. We know the Browns are not alone."[78]

Hartford's school integration plan is not perfect, nor is it fully formed. Instead, it is a work in progress where students, parents, educators, lawyers, civil rights activists, and state leaders endeavor to make the ideal of a high-quality, integrated education for all a reality. As of 2020, school integration remained a key component of struggle for racial equality in Hartford, even as citizens grappled with complications and setbacks. Elizabeth Horton Sheff affirmed, "If we do not prepare our children, give them equal access to a quality integrated education where people can come together and learn together, be American together, compete in the global economy together, then the nation is at peril." Sandra Vermont-Hollis, whose daughter thrived at a magnet school in Hartford, agreed. "In our democracy—where different racial groups are not always provided opportunities to interact with one another—an integrated school is a crucial experience that every child should have access to."[79]

Conclusion

As support for community-controlled schools receded in the mid-1970s, a consensus emerged among northern Black educational activists that school integration had a vital role to play in equalizing public schools. A new and more critical school integration movement drew on hard lessons learned in the long civil rights battles of the 1960s and early 1970s. A defining feature of this contemporary school integration movement, which continues to the present day, is that effective school integration will take much more than simply mixing Black and white students together and that the power imbalances inherent in school integration must be carefully acknowledged and addressed. Northern Black educational activists worked to revise school integration plans to ensure that Black students, families, and educators participate as equals in integrated schools and that all aspects of the school experience, from transportation to curriculum to discipline to social life, are free of racism and implicit bias. Black educational activists emphasize the importance of Black teachers, support staff, and administrators in all schools, as well as anti-racist curricula and pedagogy.

Since 1974 the Supreme Court has made it harder for school districts to create racially integrated schools and classrooms. Despite this setback, the court has not yet outlawed intentional school desegregation, and there are more than 100 school districts today that prioritize racial integration as a key component of successful, equitable education for all citizens. As the work of Black educational activists in Montclair and Hartford illustrate, these efforts are never easy, and they require persistent monitoring and constant work. However, integration can help equalize public education by equalizing access to facilities, resources, course offerings, support services, and quality teachers. School integration continues to be an integral part of the northern Black civil rights movement supported by organizations including the NAACP and the Urban League.

Conclusion

Racial segregation in American public schools has been increasing at an alarming rate for more than three decades, despite the fact that schoolchildren are more ethnically and racially diverse than in the past. Given a clear correlation between segregated and unequal schools, and solid evidence linking integrated schools to better opportunities and outcomes, it is little surprise that many Black educational activists continue to advocate school integration.

In the American political imagination, civil rights battles over school integration unfolded through dramatic conflicts in the South for two decades following the historic *Brown* ruling. This book underscores the struggle for school integration as a defining and consistent feature of Black civil rights activism in the North since the 1840s. Always present in this northern struggle was a dynamic tension between Black educational activists who advocated school integration and those who preferred separate, Black-controlled schools within a legally desegregated system. Courageous activists on both sides possessed a remarkable faith in the potential of public education to secure democracy, support Black civil rights, and advance the larger objectives of the civil rights movement. A history of these debates highlights four key findings that revitalize civil rights and educational history and have the power to inform contemporary educational policy.[1]

First, this book demonstrates that public schools have been spectacular and important sites of northern civil rights activism since the common school era. By the end of the Civil War in 1865, most northern towns and cities had free, tax-supported schools that were available to all regardless of race. This means that public schools were ubiquitous, making them highly visible and easily accessible targets of political protest. As locally funded and controlled public institutions, schools cultivated strong civic involvement and a powerful sense that educators must treat all children equally. State laws passed in the late nineteenth century specifically outlawed racial discrimination in most northern public schools, providing a formidable legal basis for demands of nondiscrimination. As a result, there have been high levels of educational activism by Black citizens eager to improve opportunities in their local schools.

Drawing on a venerable association between education and freedom, Black northerners have always been fervent supporters and avid consumers of public education. Early common schools bestowed a symbolic recognition of equal citizenship, but over time the relationship between formal education and future life chances became much more explicit. In 1954, Chief Justice Earl Warren concluded, "Today, it is a principal instrument in awakening the child to cultural values, in preparing him for later professional training, and in helping him to adjust normally to his environment. In these days, it is doubtful that any child may reasonably be expected to succeed in life if he is denied the opportunity of an education." More than fifty years later, President Barack Obama told Americans, "I believe that if you're going to be able to do whatever you want to do in your lives—if you want to become a teacher, or a doctor, or start a business, or develop the next great app, or be President—then you've got to have a great education."[2]

Such claims were not flights of judicial fancy or lofty political rhetoric. Educational attainment is a powerful indicator of employment status and earning potential in the United States. Public schools provide the vast majority of citizens the education they need to pursue vocational or higher education necessary to achieve economic security. This fact catapulted educational reform to the forefront of Black political protest and kept it there over time. Higher levels of education, professional training, and earning potential, in turn, have the potential to uplift and empower northern Black communities.[3]

Many of the people fighting for school integration or separation featured in this book would never have described themselves as civil rights activists, and yet their struggle to improve conditions in local schools advanced civil rights agendas such as enforcement of nondiscrimination legislation and equal treatment in public facilities. Whether Black educational activists fought for school integration or separation, they participated in acts of protest and civil disobedience, gained a political education, and built networks that connected local families to powerful organizations like the NAACP and the National Urban League. Educational activism knitted together families' most intimate hopes and dreams for the future with national civil rights agendas, a relationship that provided crucial resources and expertise to local communities while giving civil rights leaders the tangible examples they needed to advance litigation and policy agendas.

Women and young people were especially active in grassroots movements for educational reform. Black women like Marian Smith Williams in Dayton, Ruth Batson in Boston, and Beatrice Brown in Norwalk leveraged their moral authority as mothers to claim leadership positions on school issues. Many others participated in school boycotts, organized freedom schools, and contacted school administrators or civil rights organizations to strengthen their cause. Black teachers and school administrators like Hattie Kendrick in Cairo, Ruth Wright Hayre in Philadelphia, Julia Clark in New York City, Kate Savery in Hillburn, Phyllis Blackburn Greer in Dayton, and Barbara T. Mason in New Rochelle used their professional standing to improve opportunities for Black students. Black youth got their first taste of political organizing when they stood up to speak truth to power in their local schools. As documented by examples throughout this book, Black students challenged racist teachers, contested exclusion from extracurricular activities, insisted on equal access to all coursework, and demanded a curriculum that acknowledged African American history and culture and the fundamental right to educational self-determination. Black women and youth have always been visible on the front lines of battles for educational equality and have worked as effective organizers behind the scenes. It is impossible to understand the history of the long civil rights movement in the North without taking into account the diverse Black youth, parents, teachers, ministers, scholars, and civil rights activists who participated in local struggles to redress racial inequality in public schools.

Second, a history of northern Black debates over school integration establishes clearly that school integration was not the only—or even always the dominant—form of Black educational activism in the North, which reshapes our understanding of the relationship between educational activism and the long civil rights movement. Scholars interpret school integration as a defining feature of northern Black educational activism, with what is presented as the "exception" of the community-control movement in the late 1960s. A broader historical lens reveals that the community-control movement was not an aberration but was instead the rational development of a potent strand of educational activism with deep roots in Black nationalism that was there all along. Black separatists have powerfully shaped the contours of educational activism, including the northern struggle for school integration, since the 1840s.

The dialectical tension between school integrationists and separatists inspired and emboldened the northern Black civil rights movement for more than 150 years. In the South, African Americans had to contend with state-sponsored school segregation, but the North claimed to offer equal public schools for all. It was this expansive promise of freedom and equality that inspired so many Black families to seek better opportunities in the North, and this same promise that mobilized so many Black families, community leaders, teachers, and scholars to fight for better schools when they encountered illegal racial discrimination. The fact that different Black educational activists imagined competing visions for how public education could best serve the larger freedom struggle did not undermine Black educational reform: it made it smarter, more supple, and far more sophisticated.

The interplay between school integrationists and separatists created an especially dynamic and versatile movement for Black educational reform in the North. Even as one group of citizens claimed to have found the best answer to educational inequality, another group was poised to point out the deficiencies, oversights, risks, or untenable costs of this strategy. They offered an alternative that was convincing enough to give the other side pause, and as communities vacillated back and forth between these options, they had the chance to experiment with different tactics and objectives. There was no single reform that worked for all the thousands of diverse schools and communities throughout the North, which is why Black educational activism substantially broadened participation in the freedom struggle as students and parents in communities large and small, urban and rural and suburban, took direct action against the educational racism they personally encountered in their local schools.

Although many of the larger goals of the Black civil rights movement like equality in housing, health care, employment, and criminal justice have remained elusive, real change was possible in educational reform. Northern Black communities won meaningful victories at the local level. Over time these small victories took root and transformed American public education. To take just a few examples in the history of education in the North, the practice of segregating students by race was ended, Black teachers were hired to teach white students, Black students were permitted to take all upper level academic and vocational courses, and thousands of school districts eliminated obvious attempts to racially gerrymander school assignments. Some even experimented with creative school integration plans that resulted in significant racial mixing, even in communities with high levels of residential segregation.

Today, Black students can expect to participate freely in all extracurricular activities, Black history and literature are part of the core curriculum, schools are required to treat all students fairly in terms of counseling, course placement, and disciplinary actions, and many schools have Black Student Unions, Black Lives Matter, Natural Hair Project, or other programs to nurture and affirm Black cultures and identities. All of these gains were the result of Black educational activism by those who fought for school integration and those who fought for separate, Black-controlled schools in a legally desegregated system. A richer and more inclusive history of Black educational activism must acknowledge the contributions made by activists on both sides, as well as the unique benefits that came from the interplay between school integrationists and separatists.

A third insight from this study is that whites have been consistently opposed to Black educational equality and school integration, even in the supposedly liberal North. Just as Swedish economist Gunnar Myrdal recognized white racism as the source of the "American Dilemma" in 1944, white racism continues to fuel the African American dilemma over school integration and educational equality.

Although Black educational activists have won vital improvements and historic victories, northern whites continue to resist school integration and equalization efforts, resulting in schools that remain racially segregated and unequal today.[4]

This long history of educational discrimination has naturalized a landscape where northern public schools are either majority white or majority Black and Latinx, and white families understand it as a privilege and a right to be able to choose which of these schools to attend. For most of this history, white families could expect a "transfer" if they accidentally resided in a neighborhood that was zoned for a majority Black school. After civil rights activists convinced courts that this practice was discriminatory, school administrators established more rigid geographic boundaries with less lenient transfer policies. White families, in response, became more adept at policing school boundaries and the unequal school funding and resources that these arbitrary boundaries engendered.

As a result of more permanent school catchment zones and indelible school district boundary lines, middle-class white families can simply pick which school they want their children to attend and then rent or purchase a home there, which, again, is understood and expressed as a "civil right." White northerners voluntarily impose sky-high real estate taxes and bans on multifamily dwellings to ensure "their" schools are as exclusive as possible. Proclaiming a colorblind ideal, northern whites insist public schools are open to all, even as discriminatory real estate practices result in an enormous swath of the country where majority white and middle-class schools sit clustered on one side of an invisible line, while just down the road, the public schools are virtually all Black and Latinx with much higher rates of student poverty and lower rates of school funding.[5]

It is no accident that the North has the among highest rates of school segregation in the nation. As a white father in Greenwich, Connecticut, reflected in 2013, "We all bought our homes based on what school our kids were going to go to. If you talk to any Realtor, I'm sure in this town, but probably in any town across America, when they give you the listing for homes you have price, square footage, school district. I mean, it's not a complicated concept." Another Greenwich parent agreed it was not fair to tell a parent that their child "no longer has the right, or privilege, to attend a neighborhood school." White parents continue to insist that school integration plans, like the one in Seattle, Washington, before the 2007 Supreme Court ruling in *Parents Involved in Community Schools v. Seattle*, violate the civil rights of white children by permitting or requiring students to attend school outside of these rigid and artificial neighborhood boundaries. In virtually every instance where northern school administrators announced a school integration plan from the 1840s to today, white northerners organized to undermine this effort. Legal challenges to school desegregation plans have proven very effective, but so too have more subtle strategies that insist on colorblind policies that ignore glaring examples of institutionalized racism.[6]

Northern whites built segregated and unequal public schools and fortified them over time, and yet most white citizens refuse to acknowledge the long history of discrimination or their own complicity in maintaining this system through defense of neighborhood schools. Scholars refer to this process as hoarding, when people intentionally stockpile public resources for themselves in a way that denies an equal share to others. White northerners have significantly more economic and political power than their nonwhite neighbors. Their preference for high levels of racial and socioeconomic school segregation, which scholars describe as "double segregation," is backed up by the authority of local, state, and federal governments. Whites vote out of office school board members and elected representatives who advocate school integration or even a more equitable distribution of resources. County and state governments preserve tiny northern school districts even though larger ones would be more efficient and less expensive. Supreme Court rulings since 1974 have permitted an obscene expansion of northern school segregation, as has the near-total abandonment of school integration by mainstream political candidates.[7]

The North is long overdue for a racial reconciliation in its public schools and a robust history of Black educational activism is essential to this process. This history demonstrates that racial discrimination and segregation in the North was real, that it was enforced by local, state, and federal government agencies, and that it had quantifiable effects on the quality of public education available to Black students. Social scientists have established a clear correlation between integrated schools and improved opportunities and outcomes for Black students. For instance, a recent study by Rucker C. Johnson at the University of California, Berkeley, determined that Black students who attended integrated schools had higher achievement in high school, college success at more selective colleges, higher income, better jobs, less incarceration, and better long-term health than their demographic peers at majority minority schools. In a similar vein, a study published in the *Journal of Policy Analysis and Management* determined that the longer Black children attended racially segregated schools, the larger the achievement gap between Black and white students. More than sixty years of social science research finds that poor children benefit from attending schools in socioeconomically and racially integrated settings, which tend to have better facilities, funding, and support services. In other words, it is abundantly clear that school integration can be one effective component of educational reform if it is done well.[8]

But it is not the only one. The fourth insight gleaned from the history of turbulent debates over school integration is that the future of educational reform must draw on both traditions—school integration and separate, Black-controlled schools—to remediate the long history of educational racism and create public schools that fulfill their civic obligation to train all young people for citizenship in a multiracial democracy.

Current events suggest that both forms of activism are alive and well in northern Black educational reform. In New York City, the Alliance for School Integration and Desegregation (ASID) advocates greater racial and socioeconomic diversity in the public schools. According to its recent policy proposal, the purpose of school integration is to uproot white supremacy, preserve and spread the rich cultures of marginalized communities, and uphold the principles of democracy, equality, and human dignity that segregation curtails. The organization mobilizes parents, teachers, scholars, and non-profit foundations to support what it calls "real integration" in the schools. In June 2019, the New York City Board of Education adopted sixty-two of ASID's sixty-seven policy recommendations. ASID's vision of real integration was designed by the youth-led organization IntegrateNYC and includes five core principles: equitable resource allocation, enrollment that reflects the diversity of the community, restorative justice and non-discriminatory discipline policies, demographically representative faculty and leaders, and relationships across group identities in the classroom and curriculum. This vision of real integration draws on the long struggle for school integration as well as many of the features advocated by Black separatists, such as restorative justice and a critical mass of Black teachers. Supporters hope that it will transform public education in the nation's largest school district, improving the quality and content of education in ways that serve as an effective model for other communities.[9]

In this same northern metropolis, other Black educational activists are vocal supporters of separate, Black-controlled schools as an essential option in a formally desegregated system. Local charter school founder Rafiq R. Kalam Id-Din II insists that "when it comes to reversing the failure of educating Black students, we must stop looking to the beneficiaries of white supremacy for salvation, and instead be led by Black teachers and Black schools to solve this problem." The *New York Times* confirmed the rising popularity of Afrocentric schools in New York City in 2019. Parent activist Lurie Daniel Favors adds, "Even if integration worked perfectly—and our society spent the past 60-plus years trying—it's still not giving Black children the kind of education necessary to create the solutions our communities need."[10]

As these examples from New York City illustrate, contemporary Black educational activists draw on integrationist and separatist traditions in their quest for educational equality. Nationwide, the Black Lives Matter at School coalition promises to challenge structural racism such as school segregation and unequal distribution of resources, while also demanding an anti-racist curriculum that highlights intersectional black identities, black history, and anti-racist social movements. The Abolitionist Teaching Network's mission is to support

Figure C.1. High school students in Montclair, New Jersey, at a Black Lives Matter Rally, 2020. Photo by Chanda Hall.

educators to fight injustice within their schools and communities and secure educational freedom for all. High school students like those in Montclair, New Jersey, organize rallies and social media campaigns to make their voices heard and force school administrators to acknowledge the ongoing challenges that Black students face in public schools. They demand equal educational opportunities, but also racial justice, Black liberation, and the decolonization of curriculum and pedagogy.[11]

Gunnar Myrdal identified the American Dilemma as the nation's toxic, destructive practice of claiming liberty and justice for all while blatantly discriminating against African Americans. This book argues that a similar process unfolded in the public schools, especially in the North where school leaders promised educational equality while consigning Black youth to segregated and unequal facilities. The result was an enduring debate over whether school integration or separate, Black-controlled schools could more effectively mitigate deeply entrenched educational racism and transform public schools into institutions that would advance the larger Black freedom struggle.

A history of Black educational activism in the North reveals the enormous potential of integration to equalize school facilities, funding, and citizenship education. It also emphasizes the inherent risks of desegregating schools that remain mired in institutionalized white supremacy, and the vital importance of Black educational self-determination. The fact that the African American dilemma over school integration endures today is disturbing but not surprising given enormous racial inequalities in wealth, income, housing, employment, health care, and policing.

Perhaps the most essential lesson of this history, then, is that real change is possible when citizens organize, name racist practices, and work collaboratively to develop meaningful reforms. Educational reform must be connected to larger structural reforms designed to remedy racial injustice, uproot white supremacy, and secure Black dignity and freedom. This history serves as a solemn reminder of the unfinished battle for Black educational equality and as an impassioned call to action for all those who believe in the promise of public education to advance equal opportunities, civil rights, and justice for all.

NOTES

Introduction

1. Eleanor Roosevelt, "My Day, July 17, 1942," Eleanor Roosevelt Papers Digital Collection (2017), accessed July 3, 2019, https://www2.gwu.edu/~erpapers/myday/displaydoc. cfm?_y=1942&_f=md056240. The detailed description of the administration building and grounds comes from Bordentown Manual Training and Industrial School for Colored Youth, Application for National Register of Historic Places Registration Application, 1996, Digital Jerseyana Collection, New Jersey State Publications Digital Library, Trenton, NJ, accessed July 3, 2019, http://hdl.handle.net/10929/49171. On famous visitors to the school, see Giles R. Wright, *Afro-Americans in New Jersey: A Short History* (Trenton: New Jersey Historical Commission, 1988), 52–53.

2. At least twice, white students enrolled at the Bordentown School, but they withdrew soon after. Dr. William Valentine graduated from Montclair High School in New Jersey before attending Harvard University. Zoë Burkholder, "'Integrated Out of Existence': African American Debates over School Integration versus Separation at the Bordentown School in New Jersey, 1886–1955," *Journal of Social History* 51, no. 1 (2017): 47–79. Details on Bordentown School's course offerings and extracurricular activities are well documented in the student newspaper, *Ironsides Echo* (1898–1953), catalogs, and informational brochures (1900–1954) in Box 2, Bordentown School Records. Department of Education, Manual Training and Industrial School for Colored Youth at Bordentown Papers (Bordentown School Papers), NJ, Department of Education, SEDMA001, New Jersey State Archives, Trenton, NJ. See also interviews with Bordentown School graduates in Wynetta Devore, "The Education of Blacks in New Jersey, 1900–1915: An Exploration in Oral History," EdD diss., Rutgers University, 1980. On the school's pedagogy, see Connie Goddard, "Bordentown: Where Dewey's 'Learning to Earn' Met Du Boisian Educational Priorities: The Unique Legacy of a Once Thriving but Largely Forgotten School for Black Students," *Education and Culture* 35, no. 1 (2019): 49–70. On the complex and contested history of manual training and industrial education in the post-Reconstruction South, see Joan Malczewski, *Building a New Educational State: Foundations, Schools, and the America South* (Chicago: University of Chicago Press, 2016); William H. Watkins, *The White Architects of Black Education: Ideology and Power in America, 1865–1954* (New York: Teachers College Press, 2001); and James D. Anderson, *The Education of Blacks in the South, 1860–1935* (Chapel Hill: University of North Carolina Press, 1988).

3. "Meyner in Dispute over Negro School," *New York Times*, June 3, 1955, 11; "Integration Dooms School at Bordentown," *Afro-American*, August 7, 1954, 4; "Jersey to Close Its All-Negro School Because It Can't Get White Pupils," *New York Times*, December 17, 1954, 17.

4. Eleanor T. Smythwick to Governor Robert B. Meyner, January 19, 1955, Box 1, Folder, "Manual and Training School at Bordentown Closing," in Eleanor T. Smythwick Papers, MG 229, Schomburg Center for Research in Black Culture, New York, NY; telegram from Benjamin

A. Collier, Executive Secretary, Board of Directors, Urban League of Eastern Union County, New Jersey Commission to Study the Proposed Discontinuance of Bordentown Manual Training School, May 19, 1955, vol. 2, p. 20; B. H. Jones, Superintendent of Vocational Studies at Bordentown School, testimony at Public Hearing before the Commission to Investigate the Circumstances Surrounding the Proposed Closing of the Bordentown Manual Training School, vol. 1, May 19, 1955, pp. 20–21. On the history of racial uplift in African American history and culture, see Touré F. Reed, *Not Alms but Opportunity: The Urban League and the Politics of Racial Uplift, 1910–1950* (Chapel Hill: University of North Carolina Press, 2008); Jacqueline M. Moore, *Booker T. Washington, W.E.B. Du Bois, and the Struggle for Racial Uplift* (New York: Rowman & Littlefield, 2003); Kevin K. Gains, *Uplifting the Race: Black Leadership, Politics, and Culture in the Twentieth Century* (Chapel Hill: University of North Carolina Press, 1996).

5. It is worth emphasizing that Black civil rights activists wanted to close the school for reasons that were very different from those of white legislators. The civil rights activists objected to the outdated vocational curriculum that limited students to racially restricted "Black" jobs and to school segregation, whereas the white legislators objected to the high per-pupil costs of educating students at Bordentown School. Today the school is a state-run juvenile detention facility. Henry Lee Moon to Mary Windsor, February 14, 1955; Mary Windsor to the NAACP, February 5, 1955. Both in Folder, "School Integration," Papers of the NAACP, Part 03: The Campaign for Educational Equality, Series C: Legal Department and Central Office Records, 1951–1955, ProQuest History Vault, http://congressional.proquest.com/histvault?q=001513-012-0452; telegram from Benjamin A. Collier, Executive Secretary, Board of Directors, Urban League of Eastern Union County, New Jersey Commission to Study the Proposed Discontinuance of Bordentown Manual Training School, May 19, 1955, vol. 2, p. 20. Public Hearing. New Jersey Department of Education, Trenton, New Jersey. See also Milton Honig, "Integration Lag Cited by Forbes," *New York Times*, October 27, 1957, 66; George Cable Wright, "Costs Misfigured on Jersey School," *New York Times*, January 5, 1956, 31; "Bordentown School to Remain Open," *Philadelphia Tribune*, June 28, 1955, 12; "Republicans to Halt Closing of Bordentown Training Unit," *Afro-American*, June 18, 1955, 14; "Two Schools to Face Extinction," *Chicago Defender*, June 18, 1955, 1; "Why State Will Close Bordentown," *Afro-American*, April 16, 1955, 2; Millie Ganges, "Bordentown Citizens Hit School Closing," *Afro-American*, March 26, 1955, 6; Conrad Clark, "UNCF Forewarned by Bordentown's Closing," *Afro-American*, January 1, 1955, 5; "State May Close Down Bordentown," *Chicago Defender*, January 1, 1955, 1. On all-Black schools as a "vital sanctuary" for African Americans to cultivate Black leadership and social activism, see Jelani M. Favors, *Shelter in a Time of Storm: How Black Colleges Fostered Generations of Leadership and Activism* (Chapel Hill: University of North Carolina Press, 2019), 4–6. See Chapter 3 of this book for a complete analysis of Black northerners' responses to the closing of the Bordentown School.

6. A selection of scholarship on the long struggle for Black educational equality in the South includes Derrick P. Alridge, "Teachers in the Movement: Pedagogy, Activism, and Freedom," *History of Education Quarterly* 60, no. 1 (2020): 1–23; John L. Rury, *Creating the Suburban School Advantage: Race, Localism, and Inequality in the American Metropolis* (Ithaca, NY: Cornell University Press, 2020); Rachel Devlin, *A Girl Stands at the Door: The Generation of Young Women Who Desegregated America's Schools* (New York: Basic Books, 2018); Michelle A. Purdy, *Transforming the Elite: Black Students and the Desegregation of Private Schools* (Chapel Hill: University of North Carolina Press, 2018); Vanessa Siddle Walker, *The Lost Education of Horace Tate: Uncovering the Hidden Heroes Who Fought for Justice in Schools* (New York: New Press, 2018); Joy Ann Williamson-Lott, *Jim Crow Campus: Higher Education and the Struggle for a New Southern Social Order* (New York: Teachers College Press, 2018); Pamela Grundy, *Color and Character: West Charlotte High and the American Struggle over Educational Equality* (Chapel Hill: University of North Carolina Press, 2017); Ansley T. Erickson, *Making the Unequal Metropolis: School Desegregation and Its Limits* (Chicago: University of Chicago Press, 2016); Hilary Green, *Educational Reconstruction: African American Schools in the Urban South, 1865–1890* (New York: Fordham University Press, 2016); Adah Ward Randolph, "Presidential Address: African American Education History—A Manifestation of Faith," *History of Education Quarterly* 54, no. 1 (2014), 1–18; Tracy E. K'Meyer, *From Brown to Meredith: The Long Struggle*

for School Desegregation in Louisville, Kentucky, 1954–2007 (Chapel Hill: University of North Carolina Press, 2013); Sarah Caroline Thuesen, *Greater Than Equal: African American Struggles for Schools and Citizenship in North Carolina, 1919–1965* (Chapel Hill: University of North Carolina Press, 2013); Jeffrey L. Littlejohn and Charles H. Ford, *Elusive Equality: Desegregation and Resegregation in Norfolk's Public Schools* (Charlottesville: University of Virginia Press, 2012); Ronald E. Butchart, *Schooling the Freed People: Teaching, Learning, and the Struggle for Black Freedom, 1861–1876* (Chapel Hill: University of North Carolina Press, 2010); Christopher M. Span, *From Cotton Field to Schoolhouse: African American Education in Mississippi, 1862–1875* (Chapel Hill: University of North Carolina Press, 2009); Adam Fairclough, *A Class of Their Own: Black Teachers in the Segregated South* (Cambridge, MA: Harvard University Press, 2007); Heather Andrea Williams, *Self-Taught: African American Education in Slavery and Freedom* (Chapel Hill: University of North Carolina Press, 2005); Adam Fairclough, *Teaching Equality: Black Schools in the Age of Jim Crow* (Athens: University of Georgia Press, 2001); Matthew D. Lassiter and Andrew B. Lewis, eds., *The Moderates' Dilemma: Massive Resistance to School Desegregation in Virginia* (Charlottesville: University Press of Virginia, 1998); Vanessa Siddle Walker, *To Their Highest Potential: An African American School Community in the Segregated South* (Chapel Hill: University of North Carolina Press, 1996); Davison M. Douglas, *Reading, Writing, and Race: The Desegregation of the Charlotte Schools* (Chapel Hill: University of North Carolina Press, 1995); David S. Cecelski, *Along Freedom Road: Hyde County, North Carolina and the Fate of Black Schools in the South* (Chapel Hill: University of North Carolina Press, 1994); Henry A. Bullock, *A History of Negro Education in the South: From 1619 to the Present* (Cambridge, MA: Harvard University Press, 1967); Horace Mann Bond, *The Education of the Negro in the American Social Order* (New York: Prentice Hall, 1934).

7. A selection of scholarship on the long history of struggles for educational equality in the North includes Kabria Baumgartner, *In Pursuit of Knowledge: Black Women and Educational Activism in Antebellum America* (New York: New York University Press, 2019); Ansley T. Erickson and Ernest Morrell, eds., *Educating Harlem: A Century of Schooling and Resistance in the Black Community* (New York: Columbia University Press, 2019); Elizabeth Todd-Breland, *A Political Education: Black Politics and Education Reform in Chicago since the 1960s* (Chapel Hill: University of North Carolina Press, 2018); Richard Rothstein, *The Color of Law: A Forgotten History of How Our Government Segregated America* (New York: W.W. Norton, 2017); Russell Rickford, *We Are an African People: Independent Education, Black Power, and the Radical Imagination* (New York: Oxford University Press, 2016); Dionne Danns, *Desegregating Chicago's Public Schools: Policy Implementation, Politics, and Protest, 1965–1985* (New York: Palgrave Macmillan, 2014); Heather Lewis, *New York City Schools from Brownsville to Bloomberg: Community Control and Its Legacy* (New York: Teachers College Press, 2013); Martha Biondi, *The Black Revolution on Campus* (Berkeley: University of California Press, 2013); Jonna Perrillo, *Uncivil Rights: Teachers, Unions, and Race in the Battle for School Equity* (Chicago: University of Chicago Press, 2012); Donna Jean Murch, *Living for the City: Migration, Education, and the Rise of the Black Panther Party in Oakland, California* (Chapel Hill: University of North Carolina Press, 2010); Hilary J. Moss, *Schooling Citizens: The Struggle for African American Education in Antebellum America* (Chicago: University of Chicago Press, 2009); Jack Dougherty, *More than One Struggle: The Evolution of Black School Reform in Milwaukee* (Chapel Hill: University of North Carolina Press, 2004); Jerald Podair, *The Strike that Changed New York: Blacks, Whites, and the Ocean-Hill Brownsville Crisis* (New Haven, CT: Yale University Press, 2002); Ronald P. Formisano, *Boston against Busing: Race, Class, and Ethnicity in the 1960s and 1970s* (Chapel Hill: University of North Carolina Press, 2001); Jeffrey E. Mirel, *The Rise and Fall of an Urban School System: Detroit, 1907–81*, 2nd ed. (Ann Arbor: University of Michigan Press, 1999); Clarence Taylor, *Knocking at Our Own Door: Milton A. Galamison and the Struggle to Integrate New York City's Schools* (New York: Columbia University Press, 1997); Vincent P. Franklin, *The Education of Black Philadelphia: The Social and Educational History of a Minority Community, 1900–1950* (Philadelphia: University of Pennsylvania Press, 1979). Notably, Davison M. Douglas's *Jim Crow Moves North: The Battle over Northern School Segregation, 1865–1954* (New York: Cambridge University Press, 2005), offers a regional history that explains the role of law in accomplishing racial change in the years preceding *Brown v. Board of Education*.

8. A selection of scholarship on the history of African American struggles for school de-
segregation includes Elizabeth Gillespie McRae, *Mothers of Massive Resistance: White
Women and the Politics of White Supremacy* (New York: Oxford University Press, 2018),
Matthew F. Delmont, *Why Busing Failed: Race, Media, and the National Resistance to School
Desegregation* (Oakland: University of California Press, 2016); Dionne Danns, Michelle A.
Purdy, and Christopher M. Span, eds., *Using the Past as Prologue: Contemporary Perspectives
on African American Educational History* (Charlotte: Information Age Publishing, 2015);
Joyce A. Baugh, *The Detroit School Busing Case: Milliken v. Bradley and the Controversy over
Desegregation* (Lawrence: University of Kansas Press, 2011); Mary L. Dudziak, *Cold War
Civil Rights: Race and the Image of American Democracy*, rev. ed. (Princeton, NJ: Princeton
University Press, 2011); Sonya Douglass Horsford, *Learning in a Burning House: Educational
Inequality, Ideology, and (Dis)Integration* (New York: Teachers College Press, 2011); Rawn
James Jr., *Root and Branch: Charles Hamilton Houston, Thurgood Marshall, and the Struggle to
End Segregation* (New York: Bloomsbury Press, 2010); James E. Ryan, *Five Miles Away and a
World Apart: One City, Two Schools, and the Story of Educational Opportunity in Modern America*
(New York: Oxford University Press, 2010); Paul R. Dimond, *Beyond Busing: Reflections
on Urban Segregation, the Courts, and Equal Opportunity*, rev. ed. (Ann Arbor: University of
Michigan Press, 2005), Michael Fultz, ed., "A Special Issue on the Fiftieth Anniversary of the
Brown v. Board of Education Decision," *History of Education Quarterly* 44, no. 1 (2004): 1–171;
"Round Table: *Brown v. Board of Education*, Fifty Years Later," *Journal of American History* 91,
no. 1 (2004): 19–173; James J. Patterson, *Brown v. Board of Education: A Civil Rights Milestone
and Its Troubled Legacy* (New York: Oxford University Press, 2001); David J. Armor, *Forced
Justice: School Desegregation and the Law* (New York: Oxford University Press, 1995); Derrick
Bell, *And We Are Not Saved: The Elusive Quest for Racial Justice* (New York: Basic Books, 1987);
Mark V. Tushnet, *The NAACP's Legal Strategy against Segregated Education, 1925–1950* (Chapel
Hill: University of North Carolina Press, 1987); Derrick Bell, *Shades of Brown: New Perspectives
on School Integration* (New York: Teachers College Press, 1980); J. Harvie Wilkinson III, *From
Brown to Bakke: The Supreme Court and School Integration, 1954–1978* (New York: Oxford
University Press, 1979), James D. Anderson and Vincent P. Franklin, *New Perspectives on Black
Educational History* (Boston: G. K. Hall, 1978).

9. A selection of scholarship on Black civil rights activism in the North includes Brian Purnell,
Jeanne Theoharis, and Komozi Woodard, *The Strange Careers of the Jim Crow North: Segregation
and Struggle outside of the South* (New York: New York University Press, 2019); Jason Sokol,
All Eyes Are upon Us: Race and Politics from Boston to Brooklyn (New York: Basic Books,
2014); Clarence Taylor, ed., *Civil Rights in New York City: From World War II to the Giuliani
Era* (New York: Fordham University Press, 2011); Mark Brilliant, *The Color of America
Has Changed: How Racial Diversity Shaped Civil Rights Reform in California, 1941–1978*
(New York: Oxford University Press, 2010); ; Thomas Sugrue, *Sweet Land of Liberty: The
Forgotten Struggle for Civil Rights in the North* (New York: Random House, 2008); Peniel
E. Joseph, *Waiting 'Til the Midnight Hour: A Narrative History of Black Power in America*
(New York: Henry Holt, 2006); Jacquelyn Dowd Hall, "The Long Civil Rights Movement
and the Political Uses of the Past," *Journal of American History* 91, no. 4 (2005): 1233–1263;
Jeanne Theoharis and Komozi Woodard, eds., *Freedom North: Black Freedom Struggles outside
the South, 1940–1980* (New York: Palgrave Macmillan, 2003). Case studies of civil rights ac-
tivism in cities outside the South include Mary Lou Finely, Bernard LaFayette Jr., James R.
Ralph Jr., and Pam Smith, eds., *The Chicago Freedom Movement: Martin Luther King Jr. and Civil
Rights Activism in the North* (Lexington: University of Press of Kentucky, 2016); Patrick D.
Jones, *The Selma of the North: Civil Rights Insurgency in Milwaukee* (Cambridge, MA: Harvard
University Press, 2010); Matthew Countryman, *Up South: Civil Rights and Black Power
in Philadelphia* (Philadelphia: University of Pennsylvania Press, 2006); Kevin Mumford,
Newark: A History of Race, Rights, and Riots in America (New York: New York University Press,
2007); Scott Kurashige, *The Shifting Grounds of Race: Black and Japanese Americans in the
Making of Multiethnic Los Angeles* (Princeton, NJ: Princeton University Press, 2010); Robert
O. Self, *American Babylon: Race and the Struggle for Postwar Oakland*, revised ed. (Princeton,
NJ: Princeton University Press, 2005); Martha Biondi, *To Stand and Fight: The Struggle for Civil
Rights in Postwar New York City* (Cambridge, MA: Harvard University Press, 2003).

10. Kevin Gaines, "Whose Integration Was It?," *Journal of American History* 91, no. 1 (2004): 19–25, quote on pp. 19–20. See also, Sonya Douglass Horsford, "Whose School Integration?" *Voices in Urban Education* 49, no. 1 (2019): 21–25.

11. Gunnar Myrdal, *An American Dilemma: The Negro Problem and Modern Democracy* (New York: Harper & Row, [1944] 1962), 100. See also Mark Newman, *Black Nationalism in American History: From the Nineteenth Century to the Million Man March* (Edinburgh: Edinburgh University Press, 2018); Ashley D. Farmer, *Remaking Black Power: How Black Women Transformed an Era* (Chapel Hill: University of North Carolina Press, 2017); Charles W. Mills, *Black Rights/White Wrongs: The Critique of Racial Liberalism* (New York: Oxford University Press, 2017); Tommie Shelby, *Dark Ghettos: Injustice, Dissent, and Reform* (Cambridge, MA: Harvard University Press, 2016); Manning Marable, *Race, Reform, and Rebellion: The Second Reconstruction and Beyond in Black America, 1945–2006*, 3rd ed. (Jackson: University Press of Mississippi, 2007); Derrick Bell, *Silent Covenants: Brown v. Board of Education and the Unfulfilled Hopes for Racial Reform* (New York: Oxford University Press, 2004); Roy L. Brooks, *Integration or Separation: A Strategy for Racial Equality* (Cambridge, MA: Harvard University Press, 1996); Kevin K. Gaines, *Uplifting the Race: Black Leadership, Politics, and Culture in the Twentieth Century* (Chapel Hill: University of North Carolina Press, 1996); Evelyn Brooks Higginbotham, *Righteous Discontent: The Women's Movement in the Black Baptist Church, 1880–1920*, rev. ed. (Cambridge, MA: Harvard University Press, 1994).

12. Erica Frankenberg, Jongyeon Ee, Jennifer B. Ayscue, and Gary Orfield, "Harming Our Common Future: America's Segregated Schools 65 Years after *Brown*." Report by the Civil Rights Project of the University of California, Los Angeles, May 10, 2019. See also Paul Tractenberg, Allison Roda, Ryan Coughlan, and Deirdre Dougherty, *Making School Integration Work: Lessons from Morris* (New York: Teachers College Press, 2020); Rucker C. Johnson with Alexander Nazaryan, *Children of the Dream: Why School Integration Works* (New York: Basic Books, 2019); Eve L. Ewing, *Ghosts in the Schoolyard: Racism and School Closings on Chicago's South Side* (Chicago: University of Chicago Press, 2018); Grover J. Whitehurst, Nathan Joo, Richard V. Reeves, and Edward Rodrigue, "Balancing Act: Schools, Neighborhoods and Racial Imbalance" (Washington, DC: Brookings Institution, 2017); Monique W. Morris, *Pushout: The Criminalization of Black Girls in Schools* (New York: New Press, 2016); US Government Accountability Office, "K-12 Education: Better Use of Information Could Help Agencies Identify Disparities and Address Racial Discrimination," GAO-16-345. Report to Congressional Requesters (Washington, DC: US Government Accountability Office, 2016); Kristi L. Bowman, ed., *The Pursuit of Racial and Ethnic Equality in American Public Schools: Mendez, Brown, and Beyond* (East Lansing, MI: Michigan State University Press, 2015); Amanda E. Lewis and John B. Diamond, *Despite the Best Intentions: How Racial Inequality Thrives in Good Schools* (New York: Oxford University Press, 2015); R. L'Heureux Lewis-McCoy, *Inequality in the Promised Land: Race, Resources, and Suburban Schooling* (Stanford, CA: Stanford University Press, 2014); Richard Rothstein, "Education and the Unfinished March: For Public Schools, Segregation Then, Segregation Since" (Washington, DC: Economic Policy Institute, 2013); US Department of Education, "For Each and Every Child: A Strategy for Education Equity and Excellence" (Washington, DC: Government Printing Office, 2013); Mica Pollock, *Because of Race: How Americans Debate Harm and Opportunity in Our Schools* (Princeton. NJ: Princeton University Press, 2008); James E. Ryan, *Five Miles Away, A World Apart: One City, Two Schools, and the Story of Educational Opportunity in America* (New York: Oxford University Press, 2010); Pedro A. Noguera, *The Trouble with Black Boys . . . And Other Reflections on Race, Equity, and the Future of Public Education* (San Francisco: John Wiley, 2008); Erica Frankenberg and Gary Orfield, eds., *Lessons in Integration: Realizing the Promise of Racial Diversity in American Schools* (Charlottesville: University of Virginia Press, 2007); Jonathan Kozol, *The Shame of the Nation: The Restoration of Apartheid Schooling in America* (New York: Random House, 2005); Charles T. Clotfelter, *After Brown: The Rise and Retreat of School Desegregation* (Princeton, NJ: Princeton University Press, 2004).

13. Lawrence R. Samuel, *The American Dream: A Cultural History* (Syracuse, NY: Syracuse University Press, 2012); Noguera, *The Trouble with Black Boys*; Jim Cullen, *The American Dream: A Short History of an Idea that Shaped a Nation* (New York: Oxford University Press,

2003); Pedro Noguera, *City Schools and the American Dream: Reclaiming the Promise of Public Education* (New York: Teachers College Press, 2003).

14. Myrdal, *An American Dilemma*. See also V. P. Franklin, "The Power to Define: African American Scholars, Activism, and Social Change, 1916–2015," *Journal of African American History* 100, no. 1 (2015): 1–25; Walter A. Jackson, *Gunnar Myrdal and America's Conscience: Social Engineering and Racial Liberalism, 1938–1987* (Chapel Hill: University of North Carolina Press, 1990); David W. Southern, *Gunnar Myrdal and Black-White Relations: The Use and Abuse of An American Dilemma, 1944–1969* (Baton Rouge: Louisiana State University Press, 1987); Herbert Aptheker, *The Negro People in America: A Critique of Gunnar Myrdal's An American Dilemma* (New York: International Publishers, 1946).

15. Bettina L. Love, *Abolitionist Teaching and the Pursuit of Educational Freedom* (Boston: Beacon Press, 2019); Charles M. Payne and Carol Sills Strickland, eds., *Teach Freedom: Education for Liberation in the African American Tradition* (New York: Teachers College Press, 2008); William H. Watkins, ed., *Black Protest Thought and Education* (New York: Peter Lang, 2005).

Chapter 1

1. "Equal Suffrage or Equal School Rights?" *Douglass' Monthly*, March 1859, 37. Emphasis in original. See also Isabel Wilkerson, *Caste: The Origins of Our Discontents* (New York: Random House, 2020); David W. Blight, *Frederick Douglass: Prophet of Freedom* (New York: Simon & Schuster, 2018); Nichols Buccola, *The Political Thought of Frederick Douglass: In Pursuit of American Liberty* (New York: New York University Press, 2012); Scott C. Williamson, *The Narrative Life: The Moral and Religious Life of Frederick Douglass* (Macon, GA: Mercer University Press, 2002), 136–137; "The Company of Books," *North Star*, February 4, 1848, 2.

2. "Letter to Rev. Samuel E. Cornish, Boston," *Freedom's Journal*, November 2, 1827. See also Martin E. Dann, ed., *The Black Press: The Quest for National Identity, 1827–1890* (New York: G. P. Putnam's Sons, 1971), 293–376; "African Free Schools," *Freedom's Journal*, June 1, 1827. On the connection between abolitionists and support for Black education in the North, see George Fishman, *The African American Struggle for Freedom and Equality: The Development of a People's Identity, New Jersey, 1624–1850* (New York: Garland, 1997), 229–233.

3. Manisha Sinha, *The Slave's Cause: A History of Abolition* (New Haven, CT: Yale University Press, 2016), 65–96; Ira Berlin, *The Long Emancipation: The Demise of Slavery in the United States* (Cambridge, MA: Harvard University Press, 2015); Patrick Rael, *Eighty-Eight Years: The Long Death of Slavery in the United States, 1777–1865* (Athens: University of Georgia Press, 2015), 163–97; David Brion Davis, *The Problem of Slavery in the Age of Emancipation* (New York: Alfred A. Knopf, 2014), xi–13; Hugh Davis, *We Shall Be Satisfied with Nothing Less: The African American Struggle for Equal Rights in the North during Reconstruction* (Ithaca, NY: Cornell University Press, 2011), 72–96; Hilary J. Moss, *Schooling Citizens: The Struggle for African American Education in Antebellum America* (Chicago: University of Chicago Press, 2009), 1–13; Patrick Rael, *Black Identity and Black Protest in the Antebellum North* (Chapel Hill: University of North Carolina Press, 2002), 1–5; Carleton Mabee, *Black Freedom: The Nonviolent Abolitionists from 1830 through the Civil War* (New York: Macmillan, 1970), 139–184; Leon Litwack, *North of Slavery: The Negro in the Free States, 1790–1860* (Chicago: University of Chicago Press, 1961), 113–152.

4. Ibram X. Kendi, *Stamped from the Beginning: The Definitive History of Racist Ideas in America* (New York: Nation Books, 2016), 161–262; George M. Fredrickson, *Racism: A Short History*, rev ed. (Princeton. NJ: Princeton University Press, 2015 [2002]), 49–96; Audrey Smedley and Brian D. Smedley, *Race in North America: Origin and Evolution of a Worldview*, 4th ed. (Boulder, CO: Westview Press, 2012), 189–250; Ann Gibson Winfield, *Eugenics and Education in America: Institutionalized Racism and the Implications of History, Ideology, and Memory* (New York: Peter Lang, 2007), 45–62; John P. Jackson Jr. and Nadine M. Weidman, *Race, Racism, and Science: Social Impact and Interaction* (New Brunswick, NJ: Rutgers University Press, 2006), 29–60; Thomas F. Gossett, *Race: The History of an Idea in America*, new ed. (New York: Oxford University Press, 1997 [1963]), 54–83, 144–175, 253–386; Daryl Michael Scott, *Contempt and Pity: Social Policy and the Image of the Damaged Black Psyche, 1880–1996* (Chapel Hill: University of North Carolina Press, 1997), 1–18.

5. Leon F. Litwack, "The Emancipation of the Negro Abolitionist," in Patrick Rael, ed., *African American Activism before the Civil War: The Freedom Struggle in the Antebellum North* (New York: Routledge, 2008), 39–49; "From the Boston Olive Branch, Amalgamation Schools," *Liberator*, August 28, 1846; "Amalgamation," *Evening Post*, May 1, 1857; "Extracts from the Majority Report on the Caste Schools," *Liberator*, August 21, 1846.

6. Alexis de Tocqueville, *Democracy in America*, edited by J. P. Mayer (New York: Harper Perennial, 1988 [1835]), 343; W. E. B. Du Bois, *The Philadelphia Negro: A Social Study* (New York: Benjamin Blom, 1967 [1899]), 25–26.

7. Natasha Kohl, "Frank Webb's '*The Garies and Their Friends*' and the Struggle over Black Education in the Antebellum North," *Society for the Study of Multi-Ethnic Literature in the United States* (MELUS) 38, no. 4 (2013): 76–102; Kenneth L. Kusmer, *A Ghetto Takes Shape: Black Cleveland, 1870–1930* (Urbana: University of Illinois Press, 1976), 5; *Enos Van Camp v. The Board of Education of the Incorporated Village of Logan*. 9 Ohio St. S. Ct. 406 (1859). Ohio LEXIS 206; "Schools for Colored Children," *Liberator*, June 2, 1832. The text of the editorial from *New Jersey Freeman*, August 4, 1849, is reproduced in George Fishman, "New Jersey's Abolition Voice and the Negro—A Documentary Excerpt," *Negro History Bulletin* 31, no. 1 (18–19).

8. Kabria Baumgartner, "Love and Justice: African American Women, Education, and Protest in Antebellum New England," *Journal of Social History* 52, no. 3 (2019), 652-76; Hilary J. Moss, *Schooling Citizens*, 1–3; Edmund Fuller, *Prudence Crandall: An Incident of Racism in Nineteenth Century Connecticut* (Middletown, CT: Wesleyan University Press, 1971); Litwack, *North of Slavery*, 123–131; J. Holland Townsend, "American Caste and Common Schools," *Anglo-African Magazine* 1, no. 2 (February 1859): 80–83; "Exposition of Affairs Connected with Noyes Academy," *Liberator*, October 3, 1835; "Colored School at Canaan," *Liberator*, September 5, 1835; "Noyes Academy," *Liberator*, February 28, 1835; "Prudence Crandall's Trial," *Liberator*, November 15, 1834; "Miss Crandall's School Abandoned," *Liberator*, September 20, 1834; "Miss Crandall's School," *Liberator*, April 5, 1834; "Miss Crandall Has Been Convicted of Teaching Colored Children," *Liberator*, October 26, 1833; "Trial of Miss Crandall," *Liberator*, August 31, 1833; "Savage Barbarity! Miss Crandall Imprisoned," *Liberator*, July 6, 1833; "Institution for Colored Females: Miss Prudence Crandall," *Liberator*, April 6, 1833.

9. "The Education of the People: The Speech of Wendell Phillips, Esq.," *Liberator*, March 18, 1859; William C. Nell, "Equal School Rights for Colored Children," *Liberator*, February 20, 1857; "School for Colored Children," *Liberator*, June 2, 1832.

10. Davison M. Douglas, *Jim Crow Moves North: The Battle over Northern School Segregation, 1865–1954* (New York: Cambridge University Press, 2005), 12–60; Carleton Mabee, *Black Education in New York State: From Colonial to Modern Times* (Syracuse, NY: Syracuse University Press, 1979), 234; Horace Mann Bond, *The Education of the Negro in the American Social Order* (New York: Octagon Books, 1970 [1934]), 367–390; US Office of Education, *History of Schools for the Colored Population* (New York: Arno Press, 1969 [1871]), 301–400; Carter G. Woodson, *The Education of the Negro Prior to 1861*, 2nd ed. (New York: Arno Press, 1968 [1919]), 229–255. For the "monuments of their own degradation," quote, see Arthur O. White, "Antebellum School Reform in Boston: Integrationists and Separatists," *Phylon* 34, no. 2 (1973): 203–217, quote on p. 215.

11. Katie D. Chapman, "Mixed Schools," *Christian Recorder*, May 24, 1888; Thomas Paul Smith, "The Smith School," *Liberator*, February 15, 1850.

12. Harry C. Sicox, "Delay and Neglect: Negro Public Education in Antebellum Philadelphia, 1800–1860," *Pennsylvania Magazine of History and Biography* 97, no. 4 (1973): 444–464. In Folder 17, Box 3, Allen Ballard Collection, Charles L. Blockson Afro-American Collection, Temple University, Philadelphia, PA; Litwack, *North of Slavery*, 136-43; Woodson, *The Education of the Negro Prior to 1861*, 322–327.

13. Roy E. Finkenbine, "Boston's Black Churches: Institutional Centers of the Antislavery Movement," in Donald M. Jacobs, ed., *Courage and Conscience: Black and White Abolitionists in Boston* (Bloomington: Indiana University Press, 1993), 169–190; George A. Levesque, "White Bureaucracy, Black Community: The Contest over Local Control of Education in Antebellum Boston," *Journal of Educational Thought* 11, no. 2 (1977): 140–155.

14. Moss, *Schooling Citizens*, 1–13; Joyce A. Baugh, *The Detroit School Busing Case: Milliken v. Bradley and the Controversy over Desegregation* (Lawrence: University Press of Kansas, 2011), 57–59; Douglas, *Jim Crow Moves North*, 31–44; Steve Golin, *The Newark Teachers Strike: Hopes on the Line* (New Brunswick, NJ: Rutgers University Press, 2002), 42–43; Jack Washington, *In Search of a Community's Past: The Story of the Black Community of Trenton, New Jersey, 1860–1900* (Trenton, NJ: Africa World Press, 1990), 44–59; Giles R. Wright, *Afro-Americans in New Jersey: A Short History* (Trenton: New Jersey Historical Commission, 1988), 30–34; Carl F. Kaestle, *Pillars of the Republic: Common Schools and American Society, 1780–1860* (New York: Hill and Wang, 1983), 38–39, 171–179; Glenn Weaver, *Hartford: An Illustrated History of Connecticut's Capital* (Woodland Hills, CA: Windsor Publications, 1982), 91–92; David M. Katzman, *Before the Ghetto: Black Detroit in the Nineteenth Century* (Urbana: University of Illinois Press, 1973), 22–25, 50, 84–90; William M. Phillips Jr., *Participation of the Black Community in Selected Aspects of Educational Institutions of Newark* (New Brunswick: Rutgers University Press, 1973); John R. Anderson, "Negro Education in the Public Schools of Newark, New Jersey, during the Nineteenth Century," EdD diss., Rutgers University, 1972; Raymond B. Marcin, "Nineteenth Century De Jure School Segregation in Connecticut," *Connecticut Bar Journal*, 45 (1972): 394–400; Litwack, *North of Slavery*, 121–123; Marion T. Wright, "Mr. Baxter's School," *Proceedings of New Jersey Historical Society*, no. 224 (April 1, 1941): 116–133. Faculty Reprints, Digital Howard, Howard University. http://dh.howard.edu/reprints/224; US Office of Education, *History of Schools for the Colored Population*, 361–367, 370–383.

15. Paul J. Polgar, "'To Raise Them to an Equal Participation': Early National Abolitionism, Gradual Emancipation, and the Promise of African American Citizenship," *Journal of the Early Republic* 31, no. 2 (2011): 229–258; Moss, *Schooling Citizens*, 10–11; James Brewer Stewart, "The Emergence of Racial Modernity and the Rise of the White North, 1790–1840," in Patrick Real, ed., *African American Activism before the Civil War: The Freedom Struggle in the Antebellum North* (New York: Routledge, 2008), 220–249; Douglas, *Jim Crow Moves North*, 20–31; David Brion Davis, *The Problem of Slavery in the Age of Revolution, 1770–1823*, 2nd ed. (New York: Oxford University Press, 1999 [1975]), 15–21; William M. Banks, *Black Intellectuals: Race and Responsibility in American Life* (New York: W.W. Norton, 1996), 25–28; John L. Rury, "The New York African Free School, 1827–1836: Conflict over Community Control of Black Education," *Phylon* 44, no. 3 (1983): 187–197; Gilbert Osofsky, *Harlem: The Making of a Ghetto* (New York: Harper & Row, 1966), 10–11; Horace Bushnell, Leonard Kennedy Jr., and J. S. Eaton, "Common Schools in Cities," *Connecticut Common School Journal* 4, no. 1 (1841): 5–18.

16. "Colonization and Abolition," *Daily Courant*, August 8, 1839, 2. See also David Brion Davis, *The Problem of Slavery in the Age of Emancipation* (New York: Alfred A. Knopf, 2014), 105–125; Kohl, "Frank Webb's 'The Garies and Their Friends'"; Beverly C. Tomek, *Colonization and Its Discontents: Emancipation, Emigration, and Antislavery in Antebellum Pennsylvania* (New York: New York University Press, 2011); Nicholas Guyatt, "'The Outskirts of Our Happiness': Race and the Lure of Colonization in the Early Republic," *Journal of American History* 95, no. 4 (2009): 986–1011; Lamin O. Sanneh, *Abolitionists Abroad: American Blacks and the Making of Modern West Africa* (Cambridge, MA: Harvard University Press, 2006); Eric Burin, *Slavery and the Peculiar Solution: A History of the American Colonization Society* (Gainesville: University Press of Florida, 2005); Kenneth C. Barnes, *Journey of Hope: The Back-to-Africa Movement in Arkansas in the Late 1800s* (Chapel Hill: University of North Carolina Press, 2004); James Oliver Horton and Lois E. Horton, *In Hope of Liberty: Culture, Community, and Protest among Northern Free Blacks, 1700–1860* (New York: Oxford University Press, 1997), 177–202.

17. James Brewer Stewart, "Boston, Abolition, and the Atlantic World," in Donald M. Jacobs, ed., *Courage and Conscience: Black and White Abolitionists in Boston* (Bloomington: Indiana University Press, 1993), 101–125; Carleton Mabee, *Black Freedom: The Nonviolent Abolitionists from 1830 through the Civil War* (New York: Macmillan, 1970), 1–6; "The American Colonization Society," *North Star*, March 24, 1848, 2; "Henry Clay and African Colonization," *North Star*, February 11, 1848, 1; "Colonization," *Colored American*, January 12, 1839; "Great Anti-Colonization Meeting," *Colored American*, January 12, 1839; "Colonization," *Liberator*,

January 15, 1831; "The Colonization Society," *Freedom's Journal*, December 19, 1828; "African Colonization," *Freedom's Journal*, December 21, 1827. On Black support for colonization, see "Colonization," *Freedom's Journal*, March 14, 1829; "Our Vindication: The Change in Our Views on Colonization," *Freedom's Journal*, March 7, 1829.

18. Mabee, *Black Freedom*, 91–184.

19. Dorothy Porter Wesley, "Integration versus Separatism: William Cooper Nell's Role in the Struggle for Equality," in Donald M. Jacobs, ed., *Courage and Conscience: Black and White Abolitionists in Boston* (Bloomington: Indiana University Press, 1993), 207–224; James Oliver Horton, "Generations of Protest: Black Families and Social Reform in Ante-Bellum Boston," *New England Quarterly* 49, no. 2 (1976): 242–256; William C. Nell, "Equal School Rights," *Liberator*, April 7, 1854, 55.

20. Moss, *Schooling Citizens*, 152–159; Leonard W. Levy and Douglas L. Jones, eds., *Jim Crow in Boston: The Origin of the Separate but Equal Doctrine* (New York: Da Capo Press, 1974), vii–xxxvii; Arthur O. White, "Antebellum School Reform in Boston: Integrationists and Separatists," *Phylon* 43, no. 2 (1973): 203–217; Carleton Mabee, "A Negro Boycott to Integrate the Schools," *New England Quarterly* 41, no. 3 (1968): 341–361; Charles H. Wesley, "The Negro's Struggle for Freedom in Its Birthplace," *Journal of Negro History* 30, no. 1 (1945): 62–81.

21. Richard Fletcher, "Rights of Colored Citizens," *Liberator*, July 12, 1844; Clarkson, "The Colored School," *Liberator*, July 5, 1844; "Meeting of Colored Citizens," *Boston Courier*, July 1, 1844, 1; "The Smith School," *Liberator*, June 28, 1844; "Report," *Liberator*, June 28, 1844; "At a Meeting of the Colored Citizens of Boston," *Liberator*, June 28, 1844. "Smith School," *Daily Atlas*, May 21, 1844, 2; "Charges against a Schoolmaster," *Boston Evening Transcript*, May 15, 1844, 2.

22. "The Colored Report and Mr. Forbes," *Boston Courier*, August 1, 1844, 1. Emphasis in original. For the quote from the *Olive Branch*, see "The Schools for Colored Children," *Boston Courier*, July 10, 1845, 4. See also "Smith School," *Boston Daily Atlas*, August 2, 1844, 2; "Smith School," *Boston Daily Atlas*, May 21, 1844, 2; A similar attack on the Black community was published by the *Boston Olive Branch* and republished in the *Liberator* as evidence of the racist defense of segregated schools. See also "The Injudicious Movement of the Colored Citizens," *Liberator*, July 19, 1844, 1, and "The Smith School," *Liberator*, July 19, 1844, 1.

23. Mabee, "A Negro Boycott to Integrate the Schools"; William C. Nell, *Colored Patriots of the American Revolution* (Boston: Robert F. Wallcut, 1855), 112–113. Documents Relating to 1855. Gilder Lehrman Institute of American History, New York. GLC06132;*Reports of the Annual Visiting Committees of the Public Schools of the City of Boston, Documents of the City of Boston for the Year 1845* (Cambridge. MA: Metcalf & Co., 1846), 22; "Meeting of the Primary School Committee," *Emancipator*, July 8, 1846, 43; "Intolerance of the Primary School Committee," *Liberator*, June 27, 1845; "Meeting of the Primary School Committee," *Liberator*, June 27, 1845; "Meeting of the Primary School Committee," *Emancipator and Weekly Chronicle*, June 25, 1845, 33; "Interesting Discussion," *Emancipator and Weekly Chronicle*, June 18, 1845, 30.

24. Petition, by George Putnam, To the Primary School Committee of the City of Boston, June 15, 1846, in William Crowell, Joseph W. Ingraham, and David Kimball, *Report of the Primary School Committee on the Petition of Sundry Colored Persons for the Abolition of the Schools for Colored Children with the City Solicitor's Opinion.* City Document No. 23 (Boston: J. H. Eastburn, 1846), inside cover. Signed by eighty-five people. See also "Opinion of the City Solicitor on the Colored Schools and the Remarks of Wendell Phillips upon It," *Liberator*, August 28, 1846; "Separate Schools for Colored Children," *Liberator*, July 17, 1846.

25. John Stauffer, *The Black Hearts of Men: Radical Abolitionists and the Transformation of Race* (Cambridge, MA: Harvard University Press, 2001); Scott Hancock, "The Elusive Boundaries of Blackness: Identity Formation in Antebellum Boston," *Journal of Negro History* 84, no. 2 (1999): 115–129.

26. Crowell, Ingraham, and Kimball, *Report of the Primary School Committee*, 1846, 7. Emphasis in original.

27. Edmund Jackson and H. I. Bowditch, *Report of the Minority of the Committee of the Primary School Board on the Caste Schools of the City of Boston with Some Remarks on the City Solicitor's*

Opinion (Boston: A. J. Wright's Steam Press, 1846), 13; see also, Mabee, "A Negro Boycott to Integrate the Schools."

28. "Smith School," *Liberator*, September 4, 1846; "Extracts from the Majority Report on the Caste Schools," *Liberator*, August 21, 1846; "Minority Report," *Liberator*, August 21, 1846; "The Caste Schools," *Liberator*, August 21, 1846; "Report of a Committee of Parents and Others Interested in the Smith School, in Boston," *Boston Daily Atlas*, July 25, 1844, 1. An article in support of the Majority Report, originally published in the *Boston Olive Branch*, was printed in the *Liberator* as evidence of white animosity and open racism against the school integration movement, see "Amalgamation Schools," *Liberator*, August 28, 1846.

29. Crowell, Ingraham, and Kimball, *Report to the Primary School Committee*, 1846, 20, 38.

30. *Report of the Annual Examination of the Public Schools* (Boston, 1848): 66; (1849): 55, as cited in Mabee, "A Negro Boycott to Integrate the Schools," 347.

31. Mabee, "A Negro Boycott to Integrate the Schools," 341–361; "The Smith School," *Boston Daily Atlas*, August 15, 1849, 2; Peter Smith and Alexander Taylor, "To the Committee on the Smith School, Boston, August 10, 1848," in *Boston School Committee: Miscellaneous Papers*, 1848.

32. Jonas W. Clark, "Petition of the Colored People to the School Committee of the City of Boston," July 1849. Reproduced in Andrew Bigelow, Sampson Reed, Horace Dupree, and Edward Beecher, *Report of a Special Committee of the Grammar School Board on the Petition of Sundry Colored Persons Praying for the Abolition of the Smith School*. August 29, 1849. City Document No. 42 (Boston: J. H. Eastburn, 1849): 4–5. Originally submitted with 227 signatures, but the School Committee eliminated some of them and accepted only 202 signatures. There was also a separate integrationist petition signed by thirty-eight Black schoolchildren; see pp. 8–10, especially footnotes p. 10. Emphasis in original. See also "Manly Action: Freemen Defending Their Rights," *Pennsylvania Freeman*, August 23, 1849, 2; "Meeting of Colored Citizens: Appeal of the Colored People," *Liberator*, August 10, 1849; "Exclusive Schools," *Daily Evening Transcript*, August 8, 1849, 2.

33. White, "Antebellum School Reform in Boston," 208.

34. Bigelow, Reed, Dupree, and Beecher, *Report of a Special Committee*, 24–48.

35. Bigelow, Reed, Dupree, and Beecher, *Report of a Special Committee*, 24–48. The separatist argument was made by Thomas Paul Smith, who testified at the hearing and earned the praise of the School Committee for his "eloquence and manly bearing," p. 48. See also "Vindication," *Liberator*, October 25, 1849; "City Intelligence: Grammar School Committee," *Boston Courier*, August 30, 1849, 2; "Local Intelligence: The Smith School," *Boston Daily Atlas*, August 13, 1849, 2.

36. Bigelow, Reed, Dupree, and Beecher, *Report of a Special Committee*, 7–12.

37. Joseph M. Wightman, Esq., Chairman of the Executive Committee of the Primary School Board, to Rev. Dr. Andrew Bigelow, August 6, 1849, in Appendix of the *Majority Report of a Special Committee*, 1849, 66–67. A collection of letters of recommendation relating to Thomas Paul's scholarly and professional work can be found in the Appendix of the *Majority Report of a Special Committee*, 1849, 64–68. See also Charles T. Russell, *Report of the Minority of the Committee upon the Petitions of John T. Hilton and Others* (Boston: J. H. Eastburn, 1849).

38. Robert Johnson, Chairman of the Committee, in "On the Subject of Gal," *Liberator*, September 7, 1849.

39. "From the Liberator," *North Star*, September 14, 1849; Robert Johnson, William C. Nell, and Isaac M., Secretaries, "On the Subject of Gal," *Liberator*, September 7, 1849.

40. John H. Roberts, "On the Subject of Gal," *Liberator*, September 7, 1849. See also "Colored Schools: Boston School Report," *Liberator*, December 21, 1849; "Report on the Smith School," *Liberator*, November 16, 1849; "Riotous Proceedings," *Boston Daily Atlas*, September 19, 1849, 2; "The Smith School," *Liberator*, September 14, 1849. Black activists in Danvers, Massachusetts, sent a letter of support to Boston's school integrationists; see Daniel Foster, "The Smith School," *Liberator*, November 9, 1849.

41. "Meeting of the Colored Citizens of Boston: On the Subject of Equal School Rights," *Liberator*, September 7, 1849; "On the Subject of Gal," *Liberator*, September 7, 1849; "Meeting of the Colored Citizens: Appeal of the Colored People," *Liberator*, August 10, 1849; "Great and Enthusiastic Meeting," *Liberator*, May 11, 1849. For a description of the renovations made

to the Smith School that summer, which totaled more than $2,000, see *Report of a Special Committee of the Grammar School Board*, 1849, pp. 13–14.

42. William C. Nell, "The Smith School," *Liberator*, September 21, 1849; "Meeting of the Colored Citizens of Boston on the Subject of Equal School Rights," *North Star*, September 14, 1849; "The Smith School," *Liberator*, September 14, 1849; "Meeting of Boston on the Subject of Gal," *Liberator*, September 7, 1849; *Report of a Special Committee of the Grammar School Board on the Petition of Sundry Colored Persons Praying for the Abolition of the Smith School* (J. H. Eastburn: Boston, 1840): postscript to the Appendix, pp. 70–71; "Great and Enthusiastic Meeting," *Liberator*, May 11, 1849;

43. "The Smith School," *Liberator*, September 21, 1849, 3, 4; "All Sorts of Paragraphs," *Boston Post*, September 19, 1849, 2. See also Scott Hancock, "The Elusive Boundaries of Blackness: Identity Formation in Antebellum Boston," *Journal of Negro History* 84, no. 2 (1999): 115–129; Mabee, "A Negro Boycott to Integrate the Schools."

44. Hilary J. Moss, "The Tarring and Feathering of Thomas Paul Smith: Common Schools, Revolutionary Memory, and the Crisis of Black Citizenship in Antebellum Boston," *New England Quarterly* 80, no. 2 (2007): 218–241; James Oliver Horton and Lois E. Horton, "The Affirmation of Manhood: Black Garrisonians in Antebellum Boston," in Donald M. Jacobs, ed., *Courage and Conscience: Black and White Abolitionists in Boston* (Bloomington: Indiana University Press, 1993) 127–154; Herbert Aptheker, ed., *A Documentary History of the Negro People in the United States* (New York: Citadel Press, 1951), 19–20; "Affairs in and around the City," *Boston Daily Atlas*, July 22, 1851, 2; "Boston," *Daily Missouri Republican*, May 21, 1851, 3; "Gross Outrage," [Middletown, CT] *Constitution*, May 21, 1851, 2; "The Bold Assault upon Thomas Paul Smith," *Boston Post*, May 10, 1851, 2; "A Color of a Riot," *Daily Evening Transcript*, September 18, 1849, 2.

45. George Levesque, "Before Integration: The Forgotten Years of Jim Crow Education in Boston," *Journal of Negro Education* 48, no. 2 (1979): 113–125; George A. Levesque, "White Bureaucracy, Black Community: The Contest over Local Control of Education in Antebellum Boston," *Journal of Educational Thought* 11, no. 2 (1977): 140–155; David M. Ment, "Racial Segregation in the Public Schools of New England and New York, 1840–1940," PhD diss. Columbia University, 1975; Donald M. Jacobs, "The Nineteenth Century Struggle over Segregated Education in the Boston Schools," *Journal of Negro Education* 39, no. 1 (1970): 76–85.

46. Benjamin F. Roberts, "Our Progress in the Old Bay State," *New Era*, March 31, 1870.

47. Charles Sumner, "Equality before the Law: Unconstitutionality of Separate Colored Schools in Massachusetts. Argument before the Supreme Court of Massachusetts, in the Case of *Sarah C. Roberts v. The City of Boston*, December 4, 1849. Reproduced in Levy and Jones, *Jim Crow in Boston*, 217–232. Emphasis in original. See also "Supreme Judicial Court: Sarah Roberts vs. The City of Boston," *Liberator*, April 26, 1850; "We Have No Time for Comment on the Following Unchristian Decision," *Pennsylvania Freeman*, April 11, 1850, 3; "Argument," *North Star*, March 22, 1850; "Argument," *North Star*, February 22, 1850; William C. Nell, "Equal School Rights," *Liberator*, February 8, 1850; "Argument," *North Star*, February 1, 1850; "Constitutionality of Separate Colored Schools," *Liberator*, February 1, 1850; "Constitutionality of Separate Colored Schools," *Liberator*, January 11, 1850; "Constitutionality of Separate Colored Schools," *Liberator*, December 28, 1849; "Argument of Charles Sumner, Esq. against the Constitutionality of Separate Colored Schools," *Emancipator and Republican*, December 20, 1849, 1.

48. *Sarah C. Roberts v. The City of Boston* 5 Cush. 198 (1849).

49. George R. Price and James Brewer Stewart, "The *Roberts* Case, the Easton Family, and the Dynamics of the Abolitionist Movement in Massachusetts, 1776–1870," *Massachusetts Historical Review* 4 (2002): 89–115; James Oliver Horton and Michele Gates Moresi, "Roberts, Plessy, and Brown: The Long, Hard Struggle against Segregation," *OAH Magazine of History* 15, no. 2 (2001): 14–16; Leonard W. Levy and Harlan B. Philips, "The *Roberts* Case: Source of the Separate but Equal Doctrine," *American Historical Review* 56, no. 3 (1951): 510–18.

50. "Colored Schools," *North Star*, August 17, 1849. See also "Equal School Rights," *Frederick Douglass' Paper*, April 13, 1855; "Equal School Rights—The Smith School," *Liberator*, August 18, 1854; William C. Nell, "Equal School Rights," *Liberator*, April 7, 1854; "Disgraceful,"

Liberator, October 7, 1853; "Frederick Douglas in Boston," *Frederick Douglass' Paper*, August 12, 1853; "Equal School Privileges," *Liberator*, April 4, 1851; "Separate School System," *North Star*, April 26, 1850; "Colored School Meeting," *North Star*, December 21, 1849. "Meeting against the Colored Schools," *North Star*, December 21, 1849.

51. Lucy N. Colman, *Reminiscences* (Buffalo: H. L. Green, 1891); "Colored Schools: Report," *North Star*, August 17, 1849, 1. See also Mabee, *Black Education in New York* State, 183–187; Carleton Mabee, "Control by Blacks over Schools in New York State," *Phylon* 40, no. 1 (1979): 29–40; Judith Polgar Ruchkin, "The Abolition of 'Colored Schools' in Rochester, New York, 1832–1856," *New York History* 51, no. 4 (1970): 376–393.

52. *The General Statutes of the Commonwealth of Massachusetts, 1855*, Chapter 256, Section 1. See also Wesley, "Integration versus Separation," 211–212; Donald Jacobs, "The Nineteenth Century Struggle over Segregated Education in the Boston Schools," *Journal of Negro Education* 39, no. 1 (1970): 76–85; "Abolition of the Smith and All Other Separate Colored Schools," *Liberator*, September 14, 1855; "Abolition of Caste Schools," *Liberator*, August 31, 1855; "Colored Schools," *Liberator*, February 15, 1850.

53. "Meeting of Colored Citizens: Presentation to Mr. William C. Nell for His Efforts on Behalf of Equal School Rights," *Liberator*, December 28, 1855. Emphasis in original. Kabria Baumgartner, *In Pursuit of Knowledge: Black Women and Educational Activism in Antebellum America*. (New York: New York University Press, 2019), 142-176.

54. "Abolition of Caste Schools."

55. "Meeting of Colored Citizens: Presentation to Mr. William C. Nell for His Efforts on Behalf of Equal School Rights."

56. Edward E. Baptiste, *The Half Has Never Been Told: Slavery and the Making of American Capitalism* (New York: Basic Books, 2014), 343–397; Angela F. Murphy, *The Jerry Rescue: The Fugitive Slave Law, Northern Rights, and the American Sectional Crisis* (New York: Oxford University Press, 2014); Steven Lubat, *Fugitive Justice: Runaways, Rescuers, and Slavery on Trial* (New York: Belknap Press, 2010); Earl M. Maltz, *Fugitive Slave on Trial: The Anthony Burns Case and Abolitionist Outrage* (Lawrence: University Press of Kansas, 2010); Mark A. Graber, *Dred Scott and the Problem of Constitutional Evil* (New York: Cambridge University Press, 2006); Don E. Fehrenbacher, *The Dred Scott Case: Its Significance in American Law and Politics*, 1st paperback ed. (New York: Oxford University Press, 2001); Horton and Horton, *In Hope of Liberty*, 252–268; Litwack, *North of Slavery*, 247–280. See also *Dred Scott v. John F. A. Sanford* 60 U.S. 393 (1857).

57. Robert L. McCaul, *The Black Struggle for Public Schooling in Nineteenth Century Illinois* (Carbondale: Southern Illinois University Press, 1987), 55–72; David M. Katzman, *Before the Ghetto: Black Detroit in the Nineteenth Century* (Urbana: University of Illinois Press, 1973), 22–25, 50, 84–90; Allan H. Spear, *Black Chicago: The Making of a Negro Ghetto* (Chicago: University of Chicago Press, 1967), 53–55; "Equal School Rights, Providence," *Liberator*, March 10, 1865; "A Colored School," *Chicago Tribune*, April 1, 1864, 4; "The Colored School Question in Providence," *Liberator*, March 11, 1864; "Meeting of the Board of Education," *Chicago Tribune*, June 10, 1863, 4; "Special Meeting of the Board of Education," *Chicago Tribune*, May 9, 1863, 4; D. B. H., "Colored Children in the Providence Schools," *Liberator*, September 6, 1861; "Special Meeting of the School Committee," *Liberator*, January 29, 1858; William C. Nell, "Equal School Rights in Rhode Island," *Liberator*, December 11, 1857.

58. Mabee, *Black Education in New York State*, 98–100; Vincent P. Franklin, *The Education of Black Philadelphia: The Social and Educational History of a Minority Community* (Philadelphia: University of Pennsylvania Press, 1979), 33–34; Judy Jolley Mohraz, *The Separate Problem: Case Studies of Black Education in the North, 1900-1930* (Westport, CT: Greenwood Press, 1979), 85–107; "Negroes in Trigonometry and the Classics," *New-York Tribune*, November 13, 1866, 4.

59. Douglas, *Jim Crow Moves North*, 31–61. See also Stephen Middleton, *The Black Laws in the Old Northwest: A Documentary History* (Westport, CT: Greenwood Press, 1993); V. Jacque Voegeli, *Free but Not Equal: The Midwest and the Negro during the Civil War* (Chicago: University of Chicago Press, 1970), 2; Kusmer, *A Ghetto Takes Shape*, 5, 17, and 27.

60. *Proceedings of the National Convention of Colored Men Held in the City of Syracuse, NY October 4, 5, 6, and 7, 1864 with the Bill of Wrongs and Rights and the Address to the American People* (Boston: J. S. Rock and George L. Ruffin, 1864), 9. See also Larry E. Nelson, "Black Leaders and the Presidential Election of 1864," *Journal of Negro History* 63, no. 1 (1978): 42–58; Elsie M. Lewis, "The Political Mind of the Negro, 1865–1900," *Journal of Southern History* 21, no. 2 (1955): 189–202; "National Equal Rights League," *Christian Recorder*, December 10, 1864; "National Convention of Colored Men in America," *Christian Recorder*, October 15, 1864; "The National Convention of Colored Men," *Liberator*, October 14, 1864; "The National Convention of Colored Men," *Christian Recorder*, October 1, 1864.

61. Garrett Epps, *Democracy Reborn: The Fourteenth Amendment and the Fight for Equal Rights in Post–Civil War America* (New York: Henry Holt, 2006), 124–263; Douglas, *Jim Crow Moves North*, 62–65; James M. McPherson, "Abolitionists and the Civil Rights Act of 1875," *Journal of American History* 52, no. 3 (1965): 493–510.

62. Hugh Davis, *We Will Be Satisfied with Nothing Less: The African American Struggle for Equal Rights in the North during Reconstruction* (Ithaca, NY: Cornell University Press, 2011), 72–96; Douglas, *Jim Crow Moves North*, 68–83; Ena L. Farley, *The Underside of Reconstruction in New York: The Struggle over the Issue of Black Equality* (New York: Garland, 1993), 121–140; Katzman, *Before the Ghetto*, 84–90; "Julius C. Burrows," *Inter Ocean*, February 13, 1875, 5; "Mixed Schools: The War between Equality and Caste Must Be Fought in the Public Schools," *Inter Ocean*, January 23, 1875, 2; "The Negro Question Again: Problem of Mixed Schools," *Indianapolis Sentinel*, November 26, 1874, 6; "Mixed Schools," *Trenton State Gazette*, May 27, 1874, 2; "Brooklyn Board of Education," *New York Times*, October 8, 1873, 2; "White and Colored Schools," *New Hampshire Patriot*, July 16, 1873, 2; "Emancipation," *New York Herald*, May 16, 1873, 3; "Civil Rights in Newburg," *New York Herald*, May 5, 1873, 10; "Colored Children in the Public Schools," *New York Times*, November 30, 1872, 1; "The West: The Admission of Colored Children in White Schools," *Hartford Daily Courant*, May 8, 1872, 3; "Mixed Schools," *Leavenworth Bulletin*, February 25, 1871, 2; "Colored Children and the Common Schools," *Hartford Daily Courant*, August 1, 1868, 1; "Colored Schools," *New-York Tribune*, June 11, 1866, 4.

63. W. E. B. Du Bois, "Two Hundred Years of Segregated Schools [1955]," in Eugene F. Provenzo Jr., ed., *DuBois on Education* (New York: AltaMira Press, 2002), 157–160, quote on p. 158; Nell Irvin Painter, *Exodusters: Black Migration to Kansas after Reconstruction* (New York: Alfred A. Knopf, 1977), 49.

64. Katzman, *Before the Ghetto*, 84–90, 167–168.

65. Ferdinand L. Barnett, "Race Unity: Its Importance and Necessity: Causes Which Retard Its Development: How It May Be Secured: Our Plain Duty," *Proceedings of the National Conference of Colored Men of the United States* (Washington, DC, 1879), 85.

66. "The Color Line in Ohio," *Atlanta Constitution*, February 10, 1894, 4; "A Mixed School Experiment," *Atlanta Constitution*, February 18, 1889, 1; "The Color Line: Discord in the Town of Felicity," *San Francisco Chronicle*, December 4, 1888, 1; "Ohio's Color Line: School Boards Having Great Trouble in Mixing the Races," *Atlanta Constitution*, September 22, 1887, 1; "The Schools in Ohio," *Atlanta Constitution*, September 22, 1887, 4.

67. Douglas, *Jim Crow Moves North*, 110–122; Roger Lane, *William Dorsey's Philadelphia and Ours: On the Past and Future of the Black City in America* (New York: Oxford University Press, 1991), 134–165; Shirley Turpin-Parham, "A History of Black Public Education in Philadelphia, Pennsylvania, 1864–1914," EdD diss., Temple University, 1986: 42–61, 107–142; Harry C. Silcox, "Philadelphia Negro Educator: Jacob C. White, Jr., 1837–1902," *Pennsylvania Magazine of History and Biography*, 97, no. 1 (1973): 75–88; Mohraz, *The Separate Problem*, 86–88. Louise Kromer to Jacob C. White Jr., September 5, 1883; C. Richards to Jacob C. White Jr., October 12, 1881; Merle Nichols to Jacob C. White Jr., September 5, 1881; in Box 12G, Jacob C. White Jr. Letters, Leon Gardiner Collection of American Negro Historical Society Records, Historical Society of Pennsylvania, Philadelphia, PA.

68. Wright, *Afro-Americans in New Jersey*, 50–54; Marion M. Thompson Wright, *The Education of Negroes in New Jersey* (New York: Teachers College Press, 1941), 160–182; "Fair Haven's Colored School: The New School Building Dedicated and the Race Troubles Ended," *New York Times*, November 19, 1881, 5; "Fair Haven School Troubles Over," *New York Times*, November

17, 1881, 5; "Fair Haven School Troubles: The Colored People Agree to Accept a Separate School-House," *New York Times*, April 6, 1881, 5; "The Fair Haven School Trouble: The Excitement between the White and Colored People Still Kept Up," *New York Times*, March 31, 1881, 5; "New-Jersey Law-Making: The Fair Haven School Bill," *New York Times*, March 18, 1881, 5; "The Fair Haven Colored People," *New York Times*, March 18, 1881, 5; "Notes on Education," *Christian Recorder*, March 17, 1881; "The Fair Haven School Trouble: Stormy Meeting of White and Colored People: Negroes Obstinate," *New York Times*, March 16, 1881, 5; "A Race War in New Jersey: Endeavoring to Force Colored Scholars into Schools with White Children," *Daily Constitution*, March 5, 1881, 4; "The Following Relates to Fair Haven, NJ," *Christian Recorder*, March 3, 1881; "Race Trouble in New Jersey: The Antagonism on the School Question," *New York Times*, March 1, 1881, 5; "Fair Haven's Colored School," *New York Times*, February 27, 1881, 2; "Burning a School-House: Discontented Colored People in a New-Jersey Town," *New York Times*, February 26, 1881, 2; "Color Foolishness," *Hartford Daily Courant*, February 26, 1881, 3; "School House Burned at Fair Haven," *New York Tribune*, February 26, 1881, 2.

69. "Copy of the Item in the Report of the Secretary of the Long Branch, NJ Board of Education for the Year 1884–5, Concerning the Opening of the Brook Street School," in "School Segregation in New Jersey." Papers of the NAACP, Part 03: The Campaign for Educational Equality, Series B: Legal Department and Central Office Records, 1940–1950, ProQuest History Vault, https://congressional.proquest.com/histvault?q=001512-003-0001.

70. "52nd Annual Report of the Public Schools of Cincinnati," p. 26, as cited in Gregory Reed Corr, "Black Politics and Education in Cincinnati, 1870–1890," EdD diss., University of Cincinnati, 1984, 68–69; "Colored Schools of Ohio," *Indianapolis Leader*, October 23, 1880. See also Nikki M. Taylor, *America's First Black Socialist: The Radical Life of Peter H. Clark* (Lexington: University of Kentucky Press, 2013); Nancy Bertaux and Michael Washington, "The 'Colored Schools' of Cincinnati and African American Community in Nineteenth Century Cincinnati, 1849–1890," *Journal of Negro Education* 74, no. 1 (2005): 43–52; Nikki M. Taylor, *Frontiers of Freedom: Cincinnati's Black Community, 1802–1868* (Athens: Ohio University Press, 2005), 161–174; Herbert G. Gutman, "Peter H. Clark: Pioneer Negro Socialist, 1877," *Journal of Negro Education* 43, no. 4 (1965): 413–418; Charles Thomas Hickok, "The Negro in Ohio, 1802–1870," PhD diss. Western Reserve University, 1896, 77–122.

71. Ira Berlin, *The Making of African America: The Four Great Migrations* (New York: Penguin Books, 2010), 130–151; James R. Grossman, *Land of Hope: Chicago, Black Southerners, and the Great Migration* (Chicago: University of Chicago Press, 1991), 22–23; Corr, "Black Politics and Education in Cincinnati, 1870–1890," 34, 59–78; Kenneth L. Kusmer, *A Ghetto Takes Shape: Black Cleveland, 1870–1930* (Urbana: University of Illinois Press, 1978), 35–90; David A. Gerber, *Black Ohio and the Color Line, 1860–1915* (Urbana: University of Illinois Press, 1976), 60–92; Du Bois, *The Philadelphia Negro*, 46–72; Robert C. Weaver, *The Negro Ghetto* (New York: Russell & Russell, 1967 [1948]), 11–13.

72. Eric Foner, *Reconstruction: America's Unfinished Revolution, 1863–1877*, rev. ed. (New York: Harper Perennial, 2014); Stephen Kantrowitz, *More Than Freedom: Fighting for Black Citizenship in a White Republic, 1829–1889* (New York: Penguin Press, 2012), 382–395; Davis, *We Will Be Satisfied with Nothing Less*, 133–148; Omar H. Ali, *In the Balance of Power: Independent Black Politics and Third-Party Movements in the United States* (Athens: Ohio University Press, 2008), 54–73; August Meier, *Negro Thought in America, 1880–1915: Racial Ideologies in the Era of Booker T. Washington*, rev ed. (Ann Arbor: University of Michigan Press, 1988 [1963]), 28–30; Peter D. Klingman and David T. Geithman, "Negro Dissidence and the Republican Party, 1864–1872," *Phylon* 40, no. 2 (1979): 172–182; Philip S. Foner, "Peter H. Clark: Pioneer Black Socialist," *Journal of Ethnic Studies* 5, no. 3 (1977): 17.

73. "Left the Republican Party," *Washington Bee*, September 15, 1888; "The Colored Man in Ohio," *Eaton Democrat*, July 22, 1886; "Dividing the Negro Vote," *Springfield Republican*, July 7, 1886, 4; "Prof. Clark," *Washington Bee*, March 14, 1885; "Dr. Mr. Peter H. Clark, Principal," *Cincinnati Commercial Gazette*, September 12, 1884, 4; "Freed from Bondage: The Colored Vote Breaking Away from Political Servitude," *Wheeling Register*, August 3, 1884, 1; "Current Comment," *Washington Post*, October 4, 1883, 2; T. Thomas Fortune, "Letter to the Editor,

Complaints of the Republican Colored Voters," *New York Times*, August 14, 1883, 3; "The Negro and Republicanism: Denying that the Colored Vote Is Swinging Away from the Party," *New York Times*, August 12, 1883, 1; "Ohio's Colored Vote: Alleged Dissatisfaction among Colored Republicans, Democrats Bidding for the Vote," *New York Times*, July 7, 1882, 1; "The Workingman's Campaign," *Cincinnati Daily Star*, August 18, 1877; "Speech of Peter H. Clark," *New National Era*, April 13, 1871.

74. Taylor, *America's First Black Socialist*, 164–169; Corr, "Black Politics and Education in Cincinnati, 1870–1890," 196–201.

75. "Hon. John P. Green," *Christian Recorder*, March 27, 1884. A similar sentiment can be found in the *Western Appeal*, September 17, 1887, an African American newspaper out of St. Paul, Minnesota, "The welfare of the entire race is of more importance than the salaries of a few colored teachers."

76. "Peter H. Clark," *Christian Recorder*, April 17, 1884; "Peter H. Clark Speaks," *Christian Recorder*, April 17, 1884. On Black educators in New York City schools, see Osofsky, *Harlem*, 64–66.

77. "Peter H. Clark," *Christian Recorder*, April 17, 1884.

78. Douglas, *Jim Crow Moves North*, 174–175; Mabee, *Black Education in New York State*, 213–220; Thomas Paul Kessen, "Segregation in Cincinnati Public Education: The Nineteenth Century Black Experience," EdD diss., University of Cincinnati, 1973, 126-144; W. E. B. Du Bois, "The Black North in 1901: New York," in Dan S. Green and Edwin D. Driver, eds., *W.E.B. Du Bois: On Sociology and the Black Community* (Chicago: University of Chicago Press, 1978), 140–153; "Legislative Committee Finds Pittsburgh Education Board Guilty of Jim Crow," *Philadelphia Tribune*, June 10, 1937, 2; S. A. Virgil, "Should Pittsburgh and Allegheny County Have Colored Teachers?" *Pittsburgh Courier*, August 12, 1911, 1; "New-York's Public Schools," *New York Tribune*, May 19, 1895, 15; "In the City of New York," *Christian Recorder*, December 1, 1887; "No Separate Colored Schools in Ohio," *Boston Evening Journal*, February 17, 1887, 1; "Mixed Schools," *Christian Recorder*, August 14, 1884; B. F. Lee, "Education: The Important Subject of the Hour," *Christian Recorder*, May 1, 1884; "Colored Teachers of Ohio in Convention," *Cincinnati Commercial Tribune*, August 20, 1881, 2.

79. Taylor, *America's First Black Socialist*, 186–189; Corr, "Black Politics and Education in Cincinnati, 1870–1890," 205–225.

80. Taylor, *America's First Black Socialist*, 196–198; Booker T. Washington, *The Story of the Negro: The Rise of the Race from Slavery* (Philadelphia: University of Pennsylvania Press, 2005 [1909]), 233–250; "Dr. Benjamin W. Arnett," *Indianapolis Journal*, May 20, 1888; "No Separate Schools," *Springfield Daily Republic*, December 21, 1887; "Causing Some Friction," *New York Times*, September 22, 1887, 1; "Colored Schools in Ohio," *Chicago Daily Tribune*, September 22, 1887, 1; "They Will Not Mix," *Atlanta Constitution*, September 8, 1887, 1; "Cincinnati: Abolition of Colored High Schools," *Chicago Daily Tribune*, June 5, 1887, 18; "Race Prejudice on the School Question," *Chicago Daily Tribune*, March 20, 1887, 6; "Ohio's 'Black Laws': How Their Repeal Is Regarded by the Colored Race," *Atlanta Constitution*, March 7, 1887, 1; "Democrats and the Arnett Bill," *Cincinnati Commercial Gazette*, March 15, 1886, 3.

81. David A. Gerber, "Peter Humphries Clark: The Dialogue of Hope and Despair," in Leon Litwack and August Meier, eds., *Black Leaders of the Nineteenth Century* (Urbana: University of Illinois Press, 1988), 173–90. See also "A Mixed School Experiment in Ohio," *Watauga Democrat*, March 27, 1889; "What Is Called the Arnett Law," *Charlotte Democrat*, March 8, 1889; "A Mixed School Experiment," *Anderson Intelligencer*, February 21, 1889; "News and Notes," *Iron County Register*, February 21, 1889; "Unhappy Felicity in Ohio Town, Famous for Its Former Abolition Sentiment," *Weekly Courier-Journal*, December 24, 1888, 1.

82. Corr, "Black Politics and Education in Cincinnati, 1870–1890," 272–273; Kessen, "Segregation in Cincinnati Public Education," 123–144; Gutman, "Peter H. Clark: Pioneer Negro Socialist, 1877"; "Cincinnati Board of Education, Fifty-Eighth Annual Report of the Public Schools of Cincinnati for the School Year Ending August 31, 1887," (Cincinnati Ohio Valley Publishing and Manufacturing, 1888): xiv–xv, 65–66, 98–99; "Commencements, Graduating Exercises at Gaines High School," *Cincinnati Commercial Gazette*, June 19, 1886, 10; "Gaines High School," *Indianapolis Leader*, June 11, 1881.

83. Tina L. Ligon, "Pioneering the Change to Be Better: Jennie Davis Porter and Cincinnati's All-Black Harriet Beecher Stowe School, 1914–1935," PhD diss., Morgan State University, 2014, 33–62; Douglas, *Jim Crow Moves North*, 124–131; "Sixty-First Annual Report of the Cincinnati Public Schools," 72; "Fifty-Eighth Annual Report of the Cincinnati Public Schools," p. 87 as cited in Corr, "Black Politics and Education in Cincinnati," 272–276; Kessen, "Segregation in Cincinnati Public Education," 141–154; Mary R. Crowley, "Cincinnati's Experiment in Negro Education: A Comparative Study of the Segregated and Mixed School," *Journal of Negro Education* 1, no. 1 (1932): 25–33; "Ohio School Has 3,000 Pupils, 118 Teachers," *Afro-American*, August 31, 1929, 3; Jennie D. Porter, "The Problem of Negro Education in Northern and Border Cities," PhD diss., University of Cincinnati, 1928; "Harriet Beecher Stowe School Unique Landmark of Educational Program," *Pittsburgh Courier*, May 17, 1924, 16; "Race Principal Gets Bachelor of Science Degree," *Pittsburgh Courier*, June 23, 1923, 9.
84. William H. Manz, "Desegregation in New York: The Jamaica School War, 1895–1900," *New York State Bar Association Journal* 76, no. 4 (2004): 10–19; Carleton Mabee, "Control by Blacks over Schools in New York State, 1830–1930," *Phylon* 40, no. 1 (1979): 29–40; Carleton Mabee, "Long Island's Black 'School War' and the Decline of Segregation in New York State," *New York History* 58, no. 4 (1977): 385–411.
85. "Order from Judge Barnard on the Colored School Question," *Brooklyn Daily Eagle*, March 28, 1896, 5. See also "Long Island Notes," *New-York Tribune*, May 7, 1896, 12; "Jamaica's Color Line Fight: Man Who Claims to Be an Indian Tried under Truant Law," *New York Times*, April 17, 1896, 3; "Jamaica's School War," *New York Times*, April 15, 1896, 3; "Color Line in Jamaica Schools: Negroes Will Be Arrested for Violating Education Law," *New York Times*, April 5, 1896, 9; "No Color Line in Jamaica," *New York Times*, March 29, 1896, 9.
86. "The Negro and His Friends," *Washington Post*, June 20, 1896, 6. See a similar critique concerning Black efforts to desegregate the schools in Alton, Illinois: "Race in Education," *New York Times*, January 16, 1890, 4.
87. "Jamaica's Colored School: The Modernized Building Reopened this Morning with Appropriate Ceremonies," *Brooklyn Daily Eagle*, March 5, 1900, 7; "About the Race Problem," *New-York Tribune*, September 7, 1899, 7; "Superintendent Stevens Upheld: Colored Children in Jamaica Must Attend Their Own School," *New-York Tribune*, March 19, 1899, A2; "The Color Line in Jamaica," *New York Times*, February 5, 1899, 9; "Long Island News: Trustees Sued for Damages," *New-York Tribune*, September 18, 1896, 14; "Jamaica's School Fight," *New-York Tribune*, September 10, 1896, 12.
88. *Department Bulletin No. 1: The Consolidated School Law of the State of New York.* Chapter 492: Laws of 1900 (Albany: New York State Education Department, 1905): 185. See also Mabee, *Black Education in New York State*, 234–235; "No Color Line in Schools," *Brooklyn Daily Eagle*, April 22, 1900, 6; "The Elsberg Bill Signed," *Brooklyn Daily Eagle*, April 20, 1900, 9; "School Bills Introduced," *New York Times*, January 11, 1900, 8; "School Bills Attacked," *New York Times*, February 17, 1899, 3.
89. Manz, "Desegregation in New York"; Mabee, "Long Island's Black 'School War' and the Decline of Segregation in New York State," 397–411.

Chapter 2

1. William Edward Burghardt Du Bois, 1868–1963. "Segregated Schools," unpublished article, c. 1932. *W. E. B. Du Bois Papers* (MS312), Section 3: Articles, Special Collections and University Archives, University of Massachusetts Amherst Libraries, Amherst, MA, hereafter cited as Du Bois Papers; letter from Elizabeth Nutting to W. E. B. Du Bois, March 15, 1932, Series 1A: General Correspondence, Du Bois Papers. If anything, this letter downplays racial segregation in the Dayton schools. As early as 1920, William Pickens charged that Dayton created Jim Crow schools when school leaders removed Black children from the regular schools and assigned them to separate basements and annexes. The NAACP waged a successful battle to stop this practice between 1925 and 1926; however, this legal victory resulted in only token integration, in part because many Dayton Blacks preferred separate schools with Black teachers. "Ohio Supreme Court Bars Segregation in Dayton School," *New York Amsterdam News*, February 24, 1926, 12; "Dayton Negroes Divided on School

Segregation Fight," *Philadelphia Tribune*, February 14, 1925, 9; "Dayton Ohio Is Divided on School Fight," *Pittsburgh Courier*, February 14, 1925, 16; "Dayton People Divided on Mixed Schools," *Afro-American*, February 14, 1925, 16; "Bagnall Will Aid in Dayton School Fight," *Pittsburgh Courier*, September 27, 1924, 2; William Pickens, "Dayton Allows 'Jim Crow' in Public Schools," *Chicago Defender*, February 16, 1924, 1.

2. "McFarlane Principal of Dayton's Dunbar School," *New Journal and Guide*, September 23, 1933, 20. Du Bois, "Segregated Schools," unpublished article. Du Bois's more cautious perspective on integration and his growing interest in Black nationalism were so controversial that two years later he would quit his job as editor of the *Crisis* and resign from the NAACP. Major biographies of W. E. B. Du Bois include David Levering Lewis, *W.E.B. Du Bois: The Fight for Equality and the American Century, 1919-1963* (New York: Henry Holt, 2000); David Levering Lewis, *W.E.B. Du Bois: Biography of a Race, 1868-1919* (New York: Henry Holt, 1993); Manning Marable, *W.E.B. Du Bois: Black Radical Democrat* (G.K. Hall, 1986); W. E. B. Du Bois, *Autobiography of W.E.B. Du Bois: A Soliloquy on Viewing My Life from the Last Decade of Its First Century* (New York: International Publishers, 1968). Analyses of Du Bois's evolving views on education include Derrick P. Alridge, *The Educational Thought of W.E.B. Du Bois: An Intellectual History* (New York: Teachers College Press, 2008); Davison M. Douglas, *Jim Crow Moves North: The Battle over Northern School Segregation, 1865-1954* (New York: Cambridge University Press, 2005): 195-205; Adolph L. Reed Jr., *W.E.B. Du Bois and American Political Thought: Fabianism and the Color Line* (New York: Oxford University Press, 1997); Herbert Aptheker, ed., *DuBois: The Education of Black People: Ten Critiques, 1906-1960* (Amherst: University of Massachusetts, 1973), vii-xii.

3. Legal historian Davison Douglas offers a carefully documented study of the expansion of northern school segregation between 1890 and 1940, and debates within northern Black communities over how to respond to this segregation; see Douglas, *Jim Crow Moves North*, 123-218. Similar trends are documented in Carleton Mabee, *Black Education in New York State: From Colonial to Modern Times* (Syracuse, NY: Syracuse University Press, 1979), 247-274; see estimates in the numbers of Black children in separate schools on pp. 258-259; Marion M. Thompson Wright, *The Education of Negroes in New Jersey* (New York: Arno Press and New York Times, 1971 [1941]), 183-201.

4. Richard Rothstein, *The Color of Law: A Forgotten History of How Our Government Segregated America* (New York: W.W. Norton, 2017); Thomas J. Sugrue, *The Origins of the Urban Crisis: Race and Inequality in Postwar Detroit*, rev. ed. (Princeton, NJ: Princeton University Press, 2014); Douglas, *Jim Crow Moves North*, 5, 123-166; Kenya Davis-Hayes, "Lessons of Place: The Creation of Physical and Curricular Segregation in Chicago between 1910 and 1925," PhD diss., Purdue University, 2005; Douglas S. Massey and Nancy A. Denton, *American Apartheid: Segregation and the Making of the Underclass* (Cambridge, MA: Harvard University Press, 1993); Judy Jolley Mohraz, *The Separate Problem: Case Studies of Black Education in the North, 1900-1930* (Westport, CT: Greenwood Press, 1979); Vincent P. Franklin, *The Education of Black Philadelphia: The Social and Educational History of a Minority Community, 1900-1950* (Philadelphia: University of Pennsylvania Press, 1979); Wright, *The Education of Negroes in New Jersey*. Charles S. Johnson, *Backgrounds to Patterns of Negro Segregation* (New York: Thomas Y. Crowell, 1970 [1943]), 185; William R. Ming Jr., "The Elimination of Segregation in the Public Schools of the North and West," *Journal of Negro Education* 21, no. 3 (1952): 265-275.

5. Davis-Hayes, "Lessons of Place," 99-100; Jeffrey Mirel, *The Rise and Fall of an Urban School System: Detroit, 1907-81*, 2nd ed. (Ann Arbor: University of Michigan Press, 1999), 186-196; "Segregation Most Effective Plan for Education of Negro in North, Is Claim," *Cincinnati Enquirer*, February 25, 1929. W. E. B. Du Bois Papers (MS 312). Special Collections and University Archives, University of Massachusetts Amherst Libraries, http://credo.library.umass.edu/view/full/mums312-b182-i550; Charles H. Thompson, "The Negro Separate School," *Crisis* 42, no. 8 (1935): 230-232, 242; Horace Mann Bond, "The Only Way to Keep Public Schools Equal Is to Keep Them Mixed," *Afro-American*, March 5, 1932, 18; Lester B. Granger, "Race Relations and the School System," *Opportunity* 3, no. 35 (1925): 327-329. Granger's description of racial discrimination in New Jersey public schools is later cited

in Charles S. Johnson, *The Negro in American Civilization: A Study of Negro Life and Race Relations in the Light of Social Research* (New York: Henry Holt, 1930), 267.

6. Johnson, *Backgrounds to Patterns of Negro Segregation*, 185; Charles S. Johnson, "Source Material for Patterns of Negro Segregation in Chicago, IL, 1940," page 6, Reel 7, Sc Micro R-6534, Carnegie-Myrdal Study of the Negro in America Research Memoranda Collection, 1935–1948, Schomburg Center for Research in Black Culture, Manuscripts, Archives and Rare Books Division, New York Public Library, New York, NY; Ira De A. Reid, *Social Conditions in the Hill District of Pittsburgh* (Pittsburgh: General Committee on the Hill Survey, 1930), 82–92.

7. Leslie Pinckney Hill, "The Cheney Training School for Teachers," *Crisis* 25, no. 6 (1923): 252. The Cheyney Training School for Teachers changed its name several times, and is known today as Cheyney University of Pennsylvania, a public Historically Black College and University (HBCU). It is recognized as the nation's first HBCU.

8. Thompson, "The Negro Separate School"; Ming, "The Elimination of Segregation in the Public Schools of the North and West"; "Segregation Most Effective Plan for Education of Negro Youth in North."

9. Kenneth L. Kusmer, *A Ghetto Takes Shape: Black Cleveland, 1870–1930* (Urbana: University of Illinois Press, 1976), 182–184; David M. Ment, "Racial Segregation in the Public Schools of New England and New York, 1840–1940," PhD diss., Columbia University, 1975, 201–233; Allan H. Spear, *Black Chicago: The Making of a Negro Ghetto* (Chicago: University of Chicago Press, 1967), 45–63; Gilbert Osofsky, *Harlem: The Making of a Ghetto* (New York: Harper & Row, 1966), 19, 120–121; Gunnar Myrdal, *An American Dilemma: The Negro Problem and Modern Democracy* (New York: Harper and Row, 1962 [1944]), 191–197; Johnson, *Backgrounds to Patterns of Negro Segregation*, 173–185. Some cities, such as Newark, New Jersey, legally ended the practice of racial segregation in the public schools at this time. For instance, the Newark Public Schools passed a resolution outlawing racial segregation in 1909 with the retirement of Black principal James M. Baxter from the "colored" school on Market Street. School segregation then continued on an informal basis. See Marion T. Wright, "Mr. Baxter's School," *Proceedings of New Jersey Historical Society*, no. 224, April 1, 1941, 116–133, Faculty Reprints, Digital Howard, Howard University, http://dh.howard.edu/reprints/224; Rudy Johnson, "Last of Segregated Schools in City Abandoned in 1909," *Newark Evening News*, February 12, 1967; "Baxter Heritage," *Newark Evening News*, February 12, 1967. Both articles available on "Rise Up Newark," the Newark Public Library, Newark, NJ, http://riseupnewark.com/media-tag/newark/.

10. "The Negro and the Northern Public Schools," *Crisis* 25, no. 5 (1923): 205–206. See also "The School Transfer System and Race Children," *Chicago Defender*, November 11, 1939, 14; "Illinois Town Joins Jim Crow School List," *Chicago Defender*, September 24, 1927, 1; "'Jim Crow' School Is Legal," *Pittsburgh Courier*, April 10, 1926, 1; "Take White Students from Negro School," *Los Angeles Times*, September 16, 1923, I2; "White Supremacy League Formed in Indianapolis," *Chicago Defender*, November 25, 1922, 3; "Separate School Plot Uncovered in Gary, Indiana," *Chicago Defender*, November 6, 1920, 1; "Talk of Separate Schools for the Negro Children," *Chicago Daily Tribune*, November 14, 1903, 8, "Plan to Check Black Students," *Chicago Daily Tribune*, October 5, 1903, 3.

11. Patricia Sullivan, *Lift Every Voice: The NAACP and the Making of the Civil Rights Movement* (New York: New Press, 2009), 1–60; Touré F. Reed, *Not Alms but Opportunity: The Urban League and the Politics of Racial Uplift, 1910–1950* (Chapel Hill: University of North Carolina Press, 2008), 11–26; Mark V. Tushnet, *The NAACP's Legal Strategy against Segregated Education, 1925–1950* (Chapel Hill: University of North Carolina Press, [1987] 2004), 1–20; Michael Fultz, "'The Morning Cometh': African-American Periodicals, Education, and the Black Middle Class, 1900–1930," *Journal of Negro History* 80, no. 3 (1995): 97–112; Jess Thomas Moore Jr., *A Search for Equality: The National Urban League, 1910–1961* (University Park: Pennsylvania State University Press, 1981), 24–62; Kusmer, *A Ghetto Takes Shape*, 60–65; Spear, *Black Chicago*, 84–89; "Separate Schools Found to Benefit Whites Only," *Afro-American*, January 28, 1928, 2; "Color Line in Schools Opposed by Thoughtful Ones," *Philadelphia Tribune*, August 28, 1915, 1.

12. William Pickens, "Racial Segregation," *Opportunity* 5, no. 12 (December 1927): 364–367. See also Frank St. Claire, "Against Separate Schools," *Chicago Defender*, December 30, 1939, 12;

"Urban League and NAACP Flay Segregation Proposed for Rockville," *New York Amsterdam News*, January 29, 1930, 3; Floyd J. Calvin, "Mrs. McDougald Tells of N.Y. Mixed Schools," *Pittsburgh Courier*, March 26, 1927, B1; Chandler Owen, "Errors in Jim Crow School Argument," *Chicago Defender*, August 26, 1922, 15; "Separate Schools," *Chicago Defender*, July 1, 1916, 8; "'Jim Crow' School," *Chicago Defender*, March 29, 1913, 4.

13. José Clarana, "The Schooling of the Negro," *Crisis* 6, no. 3 (1913): 133–136. A remarkably similar quote can be found by the Pastor of the Ebenezer Baptist Church in Pittsburgh; see Rev. J. C. Austin, "Who Said, Separate Schools?" *Pittsburgh Courier*, April 14, 1923, 8.

14. "Howard 'U' Dean Forcefully Attacks School Segregation," *Pittsburgh Courier*, August 6, 1932, 2; "Randolph Urging a Mixed School System, Hits Leaders," *Philadelphia Tribune*, May 7, 1927, 1; "Bill Introduced to Change Cheney into Normal Institute," *Pittsburgh Courier*, March 28, 1925, 1; "Separate Schools Will Bring about Political Slavery," *Philadelphia Tribune*, January 26, 1924, 1; "Ministers Branded Traitors in Ohio School Upheaval," *Chicago Defender*, November 4, 1922, 1; "Race Leaders Humbly Submit to the Demon Prejudice," *Chicago Defender*, February 5, 1916, 1; "Along the Color Line," *Crisis* 2, no. 2 (1911): 51.

15. Ira Berlin, *The Making of African America: The Four Great Migrations* (New York: Penguin Books, 2010), 152–155; Isabel Wilkerson, *The Warmth of Other Suns: The Epic Story of America's Great Migration* (New York: Vintage Books, 2010); Douglas, *Jim Crow Moves North*, 184–185; James N. Gregory, *The Southern Diaspora: How the Great Migrations of Black and White Southerners Transformed America* (Chapel Hill: University of North Carolina Press, 2005), 11–42; Doug McAdam, *Political Process and the Development of Black Insurgency, 1930–1970*, 2nd ed. (Chicago: University of Chicago Press, 1999), 80; James R. Grossman, *Land of Hope: Chicago, Black Southerners, and the Great Migration* (Chicago: University of Chicago Press, 1991). See also, "Parents Fight Jim Crow School in Ohio Town," *New Journal and Guide*, December 9, 1939, 1; "Victory for Toms River," *Pittsburgh Courier*, June 25, 1927, A8; "High Court to Hear Negro School Case," *New York Times*, March 12, 1927, 13; "Pupils in Ohio Town Draw 'Color Line' on Segregation," *Pittsburgh Courier*, September 20, 1924, 2; "Along the Color Line," *Crisis* 4, no. 3 (1912): 111.

16. "Along the NAACP Battlefront," *Crisis* 45, no. 10 (1938): 336; letter from Rebecca Sebastian to Floyd Logan, March 1, 1934, Box 8, Folder 12, "Complaints from Students and their Parents," Floyd L. Logan Papers, Special Collections Research Center, Temple University Library, Philadelphia, Pennsylvania, hereafter cited as Logan Papers; Edward Robinson, "Jim Crowism Is Rampant in Asbury Park," *Afro-American*, August 8, 1931, 8; "The Year in Negro Education," *Crisis* 37, no. 8 (1930): 262–268; "Jim Crow School Burns," *Philadelphia Tribune*, May 1, 1926; William Pickens, "Dayton Allows 'Jim Crow' in Public Schools," *Chicago Defender*, February 16, 1924, A1; "Editorial," *Crisis* 1, no. 4 (1911): 21; "To Demand Separate Schools for Negroes," *New York Times*, January 18, 1911, 3; "Whites Destroy Negro School," *Los Angeles Times*, November 29, 1906, 14.

17. William Rawlings, *The Second Coming of the Invisible Empire: The Ku Klux Klan of the 1920s* (Macon, GA: Mercer University Press, 2016); Adam Laats, *The Other School Reformers: Conservative Activism in American Education* (Cambridge, MA: Harvard University Press, 2015), 34, 40, 50–58; Michael W. Homel, *Down from Equality: Black Chicagoans and the Public Schools, 1920–1941* (Urbana: University of Illinois Press, 1984), 1–26; Mohraz, *The Separate Problem*; Neil Betten and Raymond A. Mohl, "The Evolution of Racism in an Industrial City, 1906–1940: A Case Study of Gary, Indiana," *Journal of Negro History* 59, no. 1 (1974): 51–64; Wright, *The Education of Negroes in New Jersey*, 183–194, 197–198; Osofsky, *Harlem*, 120–121; *Black Chicago*, 44–49; Johnson, *The Negro in American Civilization*, 267; Chicago Commission on Race Relations, *The Negro in Chicago: A Study of Race Relations and a Race Riot* (Chicago: University of Chicago Press, 1922), 254. See also, "Victory at Toms River," *Pittsburgh Courier*, June 2, 1934, A4; Dennis A. Bethea, "The Colored Group in the Gary School System," *Crisis* 40, no. 8 (1931): 268 and 281; J. Blaine Poindexter, "Gary Revolts on Jim Crow," *Chicago Defender*, October 8, 1927, 1; "Striking White Students Win in Gary Fight," *Philadelphia Tribune*, October 6, 1927, 1; "Gary Students Ratify Peace: Back at Books," *Chicago Daily Tribune*, October 1, 1927, 9; Dewey R. Jones, "Students Strike, but Lose Demand," *Chicago Defender*, October 1, 1927, 1; "Klan to Make Fight for Ohio Organizer," *New York Times*, February 16, 1923, 8; "Education," *Crisis* 1, no. 1 (1910): 4;

"Mixture in Chicago Schools," *New York Age*, October 10, 1907, 1; "Race Problem Rends School," *Chicago Daily Tribune*, December 5, 1905, 9; "Negro Students Demand Equality," *Chicago Daily Tribune*, September 27, 1903, 3.

18. Christina Collins, *Ethnically Qualified: Race, Merit, and the Selection of Urban Teachers, 1920–1980* (New York: Teachers College Press, 2011), 13–21; Douglas, *Jim Crow Moves North*, 174–177; Jack Dougherty, *More than One Struggle: The Evolution of Black School Reform in Milwaukee* (Chapel Hill: University of North Carolina Press, 2004), 9–33; Mirel, *The Rise and Fall of an Urban School System*, 62–63, 186–188; David M. Katzman, *Before the Ghetto: Black Detroit in the Nineteenth Century* (Urbana: University of Illinois Press, 1933), 84–90; Ambrose Caliver, "Some Problems in the Education and Placement of Negro Teachers," *Journal of Negro Education* 4, no. 1 (1935): 99–112; "From the Press of the Nation," *Crisis* 42, no. 4 (1935): 115; "Along the NAACP Battlefront," *Crisis* 42, no. 2 (1935): 55–56; George Streator, "On to Asbury Park!" *Crisis* 41, no. 5 (1934): 133–134; Rayford W. Logan, "Educational Segregation in the North," *Journal of Negro Education* 2, no. 1 (1933): 65–67; "The Results of Barring Negro Teachers," *Crisis* 40, no. 9 (1933): 208; Report of a Survey by the Interracial Committee of the New Jersey Conference of Social Work, *The Negro in New Jersey* (Trenton: New Jersey State Department of Institutions and Agencies, 1932): 38–40; Clarana, "The Schooling of the Negro," 222. Although official records were not kept by the school district, one observer estimates there were between fifteen and twenty Black teachers working in the Chicago Public Schools in 1911, where, "as a rule, they are in schools where the majority of the children are Negroes." See "Employment of Colored Women in Chicago," *Crisis* 1, no. 3 (1911): 24–25. A noteworthy exception comes from New York City in 1918, where a Black man served as principal of P.S. 79 on the East Side, where the teachers and students were mostly white. See John Purroy Mitchel, "The Public Schools of New York," *Crisis* 14, no. 3 (1917): 132.

19. "Parents Fight for J.C. School," *Afro-American*, August 10, 1940, 8; Lionel B. Fraser, "Educational and Vocational Guidance of Negro Youth," *Opportunity* 8, no. 8 (1930): 241–243; De A. Reid, *Social Conditions of the Negro in the Hill District of Pittsburgh*, 90–92; "California Wins against Jim Crow," *Chicago Defender*, September 29, 1928, 2; "Citizens Say Minister for Segregation," *Philadelphia Tribune*, September 8, 1927, 9; Eva D. Bowles, "Opportunities for the Educated Colored Woman," *Opportunity* 1, no. 3 (1923): 8–10; "Along the Color Line," *Crisis* 6, no. 33 (1913): 116–117; "The Burden," *Crisis* 6, no. 31 (1913): 23; "Employment of Colored Women in Chicago," *Crisis* 1, no. 3 (1911): 24–25.

20. Dougherty, *More than One Struggle*, 9–33; Adam Fairclough, "The Costs of Brown: Black Teachers and School Integration," *Journal of American History* 91, no. 1 (2004): 43–55; Michael Fultz, "African American Teachers in the South, 1890–1940: Powerlessness and the Ironies of Expectations and Protest," *History of Education Quarterly* 35, no. 4 (1995): 401–422; John B. Reid, "'A Career to Build, a People to Serve, a Purpose to Accomplish': Race, Class, Gender, and Detroit's First Black Women Teachers, 1865–1916," in Darlene Clark Hine, Wilma King, and Linda Reed, eds., *We Specialize in the Wholly Impossible: A Reader in Black Women's History* (New York: Carlson, 1995), 303–320.

21. Myrdal, *An American Dilemma*, 305–306; C. R. Whyte, Memorandum, March 31, 1937, Folder 13, Box 1, Logan Papers.

22. Dougherty, *More than One Struggle*, 15–31.

23. J. N. Gill, "Agrees with Du Bois: Advocates Separate Schools as Means for Employment for Colored Teacher," *New Journal and Guide*, July 7, 1934, 8. See also Robert A. Crump, "Detroit Bolts at Separate Schools Idea," *New Journal and Guide*, June 23, 1934, 14; Robert A. Crump, "Detroit Resents Idea of Separate Schools," *Pittsburgh Courier*, June 23, 1934, A3.

24. Homel, *Down from Equality*, 109; Julia E. R. Clark, "Race Should Demand First-Class Separate Schools to Gain Best Education for Youth," *Pittsburgh Courier*, April 7, 1934, 2; De A. Reid, *Social Conditions of the Negro in the Hill District of Pittsburgh*, 89; Chicago Commission on Race Relations, *The Negro in Chicago: A Study of Race Relations and a Race Riot* (Chicago: University of Chicago Press, 1922), 214.

25. Garter Godwin Woodson, *The Mis-Education of the Negro* (New York: Tribeca Books, 2012 [1933]); E. Franklin Frazier, *Negro Youth at the Crossways: Their Personality Development in the Middle States* (Washington, DC: American Council on Education, 1940), 110; "Gregory

Heads N.J. Teachers' Association," *Afro-American*, May 19, 1934, 7; "The Colored High School," *Crisis* 6, no. 3 (1913): 142–143.

26. Samuel Scott, "Physical Future of the Negro, Part 2," *Crisis* 40, no. 1 (1933): 7.

27. Frazier, *Negro Youth at the Crossways*, 95–96; Josephine Mildred Buster, "Which College—White or Negro?" *Crisis* 41, no. 11 (1934): 337–338; E. Frederick Morrow, "Nordic Education for the Negro: A Curse or a Boon?" *Opportunity* 9, no. 1 (1931): 12–13; Carter G. Woodson, "The Mis-Education of the Negro," *Crisis* 40, no. 8 (1931): 266–267.

28. L. A. Pechstein, "The Problem of Negro Education in Northern and Border Cities," *Elementary School Journal* 30, no. 3 (1929): 192–199, quote on p. 198; Lester B. Granger, "Race Relations and the School System," *Opportunity* 3, no. 35 (1925): 327–329.

29. Mary R. Crowley, "Cincinnati's Experiment in Negro Education: A Comparative Study of the Segregated and Mixed School," *Journal of Negro Education* 1, no. 1 (1932): 25–33; Jennie D. Porter, "The Problem of Negro Education in Northern and Border Cities," PhD diss., University of Cincinnati, 1928; "The Negro and the Northern Public School," *Crisis* 25, no. 5 (1923): 205–206; "Northern High Schools, Colored High Schools," *Crisis* 14, no. 3 (1917): 122–124.

30. Kelly Miller, "Is the Color Line Crumbling?" *Opportunity* 7, no. 9 (1929): 282–285. See also Douglas, *Jim Crow Moves North*, 123–218; August Meier and Elliott M. Rudwick, "Early Boycotts of Segregated Schools: The Case of Springfield, Ohio, 1922–23," *American Quarterly* 20, no. 4 (1968): 744–758; August Meier and Elliott M. Rudwick, "Early Boycotts of Segregated Schools: The Alton, Illinois Case, 1897–1908," *Journal of Negro Education* 36, no. 4 (1967): 394–402; August Meier and Elliott M. Rudwick, "Early Boycotts of Segregated Schools: The East Orange, New Jersey Experience, 1899–1906," *History of Education Quarterly* 7, no. 1 (1967): 22–35; Ming, "The Elimination of Segregation in the Public Schools of the North and West."

31. Meier and Rudwick, "Early Boycotts of Segregated Schools: The Alton, Illinois Case, 1897–1908." See also "Alton School War Averted by Means of Diplomacy," *Chicago Daily Tribune*, September 9, 1908, 2; "Court Upholds Color Line," *Chicago Daily Tribune*, December 19, 1903, 3; "Negroes Lose Third Time," *Atlanta Constitution*, April 1, 1900, 4; "School War in an Illinois City," *San Francisco Chronicle*, September 25, 1897, 2; "The Alton School Controversy," *Chicago Daily Tribune*, September 25, 1897, 6; "Color Line in Illinois," *Atlanta Constitution*, September 4, 1890, 2; "The Color Line at Alton, Ill," *Chicago Daily Tribune*, February 6, 1890, 1; "The Alton Affair," *Atlanta Constitution*, January 22, 1890, 4; "The Color Line in Illinois," *Atlanta Constitution*, January 12, 1890, 18; "The Race Problem in Illinois," *Atlanta Constitution*, January 12, 1890, 18.

32. Meier and Rudwick, "Early Boycotts of Segregated Schools: The East Orange, New Jersey, Experience, 1899–1906," 32. See also Walter David Greason, *Suburban Erasure: How the Suburbs Ended the Civil Rights Movement in New Jersey* (Madison, NJ: Fairleigh Dickinson University Press, 2013), 68-71; "Negroes Win School Fight," *New York Times*, February 12, 1906, 2; "For Bucks Color Line," *New-York Tribune*, December 7, 1905, 12; "Colored Citizens Aroused," *New York Times*, October 11, 1899, 3; "The Color Line in East Orange," *New York Tribune*, September 28, 1899, 13; "Will Teach in New Jersey," *Washington Post*, June 18, 1899, 18.

33. Douglas, *Jim Crow Moves North*, 9–11, 123–166.

34. Thomas Fallace, *Race and the Origins of Progressive Education, 1880–1929* (New York: Teachers College Press, 2015); Herbert M. Kliebard, *The Struggle for the American Curriculum, 1893–1958*, 3rd ed. (New York: Routledge Falmer, 2004), 105–129; Diane Ravitch, *The Great School Wars: A History of the New York City Public Schools*, rev. ed. (Baltimore: Johns Hopkins University Press, 2000), 161–188; Mirel, *The Rise and Fall of an Urban School System*, 1–42; David B. Tyack, *One Best System: A History of Urban Public Education* (Cambridge, MA: Harvard University Press, 1974), 126–268; Lawrence A. Cremin, *The Transformation of the School: Progressivism in American Education, 1876–1957* (New York: Knopf, 1969 [1961]), 127–176.

35. Madison Grant, *The Passing of the Great Race* (New York: Charles Scribner's Sons, 1916), 13–14. See also Ibram X. Kendi, *Stamped from the Beginning: The Definitive History of Racist Ideas in America* (New York: Nation Books, 2016), 263–380; Robert Wald Sussman, *The Myth of*

Race: The Troubling Persistence of an Unscientific Idea (Cambridge, MA: Harvard University Press, 2014), 43–106; Audrey Smedley and Brian D. Smedley, *Race in North America: Origin and Evolution of a Worldview*, 4th ed. (Boulder, CO: Westview Press, 2012), 251–288; John P. Jackson and Nadine M. Weidman, *Race, Racism, and Science: Social Impact and Interaction* (New Brunswick, NJ:, Rutgers University Press, 2006), 107–119; Thomas F. Gossett, *Race: The History of an Idea in America*, new ed. (New York: Oxford University Press, 1997 [1963]), 253–286.

36. Grant, *The Passing of the Great Race*, 13–14; Arthur MacDonald, "Colored Children: A Psycho-Physical Study" (Chicago: American Medical Association Press, 1899). Children's Literature and Childhood Collection, in Nineteenth Century Collections Online, http://tinyurl.galegroup.com/tinyurl/6QJBR3; "Segregation Most Effective Plan for Education of Negro in North, Is Claim."

37. Ann Gibson Winfield, *Eugenics and Education in America: Institutionalized Racism and the Implications of History, Ideology, and Memory* (New York: Peter Lang, 2007); Vernon J. Williams Jr., *The Social Sciences and Theories of Race* (Urbana: University of Illinois Press, 2006), 16–47; George M. Fredrickson, *Racism: A Short History*, rev. ed. (Princeton, NJ: Princeton University Press, 2015 [2002]), 97–138; William H. Watkins, *The White Architects of Black Education: Ideology and Power in America, 1865–1954* (New York: Teachers College Press, 2001), 24–42; Steven Selden, *Inheriting Shame: The Story of Eugenics and Racism in America* (New York: Teachers College Press, 1999); Horace Mann Bond, *The Education of the Negro in the American Social Order* (New York: Octagon Books, 1970 [1934]), 316–336; Doxey A. Wilkerson, "Racial Differences in Scholastic Achievement," *Journal of Negro Education* 3, no. 3 (1939): 453–477; Maudelle Brown Bousfield, "Redirection of the Education of Negroes in Terms of Social Needs," *Journal of Negro Education* 5, no. 3 (1936): 412–419; Maudelle Brown Bousfield, "A Study of the Intelligence and School Achievement of Negro Children," MA thesis, University of Chicago, 1931; W. E. B. Du Bois, "Pechstein and Pecksniff," *Crisis* 36, no. 9 (1929): 313–314; "Race Intelligence," *Crisis* 20, no. 3 (1920): 118–119; W. E. B. Du Bois, "Heredity and the Public Schools" (lecture delivered at the Principals' Association of the Colored Schools in Washington, DC, in 1904), in Eugene F. Provenzo Jr., ed., *Du Bois on Education* (New York: AltaMira Press, 2002), 111–122.

38. Hugh Davis, "The Pennsylvania State Equal Rights League and the Northern Black Struggle for Legal Equality, 1864–1877," *Pennsylvania Magazine of History and Biography* 126, no. 4 (2002): 611–634; Roger Lane, *Roots of Violence in Black Philadelphia, 1860–1900* (Cambridge, MA: Harvard University Press, 1986), 16–71; Franklin, *The Education of Black Philadelphia*, 12, 30–35. Another fascinating source on the Black educational experience in antebellum Philadelphia is the novel by Frank J. Webb with a preface by Harriet Beecher Stowe, *The Garies and Their Friends* (New York: G. Routledge, 1857).

39. W. E. B. Du Bois, *The Philadelphia Negro: A Social Study* (New York: Benjamin Blom, 1967[1899]), 83–96, quotes on pp. 89 and 95; Pennsylvania Society for Promoting the Abolition of Slavery Board of Education, and Benjamin C. Bacon, *Colored School Statistics: To the Board of Education of the Pennsylvania Society for Promoting the Abolition of Slavery, Etc.* (Philadelphia: Moran, Sickels, & Co., 1853). See also Marcus Anthony Hunter, *Black Citymakers: How the Philadelphia Negro Changed Urban America* (New York: Oxford University Press, 2013); Michael B. Katz and Thomas J. Sugrue, eds., *W.E.B. Du Bois, Race, and the City: The Philadelphia Negro and Its Legacy* (Philadelphia: University of Pennsylvania Press, 1998); Adolph L. Reed Jr., *W.E.B. Du Bois and American Political Thought: Fabianism and the Color Line* (New York: Oxford University Press, 1997), 27–42.

40. *Annual Report of the Superintendent of Public Schools of the City of Philadelphia* (Philadelphia: Philadelphia Board of Education, 1907) 42–43. See also David F. Labaree, *The Making of An American High School: The Credentials Market and the Central High School of Philadelphia, 1838–1939* (New Haven, CT: Yale University Press, 1988), 64–96.

41. *Annual Report of the Superintendent of Public Schools of the City of Philadelphia.*

42. Darlene A. Thompson, "The Sociopolitical Context of the Philadelphia Public Schools 1912 to 1972: Viewed in Retrospect by Ruth Wright Hayre," PhD diss., Temple University, 1990, 53–69; Franklin, *The Education of Black Philadelphia*, 30–42; Mohraz, *The Separate Problem*, 88–90; David M. Ment, "Racial Segregation in the Schools of New England and New York,

1840-1940." Ph.D. diss. Columbia University, 1975, 247–248; Augustus Granville Dill, "The Report of the Chicago Commission on Race Relations," *Crisis* 25, no. 3 (1923): 111–112; The Chicago Commission on Race Relations, *The Negro in Chicago* (Chicago: University of Chicago Press, 1922), 241–242.

43. Robert Gregg, *Sparks from the Anvil of Oppression: Philadelphia's African Methodists and Southern Migrants, 1890–1940* (Philadelphia: Temple University Press, 1993), 27–58; Roger Lane, *Philadelphia & Ours: On the Past and Future of the Black City in America* (New York: Oxford University Press, 1991), 134–165, 231–252; Franklin, *The Education of Black Philadelphia*, 39–40; William A. Creditt, speech delivered at the National Memorial Meeting, Washington, DC, April 2, 1895, Box 36, Reel 22, Speech, Article, and Book File in Frederick Douglass Papers, 1841–1967, Manuscript Division, Library of Congress, Washington, DC. See also "Dr. William A. Creditt the Great Educator," *Philadelphia Tribune*, January 20, 1917, 2; "Anniversary of Dr. William A. Creditt," *Lincoln University Herald*, 19, no. 2 (1915): 1, Special Collection of the Langston Hughes Memorial Library, Lincoln University, Pennsylvania; "Rev. William A. Creditt, DD, Makes Strong Suggestions for the Race," *Philadelphia Tribune*, March 2, 1912, 1; "Agricultural School Meets with Success," *Philadelphia Inquirer*, March 5, 1910, 1; "Training for Negroes," *Washington Post*, October 19, 1909, 3; "Baptists of Philadelphia," *New York Age*, October 10, 1907, 1; "Inspection Day at Colored Boys' School," *Philadelphia Inquirer*, May 9, 1906, 5.

44. Franklin, *The Education of Black Philadelphia*, 51–53; Mohraz, *The Separate Problem*, 89–90; "Dr. Brumbaugh's Views on Race Schools," *Philadelphia Inquirer*, December 8, 1908, 2; "Agitation Unnecessary," *New York Age*, November 5, 1908, 5.

45. V. P. Franklin, "Voice of the Black Community: The Philadelphia Tribune, 1912–1941," *Pennsylvania History* 51, no. 4 (1984): 261–284; Mohraz, *The Separate Problem*, 9–12; "Auxiliaries of the Douglass Hospital Entertain Dr. Mossell," *Philadelphia Tribune*, April 18, 1914, 1; "They Object to Separate Schools," *Afro-American*, September 28, 1912, 1; "Along the Color Line," *Crisis* 4, no. 3 (1912): 1; "Delegation of Citizens in Lengthy Conference with Dr. Brumbaugh," *Philadelphia Tribune*, February 24, 1912, 1; "Separate School Issue," *Philadelphia Tribune*, February 17, 1912, 3. On school segregation in other northern communities, see "A Segregation of Public Schools," *Chicago Defender*, February 3, 1912, 5; "Negro Fighting Color Line," *Los Angeles Times*, June 17, 1911, I12.

46. Berlin, *The Making of African America*, 152–185; Franklin, *The Education of Black Philadelphia*, 12–24; W. E. B. Du Bois, "The Migration of Negroes," *Crisis* 14, no. 2 (1917): 63–66.

47. Daniel A. Brooks, "Veteran Principal Compares Present School Conditions with Those of World War I," *Philadelphia Tribune*, December 11, 1943, 20.

48. Davis-Hayes, "Lessons of Place," 162–164; Herbert M. Kliebard, *Schooled to Work: Vocationalism and the American Curriculum, 1876–1946* (New York: Teachers College Press, 1999), 26–54; Tyack, *The One Best System*, 217–229; Franklin, *The Education of Black Philadelphia*, 44–54; Armstrong Association of Philadelphia, *A Comparative Study of the Occupations and Wages of the Children of Working Age in Potter and Durham Schools, Philadelphia* (Philadelphia: Philadelphia Board of Education, 1913); Howard W. Odum, "Negro Children in the Public Schools of Philadelphia," *Annals of the American Academy of Political and Social Science* 49 (September 1913): 186–208, quote on page 190.

49. Watkins, *The White Architects of Black Education*, 9–23; James D. Anderson, *The Education of Blacks in the South, 1860–1935* (Chapel Hill: University of North Carolina Press, 1988); W. E. B. Du Bois, "Education," *Crisis* 10, no. 3 (1915): 132–136; emphasis in original. The *Philadelphia Tribune* reported that the Philadelphia School Board was "greatly peeved" at the editorial by Dr. Du Bois; see "Citizens Are Not Satisfied with Action of School Board," *Philadelphia Tribune*, July 10, 1915, 1. Du Bois again rails against industrial education in "The Common School," *Crisis* 16, no. 3 (1918): 111–112; "Negro Education, a Review" *Crisis* 15, no. 4 (1918): 172–173. See also Derrick P. Alridge, "Conceptualizing a Du Boisian Philosophy of Education: Toward a Model for African-American Education," *Educational Theory* 49, no. 3 (1999): 359–380.

50. "Color Line in Schools Opposed by Thoughtful Ones," *Philadelphia Tribune*, August 28, 1915, 1; "Fighting against Separate Schools," *Afro-American*, August 21, 1915, 1.

51. G. Edward Dickerson and William Lloyd Imes, "The Cheyney Training School," *Crisis* 26, no. 1 (1923): 18–21.

52. Mellie M. Brinkley, "Letter to the Tribune," *Philadelphia Tribune*, November 6, 1920, 5; "To Urge Separate Schools," *Afro-American*, April 21, 1917, 1; "Jury Verdict Sustains Action of School Board," *Philadelphia Tribune*, January 27, 1917, 1. Wartime migration caused overcrowding in the public schools serving Black students in many northern cities; see, for example, "Separate Schools in Indiana," *Afro-American*, January 25, 1924, 4; "The School Strike in Springfield, Ohio," *Opportunity* 1, no. 2 (1923): 27–28; Alvin D. Smith, "Citizens Wish for Segregation in Indianapolis," *Chicago Defender*, December 23, 1922, 3; "Separate Schools in Atlantic City," *Afro-American*, October 13, 1922, 10; "Who Caused the Jim Crow School System in Gary?" *Chicago Defender*, April 15, 1922, 8; "Negro Education Is Problem in Indiana," *Christian Science Monitor*, September 28, 1917, 3; "Refuses to Attend Separate School," *Philadelphia Tribune*, September 15, 1917, 1.

53. W. E. B. Du Bois, "Opinion," *Crisis* 20, no. 3 (1920): 117–120; W. E. B. Du Bois, "Reconstruction," *Crisis* 18, no. 3 (1919): 130.

54. Adam Ewing, *The Age of Garvey: How a Jamaican Activist Created a Mass Movement and Changed Global Black Politics* (Princeton, NJ: Princeton University Press, 2014); Manning Marable, *Malcolm X: A Life of Reinvention* (New York: Viking Press, 2011), 20–22; Adam Fairclough, *Better Day Coming: Blacks and Equality, 1890–2000* (New York: Viking Press, 2001), 111–131; Dean E. Robinson, *Black Nationalism in American Politics and Thought* (New York: Cambridge University Press, 2001), 17–79; Raymond L. Hall, *Black Separatism in the United States* (Hanover, NH: University Press of New England, 1978), 58–74; E. U. Essien-Udom, *Black Nationalism: A Search for an Identity in America* (Chicago: University of Chicago Press, 1962), 36–46; G. Grant Williams, "Marcus Garvey as We Saw Him," *Philadelphia Tribune*, October 22, 1921, 9; "Cheering Negroes Hail Black Nation," *New York Times*, August 3, 1920, 7; Horace D. Slatter, "Some Men I Have Known: Dr. J. H. Eason," *Afro-American*, August 19, 1916, 2.

55. "Negroes Told to Prepare for Bloodiest of Wars," *New-York Tribune*, February 4, 1920, 8. See also David F. Krugler, *1919, The Year of Racial Violence: How African Americans Fought Back* (New York: Cambridge University Press, 2015); Cameron McWhirter, *Red Summer: The Summer of 1919 and the Awakening of Black America* (New York: Henry Holt, 2011); Robert Whitaker, *On the Laps of Gods: The Red Summer of 1919 and the Struggle for Justice that Remade a Nation* (New York: Broadway Books, 2009); William M. Tuttle Jr., *Race Riot: Chicago and the Red Summer of 1919* (Champaign: University of Illinois Press, 1996); Augustus Granville Dill, "The Report of the Chicago Commission on Race Relations," *Crisis* 25, no. 3 (1923): 111–112; "Autumn Fair Opens Amidst Splendor of Race Achievement, Ten Thousand Hear Marcus Garvey," *Philadelphia Tribune*, October 22, 1921, 1; "Local Division of UNIA Holds Big Celebration," *Philadelphia Tribune*, April 9, 1921, 1; G. Grant Williams, "The UNI Assn. Attracts Large Crowd at Dunbar," *Philadelphia Tribune*, March 12, 1921, 1.

56. Marcus Garvey, "Address to UNIA Supporters in Philadelphia, October 21, 1919," *Negro World*, November 1, 1919. Published in Robert A. Hill, ed., *Marcus Garvey and Universal Negro Improvement Association Papers*, vol. 2, *August 1919–August 1920* (Berkeley: University of California Press, 1983), 89–98. See also Edmund David Cronon, *Black Moses: The Story of Marcus Garvey and the Universal Negro Improvement Association* (Madison: University of Wisconsin Press, 1969[1955]) 3–72.

57. "Garvey's Followers Proud of 'Jim Crow' Laws in South," *Chicago Defender*, March 31, 1923, 8; Dr. J. W. H. Eason, "Address to UNIA Meeting in New York City, October 26, 1919,"published in Hill, *Marcus Garvey and Universal Negro Improvement Association Papers*, vol. 2, 140–142. Eason, a prominent minister at Philadelphia's People's Metropolitan African Methodist Episcopal Zion Church, served as a high-ranking official in UNIA with a salary of $10,000 a year—a small fortune for the time. Due to financial mismanagement, Garvey was unable to pay the high salaries he promised to officials like Eason. In 1922, Eason quit the UNIA, sued Garvey for back wages, and traveled the country speaking out against Garvey and the UNIA. Just before Eason was scheduled to testify against Garvey in court, he was murdered in New Orleans on January 2, 1923. Although shot three times in the chest and head, Eason survived long enough to identify his assailants as two prominent members of

UNIA, who admitted to murdering Eason because he posed a threat to Garvey. Although the Black and white press predicted Eason's murder by UNIA members would mean the end of the organization, no one was ever found guilty of murdering Eason. "Eason's Suit against Garvey Continues after His Death," *Afro-American*, April 20, 1923, 6; "Dr. J. W. H. Eason Well Known Here," *New Journal and Guide*, January 20, 1923, 3; "Investigation in New Orleans," *New York Times*, January 13, 1923, 14; "Death Blow to UNIA," *New Amsterdam News*, January 10, 1923, 12; "Eason Assassinated," *New York Amsterdam News*, January 10, 1923, 1.

58. William Pickens, "Garvey on Social Equality," *Philadelphia Tribune*, April 19, 1924, 15.
59. Franklin, *The Education of Black Philadelphia*, 71–86; Logan, "Educational Segregation in the North"; letter from Membership Committee of the Philadelphia Branch of the NAACP to Members, March 29, 1923, in Folder, "Philadelphia, Pennsylvania branch operations, January–May 1923," Papers of the NAACP, Part 12: Selected Branch Files, 1913–1939, Series B: The Northeast, ProQuest History Vault, http://congressional.proquest.com/histvault?q=001425-006-1162; "Recognition of Cheyney as State Normal School," *Philadelphia Tribune*, October 30, 1920, 1.
60. Leslie Pinckney Hill, "The Cheyney Training School for Teachers," *Crisis* 25, no. 6 (1923): 252–254. See also Leslie Pinckney Hill, "The State Teachers' College at Cheyney and Its Relation to Segregation in the North," *Journal of Negro Education* 1, no. 3/4 (1932): 408–413.
61. Dickerson and Imes, "The Cheyney Training School," 20; memorandum from the Philadelphia Branch of the NAACP to Members, March 29, 1923, in Folder, "Philadelphia, Pennsylvania branch operations, January–May 1923," Papers of the NAACP. See also letter from G. Edward Dickerson to W. E. B. Du Bois, May 25, 1923; letter from G. Edward Dickerson to A. D. McDade, January 5, 1922, both in Series 1: Correspondence, Du Bois Papers.
62. W. E. B. Du Bois, "The Tragedy of Jim Crow," *Crisis* 26, no. 4 (1923): 169–172. This address was delivered first in Philadelphia at the Royal Theatre and then at Cheyney, before being published in the August issue of the *Crisis*. Positive responses to this speech and article include letter from Alice Burris to the editor of the *Crisis*, August 8, 1923; letter from Ernestine Rose to W. E. B. Du Bois, July 31, 1923, both in W. E. B. Du Bois Papers, Series 1 Correspondence; "Du Bois Speaks at Royal Theatre," *Pittsburgh Courier*, April 28, 1923, 9. For a critical response, see William Pickens, "Du Bois at Cheyney," *New York Amsterdam News*, July 25, 1923, 12; "Special: Du Bois Is Praiser of Segregation," *Chicago Defender*, July 7, 1923, 1. For more on Du Bois's views on separate versus integrated education, see Derrick P. Alridge, "On the Education of Black Folk: W.E.B. Du Bois and the Paradox of Segregation," *Journal of African American History* 100, no. 3 (2015): 473–493; Vincent P. Franklin, "W.E.B. Du Bois and the Education of Black Folk," *History of Education Quarterly* 16, no. 1 (1976): 111–118.
63. Letter from W.F.W./R.R. to Isadore Martin, July 8, 1922; letter from James W. Johnson to William Lloyd Imes, June 28, 1922; memo from William Lloyd Imes, Chairman of the Philadelphia Branch of the NAACP, et. al., Committee on Public School Education and Race Relations: A Project and a Program, June 22, 1922; letter from William Lloyd Imes to James Weldon Johnson, June 20, 1922; all found in Folder, "Philadelphia, Pennsylvania branch operations 1919–1922," Papers of the NAACP, Part 12: Selected Branch Files, 1913–1939, Series B: The Northeast, ProQuest History Vault, http://congressional.proquest.com/histvault?q=001425-006-1033. See also Thomas J. Sugrue, *Sweet Land of Liberty: The Forgotten Struggle for Civil Rights in the North* (New York: Random House, 2008), 10–12; Franklin, *The Education of Black Philadelphia*, 51, 60, 65; Meier and Rudwick, "Early Boycotts of Segregated Schools: The Case of Springfield, Ohio, 1922–23;"Anne Biddle Stirling, "Interracial Teaching in the Schools," *Opportunity* 1, no. 3 (1923): 7; "The Victory at Springfield," *Crisis* 26, no. 5 (1923): 200; "The School Strike in Springfield Ohio," *Opportunity* 1, no. 2 (1923): 27–28.
64. Letter from James Weldon Johnson to Mary Isabelle Coleman, July 27, 1923; letter from Mary Isabelle Coleman to the NAACP, July 26, 1923, both in Folder, "Segregation in Toms River, New Jersey public Schools," Papers of the NAACP, Part 3: The Campaign for Educational Equality, Series A: Legal Department and Central Office Records, 1913–1940. ProQuest History Vault, http://congressional.proquest.com/histvault?q=001509-013-0084. See also Robert W. Clark, "A History of the Philadelphia High School for Girls," PhD diss., Temple University, 1935.

65. "Why Jim Crow Schools," *Philadelphia Tribune*, May 10, 1928, 16. See also "Another Jim Crow School," *Philadelphia Tribune*, January 30, 1926, 4.
66. "Teachers in Conference Favor Separate Schools," *Philadelphia Tribune*, June 6, 1925, 1. See also "Separate School Is Discussed by Pedagogues," *Philadelphia Tribune*, May 22, 1922, 1. Howard University sociologist Kelly Miller expressed similar sentiments recognizing the value of separate schools. See Kelly Miller, "Professor Kelly Miller Flares at Pike in Ribs," *Chicago Defender*, July 29, 1922, 8; Kelly Miller, "Does Kelly Miller Advocate Jim Crow Schools in North?" *Chicago Defender*, February 11, 1922, 20.
67. E. Franklin Frazier, "A Note on Negro Education," *Opportunity* 2, no. 15 (1924): 75–77.
68. Du Bois, "The Tragedy of Jim Crow." See also "Our Graduates: Northern High Schools," *Crisis* 14, no. 3 (1917): 124.
69. Giles R. Wright, *Afro-Americans in New Jersey: A Short History* (Trenton, NJ: New Jersey Historical Commission, 1988), 67–68; Ella Lou Thornbrough, "The Indianapolis Story: School Segregation and Desegregation in a Northern City," unpublished manuscript, 1989: 42, Collection: BV 2631, Manuscript and Visual Collections Department, William Henry Smith Memorial Library, Indiana Historical Society, Indianapolis, IN; Report of a Survey by the Interracial Committee of the New Jersey Conference of Social Work, *The Negro in New Jersey* (Trenton: New Jersey State Department of Institutions and Agencies, 1932), 37; "We Should Fight for These Things," *Philadelphia Tribune*, February 20, 1926, 4; "Another Jim Crow School"; "Segregation," *Crisis* 29, no. 1 (1924): 19.
70. "Separate School Is Discussed by Pedagogues," *Philadelphia Tribune*, May 22, 1926, 1.
71. Interracial Committee of the New Jersey Conference of Social Work, *The Negro in New Jersey*, 37; "Campaign to Stop Separate School Begins," *Philadelphia Tribune*, April 3, 1926, 1.
72. O. Z. Phillips, "Prefer Separate Schools," *Philadelphia Tribune*, July 25, 1929, 16; George Blount, "Waring Heads Penna. State Teachers," *Afro-American*, June 11, 1927, 5; "Where Are the Anti-Segregationists?" *Philadelphia Tribune*, October 9, 1926, 16. See also a description of a Philadelphia school meeting written by a New Yorker, who expressed dismay at the degree of support for separate schools in Philadelphia: "Minutes of the New York Group of the Seminar on Segregation," March 8, 1934, in Folder, "NAACP on segregation," Papers of the NAACP.
73. H. Rush, "What Have You to Say?" *Philadelphia Tribune*, August 22, 1929, 16. See also "Resolution Drafted by Dr. Du Bois," March 26, 1934; NAACP, "Resolution on Segregation," March 26, 1934; both in Folder, "NAACP on segregation," Papers of the NAACP.
74. Douglas, *Jim Crow Moves North*, 172–186; Dougherty, *More than One Struggle*, 14–19; Mirel, *The Rise and Fall of an Urban School System*, 186–196, W. E. B. Du Bois, "The Black North in 1901: New York," in Dan S. Green and Edwin D. Driver, eds., *W.E.B. Du Bois: On Sociology and the Black Community* (Chicago: University of Chicago Press, 1978), 140–153; Robert A. Crump, "Detroit Bolts at Separate Schools Idea," *New Journal and Guide*, June 23, 1934, 14; "15 Colored Schools Open in Philly," *Afro-American*, September 15, 1928, 7; I. Garland Penn, "Bishop Carey Challenged to Debate," *Afro-American*, September 24, 1927, 4; Calvin, "Mrs. McDougald Tells of N.Y. Mixed School System"; "Jersey Teachers Find that Jim Crow Schools Mean Inferior Schools," *Philadelphia Tribune*, May 15, 1926, 9; "Negro Education on a Par," *Christian Science Monitor*, October 16, 1924, 8; Owen, "Errors in Jim Crow School Argument"; "Cleveland, O., Mecca for Colored People," *Philadelphia Tribune*, August 20, 1921, 1; "Answer to Mr. Loeb's Letter Fostering Separate Schools," *Chicago Defender*, August 17, 1918, 16; "Separate Schools," *Chicago Defender*, July 1, 1916, 8; "Jim Crow School," *Chicago Defender*, March 29, 1913, 4.
75. Lester B. Granger, "Ironsides: The Bordentown Vocational School," *Southern Workman* 56, no. 5 (1927): 223–231, quote on p. 227. Lester Blackwell Granger Papers, Box 2, Folder 39, Series 1: Writings, James Weldon Johnson Collection in the Yale Collection of American Literature, Beinecke Rare Book and Manuscript Library, Yale University, New Haven, CT. See also Evelyn Blackmore Duck, "An Historical Study of a Segregated School in New Jersey from 1886 to 1955," EdD diss., Rutgers University, 1984, 45–53; Ezola B. Adams, "The Role and Function of the Manual Training and Industrial School at Bordentown as an Alternative School, 1915-1955," EdD diss., Rutgers University, 1977, 1–5. Wright, *The Education of Negroes in New Jersey*, 183–188; Vishnu V. Oak and Eleanor H. Oak, "The Illegal Status of

Separate Education in New Jersey," *School and Society* 47 (May 1938): 671–673; "Large Classes at Bordentown," *New York Amsterdam News,* September 24, 1938, 17; "Bordentown Has Increased Funds," *New York Amsterdam News,* July 4, 1936, 20; "Bordentown's Head Sees 400 on Rolls," *New York Amsterdam News,* September 20, 1933, 10; Lester B. Granger, "The School and Community Leadership: The Story of Bordentown," *Opportunity* 11, no. 5 (1933): 137–140; "Lauds Program at Bordentown," *New York Amsterdam News,* June 22, 1932, 10; "Bordentown School Now a Second Tuskegee," *Chicago Defender,* January 3, 1931, 1; William Pickens, "Well-Known Jersey School Has an Educational 'Valentine,'" *New Journal and Guide,* December 27, 1930, 9.

76. Crowley, "Cincinnati's Experiment in Negro Education;"Ohio School Has 3,000 Pupils, 118 Teachers," *Afro-American,* August 31, 1929, 3; Porter, "The Problem of Negro Education in Northern and Border Cities," preface (no page number); "Harriet Beecher Stowe School Unique Landmark of Educational Program," *Pittsburgh Courier,* May 17, 1924, 16; "Race Principal Gets Bachelor of Science Degree," *Pittsburgh Courier,* June 23, 1923, 9.

77. Thornbrough, "The Indianapolis Story: School Segregation and Desegregation in a Northern City," 1–45; Lynn Ford, "Crispus Attucks High School: Despite Protests, City Created All-Black High School," *Indianapolis Star,* February 1, 2001; "Klan Fights Intermarriage and Wants Separate Schools," *Pittsburgh Courier,* September 26, 1931, 1; "T. J. Anderson Appointed Crispus Attucks Head," *Afro-American,* July 19, 1930, 17; Vivian Williams, "On Air at Attucks," *Indianapolis Recorder,* November 24, 1928, 5; Harry D. Evans, "With the Sands of the Hour Glass," *Indianapolis Recorder,* September 3, 1927, 4; "Separate Schools in Indianapolis," *Pittsburgh Courier,* June 7, 1924, 2; "Draw Color Line on School Children," *Chicago Defender,* May 20, 1916, 1.

78. Pamphlet: "Scholarship Luncheon 1984: Crispus Attucks Alumni Association Detroit Chapter," in Folder 5, Box 1, Russell A. Lane Collection, M522, Manuscript and Visual Collections Department, William Henry Smith Memorial Library, Indiana Historical Society, Indianapolis, Indiana; hereafter, Russell A. Lane Papers. Matthias Nolcox oral history interview with Jean Spears conducted in 1970, transcription in collection, Matthias Nolcox Oral History Interview, c. 1979. SC2729, Manuscript and Visual Collections Department, William Henry Smith Memorial Library, Indiana Historical Society, Indianapolis, Indiana. See also Laats, *The Other School Reformers,* 50–58.

79. Davis-Hayes, "Lessons of Place," 110–112; Dionne Danns, "Thriving in the Midst of Adversity: Educator Maudelle Brown Bousfield's Struggles in Chicago, 1920–1950," *Journal of Negro Education* 78, no. 1 (2009): 3–16, quote on p. 10; Homel, *Down from Equality,* 39–41. In 2003, the Commission on Chicago Landmarks recognized Wendell Phillips High School, Chicago's first predominantly Black high school, as a historic landmark. See Commission on Chicago Historical and Architectural Landmarks, "City of Chicago Landmark Designation Reports," September 2002, https://archive.org/stream/CityOfChicagoLandmarkDesignati onReports/WendellPhillipsHighSchool_djvu.txt; Chinta Strausberg, "City Seeks Landmark Status for Phillips, First Black High School," *Chicago Defender,* April 9, 2003, 8.

80. Crispus Attucks High School in Indianapolis *Yearbook* 1933. In Folder 6, Box 1, Russell A. Lane Papers. See also Stanley Warren, "The Evolution of Secondary Schooling for Blacks in Indianapolis, 1869–1930," in Wilma L. Gibbs, ed., *Indiana's African-American Heritage: Essays from Black History News and Notes* (Indianapolis: Indiana Historical Society, 2007), 29–50.

81. On Cairo, see Kathryn Ward, "It Ain't Got Here Yet! Intersection of Race, Economics and Civil Rights in Cairo, IL, 1828–2000," 14–16, unpublished manuscript in Folder 2, Box 22. Kendrick-Brooks Family Papers, Manuscript Division, Library of Congress, Washington, DC. See also Cheryl Lynn Greenberg, *To Ask for an Equal Chance: African Americans in the Great Depression* (Lanham, MD: Rowman & Littlefield, 2009); David B. Tyack, Robert Lowe, and Elisabeth Hansot, *Public Schools in Hard Times: The Great Depression and Recent Years* (Cambridge, MA: Harvard University Press, 1987); Jeffrey Mirel, "The Politics of Educational Retrenchment in Detroit," *History of Education Quarterly,* 24, no. 3 (1984): 323–358; S. Alexander Rippa, "Retrenchment in a Period of Defensive Opposition to the New Deal: The Business Community and the Public Schools, 1932–1934," *History of Education Quarterly* 2, no. 2 (1962): 76–82.

82. Harry W. Greene, "The Economic Crisis and Negro Education," *Opportunity* 12, no. 2 (1934): 48–50; "Secondary Education for Negroes," *Opportunity* 12, no. 11 (1934): 327; Ambrose Caliver, *Secondary Education for Negroes*, Bulletin No. 17, Monograph No. 7 (Washington, DC: Government Printing Office, 1933); Jane Addams, "The Education of Negroes," *Opportunity* 10, no. 12 (1932): 370–371; David A. Lane Jr., "The Report of the National Advisory Committee on Education and the Problem of Negro Education," *Journal of Negro Education*, 1, no. 1 (1932): 5–15; E. George Payne, "Negroes in the Public Elementary Schools of the North," *Annals of the American Academy of Political and Social Science*, 140 (November, 1928): 224–233; John W. Davis, "Education," *Opportunity* 6, no. 7 (1928): 201.
83. William M. Banks, *Black Intellectuals: Race and Responsibility in American Life* (New York: W. W. Norton, 1996), 92–117; Horace Mann Bond, "From 1905 to 1935: A Long Jump in the History of Race Progress," *Chicago Defender*, May 4, 1935, 18; E. A. Schaal, "Will the Negro Rely upon Force?" *Crisis* 40, no. 1 (1933): 8–9; W. E. B. Du Bois, "The Year in Negro Education," *Crisis* 37, no. 8 (1930): 262–268; W. E. B. Du Bois, "Along the Color Line," *Crisis* 37, no. 2 (1930): 59.
84. George F. McCray, "Education," *Crisis* 40, no. 8 (1933): 189–190; Johnson, *The Negro in American Civilization*, 267. Kelly Miller, "Is the Color Line Crumbling?" *Opportunity* 7, no. 9 (1929): 282–285.
85. Horace Mann Bond, "Charles H. Thompson Urges Legal Steps to Get Better Schools," *Pittsburgh Courier*, August 4, 1934, 7; Horace Mann Bond, "Watch Your School Budget!" *Afro-American*, March 4, 1933, 11; J. Max Barber, "The Philadelphia Public Schools," *Pittsburgh Courier*, November 7, 1931, 1.
86. Franklin, *The Education of Black Philadelphia*, 135-143.
87. Committee on Race Relations, "Summary of Seminar on Segregation, Held under the Auspices of the Committee on Race Relations, Philadelphia, Pennsylvania," January 26, 1934, in Folder, "NAACP on Segregation," Papers of the NAACP, Part 11: Special Subject Files, 1912–1939, Series B: Harding, Warren G. through YWCA, ProQuest History Vault, http://congressional.proquest.com/histvault?q=001422-029-0318. See also Robert Bagnall, "Says Whites Must Be Accepted in Negro Schools if They Apply," *Philadelphia Tribune*, July 1, 1937, 4; "303 Colored; 7,386 Whites Teach in Philly Schools," *Afro-American*, June 8, 1935, 14; William N. Jones, "Talking It Over," *Afro-American*, May 18, 1935, 13; "Philly Separate Schools Are Attacked by Howard University Professor," *Philadelphia Tribune*, August 2, 1934, 1; "Education Board Snubs Plea as Jobs Dwindle," *Philadelphia Tribune*, July 12, 1934, 1; "Throughout the State of Pennsylvania: PA Teachers to Fight Color Bar," *Afro-American*, June 16, 1934, 19; "Teachers Here Protest Closed Door Policy in High Schools," *Philadelphia Tribune*, June 14, 1934, 3; Floyd L. Logan, "Pennsylvania Law Does Not Sanction Separate Schools," *Pittsburgh Courier*, November 11, 1933, 7; "Servile Jobs Result of Jim Crow Schools," *Philadelphia Tribune*, May 26, 1932, 1; "Jim Crow Hits Ofay's Blood," *Afro-American*, April 23, 1932, 18.
88. Arnetta Barron, Oral History Interview, Atlantic City, NJ, January 23, 1979, and James Moore, Oral History Interview, Millburn, NJ, June 11, 1979, both cited in Wynetta Devore, "The Education of Blacks in New Jersey, 1900–1915: An Exploration in Oral History," EdD diss., Rutgers University, 1980, 140–141, 161–162.
89. "Jim Crow Upheld by Court in Ohio Case," *New York Amsterdam News*, June 27, 1940, 4; William D. Barbee, "High Court Will Hear School Case," *Chicago Defender*, May 11, 1940, 12; "Ohioans Fight Court's Jim-Crow School Ruling," *Chicago Defender*, January 20, 1940, 2; "Parents Fight Jim Crow School in Ohio Town"; G. James Fleming, "A Philadelphia Lawyer," *Crisis* 46, no. 11 (1939): 329–331; "Along the NAACP Battlefront," *Crisis* 45, no. 10 (1938): 336; William Pickens, "Severe Blow to James Crow in California," *Atlanta Daily World*, November 21, 1936, 7; "Branch News," *Crisis*, 41, no. 11 (1934): 370; "Jersey Parents Continue War on Jim Crow School," *Afro-American*, September 1, 1934, 11; Crump, "Detroit Bolts at Separate Schools Idea"; "Victory at Toms River"; "Jim-Crow School Plan Fought by Montclair, New Jersey, Parents," *Pittsburgh Courier*, April 28, 1934, 1; "Fight Color Line in New Jersey Schools," *Chicago Defender*, September 30, 1933, 1; "The Pittsburgh NAACP," *Crisis* 40, no. 3 (1933): 58; "Mr. James Crow," *Crisis* 40, no. 1 (1933): 17; Rayford W. Logan, "Educational Segregation in the North," *Journal of Negro Education*, 2, no. 1 (1933): 65–67;

"Pa. Town Begin Separate Schools," *Afro-American*, June 11, 1932, 5; "Segregation in Schools Fought," *New York Amsterdam News*, March 9, 1932, 10; Robinson, "Jim Crowism Is Rampant in Asbury Park"; "No Separate Schools for NJ Children," *Afro-American*, June 4, 1930, 18.

90. Johnson, *Backgrounds to Patterns of Negro Segregation*, 198; Johnson, *The Negro in American Civilization*, 271; Harry Webber, "Jersey Court Decision May Affect State's Separate Schools," *Afro-American*, March 18, 1933, 7; Ernest A. Hooton, "Is the Negro Inferior?" *Crisis* 39, no. 11 (1932): 345–346, 364; "Newark Mayor Petitioned to Drop Miss Sims," *Pittsburgh Courier*, March 17, 1928, 8; Franz Boas, "The Real Race Problem," *Crisis* 1, no. 2 (1910): 22–25.

91. Harvard Sitkoff, *A New Deal for Blacks: The Emergence of Civil Rights as a National Issue: The Depression Decade*. 30th Anniversary Edition. (New York: Oxford University Press, 2009); Lauren Rebecca Sklaroff, *Black Culture and the New Deal: The Quest for Civil Rights in the Roosevelt Era* (Chapel Hill: University of North Carolina Press, 2009); Patricia Sullivan, *Days of Hope: Race and Democracy in the New Deal Era* (Chapel Hill: University of North Carolina Press, 1996); Lizabeth Cohen, *Making a New Deal: Industrial Workers in Chicago, 1919–1939* (New York: Cambridge University Press, 1990).

92. "Jersey Parents Continue War on Jim Crow School;" William A. Nixon, "Rejoices over Berwyn School Victory," *Philadelphia Tribune*, May 17, 1934, 4; "2 Year War on Berwyn School Jim Crow Won," *Pittsburgh Courier*, May 12, 1934, 2; Joseph Rainey, "Parents Win in Long Color Bar School Fight," *Afro-American*, May 5, 1934, 12; "Jim-Crow School Plan Fought by Montclair, New Jersey Parents"; "4 Parents Jailed in Berwyn for 'Violating Code,'" *Afro-American*, October 28, 1933, 5; "Parents Defy School Boards Refusing to Enroll Children in Jim Crow Berwyn Schools," *Afro-American*, September 16, 1933, 3; "School Board Warns Parents They Face Jail," *Philadelphia Tribune*, September 7, 1933, 1; "The Pittsburgh NAACP," *Crisis* 40, no. 3 (1933): 58; Joseph Rainey, "Negroes Barred from Chester High School," *Philadelphia Tribune*, February 23, 1933, 1; "Along the Color Line," *Crisis* 20, no. 2 (1933): 39; "Mr. James Crow," *Crisis* 40, no. 1 (1933): 17; "Segregated School Suit on Main Line Lost," *Philadelphia Tribune*, December 15, 1932, 3; "Penny School Jim Crow Case in Court Dec. 6," *New Journal and Guide*, December 3, 1932, 7; "School Board Evades Issue in PA, Jim Crow," *Afro-American*, November 26, 1932, 8; "Main Line Children Refuse to Attend Segregated School," *Philadelphia Tribune*, October 6, 1932, 1; "Indignant Main Line Folk Fight Installation of 'Jim Crow' School System," *Philadelphia Tribune*, July 21, 1932, 1; "Main Line Citizens Oppose Planned Segregated School," May 19, 1932, 2.

93. "New Rochelle Hits Segregated School," *New York Amsterdam News*, September 17, 1930, 10; "Urban League and NAACP Flay Segregation Proposed for Rockville."

94. The Mayor's Commission on Conditions in Harlem, "The Negro in Harlem: A Report on Social and Economic Conditions Responsible for the Outbreak of March 19, 1935," New York, NY (1935), 67; George Streator, "Central High School, Cleveland," *Crisis* 41, no. 7 (1934): 215; George Streator, "Detroit, Columbus, and Cleveland," *Crisis* 41, no. 6 (1934): 172–173.

95. "Colored Sympathizer in Orange, NJ Battle over Segregated Schools Burns a Fiery Cross," *New Journal and Guide*, September 19, 1936, 4.

96. Charles S. Johnson, "Source Material for Patterns of Negro Segregation in Chicago, IL, 1940," page 6, Reel 7, Sc Micro R-6534, Carnegie-Myrdal Study of the Negro in America Research Memoranda Collection, 1935–1948, Schomburg Center for Research in Black Culture, Manuscripts, Archives and Rare Books Division, New York Public Library, New York, NY.

97. Charles H. Thompson, "Court Action the Only Reasonable Alternative to Remedy Immediate Abuses of the Negro Separate School," *Journal of Negro Education*, 4, no. 3 (1935): 419–434; "Color Caste in the United States," *Crisis* 40, no. 3 (1933): 59–60; Charles H. Thompson, "Introduction," *Journal of Negro Education* 1, no. 2 (1932): 101–107; Crowley, "Cincinnati's Experiment in Negro Education"; Charles H. Houston, "Editorial Comment: Why a Journal of Negro Education," *Journal of Negro Education* 1, no. 1 (1932): 1–4.

98. L. A. Pechstein, "The Problem of Negro Education in Northern and Border Cities," *Elementary School Journal* 30, no. 3 (1929): 192–199.

99. Letter from the Chicago Forum Council to Louis A. Pechstein, August 9, 1929; letter from the Chicago Forum Council to W. E. B. Du Bois, August 9, 1929; letter from W. E. B. Du Bois to Open Forum Speakers Bureau, August 7, 1929; memorandum from Walter White

to W. E. B. Du Bois: Dr. L. A. Pechstein, of University of Cincinnati, reports on survey at teachers' meeting, March 14, 1929; "Segregation Most Effective Plan for Education of Negro in the North, Is Claim," *Cincinnati Enquirer*, February 25, 1929, all in Series 1A, General Correspondence, W. E. B. Du Bois Papers.

100. Du Bois, "Pechstein and Pecksniff."

101. W. E. B. Du Bois, "Segregation," *Crisis* 40, no. 1 (1934): 2. See also, Alridge, *The Educational Thought of W. E. B. Du Bois*, 79–85; Francis J. Grimke, "Segregation," *Crisis* 41, no. 6 (1934): 173–174; W. E. B. Du Bois, "The NAACP and Race Segregation," *Crisis* 41, no. 2 (1934): 52–53.

102. Letter from W. E. B. Du Bois to NAACP Board of Directors, June 26, 1934, Series 1A, General Correspondence, Du Bois Papers; W. E. B. Du Bois, "Segregation in the North," *Crisis* 41, no. 4 (1934): 115–116.

103. Leah N. Gordon, *From Power to Prejudice: The Rise of Racial Individualism in Midcentury America* (Chicago: University of Chicago Press, 2015), 132–160; Horace Mann Bond, "The Extent and Character of the Separate School in the United States," *Journal of Negro Education* 4, no. 3 (1935): 321–327; Alain Locke, "The Dilemma of Separation," *Journal of Negro Education* 4, no. 3 (1935): 406–411; Howard Hale Long, "Some Psychogenic Hazards of Segregated Education of Negroes," *Journal of Negro Education* 4, no. 3 (1935): 336–350; Charles H. Thompson, "Editorial Comment: The Courts and the Negro Separate School," *Journal of Negro Education* 4, no. 3 (1935): 289–292.

104. W. E. B. Du Bois, "Does the Negro Need Separate Schools?" *Journal of Negro Education* 4, no. 3 (1935): 328–335.

105. Du Bois, "Does the Negro Need Separate Schools?"

106. Charles H. Thompson, "The Negro Separate School," *Crisis* 42, no. 8 (1935): 230–232; quote on p. 242. See also "Editorial: More Chickens Coming Home to Roost," *Crisis* 45, no. 1 (1938): 17.

107. Tushnet, *The NAACP's Legal Strategy against Segregated Education*, 61–81; *Alston et al. v. School Board of City of Norfolk et al.* 112F 2d 992 (4th Cir.), cert. denied, 311 U.S. 693 (1940); "Equal Salaries for Teachers," *Crisis* 47, no. 1 (1940): 10–12; Thurgood Marshall, "Equal Justice under Law," *Crisis* 46, no. 7 (1939): 199–201; *State of Missouri ex rel. Gaines v. Canada, Registrar of the University of Missouri, et al.* 305 U.S. 337 (1938); *Margaret Williams et al. v. David W. Zimmerman et al.* 172, Md. 563, 192 A.353 (1937); Charles H. Houston, "Don't Shout Too Soon," *Crisis* 43, no. 3 (1936): 79; Charles H. Houston, "Cracking Closed University Doors," *Crisis* 42, no. 12 (1935): 364, 370; Charles S. Houston, "Educational Inequalities Must Go!" *Crisis* 42, no. 10 (1935): 300–301.

Chapter 3

1. An inordinate number of northern public schools that served majority Black or all-Black student bodies were named after the Great Emancipator.

2. David Owens to Walter F. White, December 19, 1948; Franklin H. Williams to NAACP, December 22, 1948, both in Folder, "Discrimination and Segregation in East St. Louis Public Schools," Papers of the NAACP, Part 03: The Campaign for Equality, Series B: Legal Department and Central Offices Records, 1940–1950, ProQuest History Vault, http://congressional.ProQuest.com/histvault?q=001512-001-1135. See also Warrington W. Hudlin, "East St. Louis' Educational System Is Lagging Behind," *Pittsburgh Courier*, October 4, 1947, 20; "East St. Louis Girds for Fight on School Bias," *Chicago Defender*, June 28, 1947, 7.

3. For the Marshall quote, see Thurgood Marshall to James X. Ryan, no date; see also David Owens to Gloster B. Current, February 1, 1949; James X. Ryan to Ollie Harrington, January 31, 1949, all in "Discrimination and Segregation in East St. Louis Public Schools," Papers of the NAACP. See also Gloster B. Current, "Exit Jim Crow Schools in East St. Louis, Illinois," *Crisis* 57, no. 4 (1950): 209–212, 268; Albert L. Hinton, "An Open Letter to the Board of Education of East St. Louis, Illinois," *New Journal and Guide*, February 19, 1949, E10; "Children Seek to Enroll in East St. Louis Schools," *Atlanta Daily World*, February 8, 1949, 4; "White Pupils Strike over Race Issue," *New Journal and Guide*, February 5, 1949, E1. On Thurgood Marshall and the NAACP campaign against school segregation, see Rawn

James Jr., *Root and Branch: Charles Hamilton Houston, Thurgood Marshall, and the Struggle to End Segregation* (New York: Bloomsbury Press, 2010); James J. Patterson, *Brown v. Board of Education: A Civil Rights Milestone and Its Troubled Legacy* (New York: Oxford University Press, 2001), 1–45; Mark V. Tushnet, *The NAACP's Legal Strategy against Segregated Education, 1925–1950* (Chapel Hill: University of North Carolina Press, 1987); Mark V. Tushnet, *Thurgood Marshall and the Supreme Court, 1936–1961* (New York: Oxford University Press, 1994), 116–125, 150–167.

4. NAACP Press Release: Illinois NAACP Urges State and National Civil Rights Action, April 28, 1949; Gloster B. Current, NAACP Press Release: Segregated Schools on Trial in East St. Louis, March 1949; all in Folder, "Discrimination and Segregation in East St. Louis Public Schools," Papers of the NAACP.

5. W. E. B. Du Bois, *Darkwater: Voices from within the Veil* (New York: Washington Square Press, 2004 [1920]), 72; Current, NAACP Press Release: Segregated Schools on Trial in East St. Louis, March 1949, in Folder, "Discrimination and Segregation in East St. Louis Public Schools," Papers of the NAACP; East St. Louis *Journal*, February 1, 1949, as cited in Elliott Rudwick, "Fifty Years of Race Relations in East St. Louis: The Breaking Down of White Supremacy," *Midcontinent American Studies Journal* 6, no. 1 (1965): 3–15. See also Charles L. Lumpkins, *American Pogrom: The East St. Louis Race Riots and Black Politics* (Athens: Ohio University Press, 2008); Malcolm McLaughlin, "Ghetto Formation and Armed Resistance in East St. Louis, Illinois," *Journal of American Studies* 41, no. 2 (2007): 435–467; Elliot M. Rudwick, *Race Riot at East St. Louis, July 2, 1917* (Carbondale: Southern Illinois University Press, 1964).

6. June Shagaloff, "A Study of Community Acceptance of Desegregation in Two Selected Areas," *Journal of Negro Education* 23, no. 3 (1954): 330–338; "East St. Louis High Graduates 1st Negro," *Chicago Defender*, July 8, 1950, 3; "East St. Louis Schools Mixed without Incident," *Afro-American*, February 11, 1950, 1; "School Segregation Policy Ends Quietly after 85 Years in East St. Louis, IL," *New York Times*, January 31, 1950, 16; "Segregation Ends without Incident in East St. Louis, *Atlanta Daily World*, January 31, 1950, 1; "Ends Pupil Segregation," *New York Times*, January 30, 1950, 19; "New Day in East St. Louis," *Pittsburgh Courier*, December 31, 1949, 14; "East St. Louis Stops Jim Crow in Schools," *Chicago Defender*, December 31, 1949, 1; "East St. Louis Will End School Race Segregation," *New York Times*, December 22, 1949, 8; Albert L. Hinton, "Good Timing in the Court Ruling on the East St. Louis, Illinois Schools," *New Journal and Guide*, November 19, 1949, 8; "Illinois Compromise Blows Up as Wilkins Denies Approval of Deal," *Chicago Defender*, October 1, 1949, 1.

7. Memorandum from Daniel E. Byrd to Billy Jones, February 7, 1950, in Folder, "Educational Reform to End Segregation and Discrimination in East St. Louis," Papers of the NAACP, Part 03: The Campaign for Educational Equality, Series B: Legal Department and Central Office Records, 1940–1950, ProQuest History Vault, http://congressional.ProQuest.com/histvault?q=001512-001-1254; letter from Daniel E. Byrd to Thurgood Marshall, November 25, 1949, in Folder, "Discrimination and Segregation in East St. Louis Public Schools," Papers of the NAACP.

8. Gunnar Myrdal, *An American Dilemma: The Negro Problem and Modern Democracy* (New York: Harper & Row, [1944] 1962): 100. See also Leah N. Gordon, *From Power to Prejudice: The Rise of Racial Individualism in Midcentury America* (Chicago: University of Chicago Press, 2015); Mary L. Dudziak, *Cold War Civil Rights: Race and the Image of American Democracy*, new preface ed. (Princeton, NJ: Princeton University Press, 2011); Mark Brilliant, *The Color of America Has Changed: How Racial Diversity Shaped Civil Rights Reform in California, 1941–1978* (New York: Oxford University Press, 2010); Thomas J. Sugrue, *Sweet Land of Liberty: The Forgotten Struggle for Civil Rights in the North* (New York: Random House, 2008); Manning Marable, *Race, Reform, and Rebellion: The Second Reconstruction and Beyond in Black America, 1945–2006*, 3rd ed. (Jackson: University of Mississippi Press, 2007); Walter A. Jackson, *Gunnar Myrdal and America's Conscience: Social Engineering and Racial Liberalism, 1938–1987* (Chapel Hill: University of North Carolina Press, 1990); David W. Southern, *Gunnar Myrdal and Black-White Relations: The Use and Abuse of An American Dilemma, 1944–1969* (Baton Rouge: Louisiana State University Press, 1987);

Herbert Aptheker, *The Negro People in America: A Critique of Gunnar Myrdal's An American Dilemma* (New York: International Publishers, 1946).

9. New Rochelle, NY, Citizens Committee for Lincoln School, "A Report of the Findings Relative to the Lincoln School," January 11, 1949, in Folder, "Segregation and Discrimination in New Rochelle, New York Public Schools," Papers of the NAACP, Part 03: The Campaign for Educational Equality, Series B: Legal Department and Central Office Records, 1940–1950, ProQuest History Vault, http://congressional.ProQuest.com/histvault?q=001512-003-0865; newspaper clipping: "No Objection to Negro Say White Parents," November 16, 1940, in Folder, "Segregation and Discrimination in Ohio Schools and Colleges," Papers of the NAACP, Part 03: The Campaign for Educational Equality, Series B: Legal Department and Central Office Records, 1940–1950, ProQuest History Vault, http://congressional. ProQuest.com/histvault?q=001512-004-0263. See also Daryl Michael Scott, *Contempt and Pity: Social Policy and the Image of the Damaged Black Psyche, 1880–1996* (Chapel Hill: University of North Carolina Press, 1997), 71–136.

10. Richard Rothstein, *The Color of Law: A Forgotten History of How Our Government Segregated America* (New York: W.W. Norton, 2017); Patricia Sullivan, *Lift Every Voice: The NAACP and the Making of the Civil Rights Movement* (New York: New Press, 2009), 287–332; Davison M. Douglas, *Jim Crow Moves North: The Battle over Northern School Segregation, 1865–1954* (New York: Cambridge University Press, 2005), 219–273; Tushnet, *The NAACP's Legal Strategy against Segregated Education.*

11. Charles S. Johnson and Associates, *To Stem This Tide: A Survey of Racial Tension Areas in the United States* (New York: AMS Press, 1969 [1943]), 106–107. See also Linda Hervieux, *Forgotten: The Untold Story of D-Day's Black Heroes, at Home and at War* (New York: Harper Collins, 2015); William P. Jones, *The March on Washington: Jobs, Freedom, and the Forgotten History of Civil Rights* (New York: W.W. Norton, 2013); Cheryl Mullenback, *Double Victory: How African American Women Broke Race and Gender Barriers to Help Win World War II* (Chicago: Chicago Review Press, 2013); Kevin M. Kruse and Stephen Tuck, eds., *Fog of War: The Second World War and the Civil Rights Movement* (New York: Oxford University Press, 2012); Neil A. Wynn, *The African American Experience during World War II* (New York: Rowman & Littlefield, 2010); Lauren Rebecca Sklaroff, *Black Culture and the New Deal: The Quest for Civil Rights in the Roosevelt Era* (Chapel Hill: University of North Carolina, 2009); Adam Fairclough, *Better Day Coming: Blacks and Equality, 1890–2000* (New York: Viking Press, 2001), 181–201; Thomas Borstelmann, *The Cold War and the Color Line: American Race Relations in the Global Arena* (Cambridge, MA: Harvard University Press, 2001), 27–53; Ronald Takaki, *Double Victory: A Multicultural History of America in World War II* (New York: Little, Brown, 2000).

12. Margaret L. Caution, "Jersey Teachers to War on Schools' Racial Bias," *Afro-American*, June 2, 1945, 24.

13. Although her lawsuit was successful, Ms. Kendrick was fired for her political activism in 1953; see "Decision of the Cairo Board of Education, School District No. 1, July 24, 1954," in Folder 12, Box 21, and Debra Chandler Landis, "Miss Kendrick Is a Leader, Teacher, and Status-Quo Challenger," *Southeast Missourian*, August 23, 1981, 9, in Folder 10, Box 21, Kendrick-Brooks Family Papers, Manuscript Division, Library of Congress, Washington, DC. See also *Report on Educational Equality League*, 1977, Box 1, Folder 1, "History Highlights," Floyd L. Logan Papers, Special Collections Research Center, Temple University Libraries, Philadelphia, PA; Edna N. Bradley to Ella Baker, November 6, 1943, in Folder, "Segregation and Discrimination in Ohio public schools and colleges," Papers of the NAACP, Part 03: The Campaign for Educational Equality, Series B: Legal Documents and Central Office Records, 1940–1950, ProQuest History Vault, http://congressional. ProQuest.com/histvault?q=001512-004-0263; "Philadelphians Block Jim Crow School Plan," *Chicago Defender*, October 5, 1943, 1; "Colored Teachers Gets Senior High Post," *Philadelphia Tribune*, October 3, 1942, 2; Layle Lane, "Federation of School Teachers," *Crisis* 47, no. 1 (1940): 352–353; Reginald W. Pinckney to Thurgood Marshall, September 21, 1940, in Folder, "Discrimination in Pennsylvania Public Schools," Papers of the NAACP, Part 03: The Campaign for Educational Equality, Series B: Legal Department and Central Office Records, 1940–1950, ProQuest History Vault, http://congressional.ProQuest.

com/histvault?q=001512-004-0440; B. T. Gillespie, "Pittsburgh Divided on Mixed School Faculties," *Afro-American*, February 17, 1940, 6. On Hartford, see, Stacey Close, "Fire in the Bones: Hartford's NAACP, Civil Rights and Militancy, 1943–1969," *Journal of Negro History*, 86, no. 3 (2001): 228–263. On Hempstead, see Mabee, *Black Education in New York State*, 258–259.

14. NAACP Flyer: "Hillburn and Hattiesburg, Mass Rally," October 3, 1943, in Folder, "Mass meeting to protest de facto segregation in Hillburn, NY," Papers of the NAACP, Part 03: Campaign for Educational Equality, Series C: Legal Department and Central Office Records, 1951–1955, ProQuest History Vault, http://congressional.ProQuest. com/histvault?q=001513-002-0015; "Along the NAACP Battlefront: Hillburn's Attack on Jim Crow Schools," *Crisis* 50, no. 10 (1943): 308–309; "Appeal to Dewey in Hillburn Case," *Pittsburgh Courier*, September 25, 1943, 1; "Democracy Went to Sleep, Students Strike Protest of 'Jim Crow' School," *Pittsburgh Courier*, September 25, 1943, 20; "Push Court Fight on Jim Crow School," *Chicago Defender*, September 25, 1943, 5; "School Strike Continues in New York Town," *Afro-American*, September 25, 1943, 24; "Negroes Fight Jim-Crow Schools 19 Miles from New York City," *Chicago Defender*, September 18, 1943, 2; "Board Orders Segregation Ended in New York School," *Pittsburgh Courier*, September 18, 1943, 1; "Race Segregation Charged at Hillburn," *New York Times*, September 10, 1943, 25. For a scholarly account of the Hillburn School Boycott, see Sugrue, *Sweet Land of Liberty*, 163–199; Carleton Mabee, *Black Education in New York State: From Colonial to Modern Times* (Syracuse, NY: Syracuse University Press, 1979), 262–265.

15. For quotes, see "Jim Crow Is Boomerang for Hillburn Whites," *Afro-American*, January 8, 1944, 20; "The Hillburn Blot," *New York Amsterdam News*, September 18, 1943, 12. See also "Hillburn's Glory and Shame," *Crisis* 50, no. 11 (1943): 327, 344; "Hillburn White Residents Form Own Imitation of NAACP," *New Journal and Guide*, October 30, 1943, A10; "Whites Boycott Hillburn as Color Bar Falls," *Afro-American*, October 23, 1943, 1; "68 White Pupils Boycott Hillburn School Opened to Negroes," *New York Times*, October 19, 1943; "N.Y. School Board Orders Jim Crow School to Close," *Atlanta Daily World*, October 18, 1943, 1; "State Probes Hillburn Case," *Chicago Defender*, October 16, 1943, 8; "State Outlaws Jim Crow School," *New York Amsterdam News*, October 16, 1943, 1; "Hillburn Parents Win Tilt against Segregated School," *Afro-American*, October 16, 1943, 1; "Negro School in Hillburn Closed by Order of State Education Head," *New York Times*, October 12, 1943, 29; "Parents Win First Round in Hillburn School Fight," *New York Amsterdam News*, October 9, 1943, 11; "Hillburn Parents Stand Firm in School Battle," *Chicago Defender*, October 8, 1943, 8; "Parents Defy Jail Threat in Jim Crow School Dispute," *New York Amsterdam News*, October 2, 1943, 1.

16. Newspaper clippings: "Fight to Attend Hillburn School Won by Negroes," *New York Herald Tribune*, October 12, 1943; "Hillburn Schools Close as Negroes Fight Segregation," *Ramapo Valley Independent*, September 9, 1943; "Town's Negroes Strike against Jim Crow School," *PM*, September 9, 1943, 1; Patricia Bronte, "Showdown Is Due on Jim Crow School between Town's Negroes and Officials, *PM*, no date, all in Folder, "Closure of Segregated Schools in Hillburn, NY," Papers of the NAACP, Part 03: The Campaign for Educational Equality, Series B: Legal Department and Central Office Records, 1940–1950, ProQuest History Vault, http://congressional.ProQuest.com/histvault?q=001512-003-0505.

17. Sondra Astor Stave, *Achieving Racial Balance: Case Studies of Contemporary School Segregation* (Westport, CT: Greenwood Press, 1995), 45–66; Robert A. Leflar and Wylie H. Davis, "Segregation in the Public Schools: 1953," *Harvard Law Review* 67, no. 3 (1954): 377–435; Marion Thompson Wright, "Racial Integration in the Public Schools in New Jersey," *Journal of Negro Education* 23, no. 3 (1954): 282–289; Warren E. Gauerke, "The Courts and Segregation of Races in the Schools," *Elementary School Journal* 54, no. 1 (1953): 12–22; Marion Thompson Wright, "New Jersey Leads in the Struggle for Educational Integration," *Journal of Educational Sociology* 26, no. 9 (1953): 401–417; "Jim Crow School in Trenton Hit by High Court," *Chicago Defender*, February 12, 1944, 2; "Trenton School Jim Crow Illegal," *Afro-American*, February 5, 1944, 1; "Two Children Win Right to Attend "White" School," *Philadelphia Tribune*, February 5, 1944, 2; "New Jersey Negroes Win Case over School," *Christian Science Monitor*, February 1, 1944, 7; "Negroes Win School Suit," *New York Times*,

February 1, 1944, 21; *Hedgepeth and Williams v. Board of Education of Trenton*, 131 N.J.L. 153, 35 A2d 622 (1944). For quote on "Deep South," see newspaper clipping, "Jim Crow in Trenton," *New Jersey Teacher*, October 1943, "Segregation in Trenton, New Jersey Public Schools," Papers of the NAACP, Part 03: The Campaign for Educational Equality, Series B: Legal Department and Central Office Records, 1940–1950, ProQuest History Vault, http://congressional.ProQuest.com/histvault?q=001512-003-0033.

18. Earl Conrad, *Jim Crow America* (New York: Duell, Sloan and Pearce, 1947), 155–156. Emphasis in original. On the growth of Black civil rights activism after 1945, see Abigail Perkiss, *Making Good Neighbors: Civil Rights, Liberalism, and Integration in Postwar Philadelphia* (Ithaca, NY: Cornell University Press, 2014); Clarence Taylor, ed., *Civil Rights in New York City: From World War II to the Guiliani Era* (New York: Fordham University Press, 2011); Marable, *Race, Reform, and Rebellion*, 12–37; Martha Biondi, *To Stand and Fight: The Struggle for Civil Rights in Postwar New York City* (Cambridge, MA: Harvard University Press, 2003).

19. Conrad, *Jim Crow America*, 156.

20. Joseph L. Bustard, "The New Jersey Story: The Development of Racially Integrated Public Schools," *Journal of Negro Education* 21, no. 3 (1952): 275–285.

21. "Pennsylvania District Teachers Groups Combine," *Philadelphia Tribune*, October 17, 1950, 5; Margaret L. Caution, "Jersey Teachers to War on Schools' Racial Bias," *Afro-American*, June 2, 1945, 24.

22. Bonita H. Valien, "Racial Desegregation of the Public Schools in Southern Illinois," *Journal of Negro Education* 23, no. 3 (1954): 303–309, quote on pp. 305–306; William R. Ming Jr., "The Elimination of Segregation in the Public Schools of the North and West," *Journal of Negro Education* 21, no. 3 (1952): 265–275. Northern Black teachers came to support school integration in general in the postwar period, as indicated by their support for local school campaigns and statements issued by professional associations. However, individual Black teachers continued to express reservations about school integration for various reasons. See Jonas O. Rosenthal, "Negro Teachers' Attitudes toward Desegregation," *Journal of Negro Education* 26, no. 1 (1957): 63–71.

23. Ella Lou Thornbrough, "The Indianapolis Story: School Segregation and Desegregation in a Northern City," unpublished manuscript, 1989: 42, Collection: BV 2631, Manuscript and Visual Collections Department, William Henry Smith Memorial Library, Indiana Historical Society, Indianapolis, IN; Norma Jensen, "A Survey of Segregation Practices in the New Jersey School System," *Journal of Negro Education* 17, no. 1 (1948): 84–88; Shagaloff, "A Study of Community Acceptance of Desegregation in Two Selected Areas"; "Along the NAACP Battlefront: Salary Suit Cases," *Crisis* 52, no. 5 (1945): 143. See also "School Population Philadelphia," NAACP Philadelphia Branch, June 1946, in Folder, "Discrimination in Pennsylvania Public Schools," Papers of the NAACP; Norma Jensen, The Emergency Committee for Better Schools for New York City's Children, 1945, in Folder, "Discrimination and segregation in New York schools and colleges," Papers of the NAACP, Part 03: The Campaign for Educational Equality, Series B: Legal Department and Central Office Records, 1940–1950, ProQuest History Vault, http://congressional.ProQuest.com/histvault?q=001512-003-0168; Warren Chew to Walter White, September 21, 1945 (includes petition by parents in Wayne, PA), in Folder, "Discrimination in Pennsylvania Public Schools," Papers of the NAACP.

24. Charles P. Lucas to Thurgood Marshall, November 27, 1945, in Folder, "Segregation and Discrimination in Ohio Public Schools," Papers of the NAACP Part 03: The Campaign for Educational Equality, Series B: Legal Department and Central Office Records, 1940–1950, ProQuest History Vault, http://congressional.ProQuest.com/histvault?q=001512-004-0203.

25. Minutes of State Conference of Branches of the NAACP, J. Maynard Dickerson, January 12, 1946; Thurgood Marshall to Charles P. Lucas, December 15, 1945, both in Folder, "Segregation and Discrimination in Ohio Public Schools and Colleges," Papers of the NAACP, Part 03: The Campaign for Educational Equality, Series B: Legal Department and Central Office Records, 1940–1950, ProQuest History Vault, http://congressional.proquest.com/histvault?q=001512-004-0263.

26. Mary E. Crawford, "Bainbridge, Ohio School Investigation," March 15, 1946, "Segregation and Discrimination in Ohio Public Schools"; Cleveland Branch NAACP, "Summary of the Chagrin Falls Park School Case," January 11, 1946, all in Folder, "Segregation and Discrimination in Ohio Public Schools and Colleges," Papers of the NAACP.

27. Thurgood Marshall to Charles P. Lucas, December 15, 1945, in Folder, "Segregation and Discrimination in Ohio Public Schools and Colleges," Papers of the NAACP.

28. "Summary of the Chagrin Falls Park School Case"; George V. Johnson to Robert L. Carter, September 7, 1946, both in Folder, "Segregation and Discrimination in Ohio Public Schools and Colleges," Papers of the NAACP.

29. Douglas, *Jim Crow Moves North*, 258. See also NAACP Memorandum, "Segregation in Education," c. 1952, Folder 375, Box 19, National Association for the Advancement of Colored People, Philadelphia Branch Records, SCRC 15, Special Collections Research Center, Temple University Libraries, Philadelphia, PA; hereafter, "NAACP Philadelphia Branch Records."

30. Phyllis Blackburn Geer, 1972, as cited in Paul R. Dimond, *Beyond Busing: Reflections on Urban Segregation, the Courts, and Equal Opportunity*, rev ed. (Ann Arbor: University of Michigan Press, 2005), 8; William Edward Burghardt Du Bois, 1868–1963, "Segregated Schools, unpublished article," c. 1932. *W. E. B. Du Bois Papers* (MS312), Section 3: Articles, Special Collections and University Archives, University of Massachusetts Amherst Libraries, Amherst, MA.

31. Phyllis Blackburn Geer, 1972, as cited in Dimond, *Beyond Busing*, 9. See also Joseph Watras, "The Racial Desegregation of Dayton, Ohio, Public Schools, 1966–2008," *Ohio History* 117 (August 2010): 93–107; Harriet Elaine Glosson, "Trends in School Desegregation: An Historical Case Study of Desegregation in Dayton, Ohio; Denver, Colorado; Los Angeles, California; and Seattle, Washington," PhD diss., Brigham Young University, 1986, 192–202.

32. Marian Smith Williams to W. E. B. Du Bois, August 6, 1945, Series 1A: General Correspondence, W. E. B. Du Bois Papers, Special Collections and University Archives, University of Massachusetts Amherst Libraries, Amherst, MA. The Dayton Branch of the NAACP also protested the racial transformation of Wogaman Elementary. See Marian Smith Williams to Walter White, October 23, 1945; Miley O. Williamson to Thurgood Marshall, June 7, 1945; both in Folder, "Segregation and Discrimination in Ohio Public Schools and Colleges," Papers of the NAACP, Part 03: The Campaign for Educational Equality, Series B: Legal Department and Central Office Records, 1940–1950, ProQuest History Vault, https://congressional.ProQuest.com/histvault?q=001512-004-0263. Additional reports documenting the racial segregation at Wogaman can be found in Theodore M. Berry to Matral Reese, November 5, 1945; NAACP Press Release, "NAACP Seeks Clarification of Wogaman School Policy," August 25, 1945, both in Folder, "Segregation and Discrimination in Ohio Public Schools and Colleges," Papers of the NAACP. Principal MacFarlane's name is alternatively spelled "McFarlane" in some sources.

33. W. E. B. Du Bois to Marian S. Williams, August 31, 1945, Series 1A: General Correspondence, W. E. B. Du Bois Papers.

34. Marian S. Williams to W. E. B. Du Bois, September 19, 1945, Series 1A: General Correspondence, W. E. B. Du Bois Papers.

35. W. E. B. Du Bois, "The Question of Jim Crow Schools," *Chicago Defender*, October 6, 1945, 15. See also Marian S. Williams and Miley O. Williamson to Walter White, January 11, 1946; memorandum from Walter White to Thurgood Marshall, October 29, 1945, both in Folder, "Segregation and Discrimination in Ohio Public Schools and Colleges," Papers of the NAACP.

36. Theodore M. Berry to Matral Reese, November 5, 1945, in Folder, "Segregation and Discrimination in Ohio Public Schools and Colleges," Papers of the NAACP. See also Douglas, *Jim Crow Moves North*, 256. On December 1, 1972, Theodore M. "Ted" Berry would be sworn in as the first Black mayor of Cincinnati. See the finding aid of the Theodore M. Berry Papers, Archives and Rare Books Library, University of Cincinnati, OH, http://ead.ohiolink.edu/xtf-ead/view?docId=ead/OhCiUAR0135.xml;chunk.id=headerlink;brand=default.

37. P. Barton Myers, *Eighty-Five Years after Lincoln* (Dayton, OH: Phineas B. Byers, Jr. Publishing, 1950), 33–34; "Dayton Fans Pleased with Way Negroes Officiate," *New York Amsterdam News*, December 11, 1946, 12; "Basketball," *Chicago Defender*, January 20, 1945, 7; "Charles Thomas, New Captain of Boston U. Basketball Team, 2nd Negro so Honored," *New York Amsterdam News*, June 21, 1941, 18; M. Turner, "Article 7," *Chicago Defender*, May 14, 1938, 23.

38. Sally Remaley, "NAACP Meets, Tangles with School Problems," *Chicago Defender*, August 8, 1963, 1.

39. For "pioneer" quote, see Jeanne Rogers, "Integration Called Success in 24 'North-Fringe' Towns," *Washington Post*, November 20, 1954, 23. See also Harry S. Ashmore, *The Negro and the Schools* (Chapel Hill: University of North Carolina Press, 1954), 66–71; Dwight W. Culver, "Racial Desegregation in Education in Indiana," *Journal of Negro Education* 23, no. 3 (1954): 296–302; Lester B. Granger, "Does the Negro Want Integration?" *Crisis* 58, no. 2 (1951): 73–78.

40. Hugh H. Smythe and Rufus Smith, "Section C: Race Policies and Practices in Selected Public School Systems of Pennsylvania," 1952–1953, reprinted brochure from *Journal of Negro Education*, 1948, in Folder 375, Box 19, NAACP Philadelphia Branch Records. See also "Probe of Alleged Segregated in Pennsylvania Schools Asked," *New Journal and Guide*, June 19, 1948, 18; "PA Schools Practice Bias—NAACP Survey," *Atlanta Daily World*, June 4, 1948, 3.

41. Ashmore, *The Negro and the Schools*, 69, 74–75. The towns with separate schools included Atlantic City, Egg Harbor, Pleasantville, Hackensack, Beverly City, Bordentown, Burlington, Cinnaminson Township, Florence, Mount Holly, Riverside, Berlin, Camden, Cape May, Whitesboro, Port Norris, Mullica Hill, Princeton, Fair Haven, Freehold, Tom's River, Penns Grove, Salem, Swedesboro, and Woodstown. See "A Survey of the public school systems in the State of New Jersey, made under the direction of the NJ State Conference of NAACP Branches," February 28, 1947, in Folder, "School Segregation in New Jersey," Papers of the NAACP Part 03: Campaign for Educational Equality, Series B: Legal Department and Central Office Records, 1940–1950, ProQuest History Vault, http://congressional. ProQuest.com/histvault?q=001512-003-0001; US Commission on Civil Rights, "Report of the United States Commission on Civil Rights, 1959" (Washington, DC: US Government Printing Office, 1959), 245–264; "Segregation without Protest," *Pittsburgh Courier*, April 19, 1947, 6; "Segregated Negro Schools in N.J. Protested by NAACP," *Atlanta Daily World*, April 15, 1947, 1; "New Jersey School Jim Crow Worst Outside the Deep South," *Chicago Defender*, February 15, 1947, 5.

42. Educational Equality League Memorandum: "Some Pertinent Facts about Philadelphia Public Schools," c. 1953, in Folder 375, Box 19, NAACP Philadelphia Branch Records. See also "Report on Educational Equality League," Folder 1, Box 1, Floyd L. Logan Papers, Special Collections Research Center, Temple University Libraries, Philadelphia, PA.

43. NAACP Press Release, March 1949, Gloster B. Current, "Segregated Schools: On Trial in East St. Louis"; NAACP Press Release, April 28, 1949 Peoria, IL, "Illinois NAACP urges state and national civil rights action," both in Folder, "Discrimination and Segregation in East St. Louis Public Schools," Papers of the NAACP; memorandum from Mr. Marshall to Mr. Wilkins, December 14, 1948, in Folder, "Discrimination and Segregation in Illinois Public Schools," Papers of the NAACP.

44. Thomas J. Sugrue find that battles over school integration in the postwar era most often erupted in small northern cities and suburbs with Black populations and skipped over the larger cities until later. See *Sweet Land of Liberty: The Forgotten Struggle for Civil Rights in the North* (New York: Random House, 2008), 174–175. For quote, see Virgil A. Clift, "Democracy and Integration in Public Education," *Crisis* 59, no. 7 (1952): 414–420, 472. On local various northern school integration battles, see Ronald D. Cohen, "The Dilemma of School Integration in the North: Gary, Indiana, 1945–1960," *Indiana Magazine of History* 82, no. 2 (1986): 161–184; Ashmore, *The Negro in the Schools*, 66–75; "Albion Closes Jim Crow School," *Pittsburgh Courier*, October 31, 1953, 20; "Editorials: School Paradoxes," *Crisis* 60, no. 8 (1953): 485; "Along the NAACP Battlefront: Schools," *Crisis* 59, no. 9 (1952): 586–587; "N.J. Schools Held Model," *Afro-American*, August 15, 1953, 8; "Cairo

School Situation," *Crisis* 59, no. 3 (1952): 143–144; June Shagaloff and Lester P. Bailey, "Cairo—Illinois' Southern Exposure," *Crisis* 59, no. 4 (1952): 208–213, 262–265; "Cairo, IL Parents Turn to Courts in School Fight," *Philadelphia Tribune*, February 19, 1952, 3; "Officials Fight Cairo School Discrimination," *Atlanta Daily World*, January 30, 1952, 6; "Illinois Town Ends Separate School System," *New Journal and Guide*, December 1, 1951, A11; "Along the NAACP Battlefront: Segregation," *Crisis* 58, no. 10 (1951): 676–677; "N.J. Mixed School Drive Nearly Complete—Driscoll," *Afro-American*, May 27, 1950, 14; "Along the NAACP Battlefront: School," *Crisis* 57, no. 1 (1950): 37–40; Berni Fisher, "Blast Hub Jim Crow School Set Up," *Newsday*, November 10, 1949, 3; Berni Fisher, "NAACP Asks Hearing on Hempstead School Case," *Atlanta Daily World*, October 30, 1949, 8; "Mothers Stage Walkout: Close Jim Crow School," *Philadelphia Tribune*, September 10, 1949, 1; "Progress in Eliminating School JC Cited in NJ," *Afro-American*, May 28, 1949, A1; "NJ School Systems almost 100 Per Cent Integrated," *Philadelphia Tribune*, May 17, 1949, 3; "Pupils' Dignity Protected by School Officials Move," *Afro-American*, February 19, 1949, C3; "Start Fight against Segregated School," *Newsday*, September 14, 1949, 35; "Indianapolis Jim Crow School Battle Rages," *Chicago Defender*, October 2, 1948, 5; "Plan Will End Segregation in Colored School," *New Journal and Guide*, August 21, 1948, 4; A. Ritchie Low, "Indianapolis Citizens Want Democratic Schools," *Afro-American*, May 22, 1948, B5; "Irate Parents Block Return of Pupils to Segregated School," *Afro-American*, October 4, 1947, 18; "Indianapolis Minister Challenges Jim Crow School," *Atlanta Daily World*, October 9, 1947, 1; "Fight on Segregated School Board in Indiana Goes on," *Atlanta Daily World*, September 9, 1947, 3; "Alton Citizens, NAACP Fight Segregated School System," *Chicago Defender*, December 28, 1946, 7; "Jim Crow School Goes Interracial," *New York Amsterdam News*, October 5, 1946, 4; "Chester Citizens Oppose Jim Crow School Classes," *Afro-American*, September 23, 1944, 6; "Whites Fight Mixed School," *Chicago Defender*, September 14, 1946, 9; "NJ High Court Weighs Jim Crow School Case," *Chicago Defender*, December 18, 1943, 13; "Hillburn Parents Pledge Fight to the Finish," *Pittsburgh Courier*, September 25, 1943, 20; "Ohioans Fight Court's Jim Crow School Ruling," *Chicago Defender*, January 20, 1940, 2. Some northern communities, like Cadiz, Ohio, decided to end separate schools as "an economy move"; see "Ohio Town to Get First Mixed School since '53," *Afro-American*, July 28, 1951, 5.

45. Memorandum from Franklin H. Williams, July 21, 1947, in Folder, "Segregation and Discrimination in New Jersey Public Schools and Colleges," Papers of the NAACP, Part 03: The Campaign for Educational Equality, Series B: Legal Department and Central Office Records, 1940–1950, ProQuest History Vault, http://congressional.ProQuest.com/histvault?q=001512-002-1222.

46. "Report on Educational Equality League, 1977," in Folder 1, Box 1, Floyd L. Logan Papers. Ethel L. Puryear to NAACP September 15, 1947; memorandum from Franklin H. Williams to Thurgood Marshall, September 15, 1947, both in Folder, "Segregation and Discrimination in New Jersey Public Schools and Colleges," Papers of the NAACP. See also Douglas, *Jim Crow Moves North*, 219–273.

47. "Integrate Now, Urges Dr. Caliver," *Afro-American*, April 16, 1955, 9; *Brown v. Board of Education of Topeka, Kansas.* 347 U.S., 483 (1954). See also Derrick Bell, *Silent Covenants: Brown v. Board of Education and the Unfulfilled Hopes for Racial Reform* (New York: Oxford University Press, 2005); James D. Anderson, Dara N. Byrne, and Tavis Smiley, *The Unfinished Agenda of Brown v. Board of Education* (Hoboken, NJ: Wiley, 2004); Richard Kluger, *Simple Justice: The History of Brown v. Board of Education and Black America's Struggle for Equality* (New York: Vintage Books, 2004 [1974]); Patterson, Brown v. Board of Education; Harvie J. Wilkinson, *From Brown to Bakke: The Supreme Court and School Integration, 1954–1978* (New York: Oxford University Press, 1989 [1979]).

48. "Leaders Comment on Supreme Court School Decision," *Afro-American*, May 29, 1954, 9; Horace Mann Bond, "Educators Comment on School Decision," *Chicago Defender*, May 22, 1954, 5. On the relationship between the Cold War and *Brown*, see Dudziak, *Cold War Civil Rights*; Thomas Borstelmann, *The Cold War and the Color Line: American Race Relations in the Global Arena* (Cambridge, MA: Harvard University Press, 2001), 27–53.

49. W. E. B. Du Bois, speech at National Guardian Dinner, November 21, 1957, W. E. B. Du Bois Papers (M.S. 312), Special Collections and University Archives, University of Massachusetts,

Amherst, MA, http://credo.library.umass.edu/view/full/mums312-b205-i053. For more on Du Bois's response to the Brown ruling, see W. E. B. Du Bois, "Two Hundred Years of Segregated Schools [1955]," in Eugene F. Provenzo Jr., ed., *DuBois on Education* (New York: AltaMira Press, 2002), 157–160; W. E. B. Du Bois, *The Autobiography of W.E.B. Du Bois: A Soliloquy on Viewing My Life from the Last Decade of Its First Century* (New York: International Publishers, 1968), 333.

50. Doxey A. Wilkerson, *The People versus Segregated Schools* (New York: New Century Publishers, 1955), 5.

51. Charles T. Clotfelter, *After* Brown: *The Rise and Retreat of School Desegregation* (Princeton, NJ: Princeton University Press, 2004), 1–22; Patterson, Brown v. Board of Education, 64–69; Gary Orfield and Susan E. Eaton, *Dismantling Desegregation: The Quiet Reversal of* Brown v. Board of Education (New York: W.W. Norton, 1996). The Batson quote is from an unpublished copy of a book manuscript, Ruth Batson, *The Black Educational Movement in Boston: A Sequence of Historical Events,* pp. 47–48, in Folder 1, Box 2, the Papers of Ruth Batson, 1919–2003, Arthur and Elizabeth Schlesinger Library on the History of Women in America, Radcliffe Institute for Advanced Study, Harvard University, Cambridge, MA. The book was published by Northeastern University Press in 2001.

52. For "Philadelphia, as in Little Rock" quote, see "Separate School Cheats Children," *Philadelphia Tribune,* June 14, 1958, 4. For NAACP quote: "Implementing the Supreme Court Decision: Report of the NAACP Workshop, Action Program for Northern Branches," July 1, 1954. Both in Folder 377, Box 19, NAACP Philadelphia Branch Records. Drafts of similar documents include "Desegregation in Northern Areas: The Public Schools," produced by the Legal Defense and Educational Fund and distributed to various community organizations such as the American Jewish Congress. Enclosed with Don J. Hager to Gloster B. Current, January 8, 1957; memorandum from June Shagaloff to Robert L. Carter, "NAACP Program on De Facto Segregated Public Schools," August 28, 1959; both in Folder, "De facto segregation and desegregation efforts in Northern and Western states," Papers of the NAACP, Part 03: The Campaign for Educational Equality, Series D: Central Office Records, 1956–1965, ProQuest History Vault, http://congressional.proquest.com/histvault?q=001516-003-0001. See also Robert I. Weil, "Pennsylvania State Conference," *Crisis* 65, no. 10 (1958): 607–611; Lewis G. Watts, "Racial Trends in Seattle, Washington, 1958," *Crisis* 65, no. 6 (1958): 333–338; "Along the NAACP Battlefront: School Investigation," *Crisis* 65, no. 3 (1958): 164–165; "Looking and Listening: Race and the Schools," *Crisis* 65, no. 2 (1958): 100–102; Rachelle Marshall, "Concrete Curtain—East Palo Alto Story," *Crisis* 64, no. 9 (1957): 543–548.

53. On the Englewood, New Jersey, struggle see "Englewood Shows Slight Integration," *New York Amsterdam News,* October 8, 1955, 20; "The Englewood Pattern," *Pittsburgh Courier,* June 4, 1955, 6; "Discrimination Charged in Suit at Englewood," *Philadelphia Tribune,* February 8, 1955, 8; "Englewood City Board Denies Bias," *Afro-American,* November 6, 1954, 6; "Englewood Parents Decry School Bias," *New York Amsterdam News,* October 30, 1954, 38; "School Bias Case Heard in Jersey," *New York Times,* October 21, 1954, 30; "School Bias Probed in Englewood, NJ," *Philadelphia Tribune,* September 11, 1954, 12; "Englewood Faces School Bias Case," *New York Times,* September 4, 1954, 13. See also Emily Joy Jones McGowan, "A Case Study of Dwight Morrow High School and the Academies at Englewood: An Examination of School Desegregation Policy from a Critical Race Perspective," PhD diss., Rutgers University, 2011. Charles Anthony Cobb, "Segregation, Desegregation and Race: A Case Study of the Englewood, New Jersey Public School District, 1962–2000," EdD diss., Fordham University, 2007, 79–86. On other northern communities, see "Negro Progress in 1961," *Ebony,* January 1962, 22–27; "Danger in Sudden Integration of Teachers Staffs," *Philadelphia Tribune,* May 31, 1958, 2; "Chicago Wants More School Integration," *Afro-American,* November 9, 1957, 19; Leo Shapiro, "Boston Integration Problem Serious, Says Negro Leader," *Boston Globe,* October 21, 1957, 6; Everett G. Martin, "Detroit's Orderly Integration Tied to Firm Policy," *Christian Science Monitor,* October 10, 1957, 3; Robert E. Baker, "Integration Difficulties Embarrass New York," *Washington Post,* August 25, 1957, E1; Frank Johnson, "Bar White Girl's Shift from 7–1 Negro School," *Newsday,* August 16, 1957, 7; "New York Tension High over School Integration," *Hartford Courant,* April 30, 1957, 22E; Paul Sampson, "Segregation Troublesome to N.Y. City," *Washington Post,* February 25,

1957, B1; "New York Moves Tan Pupils by Bus to Mixed School," *Afro-American*, February 16, 1957, 17; "Would You Believe It, School Integration Trouble in New York?" *Pittsburgh Courier*, November 10, 1956, 15; "New York Launches Master Plan of Integration," *New Journal and Guide*, August 4, 1956, 3; "School Segregation Here?" *New York Times*, November 8, 1955, 30; "Deny Aid to Segregated School, Teachers Urge," *Philadelphia Tribune*, October 11, 1955, 3; "School Board Asked to Redistrict for Full Integration," *Philadelphia Tribune*, March 8, 1955, 3.

54. For Carter quote, see memorandum from Robert L. Carter to Roy Wilkins, June 26, 1959, in Folder, "De facto segregation and desegregation efforts in Northern and Western states," Papers of the NAACP, Part 03: The Campaign for Educational Equality, Series D: Central Office Records, 1956–1965, ProQuest History Vault, http://congressional.ProQuest.com/histvault?q=001516-003-0001. On Cairo and Colp, Illinois, school integration in the wake of *Brown*, see Leo Shapiro, "Boston Integration Problem Serious, Says Negro Leader," *Boston Globe*, October 21, 1957, 6; "Battle Looms in Ill. Town over School Mixing," *Chicago Defender*, July 27, 1957, 20; Duke Kaminski, "State Finds Segregation in Three School Districts," *Evening Bulletin* [Philadelphia, PA], May 15, 1957; "School Segregation Survey Cloaked by Ten Week Silence," *Philadelphia Inquirer*, February 6, 1957, 1; Harrison W. Fry, "Leader Orders State Survey of School Desegregation," *Evening Bulletin* [Philadelphia], November 20, 1956; "School Board Asked to Redistrict for Full Integration," *Philadelphia Tribune*, March 8, 1955, 3; "Los Angeles School Board Rids City of Final Segregation," *Atlanta Daily World*, July 14, 1954, 1; "Few Illinois Schools Have Segregation," *Chicago Daily Tribune*, May 18, 1954, 10. See also Kathryn Anne Schumaker, "Civil Rights and Uncivil Society: Education, Law, and the Struggle for Racial Equity in the Midwest, 1965–1980," PhD diss., University of Chicago, 2013, 164–167. See also "School Segregation Stirs Storm in North," *Los Angeles Times*, December 2, 1962, 14. Similar ideas are expressed in G. W. Foster Jr., "The North and West Have Problems, Too," originally published in *Saturday Review*, April 20, 1963, in George Henderson, ed., *America's Other Children: Public Schools Outside Suburbia* (Norman: University of Oklahoma Press, 1971), 355–366; Ted Princiotto, "Battle over Schools Reaches North, West," *Cleveland Plain Dealer*, March 7, 1962, 1 and 6; "Looking and Listening: Racial Integration," *Crisis* 68, no. 8 (1961): 489–491; L. H. Holman, "How the Illinois NAACP Fights School Segregation," *Crisis* 68, no. 5 (1961): 294–297; "Looking and Listening: Integration NYC Schools," *Crisis* 67, no. 8 (1960): 530–531; James R. Dumpson, "A Changing City—New Issues and New Relationships," *Crisis* 67, no. 2 (1960): 69–76.

55. Commission on School Integration of the National Association of Intergroup Relations Officials, *Public School Segregation and Integration in the North: Analysis and Proposals* (Washington, DC: National Association of Intergroup Relations Officials, 1963), 1–17.

56. For local NAACP school integration campaigns in the North, see memorandum: June Shagaloff, March 1, 1962, Folder, "School desegregation progress and demand for removal of June Shagaloff as NAACP educational specialist," Papers of the NAACP, Part 03: The Campaign for Educational Equality, Series D: Central Office Records, 1956–1965, ProQuest History Vault, http://congressional.ProQuest.com/histvault?q=001516-013-0944. See also Memorandum from June Shagaloff, "Public School Desegregation in the North and West," January [no number], 1963; memorandum from June Shagaloff and L. H. Holman to Branch Presidents and Officers of the NAACP, March 14, 1962. The American Jewish Congress documented de facto school segregation in Chicago, Cincinnati, Cleveland, Detroit, Los Angeles, New York, Philadelphia, and San Francisco in 1957, see "Predominantly Negro Schools in Eight Northern Cities," enclosed with Memorandum from June Shagaloff to Messrs. Current, Jones, Moon, Morsell, and Wilkins, December 9, 1957. All three texts in Folder, "De facto segregation and desegregation efforts in Northern and Western states," Papers of the NAACP.

57. "Freedom Day Boycott of Schools Is Set," *Chicago Tribune*, October 13, 1965, 2; Board of Education of the City of New York, "Action toward Quality Integrated Education," May 28, 1964. [Pamphlet collection, NYU Tamiment]; "Report of the United States Commission on Civil Rights, 1959," 256–257; William R. Clabby, "With None of the South's Strife, Many Illinoisans Thwart Integration," *Wall Street Journal*, October 15, 1958, 1; "Pupil Boycott May Shut Down All-Negro School," *Boston Globe*, October 5, 1958, 22; "Seeks to Close Integrated

School in Colp," *Chicago Defender*, September 22, 1958, A9; "White Pupils Boycott New Integrated School in Colp," *Chicago Defender*, August 28, 1957, 4; "Segregationists Lose Downstate Court Case," *Chicago Defender*, August 7, 1958, 4; Robert E. Baker, "Cairo, Illinois Schools Remain Segregated," *Washington Post*, June 28, 1956, 52; Leslie H. Fishel Jr., "Can Segregated Schools Be Abolished?" *Journal of Negro Education* 23, no. 2 (1954): 109–116, quote on p. 112.

58. Zoë Burkholder, "'Integrated Out of Existence': African American Debates over School Integration versus Separation at the Bordentown School in New Jersey, 1886–1955," *Journal of Social History* 51, no. 1 (2017): 47–79. See also Dr. Booker T. Washington's *Report on Bordentown*, printed in the weekly issue of *Bordentown Manual Training and Industrial School*, No. 2, December 28, 1920, in Folder, Dr. Washington's Report on Bordentown, Box 1, Department of Education, Manual Training and Industrial School for Colored Youth at Bordentown Papers (Bordentown School Papers), NJ, Department of Education, SEDMA001, New Jersey State Archives, Trenton, NJ. Details on Bordentown School's course offering and extracurricular activities are well documented in the student newspaper, *The Ironsides Echo* (1898–1953), catalogs, and informational brochures (1900–1954) in Box 2, Bordentown School Records. For newspaper coverage, see "New Interest Taken in the Bordentown School," *Afro-American*, July 5, 1913, 2. See also "Must Ignore Politics: Booker T. Washington Sounds Warning for Bordentown School," *New York Times*, August 12, 1913, 4. "New Jersey to Have a Tuskegee Institute," *New York Times*, June 29, 1902, 29. See also Lester B. Granger, "Ironsides: The Bordentown Vocational School," *Southern Workman* 56, no. 5 (1927): 223–231, quotes on pp. 227 and 229, Series 1: Writings, Box 2, Folder 39, Lester Blackwell Granger Papers, Yale University, New Haven, CT. "For Colored Youths' School," *New York Times*, August 24, 1902, 3; "Celebration at Bordentown," *New York Times*, October 22, 1897, 12.

59. "Jersey to Close All-Negro School Because It Can't Get White Pupils," *New York Times*, December 18, 1954, 17. See also "Integration Dooms School at Bordentown," *Afro-American*, August 7, 1954, 6; Conrad Clark, "UNCF Forewarned by Bordentown's Closing," *Afro-American*, January 1, 1955, 5; "State May Close Bordentown," *Chicago Defender*, January 1, 1955, 1.

60. For more on Black support for separate schools, see Adam Fairclough, *A Class of Their Own: Black Teachers in the Segregated South* (Cambridge, MA: Harvard University Press, 2007); Jack Dougherty, *More Than One Struggle: The Evolution of Black School Reform in Milwaukee* (Chapel Hill: University of North Carolina Press, 2004); Vanessa Siddle Walker, *To Their Highest Potential: An African American School Community in the Segregated South* (Chapel Hill: University of North Carolina Press, 1996); David S. Cecelski, *Along Freedom Road: Hyde County, North Carolina, and the Fate of Black Schools in the South* (Chapel Hill: University of North Carolina Press, 1994). See also "Bordentown School Closing Is Delayed," *Philadelphia Tribune*, April 12, 1955, 3; "Assemblyman Seeks to Halt Bordentown's Closing," *Philadelphia Tribune*, April 5, 1955, 13; "Feud at Bordentown: Alumni Hit State, Ask Investigation," *Afro-American*, March 5, 1955, 2; "Bordentown School Alumni Hit Closing," *Afro-American*, February 19, 1955, 14.

61. Minutes of New Jersey Commission to Study the Proposed Discontinuance of Bordentown Manual Training School, May 19, 1955, vols. 1 and 2, Public Hearing, New Jersey Department of Education, Trenton, New Jersey. See also interviews with Bordentown School graduates in Wynetta Devore, "The Education of Blacks in New Jersey, 1900–1915: An Exploration in Oral History," EdD diss., Rutgers University, 1980.

62. James W. McGrew, Research Director for the New Jersey State Chamber of Commerce, testimony at Public Hearing before The Commission to Investigate the Circumstances Surrounding the Proposed Closing of the Bordentown Manual Training School, May 19, 1955, vol. 1, pp. 1–2, in Folder, "Legislation and Commission Reports on School Closure," Box 4, Bordentown School Records.

63. B. H. Jones, Superintendent of Vocational Studies at Bordentown School, testimony at Public Hearing before The Commission to Investigate the Circumstances Surrounding the Proposed Closing of the Bordentown Manual Training School. May 19, 1955, 20–21, vol. 1.

64. Major V. Daniels, Dean of Boys at Bordentown School, testimony at Public Hearing before The Commission to Investigate the Circumstances Surrounding the Proposed Closing of the Bordentown Manual Training School, May 19, 1955, 22–23, vol.1.

65. Milton Honig, "Integration Lag Cited by Forbes," *New York Times*, October 27, 1957, 66; George Cable Wright, "Costs Misfigured on Jersey School," *New York Times*, January 5, 1956, 31; "Bordentown School to Remain Open," *Philadelphia Tribune*, June 28, 1955, 12; "Republicans to Halt Closing of Bordentown Training Unit;" *Afro-American*, June 18, 1955, 14; "Two Schools to Face Extinction," *Chicago Defender*, June 18, 1955, 1; "Why State Will Close Bordentown," *Afro-American*, April 16, 1955, 2; Millie Ganges, "Bordentown Citizens Hits School Closing," *Afro-American*, March 26, 1955, 6; Conrad Clark, "UNCF Forewarned by Bordentown's Closing," *Afro-American*, January 1, 1955, 5; "State May Close Down Bordentown," *Chicago Defender*, January 1, 1955, 1.

66. Henry Lee Moon to Mary Windsor, February 14, 1955; Mary Windsor to the NAACP, February 5, 1955; both in Folder, "School Integration," Papers of the NAACP, Part 03: The Campaign for Educational Equality, Series C: Legal Department and Central Office Records, 1951–1955, ProQuest History Vault, http://congressional.ProQuest.com/ histvault?q=001513-012-0452; telegram from Benjamin A. Collier, Executive Secretary, Board of Directors, Urban League of Eastern Union County, New Jersey Commission to Study the Proposed Discontinuance of Bordentown Manual Training School, May 19, 1955, vol. 2, p. 20.

67. Edward "Sonny" Murrain, "Sonny Side Up," *Chicago Defender*, June 22, 1955, 8. For insight into the experiences of Black teachers and administrators in the North following *Brown*, see Elizabeth Flemister Hood, "The Responsibility of Negro Teachers in Urban Communities," *Crisis* 69, no. 4 (1962): 201–207; Henry Hardy, "Interview with a Negro Teacher," *Crisis* 66, no. 5 (1959): 283–287. See also Evelyn Blackmore Duck, "An Historical Study of a Segregated School in New Jersey from 1886 to 1955," EdD diss., Rutgers University, 1984; Ezola B. Adams, "The Role and Function of the Manual Training and Industrial School at Bordentown as an Alternative School, 1915–1955," EdD diss., Rutgers University, 1977; "Bordentown School to Remain Open," *Philadelphia Tribune*, June 28, 1955, 12; "Republicans to Halt Closing of Bordentown Training Unit," *Afro-American*, June 18, 1955, 14; "Two Schools to Face Extinction," *Chicago Defender*, June 18, 1955, 1; "Why State Will Close Bordentown," *Afro-American*, April 16, 1955, 2; Millie Ganges, "Bordentown Citizens Hits School Closing," *Afro-American*, March 26, 1955, 6; Conrad Clark, "UNCF Forewarned by Bordentown's Closing," *Afro-American*, January 1, 1955, 5; "State May Close Down Bordentown," *Chicago Defender*, January 1, 1955, 1.

68. Dan W. Dodson, *Crisis in the Public Schools: Racial Segregation Northern Style* (New York: Council for American Unity, 1965); "New Rochelle Parents Fight Segregated School," *New York Amsterdam News*, April 27, 1957, 17; NAACP Statement, March 21, 1957, pp. 1–11. In Folder, "New Rochelle, New York School Desegregation Efforts," Papers of the NAACP, Part 03: The Campaign for Educational Equality, Series D: Central Office Records, 1956–1965, ProQuest History Vault, http://congressional.ProQuest.com/histvault?q=001516-006-0721; "New Rochelle Criticized on School Bias," *New York Times*, April 2, 1957, 33; "Race Issue Posed by a New School," *New York Times*, March 23, 1957, 21; "New Rochelle Asks Big School Project," *New York Times*, December 20, 1956, 46; "Doom School Bias in New Rochelle," *New York Amsterdam News*, October 20, 1956, 6; "Hearing Set in New Rochelle School Case," *New Journal and Guide*, January 1950, 17; "New Rochelle Hits Segregated School," *New York Amsterdam News*, September 17, 1930, 10; "Protest to Governor on 'Jim Crow' Schools, *New York Times*, September 10, 1930, 22. On the history and development of the New Rochelle Public Schools, see Austin D. Devane, "History of the New Rochelle Public Schools, 1795–1952," PhD diss., Columbia University, 1953.

69. *Taylor v. Board of Education of City School District of City of New Rochelle*, 195, F. Supp. 231 (1961). See also Sugrue, *Sweet Land of Liberty*, 190–199; "New Rochelle Is Ordered to End Segregation," *Hartford Courant*, January 25, 1961, 2; Harvey Aronson, "New Rochelle Decision Points Up Bias in North," *Newsday*, January 25, 1961, 4; "Negroes Rejoice in New Rochelle," *New York Times*, January 26, 1961, 20; "Editorials: New Rochelle," *Crisis* 68, no. 2 (1961): 98–99.

70. School integration cases followed in Hempstead, New York: *Vetere v. Allen*, 15 N.Y. 2d 259, 206 N.E. 2d 174 (1965); Plainfield, New Jersey: *Booker v. Board of Education of Plainfield*, 212 A. 2d 1, 45 N.J. 161 (1965); Manhasset, New York: *Blocker v. Board of Education of Manhasset, New York*, 226 F. Supp. 208, 228, 229, F. Supp. 709, 229 F. Supp. 714 (E.D.N.Y. 1964); Springfield, Massachusetts: *Barksdale v. Springfield School Committee*, 237 F. Supp. 543 (D. Mass. 1965); Gary, Indiana: *Bell v. School City of Gary*, 213 F. Supp. 819 (1963), 324 F. 2d 209 (7th Cir. 1963), *cert. den.*, 377 U.S. 924 (1964); Cincinnati, Ohio: *Deal v. Cincinnati Board of Education*, 224 F. Supp. 572 (1965), 369 F. 2d 55 (6th Cir. 1966), *cert. den.*, 389 U.S. 847 (1967), 419 F. 2d 1387 (6th Cir. 1969), *cert. den.*, 402 U.S. 962 (1971); Pontiac, Michigan: *Henry v. Godsell*, 165 F. Supp. 87 (E.D. Mich. 1958). Not all of these court cases were successful in their effort to challenge de facto school segregation; see Robert L. Herbst, "The Legal Struggle to Integrate Schools in the North," *Annals of American Academy of Political and Social Science* 407 (May, 1973): 43–62; Robert A. Dentler, "Barriers to Northern School Desegregation," *Daedalus* 95, no. 1 (1966): 45–63; Robert L. Carter, "De Facto School Segregation: An Examination of the Legal and Constitutional Questions Presented," *Western Reserve Law Review* 16 (1965): 502, 516; Doxey A. Wilkerson, "School Integration, Compensatory Education and the Civil Rights Movement in the North," *Journal of Negro Education* 34, no. 3 (1965): 300–309; "Along the NAACP Battlefront: New York School Ruling," *Crisis* 71, no. 3 (1964): 178; "Along the NAACP Battlefront: De Facto School Segregation," *Crisis* 70, no. 8 (1963): 482–483; June Shagaloff, "Public Desegregation—North & West," *Crisis* 70, no. 2 (1963): 92–95, 103; "Along the NAACP Battlefront: Northern and Western Cities Slated to End School Segregation," *Crisis* 69, no. 8 (1962): 481–484; "Along the NAACP Battlefront: Plainfield Schools," *Crisis* 69, no. 7 (1962): 414; "Along the NAACP Battlefront: School Bias," *Crisis* 69, no. 6 (1962): 347–350; "Editorial: NAACP Leads Northern School Program," *Crisis* 69, no. 4 (1962): 230–231.

71. Merrill Folsom, "Appeal Is Voted by New Rochelle," *New York Times*, February 8, 1961, 33. See also "Ruling Appealed in New Rochelle," *New York Times*, March 21, 1961, 39; "New Rochelle to Fight," *Newsday*, February 8, 1961, 52.

72. Perry Morgan, "The Case for the White Southerner," in George Henderson, ed., *America's Other Children* (Norman: University of Oklahoma Press, 1971), 315–324. Originally published in *Esquire*, January 1962, 315. Jason Sokol argues that Springfield, Massachusetts, school leaders disingenuously used a "colorblind" defense of school segregation during the same era: *All Eyes Are Upon Us: Race and Politics from Boston to Brooklyn: The Conflicted Soul of the Northeast* (New York: Basic Books, 2014), 71–102. See also "Court Denies New Rochelle Stay," *New York Times*, August 31, 1961, 12; "New Rochelle Asks Stay by High Court," *New York Times*, August 18, 1961, 21; "Stubborn New Rochelle Board of Education to Appeal Case," *New York Amsterdam News*, August 12, 1961, 34; Edward Ranzal, "School Case Lost by New Rochelle," *New York Times*, August 3, 1961, 25; "New Rochelle Education Board Fights Order to Desegregate," *Boston Globe*, August 5, 1961, 2; "School in New Rochelle Segregated Deliberately, Appeals Court Rules," *Hartford Courant*, August 3, 1961, 25; "The New Rochelle School Battle," *New York Amsterdam News*, July 22, 1961, 8; "Appeal Is Argued by New Rochelle," *New York Times*, July 19, 1961, 34.

73. For quote, see Merrill Folsom, "Schools in Crisis in New Rochelle," *New York Times*, November 11, 1962, 132. See also Lou Bertha Viola Mckenzie-Wharton, "Case Study: New Rochelle Board of Education's Policy Toward Racial Imbalance at the Lincoln Elementary School, 1947–1962," EdD diss., Columbia University, 1973; "New Rochelle to End Jim Crow Schools, Pay Integration Costs," *Chicago Defender*, May 20, 1963, 13; Merrill Folsom, "End to Racial Imbalance Sought in New Rochelle School Program," *New York Times*, May 15, 1963, 26; "New Rochelle School Shifts 267 Students," *Washington Post*, September 7, 1961, A10; Merrill Folsom, "267 New Rochelle Negro Pupils Are Transferring from Lincoln," *New York Times*, September 7, 1961, 29; "Pupils Shift Thursday," *New York Times*, September 2, 1961, 18.

74. For quote, see Bernard Stengren, "Race Criteria Irk Negro Educator," *New York Times*, November 30, 1960, 32. See also US Commission on Civil Rights, "Civil Rights USA: Public Schools North and West 1962" (Washington, DC: US Government Printing Office, 1962), 56–57; "Boycott of Realtors Advised by Principal," *New York Amsterdam News*, September 24,

1960, 19; Merrill Folsom, "Negro Principal Rebuffs Negroes," *New York Times*, September 16, 1960, 33.

75. US Commission on Civil Rights, "Civil Rights USA: Public Schools North and West 1962," 56–57.

76. Foster, "The North and West Have Problems, Too," 362–363; US Commission on Civil Rights, "Civil Rights USA: Public Schools North and West 1962," 91–92.

77. US Commission on Civil Rights, "Civil Rights USA: Public Schools North and West 1962," 92–93. For Zuber quote, see front page of the *Standard Star*, September 27, 1960, as quoted in Mckenzie-Wharton, "Case Study: New Rochelle Board of Education's Policy toward Racial Imbalance at the Lincoln Elementary School, 1947–1962," 121. The local NAACP and the local Urban League rebuked Zuber for his choice of words.

78. US Commission on Civil Rights, "Civil Rights USA: Public Schools North and West 1962," 1–2; "Editorial: NAACP Leads Northern School Program," *Crisis* 69, no. 4 (1962): 230–231.

79. "Along the NAACP Battlefront: Northern and Western Cities Slated to End School Segregation," *Crisis* 69, no. 8 (1962): 481–484, quote on p. 481.

80. Richard Rothstein explores the meaning and history of "ghetto" formation through deliberate, state-sponsored racial discrimination in *The Color of Law: A Forgotten History of How Our Government Segregated America* (New York: W.W. Norton, 2017), xvi–xvii. See also Ira Berlin, *The Making of African America: The Four Great Migrations* (New York: Penguin Books, 2010), 152–200; David M. P. Freund, *Colored Property: State Policy and White Racial Politics in Suburban America* (Chicago: University of Chicago Press, 2007); Charles T. Clotfelter, *After Brown: The Rise and Retreat of School Desegregation* (Princeton, NJ: Princeton University Press, 2004), 17–22; Andrew Weise, *Places of Their Own: African American Suburbanization in the Twentieth Century* (Chicago: University of Chicago Press, 2004); Alice O'Connor, *Poverty Knowledge: Social Science, Social Policy and the Poor in Twentieth-Century America* (Princeton, NJ: Princeton University Press, 2001), 74–98; Douglas S. Massey and Nancy A. Denton, *American Apartheid: Segregation and the Making of the Underclass* (Cambridge, MA: Harvard University Press, 1993); Jon C. Teaford, *The Rough Road to Renaissance: Urban Revitalization in America, 1940–1985* (Baltimore: Johns Hopkins University Press, 1990); Kenneth Fox, *Metropolitan America: Urban Life and Urban Policy in the United States, 1940–1980* (New Brunswick, NJ: Rutgers University Press, 1985); Katherine M. Borman and Joel H. Spring, *Schools in Central Cities: Structure and Process* (New York: Longman, 1984); Raymond C. Hummell and John M. Neagle, *Urban Education in America: Problems and Prospects* (New York: Oxford University Press, 1973); Robert C. Weaver, *The Negro Ghetto* (New York: Russell and Russell, 1967 [1949]; US Commission on Civil Rights, "1963 Staff Report: Public Education, December 1963" (Washington, DC: US Government Printing Office, 1963), 80–82.

81. For a list of the correlations between racially segregated schools and negative effects for Black students, see Commission on School Integration of the National Association of Intergroup Officials, *Public School Segregation and Integration in the North*, 21–27.

82. Commission on School Integration of the National Association of Intergroup Relations Officials, *Public School Segregation and Integration in the North*, 41–42. See also Andrew R. Highsmith, *Demolition Means Progress: Flint, Michigan, and the Fate of the American Metropolis* (Chicago: University of Chicago Press, 2015); Thomas J. Sugrue, *The Origins of the Urban Crisis: Race and Inequality in Postwar Detroit*, rev. ed., (Princeton, NJ: Princeton University Press, 2014); Dionne Danns, *Desegregating Chicago's Public Schools: Policy Implementation, Politics, and Protest, 1965–1985* (New York: Palgrave Macmillan, 2014); Heather Lewis, *New York City Public Schools from Brownsville to Bloomberg: Community Control and Its Legacy* (New York: Teachers College Press, 2013); Dougherty, *More than One Struggle*; Matthew J. Countryman, *Up South: Civil Rights and Black Power in Philadelphia* (Philadelphia: University of Pennsylvania Press, 2006), 223–257; Jerald E. Podair, *The Strike that Changed New York: Blacks, Whites, and the Ocean Hill-Brownsville Crisis* (New Haven, CT: Yale University Press, 2002); Jeffrey Mirel, *The Rise and Fall of an Urban School System*, 2nd ed. (Ann Arbor: University of Michigan Press, 1999 [1993]); Diane Ravitch, *The Great School Wars: A History of the New York City Public Schools*, rev. ed. (Baltimore: Johns Hopkins University Press,

2000): 251–380; Michael W. Homel, *Down from Equality: Black Chicagoans and the Public Schools, 1920–1941* (Urbana: University of Illinois Press, 1984).

83. On most racially segregated city quote, see "Report of the U.S. Commission on Civil Rights, 1959," 365. John L. Rury, "Race, Space, and the Politics of Chicago's Public Schools: Benjamin Willis and the Tragedy of Urban Education," *History of Education Quarterly* 39, no. 2 (1999): 117–142.

84. For Willis quote, see "Willis Defends Jim Crow School Policy Here," *Chicago Defender*, December 7, 1961, 5. See also Danns, *Desegregating Chicago's Public Schools*, 7–12; John F. Lyons, *Teachers and Reform: Chicago Public Education, 1929–1970* (Urbana: University of Illinois Press, 2008), 133–170; Dionne Danns, *Something Better for Our Children: Black Organizing in Chicago's Public Schools, 1963–1971* (New York: Routledge, 2003); James R. Ralph Jr., *Northern Protest: Martin Luther King, Jr., Chicago, and the Civil Rights Movement* (Cambridge, MA: Harvard University Press, 1993); Alan Anderson and George W. Pickering, *Confronting the Color Line: The Broken Promise of the Civil Rights Movement in Chicago* (Athens: University of Georgia Press, 1986), 44–104. On the racial transition of urban schools and neighborhoods, see Robert G. Wegmann, "Neighborhoods and Schools in Racial Transition," *Growth and Change*, July 1975, pp. 3–8.

85. US Commission on Civil Rights, "Report 2: Education" (Washington, DC: US Government Printing Office, 1961), 115; "De Facto Segregation in Chicago Public Schools," *Crisis* 65, no. 2 (1958): 87–93, 126–127, quote on p. 89. See also "School Head Scored by Chicago N.A.A.C.P," *New York Times*, June 28, 1961, 24; "Chicago School Committee," *Chicago Defender*, February 6, 1961, 10; "The Chicago School System," *Chicago Defender*, December 23, 1958, 11; "How About Chicago Schools?" *Chicago Defender*, August 25, 1958, A11; "Integration and Chicago Schools," *Chicago Defender*, May 27, 1958, 11; "Majority of Chicago Schools Segregated 'De Facto,'" *New York Amsterdam News*, February 8, 1958, 3; "School Equality Is Urged in Chicago," *Afro-American*, January 11, 1958, 17; "NAACP Praises Chicago School Integration Study," *Afro-American*, November 9, 1957, 19; Robert L. Birchman, "Chicago High Schools 70% Jim Crow," *Chicago Defender*, September 21, 1957, 5; James K. Sparkman, "NAACP Pushes Bid for Chicago Mixed Schools," *Christian Science Monitor*, March 20, 1957, 5; "Our Opinions, Are Chicago Schools Integrated?" *Chicago Defender*, March 16, 1957, 10; "NAACP Hits Chicago School Inequality," *New York Amsterdam News*, January 19, 1957, 6; "NAACP Wants Chicago Schools Desegregated," *Chicago Defender*, December 15, 1956, 10. The statistics on "de facto" segregated schools in Chicago were mirrored in other cities. The US Commission on Civil Rights found that in 1960 in New York City, about 20 percent of the elementary and junior high schools enrolled 85 percent or more Black and Puerto Rican students while 48 percent of the elementary and 44 percent of the junior high schools enrolled 85 percent or more white pupils. In Philadelphia, 14 percent of the public schools had enrollment that was 99 percent or more Black, and in Pittsburgh, half of the Black students in the district attended schools that were 80 percent or more Black. Meanwhile in Pittsburgh, 60 percent of white children in elementary school and 35 percent in secondary schools attended public schools that had less than 5 percent Black students. See US Commission on Civil Rights, "Report 2: Education" (Washington, DC: US Government Printing Office, 1961), 99–100. The NAACP found the same kind of school segregation and inequality in Newark, New Jersey, in 1961; see Education Committee of the Newark Branch, NAACP, "A Report on Newark Public Schools," 1961, in Rise Up Newark, http://riseupnewark.com/a-report-on-newark-public-schools-by-the-education-committee-of-the-newark-naacp-nov-1961-ilovepdf-compressed-2/?mode=grid. See also press release, "Majority of Chicago Schools Segregated De Facto," January 30, 1958; press release, "Chicago NAACP Carries School Fight to State Legislature," March 28, 1957," both in Folder, "Illinois School Desegregation Efforts," Papers of the NAACP, Part 03: The Campaign for Educational Equality, Series D: Central Office Records, 1956–1965, ProQuest History Vault, http://congressional.ProQuest.com/histvault?q=001516-005-0001.

86. Rury, "Race, Space, and the Politics of Chicago's Public Schools," 124–125; Anderson and Pickering call Willis's stance "intransigent innocence," *Confronting the Color Line*, 85–102. For Willis quote, see "Willis Defends Jim Crow School Policy Here."

87. Danns, *Desegregating Chicago's Public Schools*, 12–14; Alvin Adams, "School Integration Problems Move North," *JET*, September 21, 1961, 24–27.

88. Sugrue, *Sweet Land of Liberty*, 451–454; Anderson and Pickering, *Confronting the Color Line*, 84–90; memorandum: June Shagaloff to Roy Wilkins, December 28, 1961, Folder, "School desegregation progress and demand for removal of June Shagaloff as NAACP educational specialist," Papers of the NAACP, Part 03: The Campaign for Educational Equality, Series D: Central Office Records, 1956–1965, ProQuest History Vault, http://congressional.ProQuest.com/histvault?q=001516-013-0944.

89. *James William Webb, Jr. et al. v. Board of Education of City of Chicago and Benjamin Willis* 61C1569 (1961); "School Suit Answered," *New York Times*, December 16, 1961, 15; "Alderman, City Leaders Blast Away at Education Setup in Chicago Schools," *Chicago Defender*, October 28, 1961, 19; "Officials Deny Bias," *New Journal and Guide*, October 4, 1961, 2; Donald Janson, "School Quarrel Grows in Chicago," *New York Times*, October 1, 1961, 58; "TWO Throws Full Support Behind Efforts to End Segregation in Chicago Schools," *Chicago Defender*, September 25, 1961, 5; "Chicago Schools Sued by Negroes," *New York Times*, September 19, 1961, 21; Donald Janson, "Chicago Schools Set to Integrate," *New York Times*, September 17, 1961, 67; "Chicago Schools Rebuff Negroes," *New York Times*, September 7, 1961, 28; "NAACP Accuses Chicago of School Discrimination," *Washington Post*, August 28, 1961, A4.

90. Press Release "Chicago Parents Arrested in School Demonstrations," January 19, 1962, in Folder, "Illinois School Desegregation Efforts," Papers of the NAACP. See also "The People Speak on School Superintendent," *Chicago Defender*, March 31, 1962, 1; "Chicago Is Lambasted for Lagging in Drive for Integration of Schools," *Chicago Defender*, March 26, 1962, 3; Adolph J. Slaughter, "How Segregated Are Chicago's Schools?" *Chicago Defender*, February 14, 1962, 2; Kenneth C. Field, "How Segregated Are Chicago's Schools?" *Chicago Defender*, February 12, 1962, 1; "Chicago Parents Go to Jail over School Protests," *Pittsburgh Courier*, January 27, 1962, A3.

91. *Branche v. Board of Education of Town of Hempstead*, 204 F. Supp. 150 (E.D.N.Y. 1962). For quote in Gary see Austin C. Wehrwein, "NAACP Opens Gary School Suit," *New York Times*, September 11, 1962, 21. See also Sugrue, *Sweet Land of Liberty*, 454–463; Anderson and Pickering, *Confronting the Color Line*, 99–100; Robert L. Herbst, "The Legal Struggle to Integrate Schools in the North," *Annals of the American Academy of Political and Social Science*, 407 (May 1973): 43–62; "Predicts Integration of Schools Coming Here," *Chicago Defender*, August 20, 1962, 2; "NAACP Files School Suit in Gary, Indiana," *Atlanta Daily World*, June 21, 1962, 2; "ACLU Urges School Board: Push Integration in Chicago," *Chicago Defender*, June 21, 1962, 1; Ed Cony, "Integration Shift," *Wall Street Journal*, May 28, 1962, 1; "Chicago Not Alone in School Segregation Row," *Chicago Defender*, April 14, 1962, 1.

92. "Chicago School Integration Plan Stirs Criticism," *Atlanta Daily World*, August 30, 1962, 3.

93. For activist quotes, see "Integration of Chicago Schools Arouses Both Sides in Dispute," *New York Times*, February 15, 1964, 11. See also Elizabeth Todd-Breland, *A Political Education: Black Politics and Education Reform in Chicago since the 1960s* (Chapel Hill: University of North Carolina Press, 2018), 27; Danns, *Desegregating Chicago's Public Schools*, 13–15; Danns, *Something Better for Our Children*, 44–48; "Negro Kids Hurt by Jim Crow Schools," *Chicago Defender*, April 2, 1962, 1; Ernestine Cofield, "Say Residential Bias Is Key to School Integration," *Chicago Defender*, July 22, 1963, A9. See also Jakobi Williams, *From the Bullet to the Ballot: The Illinois Chapter of the Black Panther Party and Racial Coalition Politics in Chicago* (Chapel Hill: University of North Carolina Press, 2013), 15–42.

94. Breland-Todd, *A Political Education*, 27–40; Jeanne Theoharis, *A More Beautiful and Terrible History: The Uses and Misuses of Civil Rights History* (Boston: Beacon Press, 2018), 31–61; Danns, *Desegregating Chicago's Public Schools*, 14–16; Robert B. McKersie, *A Decisive Decade: An Insider's View of the Chicago Civil Rights Movement during the 1960s* (Carbondale: Southern Illinois University Press, 2013), 47–65; John Hall Fish, *Black Power, White Control: The Struggle of The Woodlawn Organization in Chicago* (Princeton, NJ: Princeton University Press, 1973), 175–234; Rury, "Race, Space, and the Politics of Chicago's Public Schools," 33–34; "Battle Front: Gains in Northern School Drive," *Crisis* 72, no. 6 (1965): 380–384; "A School Boycott Called in Chicago," *New York Times*, May 29, 1965, 10; "2,500 March in Chicago in a Protest over Schools," *New York Times*, April 17, 1965, 7; "Chicago Ministers Protest School "Racial Injustices," *New York Times*, March 11, 1965, 20; Lillian S. Calhoun, "80 Clerics March against Ben Willis," *Chicago Defender*, March 4, 1965,

1; "Battle Front: Segregated Schools Banned in Springfield," *Crisis* 72, no. 3 (1965): 163–164; "Freedom News: Judge Bans Segregated Mass. Schools," *Crisis* 72, no. 2 (1965): 117; Dorothea Kahn Jaffe, "Chicago School Protests Fade into Talks," *Christian Science Monitor*, October 15, 1964, 5; "Along the NAACP Battlefront: Northern School Drive," *Crisis* 71, no. 8 (1964): 558–560; "Highlights in School Desegregation, 1936–1963," *Crisis* 71, no. 5 (1964): 285–290; John Herbers, "Freedom School Held under Tree," *New York Times*, July 3, 1964, 8; "Chicago Tackles School Problems," *New York Times*, May 31, 1964, 46; "Along the NAACP Battlefront: Boston School Boycott," *Crisis* 71, no. 4 (1964): 261–262; "Along the NAACP Battlefront: New York School Ruling," *Crisis* 71, no. 3 (1964): 178; "125,000 in School Boycott," *Chicago Tribune*, February 26, 1964, 1; Austin C. Wehrwein, "School Boycotts Are Set in 5 Cities," *New York Times*, January 26, 1964, 39; "School Boycott May Hit 5 Cities," *Afro-American*, January 25, 1964, 1; Fred Powledge, "5 Cities May Join in School Boycott," *New York Times*, January 15, 1964, 21; "Plan Nationwide School Boycott," *Chicago Defender*, January 6, 1964, 1; "2nd School Boycott Possible," *Chicago Defender*, January 2, 1964, 1; "Schools Boycott Set in N.Y. a la Chicago," *Chicago Defender*, December 24, 1963, 18; "Negro Leaders in Chicago Hail Impact of Mass School Boycott," *New York Times*, October 24, 1963, 25; "The School Boycott," *Chicago Tribune*, October 22, 1963, 14; "Church, Civic Groups Support School Boycott, Blast Willis," *Chicago Defender*, October 21, 1963, 4; "Freedom Day Boycott of Schools Is Set," *Chicago Tribune*, October 13, 1963, 2.

95. The National Advisory Commission on Civil Disorders, *Report of the National Advisory Commission on Civil Disorders* (New York: Bantam Books, 1968), 38–39.

96. For chanting white students, see "White Students Put on an Anti-Integration Rally," *Los Angeles Times*, September 10, 1963, 19; "Chicago Whites Picket a School," *New York Times*, September 10, 1963, 29. For "bad reputation," see "White Parents Say No to Local 'Negro' School," *Chicago Defender*, February 4, 1964, A7. For "Negro Revolution," see "School Boycotts Sweep U.S.," *Chicago Defender*, January 18, 1964, 1. One white parents' association, the Beverly Area Planning Association, surveyed 1,000 parents in 1964 and reported that 99.7 percent of parents surveyed were in favor of neighborhood schools, 95.3 percent supported Superintendent Willis, and 95.8 percent were opposed to the Hauser Report and its modest suggestions for school integration such as "cluster plans" of enlarged school catchment zones. See Nelson C. Blackfrod, Executive Secretary of the Beverly Area Planning Association, to Frank Whiston, President, Chicago Board of Education, January 12, 1965n in "Schools—General Correspondence, 1965–1966," Folder 190, Box 11, Beverly Area Planning Association Records MSBAPA75, Special Collections and University Archives, University of Illinois, Chicago, IL. On white resistance to school integration, see Andrew J. Diamond, *Mean Streets: Chicago Youths and the Everyday Struggle for Empowerment in the Multiracial City, 1908–1969* (Los Angeles: University of California Press, 2009), 231–251; Thomas J. Sugrue, "Crabgrass-Roots Politics: Race, Rights, and the Reaction against Liberalism in the Urban North, 1940–1964," *Journal of American History*, 82 no. 2 (1995): 551–578.

97. Lillian S. Calhoun, "Confetti," *Chicago Defender*, February 3, 1964, 9. See also Lillian Calhoun, "Local NAACP Drags Its Feet in School Suit," *Chicago Defender*, October 22, 1964, 2.

98. Paul B. Zuber to Roy Wilkins, August 5, 1963, in Folder, "Illinois School Desegregation Cases, NAACP Special Conference on Education, and Discrimination by University of Illinois Fraternities," Papers of the NAACP, Part 03: Campaign for Educational Equality, Series D: Central Office Records, 1956–1965, ProQuest History Vault, http://congressional.ProQuest.com/histvault?q=001516-011-0631.

99. For "white masters" quote, see "Politicians Using NAACP, Urban League to Fight Chicago's School Boycott," *Chicago Defender*, February 5, 1964, 3. For anger and frustration quote, see Nobuo Abiko, "Chicago Negroes Adamant," *Christian Science Monitor*, February 27, 1964, 3. See also "Politicians Using NAACP, Urban League to Fight Chicago's School Boycott," *Chicago Defender*, February 5, 1964, 3; "NAACP Boycotts School Boycott," *Chicago Defender*, January 20, 1964, 1.

100. Georgie Anne Geyer, "Negro Leaders Split over Rights Tactics," *Chicago Daily News*, (no date). Clipping in Folder, "Illinois School Desegregation Cases, NAACP Special Conference on Education, and Discrimination by University of Illinois Fraternities," Papers of the NAACP.

101. Geyer, "Negro Leaders Split over Rights Tactics."

102. Chicago Urban League Research Report, "Public School Segregation: City of Chicago, 1964–1965" (Chicago: Urban League, 1965); Chicago Urban League Research Report, "Public School Segregation: City of Chicago, 1963–1964" (Chicago: Urban League, 1964), both in "Annual Reports, 1958–1968," Folder 33, Series I, Box 2, Chicago Urban League Records, Special Collections and University Archives, University of Illinois at Chicago. On anti-busing rally in New York City, see Jerald E. Podair, *The Strike that Changed New York: Blacks, Whites, and the Ocean-Hill Brownsville Crisis* (New Haven, CT: Yale University Press, 2002), 28–29; Fred Powledge, "Oppose Shifting of Pupils," *New York Times*, March 13, 1964, 1. On quote by New York Council of Supervisory Associations, see Leonard Buder, "School Supervisors Assail Board's Pairing Proposals," *New York Times*, March 26, 1964, 1.

103. Matthew F. Delmont, *Why Busing Failed: Race, Media, and the National Resistance to School Desegregation* (Oakland: University of California Press, 2016), 54–76; Danns, *Desegregating Chicago's Public Schools*, 1–15; Danns, *Something Better for Our Children*, 50–53; Chicago Urban League Research Report, "Racial Segregation in the Chicago Public Schools, 1965–1966" (Chicago: Chicago Urban League, 1966), Special Collections and University Archives, University of Illinois, Chicago; "Editorial: Accelerating School Desegregation," *Crisis* 72, no. 4 (1965): 211–212; "Chicago Tackles School Problems," *New York Times*, May 31, 1964, 46. On the degree of school segregation in the North, see the study of 380 northern communities reported by Herman Long for the National Association of Intergroup Relations Officials, in *New York State Commission's Conference on Race and Education*, State Education Department, Albany, NY, 1964. See also Nathan Kantrowitz, "Ethnic and Racial Segregation in the New York Metropolis, 1960," *American Journal of Sociology* 74, no. 6 (1969): 685–695; Robert A. Dentler, "Community Behavior and Northern School Desegregation," *Journal of Negro Education* 34, no. 3 (1965): 258–267.

104. Robert L. Carter, "De Facto School Segregation Conference," *Crisis* 73, no. 10 (1966): 514–517; "Battle Front: School Desegregation Guidelines," *Crisis* 73, no. 4 (1966): 217–219; Dentler, "Community Behavior and Northern School Desegregation"; "Southern Schools Complying with Civil Rights Act," *Newark Herald News*, November 6, 1965, 8; J. Skelly Wright, "Public School Desegregation: Legal Remedies for De Facto Segregation," *New York University Law Review* 40 (1965): 285–309; "High Court Lets Stand Ruling in Gary, Indiana," *Wall Street Journal*, May 5, 1964, 4.

105. Michael Clapper, "The Constructed World of Postwar Philadelphia Area Schools: Site Selection, Architecture, and the Landscape of Inequality," PhD diss., University of Pennsylvania, 2008, 8. For Hicks quote, see "Integration Plan Scored in Boston," *New York Times*, April 16, 1965, 57. For Meinke quote, see "School Integration Decried in Hartford," *New York Times*, November 19, 1964, 39.

106. Mary Lou Finley, Bernard Lafayette Jr., James R. Ralph Jr., and Pam Smith, eds., *The Chicago Freedom Movement: Martin Luther King Jr. and Civil Rights Activism in the North* (Lexington: University of Kentucky Press, 2016); Taylor Branch, *At Canaan's Edge: America in the King Years, 1965–1968* (New York: Simon and Schuster, 2006), 501–522;, "Programmatic Action Proposal for Chicago," September [no date],1965, King Library and Archives, The Martin Luther King, Jr., Center for Nonviolent Social Change, Atlanta, GA, digital archive, http://www.thekingcenter.org/archive/document/proposal-chicago-schools#. For the quote from the New Jersey NAACP, see William Smith, "School News and Views," *Newark Herald News*, October 30, 1965, 8.

107. Irving Adler, "Our Northern Cities: Toward Integration, or Segregation?" *Strengthening Democracy* 18, no. 1 (1965): 1, in Box 31, Folder 39, United Federation of Teachers Records, WAG 22. See also Board of Education of New York City, "Better Education through Integration," January 29, 1964, New York, NY, in Box 31, Folder 40, UFT Records.

108. Todd-Breland, *A Political Education*, 35–37; Robert Levy, "A Decade after School Desegregation Decision," *Boston Globe*, May 17, 1964, 6A.

Chapter 4

1. For "arbitrary" quote, see "School Boycott Likely if Negroes Bused: CORE," *Hartford Courant*, July 11, 1968, 27A; "2 Groups Sue Board, Charge Discrimination," *Hartford Courant*, July 10, 1968, 10. For Yates quote, see William Borders, "Negroes Sue in Norwalk to End Busing and Reopen Black School," *New York Times*, August 28, 1968, 28. For 1963 school desegregation plan, see "Council Votes Housing Discrimination Ban: Norwalk First City to Follow JFK Order," *Norwalk Hour*, November 28, 1962, 1–2, in Folder, "Organization Department Chapter Files: Norwalk, Connecticut," Congress of Racial Equality Papers, Addendum, 1944–1967, Black Freedom Struggle in the 20th Century: Organizational Records and Personal Papers, Part 2, ProQuest History Vault, https://congressional.ProQuest.com/histvault?q=252252-017-1091; Andrew J. Wise to Robert Carter, June 3, 1964, and June Shagaloff, memorandum, January 1965, both in Folder, "Connecticut School Desegregation Plans," Papers of the NAACP, Part 03: The Campaign for Educational Equality, Series D: Central Office Records, 1956–1965, ProQuest History Vault, https://congressional.ProQuest.com/histvault?q=001516-002-0883. See also Andrew J. Wise to Robert Carter, June 3, 1964, and June Shagaloff, memorandum, January 1965, both in Folder, "Connecticut School Desegregation Plans," Papers of the NAACP, Part 03: The Campaign for Educational Equality, Series D: Central Office Records, 1956–1965, ProQuest History Vault, https://congressional.ProQuest.com/histvault?q=001516-002-0883. See also Legal Complaint filed by Norwalk Congress of Racial Equality (CORE) and Roodner Court Fair Rent Association against Norwalk Board of Education, June 25, 1968, US District Court in New Haven, Connecticut, Civil Action no. 12624 and the answer by the court, which denied relief, both in Folder, "CORE v. Norwalk Board of Education Case," Papers of the NAACP, Supplement to Part 23: Legal Department Case Files, 1960–1972, Series B: The Northeast, Section I: Connecticut, Delaware, District of Columbia, Maine, Massachusetts, New Hampshire, New Jersey, Pennsylvania, and Rhode Island, https://congressional.ProQuest.com/histvault?q=016310-003-0637.

2. For Beatrice Brown quote, see Borders, "Negroes Sue in Norwalk to End Busing and Reopen Black School." For Yates quote, see Richard D. McNeill, "Norwalk School Dispute Splits CORE and NAACP," *Hartford Courant*, August 3, 1968, 7. See also *Norwalk CORE et al. v Norwalk Board of Education* 423 F. 2d 121 (1970). Wilber G. Smith to Robert Carter, August 6, 1968, in Folder, "CORE v. Norwalk Board of Education Case," Papers of the NAACP, ProQuest History Vault in Folder, "CORE v. Norwalk Board of Education Case," Papers of the NAACP, Supplement to Part 23: Legal Department Case Files, 1960–1972, Series B: The Northeast, Section I: Connecticut, Delaware, District of Columbia, Maine, Massachusetts, New Hampshire, New Jersey, Pennsylvania, and Rhode Island, https://congressional.ProQuest.com/histvault?q=016310-003-0637.

3. On July 4, 1966, CORE declared its independence from the civil rights movement and dedicated itself to Black power, defined as race pride, economic independence, and political power. Both CORE and the Student Nonviolent Coordinating Committee (SNCC) expelled white members, rejected integration as a strategy and a goal, and declared that non-violent direct action was a "dying philosophy." Ashley D. Farmer, *Remaking Black Power: How Black Women Transformed an Era* (Chapel Hill: University of North Carolina Press, 2017), 50–92; Manning Marable, *Race, Reform, and Rebellion: The Second Reconstruction and Beyond in Black America, 1945–2006*, 3rd ed. (Jackson: University Press of Mississippi, 2007), 112–145; Peniel E. Joseph, *Waiting 'Til the Midnight Hour: A Narrative History of Black Power in America* (New York: Henry Holt, 2006), 146–150; August Meier and Elliott Rudwick, *CORE: A Study of the Civil Rights Movement, 1942–1968* (New York: Oxford University Press, 1973), 412–415; Nathan Wright Jr., *Let's Work Together* (New York: Hawthorne Books, 1968). On the tremendous diversity of grassroots Black power campaigns, see the collection of essays in Peniel E. Joseph, ed., *Neighborhood Rebels: Black Power at the Local Level* (New York: Palgrave Macmillan, 2010).

4. Robert C. Weaver, "Introduction," in Betty Lanier Jenkins and Susan Phillis, eds., *Black Separatism: A Bibliography* (Westport, CT: Greenwood Press, 1976), xxiv–xxv.

5. Charles V. Hamilton, "Race and Education: A Search for Legitimacy," *Harvard Educational Review* 38, no. 4 (1968): 669–684.

6. Robert S. Browne, "The Case for Two Americas—One Black, One White," *New York Times,* August 11, 1968, SM12. Scholarship documenting widespread support for community-controlled schools in the North includes Peter K. Eisinger, "Community Control and Liberal Dilemmas," *Publius* 2, no. 2 (1972): 129–148; Leonard Fein, *The Ecology of the Public Schools: An Inquiry into Community Control* (New York: Pegasus, 1971); Alan Altshuler, *Community Control: The Black Demand for Participation in Large American Cities* (New York: Pegasus, 1970); Mario Fantini, Marilyn Gittell, and Richard Magat, *Community Control and the Urban School* (New York: Praeger, 1970); Milton Kotler, *Neighborhood Government: The Local Foundations of Political Life* (Indianapolis: Bobbs-Merrill, 1969). A special issue of *Ebony* magazine explored whether integration or separation was best positioned to advance Black liberation; see "Separation? Integration? Liberation? Which Way Black America?" Special Issue, *Ebony* 25, no. 10 (August 1970): 33–180.

7. Albert L. Alford, "The Elementary and Secondary Education Act of 1965: What to Anticipate," *Phi Delta Kappan* 46, no. 10 (1965): 483–488, quote on p. 483; Philip Dodd, "Johnson Signs Bill at Old Schoolhouse," *Chicago Tribune,* April 12, 1965, 18; Carol Kilpatrick, "Johnson, at Old School, Signs Education Aid Bill," *Washington Post,* April 12, 1965, 1; Alan Spivak, "Johnson Signs Aid to Education Bill into Law," *Chicago Defender,* April 12, 1965, 3. See also Laurence Parker, ed., *The Elementary and Secondary Education Act at 40: Reviews of Research, Policy Implantation, Critical Perspectives, and Reflections* (Washington, DC: American Educational Research Association, 2005); Alice O'Connor, *Poverty Knowledge: Social Science, Social Policy, and the Poor in Twentieth-Century America* (Princeton, NJ: Princeton University Press, 2001), 74–123; Julie Roy Jeffrey, *Education for Children of the Poor: A Study of the Origins and Implementation of the Elementary and Secondary Education Act of 1965* (Columbus: Ohio State University Press, 1978).

8. For the statistic on northern school segregation in 1964, see Robert A. Dentler, "Community Behavior and Northern School Desegregation," *Journal of Negro Education* 34, no. 3 (1965): 258–267. Davison Douglas argues northern school segregation increased after World War II; *Jim Crow Moves North,* 219–221. See also Marable, *Race, Reform, and Rebellion,* 80–83; C. Vann Woodward, *The Strange Career of Jim Crow,* commemorative ed. (New York: Oxford University Press, 2002), 186–187; Advisory Committee on Racial Imbalance and Education, *Because It's Right: Springfield, Massachusetts* (Springfield: Massachusetts Board of Education, 1965), 77–86; Urban League of Greater New York, *A Study of the Problems of Integration in New York City Public Schools since 1955* (New York: Urban League of Greater New York, 1963); Public Education Association, *The Status of the Public School Education of Puerto Rican and Negro Children in New York City* (New York: Public Education Association, 1955).

9. *Wilfred Keyes et al. v. School District No. 1, Denver, Colorado, et al.* 413 U.S. 189 (1973); *Swann v. Charlotte-Mecklenburg Board of Education,* 402 U.S. 1 (1971). See also Joyce A. Baugh, *The Detroit School Busing Case: Milliken v. Bradley and the Controversy over Desegregation* (Lawrence: University of Kansas Press, 2011); David J. Armor, *Forced Justice: School Desegregation and the Law* (New York: Oxford University Press, 1995), 34–38; J. Harvie Wilinson III, *From Brown to Bakke: The Supreme Court and School Integration, 1954–1978* (New York: Oxford University Press, 1979), 193–239; Margo Evans, "From Denver to Dayton: The Evolution of Constitutional Doctrine in Northern School Desegregation Litigation," *University of Dayton Law Review* 3, no. 1 (1978): 115–152; Robert L. Herbst, "The Legal Struggle to Integrate Schools in the North," *Annals of the American Academy of Political and Social Science* 407 (May 1973): 43–62; US Commission on Civil Rights, "Five Communities: Their Search for Equal Education," December 1972 (Washington, DC: US Government Printing Office, 1972); Owen M. Fiss, "The Charlotte Mecklenburg Case: Its Significance for Northern School Desegregation," *University of Chicago Law Review* 38, no. 4 (1971): 697–709; US Commission on Civil Rights, "Understanding School Desegregation" (Washington, DC: US Government Printing Office, 1971).

10. There were 163 rebellions in 1967 alone, capped by deadly clashes between Black citizens and the National Guard and the US Army in Detroit and Newark. Dozens of uprisings also took place in small cities, small towns, and suburbs in the North. See Scott Kurashige, *The Fifty Year Rebellion: How the U.S. Political Crisis Began in Detroit* (Oakland: University of California Press, 2017); Malcolm McLaughlin, *The Long Hot Summer of 1967: Urban*

Rebellion in America (New York: Palgrave Macmillan, 2014); Joe T. Darden and Richard W. Thomas, *Detroit: Race Riots, Racial Conflicts, and Efforts to Bridge the Racial Divide* (East Lansing: Michigan State University Press, 2013); Kevin Mumford, *Newark: A History of Race, Rights, and Riots in America* (New York: New York University Press, 2007); Ronald Porambo, *No Cause for Indictment: An Autopsy of Newark* (New York: Melville House Books, 2007); Thomas J. Sugrue and Andrew P. Goodman, "Plainfield Burning: Black Rebellion in the Suburban North," *Journal of Urban History* 33, no. 4 (2007): 568–601; Otto Kerner et. al., "Report of the National Advisory Commission on Civil Disorders" (Washington, DC: US Government Printing Office, 1968), 75–81.

11. Russell Freeburg, "Carmichael, Brown Share Violent World," *Chicago Tribune*, July 30, 1967, 14. See also Daryl Michael Scott, *Contempt and Pity: Social Policy and the Image of the Damaged Black Psyche, 1880–1996* (Chapel Hill: University of North Carolina Press, 1997): 161–185.

12. Bayard Rustin, "A Negro Leader Defines a Way Out of the Exploding Ghetto," *New York Times*, August 13, 1967, 20. See also Harvard Sitkoff, *The Struggle for Black Equality*, rev. ed. (New York: Hill & Wang, 2008), 184–209; Joseph, *Waiting 'til the Midnight Hour*, 174–191; John D'Emilio, *Lost Prophet: The Life and Times of Bayard Rustin* (New York: Free Press, 2003), 440–471; Adam Fairclough, *Better Day Coming: Blacks and Equality, 1890–2000* (New York: Viking Penguin, 2001), 310–321; Paul Good, "Odyssey of a Man—And a Movement," *New York Times*, June 25, 1967, SM3; "The Backlash: After Progress and Riots, Protest at the Polls," *New York Times*, October 2, 1966, 203; Emmet John Hughes, "Three Rs We Must Not Teach: Rancor, Riot and Revenge Are Black Power Pitfalls," *Boston Globe*, August 14, 1966, A5; Jack Nelson, "Black Power: The 'Color' Line Closes in on King," *Los Angeles Times*, July 3, 1966, B1. See also Bayard Rustin, "The Failure of Black Separatism," *Harper's Magazine* (January 1970), 25–34. A collection of Rustin's reflections on the urban rebellions can be found in Folder, "Bayard Rustin Writings on Race Riots in the 1960s," Bayard Rustin Papers, ProQuest History Vault, https://congressional.ProQuest.com/histvault?q=001581-018-1251.

13. Elizabeth Gillespie McRae, *Mothers of Massive Resistance: White Women and the Politics of White Supremacy* (New York: Oxford University Press, 2018), 217–241; Matthew F. Delmont, *Why Busing Failed: Race, Media, and the National Resistance to School Desegregation* (Oakland: University of California Press, 2016); Ernest Conine, "Can the White Majority Accept True Integration?" *Los Angeles Times*, August 24, 1966, A5. For Cimmino quote, see William Borders, "Day of Doom—or Hope: Integration Plan Is Due by March 15, and Mt. Vernon Faces a New Split," *New York Times*, February 14, 1966, 22. For Rochester mother, see Lucia Johnson, "Rochester, NY Focuses Effort on the Inner City Schools," *Christian Science Monitor*, July 10, 1968, 3. For Queens activist, see Warren Berry and Ramona Negron Hamill, "School Busing: Black, White, or Gray," *Boston Globe*, October 3, 1966, 2. For white teacher, see Robert Coles, *The South Goes North*, vol. 3 of *Children of Crisis* (New York: Little, Brown, 1971), 457. On the discriminatory meaning of the concept of neighborhood school, see Michael Hilton, "Neighborhood Schools—An Etymology," *Poverty & Race* 24, no. 6 (November/December 2015): 12–13.

14. Joshua Zeitz, *Building the Great Society: Inside Lyndon Johnson's White House* (New York: Viking, 2018), 242, emphasis in original. For Dentler quote, see "Community Behavior and Northern School Desegregation," 265. Robert Coles documents both white and Black perspectives on school integration and busing in the North. His study captures the very wide range of responses by both groups, including intimate portrayals of the experiences of young children, their parents, and their teachers. See Coles, *The South Goes North*, 421–536.

15. Conine, "Can the White Majority Accept True Integration?" For Malverne mothers, see "Seek Reversal in Albany on Pupil Transfer," *Newsday*, March 1, 1966, 2; "Parents, Kids Rip New York School Busing," *Chicago Defender*, February 24, 1966, 56. For Harsdale father, see William Borders, "Hartsdale in Ferment," *New York Times*, April 15, 1966, 80. See also McRae, *Mothers of Massive Resistance*; Delmont, *Why Busing Failed*, 23–53.

16. George R. Metcalf, *From Little Rock to Boston: The History of School Desegregation* (Westport, CT: Greenwood Press, 1983), 3–16; US Commission on Civil Rights, "Your Child and Busing," May 1972 (Washington, DC: US Government Printing Office, 1972); John Herbers, "Integration Gains but Storm Signs Grow across U.S.," *New York Times*, January 11, 1967,

NOTES TO PAGES 135–137

27; Robert Coles, "The White Northerner: Pride and Prejudice," *Newsday*, October 8, 1966, 8W; "Riots Engender Pessimism," *Philadelphia Tribune*, October 8, 1966, 24; Dick Zander, "Nassau Dems Spurn Busing," *Newsday*, September 30, 1966, 5.

17. President Nixon released two official statements detailing his policy on busing: Richard Nixon, "Statement about the Busing of School Children," August 3, 1971, online by Gerhard Peters and John T. Woolley, *The American Presidency Project*, https://www.presidency.ucsb.edu/documents/statement-about-the-busing-schoolchildren; Richard Nixon, "Statement about Desegregation of Elementary and Secondary Schools," March 24, 1970, online by Gerhard Peters and John T. Woolley, *The American Presidency Project*, https://www.presidency.ucsb.edu/documents/statement-about-desegregation-elementary-and-secondary-schools. This stance ostensibly supported Supreme Court rulings on school integration, while in reality it signaled his opposition to the most effective measure—transporting students to schools—available to overcome school segregation. It also established his opposition to efforts to overcome northern de facto school segregation. See Rick Perlstein, *Nixonland: The Rise of a President and the Fracturing of America* (New York: Simon & Schuster, 2008), 223–284 and 610-646; Gary Orfield and Susan E. Eaton, *Dismantling Desegregation: The Quiet Reversal of Brown v. Board of Education* (New York: New Press, 1997), 4–32; 311–139; Metcalf, *From Little Rock to Boston*, 7–229; see also Robert O. Self, *All in the Family: The Realignment of American Democracy since the 1960s* (New York: Hill and Wang, 2012); Daniel T. Rodgers, *The Age of Fracture* (New York: Belknap Press, 2011); Jefferson Cowie, *Stayin' Alive: The 1970s and the Last Days of the Working Class* (New York: New Press, 2010); Bruce J. Shulman, *The Seventies: The Great Shift in American Culture, Society, and Politics* (New York: Da Capo Press, 2002); Maurice Isserman and Michael Kazin, *America Divided: The Civil War of the 1960s*, 2nd ed. (New York: Oxford University Press, 2004).

18. Gerald Grant, "An Educational Time Bomb: Coleman Report Jolts Some Time-Honored Premises," *Washington Post*, December 26, 1966, A4. Another influential piece of social science scholarship was Daniel Patrick Moynihan, "The Negro Family: The Case for National Action," Office of Policy Planning and Research, US Department of Labor (Washington, DC: US Government Printing Office, 1965).

19. Joseph Alsop, "A Report Disputes a Cure," *Boston Globe*, January 23, 1967, 15; Grant, "An Educational Time Bomb"; James S. Coleman et al., *Equality of Educational Opportunity* (Washington, DC: Government Printing Office, 1966). See also "U.S. Study Finds Racial Inequality Grows in School," *New York Times*, September 18, 1966, 72; and Patrick J. Sloyan, "Education: Is Minority Child Still Shut Out?" *Chicago Defender*, September 24, 1966, 6.

20. William E. Nelson Jr., "School Desegregation and the Black Community," *Theory into Practice* 17, no. 2 (1978): 122–130; Frederick Mosteller and Daniel P. Moynihan, eds., *On Equal Educational Opportunity: Papers Deriving from the Harvard University Faculty Seminar on the Coleman Report* (New York: Random House, 1972); Harvard Educational Review, eds., *Equal Educational Opportunity* (Cambridge, MA: Harvard University Press, 1969); Charles H. Thompson, "Race and Equality of Educational Opportunity: Defining the Problem," *Journal of Negro Education* 37, no. 3 (1968): 191–203; Earle H. West, "Progress toward Equality of Opportunity in Elementary and Secondary Education," *Journal of Negro Education* 37, no. 3 (1968): 212–219; Kenneth Clark, "Alternative Public School Systems," *Harvard Educational Review* 38, no. 1 (1968): 100–113; Daniel Moynihan, "Sources of Resistance to the Coleman Report," *Harvard Educational Review* 38, no. 1 (1968), 23–36; Thomas Pettigrew, "Race and Equal Educational Opportunity," *Harvard Educational Review* 38, no. 1 (1968), 66–76.

21. Harrell R. Rodgers Jr. and Charles S. Bullock III, "School Desegregation: Successes and Failures," *Journal of Negro Education* 43, no. 2 (1974): 139–154, 141; Christopher Jencks et al., *Inequality: A Reassessment of the Effect of Family and Schooling in America* (New York: Harper & Row, 1972); Robert L. Crain, "School Integration and the Academic Achievement of Negroes," *Sociology of Education* 44, no. 1 (1971): 1–26. The Coleman Report also fueled a backlash against school integration from a growing number of white neoconservative social scientists like Nathan Glazer and Daniel Patrick Moynihan. These scholars once identified as racial liberals but grew skeptical as race relations seemed to deteriorate alongside the rise of the Black Power movement and urban rebellions of the late 1960s. Moynihan insisted that liberals were making a mistake by focusing on social relations like discrimination in housing

and employment instead of what he viewed as the more important factors of individual responsibility and the deterioration of the Black family. He read Coleman's findings as justification that the family was more important than government services, such as public education. See Daryl Michael Scott, *Contempt and Pity: Social Policy and the Image of the Damaged Black Psyche, 1880–1996* (Chapel Hill: University of North Carolina Press, 1997), 170–177.

22. Grant, "An Educational Time Bomb"; and Coleman et al., *Equality of Educational Opportunity*, 23–24.

23. Nathan Wright Jr., *Ready to Riot* (New York: Holt, Rinehart and Winston, 1968), 130; Floyd McKissick, "Is Integration Necessary?" *New Republic*, December 3, 1966, 33–36.

24. "Report of the National Advisory Commission on Civil Disorders," 236–277, 424–456; Hamilton, "Race and Education"; "Clark Tells NAACP Shift School Emphasis," *New Jersey Herald News*, October 29, 1966, 7.

25. Lewis M. Steel, memorandum, October 1, 1968, in Folder, "CORE v. Norwalk Board of Education Case," Papers of the NAACP, ProQuest History Vault in Folder, "CORE v. Norwalk Board of Education Case," Papers of the NAACP, Supplement to Part 23: Legal Department Case Files, 1960–1972, Series B: The Northeast, Section I: Connecticut, Delaware, District of Columbia, Maine, Massachusetts, New Hampshire, New Jersey, Pennsylvania, and Rhode Island, https://congressional.ProQuest.com/histvault?q=016310-003-0637.

26. On white student protests in Rochester, New York, see "Closing of Rochester School, Ends Furor on Busing," *New York Times*, June 21, 1972, 47. See also Lucia Johnson, "Rochester, NY Focuses Effort on the Inner City School," *Christian Science Monitor*, July 10, 1968, 3; Lucia Johnson, "Inner and Outer City Pupils Cross Bus," *Christian Science Monitor*, July 3, 1968, 3; Lucia Johnson, "Rochester Integration: Miles to Go," *Christian Science Monitor*, June 25, 1968, 1. See also Sondra Astor Stave, *Achieving Racial Balance: Case Studies of Contemporary School Desegregation* (Westport, CT: Greenwood Press, 1995), 23–44; Herman R. Goldberg, *Grade Reorganization and Desegregation of the Rochester Public Schools: A Report to the Board of Education* (Rochester, NY: City School District, 1969). On Black school closing and job loss, see Derrick A. Bell Jr., "The Burden of Brown on Blacks: History-Based Observations on a Landmark Decision," *North Carolina Central Law Review* 7 (1975): 25–38; "Judge Orders One-Teacher Schools Closed," *New Jersey Herald News*, March 5, 1966, 6; "Report Shows Negro Teacher Subject to Ouster by South," *New Jersey Herald News*, January 1, 1966, 2; "Fund to Aid Negro Teachers from South Is Operational," *New Jersey Herald News*, January 1, 1966, 2.

27. John Sharnick, "When Things Go Wrong All Blacks Are Black and All Whites Are Whitey," *New York Times*, May 25, 1969, SM30. For more examples of why Black northerners supported community-controlled schools, see Coles, *The South Goes North*, 421–536; US Commission on Civil Rights, *What Students Perceive*, Clearing House Publication No. 24 (Washington, DC: US Government Printing Office: 1970). For more on Black educational activism in Norwalk and the struggle to preserve Black neighborhood schools, see "Equal Protection of the Laws," *Harvard Law Review* 83, no. 6 (1970): 1434–1440.

28. Peniel E. Joseph, *Stokely: A Life* (New York: Basic Books, 2014), 101–125; Fairclough, *Better Day Coming*, 310–315.

29. Stokely quote in Ken Byerly and John Cummings, "Pickets, Police Clash as Principal Returns," *Newsday*, September 21, 1966. Parenthetical interpretation in original. See also Joyce Egginton, "A Little Rock in Reverse," *Observer*, September 25, 1966, 13; John Goldman, "N.Y. Negroes Defy Carmichael," *Boston Globe*, September 23, 1966, 2; "Principal Returns, Five Seized," *Chicago Tribune*, September 22, 1966, 12; "N.Y. Pickets Protest Return of Principal," *Hartford Courant*, September 22, 1966, 4; "SNCC Leader, Pickets Try to Oust Principal," *Los Angeles Times*, September 22, 1966, 12; Thomas A. Johnson, "Militant Negro Groups Moving to Aid Parents in School Fight," *New York Times*, September 22, 1966, 50; "Harlem School Melee Brings Arrest of Five," *Washington Post*, September 22, 1966, A2.

30. Latinx is a preferred contemporary, gender-neutral term embraced by many younger Americans who are either from, or who have family from, Latin America. Since this term is new, it would not have been used by people living in the historical era covered in this chapter, who would have been more likely to use specific ethnic designations like Mexican American or Puerto Rican, or Hispanic, Latin, or Latino.Ed Morales, *Latinx: The New Force in American*

Politics and Culture (New York: Verso, 2018); Paul Ortiz, *An African American and Latinx History of the United States* (New York: Beacon Press, 2018); Catalina (Kathleen) M. deOnís, "What's in an 'x'?: An Exchange about the Politics of 'Latinx,'" *Chiricú Journal: Latina/o Literatures, Arts, and Cultures* 1, no. 2 (2017): 78-91.

31. Preston Wilcox, "The Kids Will Decide—And More Power to Them," *Ebony* 25, no. 10 (August 1970): 134-137. For statistics on school segregation, see Mario Fantini, Marilyn Gittell, and Richard Magat, *Community Control and the Urban School* (New York: Praeger, 1970), 6-7; Board of Education of the City of New York, "Action toward Quality Integrated Education," May 28, 1964, 25-26 [PAM 1853 Tamiment Pamphlet Collection]. On residential segregation in New York City, see Nathan Kantrowitz, "Ethnic and Racial Segregation in the New York Metropolis, 1960," *American Journal of Sociology* 74, no. 6 (1969): 685-695. See also Clarence Taylor, "Conservative and Liberal Opposition to the New York City School-Integration Campaign," in Clarence Taylor, ed., *Civil Rights in New York City: From World War II to the Giuliani Era* (New York: Fordham University Press, 2011), 95-117; Martha Biondi, *To Stand and Fight: The Struggle for Civil Rights in Postwar New York City* (Cambridge, MA: Harvard University Press, 2003), 223-249; Jerald E. Podair, *The Strike that Changed New York: Blacks, Whites, and the Ocean-Hill Brownsville Crisis* (New Haven, CT: Yale University Press, 2002), 22-27; Diane Ravitch, *The Great School Wars: A History of the New York City Public Schools*, rev. ed. (Baltimore: Johns Hopkins University Press, 2000), 251-380; Doxey A. Wilkerson, "School Integration, Compensatory Education and the Civil Rights Movement in the North," *Journal of Negro Education* 34, no. 3 (1965): 300-309; Board of Education of the City of New York, "The Open Enrollment Program in the New York City Public Schools: Progress Report," September 1960-September 1963 (New York: Board of Education of the City of New York, 1963), Tamiment Pamphlet Collection TAM 1854.

32. Fantini, Gittell, and Magat, *Community Control and the Urban School*, 4.

33. Kenneth Clark, "Introduction" to Fantini, Gittell, and Magat, *Community Control and the Urban School*, ix-xi, quote on p. x; Arthur Siddon, "Black Separatism Move on the Rise," *Chicago Tribune*, July 30, 1968, A3. See also Russell Rickford, *We Are an African People: Independent Education, Black Power, and the Radical Imagination* (New York: Oxford University Press, 2016), 23-33.

34. For Hamilton quote, see Marilyn Bain, "Community Control Advised for Schools," *Hartford Courant*, April 19, 1970, 15C. For Black senator quote, see Siddon, "Black Separatism Move on the Rise." See also Congress of Racial Equality (CORE), "CORE and I.S. 201," undated, in Folder, "Education and 'CORE and I.S. 201,' Community Relations Department Subject Files," Congress of Racial Equality Papers, Addendum, 1944-1968, Congress of Racial Equality Papers, Martin Luther King, Jr. Center for Nonviolent Social Change, Inc., Atlanta, GA, ProQuest History Vault, https://congressional.ProQuest.com/histvault?q=252252-014-0144.

35. Sara Slack, "Living Legend Rhody McCoy Continues Education Battles," *New York Amsterdam News*, March 28, 1970, 32; "100 Black Men's Plan Backs Community Control," *New York Amsterdam News*, March 29, 1969, 4; Sydney H. Schanberg, "O'Dwyer Favors Community Control of Schools," *New York Times*, October 8, 1968, 32.

36. Jack D. Forbes, "Segregation and Integration: The Multi-Ethnic or Uni-Ethnic School," *Phylon* 30, no. 1 (1969): 34-41, quote on p. 35. For African American Teachers Association quote, see C. Gerald Fraser, "Negro Teachers Define their Stand," *New York Times*, September 21, 1967, 52. See also "Roxbury's Cry: Action Now!" *Boston Globe*, March 19, 1968, 28A; Leonard Buder, "Harlem Parents Fight New School," *New York Times*, September 9, 1966, 47. See also Christopher Jenks, "Private Schools for Black Children," *New York Times*, November 3, 1968, SM30-31; Fred M. Hechinger, "Education: A Storm Gathers across the Land," *New York Times*, September 8, 1968, E1.

37. For Martin quote, see Leonard Buder, "Teacher Ousted over US 201 Show," *New York Times*, February 28, 1968, 50. See also "McKissick Asserts 'Shock' Is Necessary to Gain Negro Goal," *New York Times*, October 2, 1966, 69; Gerald Grant, "Harlem School Moderates Undercut," *Washington Post*, September 26, 1966, A4.

38. Jon Shelton, *Teacher Strike: Public Education and the Making of a New American Political Order* (Urbana: University of Illinois Press, 2017), 34-37; Jonna Perrillo, *Uncivil Rights: Teachers,*

Unions, and Race in the Battle for School Equity (Chicago: University of Chicago Press, 2012), 116–147; Daniel Perlstein, *Justice, Justice: School Politics and the Eclipse of* Liberalism (New York: Peter Lang, 2004), 81–96. The Anti-Defamation League (ADL) documented sharply increased anti-Semitism in the New York City public schools from 1967 to 1969 and concluded that this surge in anti-Semitism was "perpetrated largely by Black extremists." The ADL also supported decentralization in New York City but was "unalterably opposed" to community control. See "ADL: Anti-Semitism at Crisis Level in New York City Schools" and "Decentralization Favored, but not Community Control," both in *The Metropolitan Star*, 24, no. 8 (January 1969), 1. In Box 58, Folder 8, United Federation of Teachers (UFT) Records, Papers, Black civil rights leaders Bayard Rustin and A. Philip Randolph continued to support the UFT and school decentralization in New York City when many other Black civil rights activists did not. See Bayard Rustin, speech: "Integration within Decentralization: Acceptance Speech for the 1968 John Dewey Award of the UFT," April 6, 1968; A. Philip Randolph and Bayard Rustin, Letter to the Editor, *New York Times*, October 6, 1967; Bayard Rustin, "Why I Support the UFT," *New York Amsterdam News*, September 23, 1967. All three in Box 84, Folder 16, United Federation of Teachers Records.

39. Clarence Taylor, *Knocking at Our Door: Milton A. Galamison and the Struggle to Integrate New York City Schools* (New York: Columbia University Press, 1997), 176–207; Sara Slack, "New Administrator Wants Parents' Aid," *New York Amsterdam News*, October 28, 1067, 25. See also George Todd, "Hail Education Board's New Principal Selection," *New York Amsterdam News*, September 2, 1967, 23; "Group Assails Demonstration Principal's Post," *New York Times*, August 26, 1967, 21; M. A. Farber, "Board of Education Creates Post of Demonstration School Principal in Three Districts," *New York Times*, August 25, 1967, 21; M. A. Farber, "Group Threatens to Shut 7 Schools," *New York Times*, August 12, 1967, 25.

40. "Ambitious Educator, Rhody Arnold McCoy, Jr.," *New York Times*, May 14, 1968, 44; Paul Hofmann, "Ousted Teachers Get Mixed Advice," *New York Times*, May 13, 1968, 39; "NY Firing of Teachers Stirs Storm," *Boston Globe*, May 11, 1968, 4. See also Board of Education of the City of New York, memorandum, September 20, 1968, and Harold Siegel, Secretary of the New York City Board of Education to Rhody McCoy, September 15, 1968, both in Folder, "Ocean Hill-Brownsville Governing Board v. Board of Education case, general case material," in Papers of the NAACP, Supplement to Part 23: Legal Department Case Files, 1960–1972, Series B: The Northeast, Section II: New York, ProQuest History Vault, https://congressional.ProQuest.com/histvault?q=100243-026-0050.

41. For quotes, see "100 Teachers Stay Out in City 'Firing' Dispute," *Newsday*, May 14, 1968, 65. See also George H. Favre, "Brooklyn Uproar Tests School Plan," *Christian Science Monitor*, May 16, 1968, 10; Pat Patterson, "School Is Closed after Cops Lead Teachers In," *Newsday*, May 15, 1968, 7.

42. Little Rock reference, see "100 Teachers Stay Out in City 'Firing' Dispute." For McCoy quote, see C. Gerald Fraser, "Members of Troubled School Board Tell of Agony," *New York Times*, May 17, 1968, 37. See also "Color Test," *Washington Post*, May 18, 1968, A14. Various community groups weighed in on the teachers strike as well. Union groups, including the Black Trade Unionists, insisted the teachers strike had merit since workers had been fired without due process, while many Black civil rights and educational groups, including the New York Association of Black School Supervisors and Administrators and the National Urban League, wrote letters in support of Rhody McCoy and the Ocean Hill-Brownsville Community Board of Education. "To try to make Black people think the UFT teacher strike is not racial is a damn lie," wrote Edward Urquhart, a self-identified Black civil servant and union member on September 19, 1968. For a collection of these letters for and against the UFT strike, see Folder, "United Federation of Teachers Strike, September 1968," Bayard Rustin Papers, ProQuest History Vault, https://congressional.ProQuest.com/histvault?q=001581-006-0001. For more on how and why various constituencies responded to this strike, see Perlstein, *Justice, Justice*.

43. For quote, see "The School Mess," *New York Amsterdam News*, September 14, 1968, 14. See also George Todd, "10 Policemen Hurt in Model Schools Area," *New York Amsterdam News*, October 5, 1968, 23.

44. Joseph Featherstone, "Community Control: Down but Not Out," *New Republic*, August 9, 1969, 11–12. See also Ravitch, *The Great School Wars*, 362–380.

45. Michael B. Katz, "Why Don't American Cities Burn Very Often," *Journal of Urban History* 34, no. 2 (2008): 185–208; Ravitch, *The Great School Wars*, 381–387; Ira Katznelson, *City Trenches: Urban Politics and the Patterning of Class in the United States* (Chicago: University of Chicago Press, 1981), 179, 187; Sydney H. Schanberg, "City School Bill Voted in Albany," *New York Times*, May 1, 1969, 1; Nathan Glazer, "For White and Black, Community Control Is the Issue," *New York Times*, April 27, 1969, SM36.

46. On the varied and pragmatic approach of Black educational activists in the late 1960s and early 1970s, see Matthew J. Countryman, *Up South: Civil Rights and Black Power in Philadelphia* (Philadelphia: University of Pennsylvania Press, 2006), 223–257; Theoharis and Woodard, eds., *Freedom North*, especially Jeanne Theoharis, "I'd Rather Go to School in the South: How Boston's School Desegregation Complicates the Civil Rights Paradigm," 125–152. On new fissures between and among Black civil rights activists, labor unions, and Jews, see Perrillo, *Uncivil Rights*, 138–147; Daniel Perlstein, "The Dead End of Despair: Bayard Rustin, the 1968 New York School Crisis and the Struggle for Racial Justice," in Clarence Taylor, ed., *Civil Rights in New York City: From World War II to the Giuliani Era* (New York: Fordham University Press, 2011), 95–117; Perlstein, *Justice, Justice*, 7–13; Podair, *The Strike that Changed New York*, 5–7; Ravitch, *The Great School Wars* 362–378; Jeffrey Mirel, *The Rise and Fall of an Urban School System: Detroit, 1907–81*, 2nd ed. (Ann Arbor: University of Michigan Press, 1999), 298–313.

47. Taylor, "Opposition to the New York City School-Integration Campaign"; Thomas Sugrue, *The Origins of the Urban Crisis: Race and Inequality in Postwar Detroit* (Princeton, NJ: Princeton University Press, 2014), 268.

48. M. Costello, "School Busing and Politics," *Editorial Research Reports*, March 1, 1972, Editorial Research Reports 1972 (vol. 1) (Washington, DC: CQ Press, 1972), http://library.cqpress.com/cqresearcher/cqresrre1972030100; Babette Edwards and Preston Wilcox, "What Happened to Community Control of Our Schools," *New York Amsterdam News*, December 11, 1971, A7 (parentheses and emphasis in original).

49. Rickford, *We Are an African People*, 2, 38–41; Stokely Carmichael, *Stokely Speaks: From Black Power to Pan-Africanism* (Chicago: Chicago Review Press, 2007[1971]), 23. For Pulley quote, see Len Lear, "Black Community Control Is a Must," *Philadelphia Tribune*, September 30, 1972, 27.

50. Hope Justus, "Chicago's Public Schools and Community Control," *Chicago Tribune*, July 4, 1971, A1; Ewell W. Finley, "Why Desegregating LI Schools Is a Must," *Newsday*, June 7, 1971, 41; Michael B. Trister and P. Kent Spriggs, "The Debate over School Integration," *New Republic*, March 28, 1970, 25–28, quote on p. 27, emphasis in original; "Fight School Bias in North," *Chicago Defender*, January 21, 1970, 4. On rising tide of anti-integration among Congress and President Nixon, see Delmont, *Why Busing Failed*, 114–141; Metcalf, *From Little Rock to Boston*, 130–147.

51. James A. Banks, "Quality Education for Black Students," in Norene Harris, Nathaniel Jackson, and Carl E. Rydingsword, eds., *The Integration of American Schools: Problems, Experiences, Solutions* (Boston: Allyn & Bacon, 1975), 165–175; US Commission on Civil Rights, *What Students Perceive*, 13; Mirel, *The Rise and Fall of an Urban School System*, 326–345.

52. For Chicago quote, see John Hall Fish, *Black Power, White Control: The Struggle of the Woodlawn Organization in Chicago* (Princeton, NJ: Princeton University Press, 1973), 175. For Philadelphia quote, see John Wilder, "All-Black Disciplinary School," *Philadelphia Tribune*, May 2, 1970, 40. See also Thomas J. Sugrue and Andrew P. Goodman, "Plainfield Burning: Black Rebellion in the Suburban North," *Journal of Urban History* 33, no. 4 (2007): 568–601; "21 Reported Injured in Racial Fighting at Plainfield School," *New York Times*, February 3, 1970, 19; Richard J. H. Johnson, "Disorders Erupt and Subside at High Schools across New Jersey," *New York Times*, March 14, 1969, 27; "NAACP Rips School Plan," *New Jersey Herald News*, November 26, 1966, 1–2. On financial crisis and dilapidated conditions in urban schools, see Mirel, *The Rise and Fall of an Urban School System*, 313–325; James Luther Jones Jr., "Budget Reduction in School Districts," EdD diss., University of Southern California, 1973; Leonard Butler, "Less for Those that Need More," *New York*

Times, December 10, 1972, E5; Ralph E. Winter, "Budget Battle," *Wall Street Journal*, October 29, 1971, 1; Martin Tolchin, "School Budget Crisis," *New York Times*, March 4, 1971, 26.

53. Reynolds Farley, "Residential Segregation and Its Implications for School Integration," *Law and Contemporary Problems* 39, no. 1 (1975): 164–193; "Court: Desegregate All Black Brooklyn School," *New York Amsterdam News*, January 12, 1974, C1; "Michigan City Has All-Black School," *Los Angeles Times*, April 20, 1972, A11; William E. Farrell, "Chicago, A City That Works, Faces Some Hard Realities," *New York Times*, April 1, 1975, 37; Robert Reinhold, "Study Discounts Gains on Busing," *New York Times*, May 23, 1972, 8; Louise Hutchinson, "All Black Schools Show Increase Here," *Chicago Tribune*, January 22, 1972, 13; Seth S. King, "Chicago Reports Segregation Is Up," *New York Times*, November 28, 1971, 69; Anthony Ripley, "Detroit Integration Drive Fails as Whites Quit 3 School Areas," *New York Times*, April 15, 1968, 27; Dorothea Kahn Jaffe, "One Answer: Improve City Inner City Schools," *Christian Science Monitor*, March 2, 1968, 12.

54. For quotes by white students, see US Commission on Civil Rights, *What Students Perceive*, 10. For additional quotes, see William Borders, "New Haven Acts on School Clash," *New York Times*, February 7, 1968, 32; William Borders, "Negro Students Disrupt School," *New York Times*, December 16, 1967, 37. See also "New Haven Minorities Form Own Protection Patrol," *Afro-American*, May 9, 1970, 18; "Demand Probe of School Violence Here," *Chicago Defender*, February 14, 1970, 1; Gene Currivan, Brooklyn High School Closed after Student Riot," *New York Times*, April 19, 1969, 67; Richard J. H. Johnson, "Blacks Rampage in Jersey School," *New York Times*, March 19, 1969, 34; "School Is Reopened as Racial Tensions Let Up in Westbury," *New York Times*, April 4, 1968, 30; "Schools Close in White Plains," *New York Times*, April 4, 1968, 30; Kenneth G. Gehret, "Philadelphia Racial Outlook Brighter," *Christian Science Monitor*, March 21, 1968, 16; "Racial Fights Close Trenton High School," *New York Times*, February 29, 1968, 45; Ralph Blumenthal, "Negroes Protest Mount Vernon Buses," *New York Times*, February 17, 1968, 30; "Chicago Brawl Empties School," *New York Times*, October 9, 1965, 2. On the history of school integration in New Haven, see Thomas Foster Harbison, "Reconsidering Public School Reform in New Haven, Connecticut: A Historical Analysis of the Evolution of the Community School, 1890–2000," master's thesis, Southern Connecticut State University, 2003; Samuel Nash et al., "New Haven, Connecticut: New Haven Chose to Desegregate," in Harris, Jackson, and Rydingsword, *The Integration of American Schools*, 93–108.

55. Robert C. Weaver, "Introduction," in Jenkins and Phillis, *Black Separatism*, xxiv–xxv; "Blacks' School Goals Changing," *Boston Globe*, July 12, 1968, 10.

56. Jenkins and Phillis, *Black Separatism*, xiii–xxv.

57. Jerry M. Flint, "Michigan Blacks Wary on School Change," *New York Times*, October 4, 1970, 60; John Landry, "Blacks See Need of Activism," *Hartford Courant*, March 1, 1970, 38A; "Negro Educator Group Plans All-Day Meeting," *Hartford Courant*, September 25, 1968, 3; "Blacks' School Goals Changing," *Boston Globe*, July 12, 1968, 10. Philadelphia public schools issued a mandate requiring all schools to provide African and African American history for every child; see Lillian Safiasha Gaskins-Green, "A Critical Analysis of the Implementation Process Used to Enforce the 1969 Policy to Infuse the African/African-American History and Culture in the Curriculum of the School District of Philadelphia from 1969–1994," PhD diss., Temple University, 1998, 94–102.

58. *Milliken v. Bradley*, 418 U.S. 717 (1974). See also Baugh, *The Detroit School Busing Case*, 86–137; Mirel, *The Rise and Fall of an Urban School System*, 345–369.

59. For quote, see Komozi Woodard, "Amiri Baraka and the Black Power Experiment," in Jeanne Theoharis and Komozi Woodard, *Freedom North: Black Freedom Struggles Outside the South, 194–1980* (New York: Palgrave Macmillan, 2003), 287–312, quote on p. 288. See also Peniel E. Joseph, *Dark Days, Bright Nights: From Black Power to Barack Obama* (New York: BasicCivitas Books, 2010), 156–160; Sitkoff, *The Struggle for Black Equality*, 201–214; Marable, *Race, Reform, and Rebellion*, 103–110; Joseph, *Waiting 'til the Midnight Hour*, 241–275; Fairclough, *Better Day Coming*, 295–322; Robert O. Self, *All in the Family: The Realignment of American Democracy since the 1960s* (New York: Hill & Wang, 2012); John Hall Fish, *Black Power, White Control: The Struggle of The Woodlawn Organization in Chicago*

(Princeton, NJ: Princeton University Press, 1973); Harold Cruse, *The Crisis of the Negro Intellectual* (New York: William Morrow, 1967), 402–405.

60. Jeffrey R. Henig and Wilbur C. Rich, eds., *Mayors in the Middle: Politics, Race, and Mayoral Control of Urban Schools* (Princeton, NJ: Princeton University Press, 2004); Wilbur C. Rich, *Black Mayors and School Politics: The Failure of Reform in Detroit, Gary, and Newark* (New York: Routledge, 1996); John O'Shea, "Newark: Negroes Move Toward Power," *Atlantic Monthly*, November 1965, 90. On Black power in Newark, see Nathan Wright Jr., *Black Power and Urban Unrest: Creative Possibilities* (New York: Hawthorne Books, 1967). This book summarizes the work of the National Conference on Black Power in Newark, held in 1967 shortly after the rebellion. The meeting included more than 1,100 delegates representing 42 cities and 197 Black organizations. Delegates specifically addressed the failure of urban public schools to educate Black youth and called for "a demand to be put into a position where the power and assets of Black people may enrich the lives of all" (88).

61. Cordell S. Thompson, "It's 'Nation Time' in Newark," *JET*, July 2, 1970: 14–18; "Kenneth A. Gibson," *Crisis* 77, no. 6, (1970): 217–218. On racial tensions during the election, see Cordell S. Thompson, "Whites Engage in Hate Campaign," *JET*, June 18, 1970: 14–18. See also Junius Williams, *Unfinished Agenda: Urban Politics in the Era of Black Power* (Berkeley, CA: North Atlantic Books, 2014): 245–272; Mfanya D. Tryman, "Black Mayoralty Campaigns: Running the 'Race,'" *Phylon* 35, no. 4 (1974): 346–358. Some of the racist flyers circulated on the streets against Ken Gibson tended to associate him with violent Black radicals and militants. One flyer, for example, featured the sensationalist title: "Le Roi Jones Gibson's Chief Aide Says 'Kill Whites Right Now.'" Another said, "All That Is Black Is Not Beautiful." See Folder 2 and Folder 8, Box 9, Barbara J. Kukla Papers, Charles F. Cummings New Jersey Information Center, Newark Public Library, Newark, NJ; hereafter, "Kukla Papers."

62. For description of Newark, see Fox Butterfield, "Newark Held an Angry and Anguished City," *New York Times*, April 12, 1971, 31. On Kenneth Gibson's catch phrase, see Fred J. Cook, "Mayor Kenneth Gibson Says Wherever the Central Cities Are Going, Newark Is Going to Get There First," *New York Times*, July 25, 1971, SM 7. Robert Curvin, *Inside Newark: Decline, Rebellion, and the Search for Transformation* (New Brunswick, NJ: Rutgers University Press, 2014), 129–133; Brad R. Tuttle, *How Newark Became Newark: The Rise, Fall and Rebirth of an American City* (New Brunswick: Rutgers University Press, 2009), 190–195; Mumford, *Newark*, 197–212; "Gibson Calls on Newark's People Black and White to Build a New City,'" *New York Times*, June 18, 1970, 51; Ronald Sullivan, "Gibson Defeats Addonizio in Newark Mayoral Race," *New York Times*, June 17, 1970, 1; Wright, *Ready to Riot*.

63. Christina Collins, *Ethnically Qualified: Race, Merit, and the Selection of Urban Teachers, 1920–1980* (New York: Teacher College Press, 2011); W.M. Phillips Jr., *Participation of the Black Community in Selected Aspects of the Educational Institution of Newark, 1958–1972* (New Brunswick, NJ: Rutgers University Press, 1973), 38–42; Education Committee of the Newark Branch of the NAACP, "A Report on Newark Public Schools," 1961, 12, hosted on digital archive, Rise Up North: Newark, http://riseupnewark.com/a-report-on-newark-public-schools-by-the-education-committee-of-the-newark-naacp-nov-1961-ilovepdf-compressed-2/?mode=grid. Although local NAACP leaders believed a higher degree of school integration would help alleviate educational inequality in Newark, the Black masses did not. A 1959 survey found that 52 percent of Black residents thought the schools reflected an appropriate degree of integration, and another 33 percent had no opinion on the matter; Mayor's Commission on Group Relations "Newark: A City in Transition," vol. 3, June 1959, Box 1, Alexander Mark Collection, Newark Public Library, Newark, New Jersey.

64. Williams, *Unfinished Agenda*, 324. See also Tuttle, *How Newark Became Newark*, 198–201; Steve Golin, *The Newark Teachers Strikes: Hopes on the Line* (New Brunswick, NJ: Rutgers University Press, 2002), 108–177; William M. Phillips Jr., *Participation of the Black Community in Selected Aspects of the Educational Institutions of Newark* (New Brunswick: Rutgers University Press, 1973), 63, 74–90. Although a substantial number, about one-third, of Newark's teaching force was Black, most Black teachers were not fully credentialed because of discriminatory oral exams required for teacher certification. Most Black teachers, therefore,

were permanent substitutes earning less money and with fewer job protections than their fully credentialed, mostly white counterparts.

65. Cook, "Mayor Kenneth Gibson Says."

66. Mumford, *Newark*, 171–181; Komozi Woodard, *A Nation within a Nation: Amiri Baraka (LeRoi Jones) and Black Power Politics* (Chapel Hill: University of North Carolina Press, 1999); "Newark Drunk after King's Murder," *Black Newark*, 1, no. 1 (April 1968): 1, available on Rise Up North: Newark digital archive, http://riseupnewark.com/Black-new-ark-april-1968/.

67. Mumford, *Newark*, 170–190; Golin, *The Newark Teachers Strikes*, 40–47; for quotes by the New Jersey ACLU, see Ronald Sullivan, "Newark's White Citizens Patrol, Opposed by Governor, Sees Itself as Antidote to Fear and Riots," *New York Times*, June 24, 1968, 23. For quotes by Anthony Imperiale, see Paul Goldberger, "Tony Imperiale Stands Vigilant for Law and Order," *New York Times*, September 29, 1968, SM30. A collection of newspaper clippings on Anthony Imperiale detailing his popularity among whites in Newark and his opposition to Black educational activists in 1970 and 1971 can be found in Folder 10, Box 9, Kukla Papers.

68. Mumford, *Newark*, 179, Woodard, "Amiri Baraka and the Black Power Experiment," 304–305.

69. Golin, *The Newark Teachers Strikes*, 124–125. Clarence Coggins, interview with Norman Eiger, Newark, November 7, 1974, as cited in Norman Eiger, "The Newark School Wars: A Sociohistorical Study of the 1970 and 1971 Newark School System Strikes," EdD diss., Rutgers University, 1976, 499.

70. Tuttle, *How Newark Became Newark*, 198–199; Golin, *The Newark Teacher Strikes*, 108–139.

71. Lawrence Feinberg, "A Battle for Control of Schools," *Washington Post*, March 22, 1971, A3. Parenthetical reference in the original. See also Golin, *The Newark Teacher Strikes*, 124–125.

72. For David Barrett quotes, see Cook, "Mayor Kenneth Gibson Says"; "10-week Teacher Strike Continues in Newark, NJ," *Afro-American*, April 17, 1971, 12. For Felix Arnstein quotes, see Felix G. Arnstein, "Newark: City of the Future?" *Crisis* 82, no. 1 (1975): 18–21.

73. "Newark Teachers Ignore Mayor's Plea on Strike," *JET*, February 25, 1971, 48.

74. For Graves quote, see "Newark Teachers Strike," *Newsday*, February 2, 1971, 9. See also William M. Phillips Jr. and Joseph M. Conforti, *Social Conflict: Teachers' Strikes in Newark, 1964–1971* (Trenton: New Jersey State Department of Education, 1972); "Newark Teachers Strike Again," *Boston Globe*, February 2, 1971, 2; "Teachers Begin Strike in Newark," *Washington Post*, February 2, 1971, A4; Frank Fiorito, *The Anatomy of a Strike: The Newark Teachers Union, February 1, 1970 to February 25, 1970* (Newark: Newark Teachers Union, 1970), in Charles E. Cummings New Jersey Information Center, Newark Public Library, Newark, NJ.

75. Fox Butterfield, "Newark School Strike Splits Blacks," *New York Times*, February 14, 1971, 45; Ronald Sullivan, "Crisis for Mayor Gibson," *New York Times*, February 4, 1971, 39; "Newark Teachers Vote to Strike if They Fail to Get Contract," *New York Times*, February 1, 1971, 32.

76. For press release, see Victor Riesel, "Terror Hits Teachers, Blood Flows as Extremists' Flying Squads Slug Way toward Control of Education," *Inside Labor*, February 4, 1971, Jewish Labor Committee Records, Part III (hereafter JLC Records), WAG.025.003, Box 155, Folder 13, Tamiment Library & Robert F. Wagner Labor Archives, New York University, NY. For Maciante quote, see "Violence Mars Newark Teachers Strike," *Chicago Defender*, February 4, 1971, 7. On support by organized labor, see telegram from Jewish Labor Committee to Mayor Kenneth A. Gibson, City Hall, February 3, 1971, in JLC Records, Box 155, Folder 13. Dozens of letters of support from different unions can be found in New York City Central Labor Council Records; WAG 049, Box 14, Folder, "Newark Teachers Strike," Tamiment Library & Robert F. Wagner Labor Archives, New York University, New York.

77. Peter Bridge, "No Settlement in Sight," *Christian Science Monitor*, March 8, 1971, 5. For striking teacher in Feinberg quote, see "A Battle for Control of Schools;" for Jacobs quote, see Butterfield, "Newark Held an Angry and Anguished City."

78. "Newark Teachers Strike," *Inner-City Voice* 3, no. 2 (April, 1971), 11. The Black Power Movement: The League of Revolutionary Black Powers, 1965–1976, Series 9, Oversize Materials, Black Freedom Struggle in the 20th Century: Organizational Records and Personal Papers, Part 1, ProQuest History Vault, https://congressional.ProQuest.com/histvault?q=100388-003-0606. Other Black activists were critical of Mayor Gibson and

Amiri Baraka. For instance, a study by William M. Phillips and Joseph M. Conforti found that the Nation of Islam officially criticized Board of Education President Jesse Jacobs "for attempting to break the union, Mayor Gibson for failing to exercise leadership in resolving the strike, and Imamu Baraka for being a racist." They also found that the Black Panther Party expressed support for the Newark Teachers Union, as it felt the teachers' union grievances were valid and represented progressive changes for Blacks in Newark, Philips and Conforti, *Social Conflict*, 45.

79. Butterfield, "Newark School Strike Splits Blacks."

80. Williams, *Unfinished Agenda*, 324–326; Golin, *The Newark Teachers Strikes*, 167–181; Phillips and Conforti, *Social Conflict*, 54–57. A stark example of these continuing hostilities is evident in a program hosted by the Newark Teachers Union on May 11, 1974, called "The Future of Public Education." According to the program flyer, this event featured a panel entitled "The Role of the Community," moderated by Connie Woodruff of the International Ladies' Garment Workers' Union (ILGWU). The questions this panel addressed included "Who is the community?" and "Are community spokesmen addressing themselves to the real needs of the community?" The NTU was skeptical of Black citizens' efforts to seize community control of public schools. The program featured a half-page add by state senator Anthony Imperiale with a note that read "From one dedicated to improving the city to many dedicated to educating its people"; see Newark Teachers Union Local 481 AFT, "The Future of Public Education," May 11, 1974, in Box 8, Folder 13, Kukla Papers.

81. For Black city official quote, see Fox Butterfield, "Opening of Marcus Garvey School in Newark Reflects Growing Blackness of City," *New York Times*, September 8, 1971, 50. On Black Panther and Nation of Islam objections to Baraka, see "Newark Teachers Strike," *Inner-City Voice*; Phillips and Conforti, *Social Conflict*, 45.

82. For quotes, see Butterfield, "Opening of Marcus Garvey School in Newark Reflects Growing Blackness of City." See also Phillips and Conforti, *Social Conflict*, 53–57; Jo Ann Levine, "Newark Teachers Pack for Jail," *Christian Science Monitor*, December 23, 1971, 2; "Schools in Newark Restrained from Putting Up Black Flags," *New York Times*, December 4, 1971, 24; Daniel Hays, "Newark's Black Flag Hassle Reaches Legislature," *Washington Post*, December 4, 1971, A25; Stanley E. Terrell, "Newark Classroom Goes Experimental," September 20, 1970, 43, in news clippings, Folder 3, Box 8, Kukla Papers. On Gibson's appointment of Hamm to the Board of Education, which he came to regret, see Rich, *Black Mayors and School Politics*, 101.

83. For quote, see "School Safety," September 18, 1972, in collection of local news clippings in Folder 3, Box 8, Kukla Papers. Other articles include "Repairs Prompt Shift of Students," September 13, 1972, 11; Lawrence H. Hall, "Newark School to Close One Month for Repairs," September 12, 1972, 8; Bob Smart, "School's Out: Newark Board Shuts Building after Ceiling Collapses," September 11, 1972, 5. On the fiscal and political crisis in Newark Public Schools between 1971 and 1995, the year the State of New Jersey took over the public schools, see Rich, *Black Mayors and School Politics*, 100–127. On the retreat of Black and white middle-class families to the suburbs in pursuit of lower taxes and better schools, see Wright Jr., *Ready to Riot*, 1–55. See also Leah Platt Boustan, *Competition in the Promised Land: Black Migrants in Northern Cities and Labor Markets* (Princeton, NJ: Princeton University Press, 2017), 122–164; Jon C. Teaford, *The Metropolitan Revolution: The Rise of Post-Urban America* (New York: Columbia University Press, 2006), 90–164; Andres Duany, Elizabeth Plater-Zyberk, and Jeff Speck, *Suburban Nation: The Rise and Decline of the American Dream* (New York: Farrar, Straus and Giroux, 2000), 153–182; Kenneth Jackson, *The Crabgrass Frontier: The Suburbanization of the United States* (New York: Oxford University Press, 1985), 190–230.

84. Phillips and Conforti, *Social Conflict*, 54; "Clergymen Point at Baraka as 'Racially Dividing City,'" *Afro-American*, January 29, 1972, 20. See also "Black Ministers to Oppose Jones," *New York Times*, January 14, 1972, 37.

85. Williams, *Unfinished Agenda*, 326; Rich, *Black Mayors and School Politics*, 94.

86. Tracy L. Steffes, *School, Society, and State: A New Education to Govern Modern America, 1890–1940* (Chicago: University of Chicago Press, 2012), 155–194; David B. Tyack, *The One Best*

System: A History of American Urban Education (Cambridge, MA: Harvard University Press, 1974), 126–176.

87. Irving Ankler, "Chancellor's Report on Programs and Problems Affecting Integration of the New York City Public Schools," February 1974 (New York: New York City Board of Education, 1974), 35–36, in Box 31, Folder 40, United Federation of Teachers Records, WAG 022; Select Committee on Equal Educational Opportunity, United States Senate, "Toward Equal Educational Opportunity," Report No. 92-000, 92nd Congress, 2nd Session, December 31, 1972, 102–104, 110–111, 114–117.

88. For both quotes, see William E. Farrell, "School Integration Resisted in Cities of the North," *New York Times,* May 13, 1974, 24. See also Stave, *Achieving Racial Balance;* US Commission on Civil Rights, "Title IV and School Desegregation: A Study of a Neglected Federal Program," January 1973 (Washington, DC: US Government Printing Office, 1973).

89. Nathaniel R. Jones, "*Milliken v. Bradley:* A Judicial Betrayal of *Brown,*" in Kristi L. Bowman, ed., *The Pursuit of Racial and Ethnic Equality in American Public Schools: Mendez, Brown, and Beyond* (East Lansing: University of Michigan Press, 2015), 171–176.

90. *Milliken, Governor of Michigan, et al. v. Bradley, et al.* 418 U.S. 717 (1974). See also NAACP Press Release, "Supreme Court Detroit Ruling 'Unfortunate' NAACP Declares," July 25, 1974, in Folder, "Bradley v. Milliken Segregation Case, General Case Material," Papers of the NAACP, Supplement to Part 23: Legal Department Case Files, 1960–1972, Series C: The Midwest, Section II: Illinois, Indiana, Iowa, Kansas, Michigan, Minnesota, Missouri, Nebraska, West Virginia and Wisconsin, ProQuest History Vault, https://congressional. ProQuest.com/histvault?q=100488-017-0345.

91. *Milliken v. Bradley* (1974); for Coleman Young quote, see Agis Salpukas, "Joy Is Expressed in the Suburbs, Reactions in Detroit Divided," *New York Times,* July 26, 1974, 17. See also Charles T. Clotfelter, "Milliken and the Prospects for Racial Diversity in U.S. Public Schools," in Kristi L. Bowman, ed., *The Pursuit of Racial and Ethnic Equality in American Public Schools: Mendez, Brown, and Beyond* (East Lansing: University of Michigan Press, 2015), 195–212; Baugh, *The Detroit School Busing Case,* 138–171; Wilkinson, *From Brown to Bakke,* 216–249; Eleanor P. Wolf, *Trial and Error: The Detroit School Segregation Case* (Detroit: Wayne State University Press, 1981); Conference before the US Commission on Civil Rights, "*Milliken v. Bradley:* The Implications for Metropolitan Desegregation," November 9, 1974 (Washington, DC: US Government Printing Office, 1974); Warren Weaver, "Decision by 5 to 4," *New York Times,* July 26, 1974, 1.

92. Editorial board, "Detroit's School Dilemma," *New York Times,* August 23, 1975, 20; William K. Stevens, "Many White Parents Now See Their Children as Safe," *New York Times,* July 27, 1974, 60.

93. Jeanne Theoharis and Matthew Delmont, "Introduction: Rethinking the Boston 'Busing Crisis,'" *Journal of Urban History* 43, no. 2 (2017): 191–203; Delmont, *Why Busing Failed,* 190–208; Ronald P. Formisano, *Boston against Busing: Race, Class, and Ethnicity in the 1960s and 1970s* (Chapel Hill: University of North Carolina Press, 2001); J. Anthony Lukas, *Common Ground: A Turbulent Decade in the Lives of Three American Families* (New York: First Vintage Books, 1986); US Commission on Civil Rights, "School Desegregation in Boston" (Washington, DC: US Government Printing Office, 1975).

94. John Kifner, "New Boston Area Hit by Violence," *New York Times,* September 20, 1974, 42; John Kifner, "Boston School Buses Stoned a 2nd Day, but City Is Mostly Calm," *New York Times,* September 14, 1974, 13; Denton L. Watson, "The Detroit School Challenge," *Crisis* 81, no. 6 (1974), 188–194.

95. Paul Delaney, "Blacks' Anger Rising in South Boston as Violence over Schools Spreads," *New York Times,* May 2, 1976, 32. Similar accounts by Black students in Boston can be found in Pamela Bullard and Judith Stoia, *The Hardest Lesson: Personal Accounts of a School Desegregation Crisis* (Boston: Little, Brown, 1980). See also US Commission on Civil Rights, "School Desegregation in Boston."

96. Derrick A. Bell Jr., "The Burden of Brown on Blacks: History-Based Observations on a Landmark Decision," *North Carolina Central Law Review* 7 (1975): 25–38, quotes on pp. 25, 30–31.

97. Bell, "The Burden of Brown on Blacks: History-Based Observations on a Landmark Decision," 36–37.

Chapter 5

1. Simon Anekwe, "Twenty-One Years Is Too Long to Wait," *New York Amsterdam News*, May 28, 1975, A2; John Kifner, "Tensions and Violence in Boston Schools Are Rooted in Traditions of White Ethnic Neighborhoods," *New York Times*, May 18, 1975, 48. See also Thomas Adams Upchurch, *Race Relations in the United States, 1960–1980* (Westport, CT: Greenwood Press, 2008), 128–129.

2. Roy Wilkins, "Integration Is the Only Way, March 22, 1975," in Marcus D. Pohlmann, ed., *African American Political Thought* (New York, Routledge, 2003), vol. 6, 367–369; Vernon E. Jordan, "The Black Underclass Untouched by Brown," *Howard Law Journal*, 23 (1980): 61–66, quote on p. 62.

3. For Ellena Ross quote, see William Chapman, "Boston Debates Order for Fall School Busing," *Washington Post*, April 7, 1974, A2. For Mrs. Hale and Rev. Ross quotes, see Robert Reinhold, "2 Boston Areas Point Up School Dilemma," *New York Times*, July 8, 1974, 22.

4. "2 Boston Areas Point Up School Dilemma." For Ruth Batson quote, see "Integration Plan Angers, Scares Boston School System's Parents," *Hartford Courant*, August 18, 1974, 47A.

5. John H. Stanfield, "Urban Public School Desegregation: The Reproduction of Normative White Domination," *Journal of Negro Education* 51, no. 2 (1982): 90–100, quote on p. 95. See also William E. Nelson Jr., "School Desegregation and the Black Community," *Theory into Practice* 26 (December 1987): 450–458; John U. Ogbu, "School Desegregation in Racially Stratified Communities: A Problem of Congruence," *Anthropology & Education Quarterly* 9, no. 4 (1978): 290–292.

6. "Freedom House Institute on Schools and Education, Position Paper on Phase II of Boston Public School Desegregation," c. 1975–1977, Boston Desegregation Project, Archives and Special Collections, Northeastern University Library, Boston, MA, http://hdl.handle.net/2047/D20201270; "Backdrop to Boston," *Crisis* 82, no. 1 (January 1975): 7–11. See also Gary Orfield, Jennifer Arenson, Tara Jackson, Christine Bohrer, Dawn Gavin, and Emily Kalejs, *City-Suburban Desegregation: Parent and Student Perspectives in Metropolitan Boston* (Cambridge, MA: Harvard Civil Rights Project, 1997), 26–32. US Commission on Civil Rights, *Fulfilling the Letter and Spirit of the Law: Desegregation of the Nation's Public Schools* (Washington, DC: US Government Printing Office, 1976), 25–51.

7. Kristi L. Bowman, ed., *The Pursuit of Racial and Ethnic Equality in American Public Schools: Mendez, Brown, and Beyond* (East Lansing: University of Michigan Press, 2015); Davison M. Douglas, "Brown v. Board of Education and Its Impact on Black Education in America," in Peter F. Lau, ed., *From the Grassroots to the Supreme Court: Brown v. Board of Education and American Democracy* (Durham, NC: Duke University Press, 2004), 361–382; Mark V. Tushnet, "The 'We've Done Enough' Theory of School Desegregation," *Howard Law Journal* 39 (1996): 767–779; Christine H. Rossell, "The Convergence of Black and White Attitudes on School Desegregation Issues during the Four Decade Evolution of the Plans," *William & Mary Law Review* 36 (1995): 613–663; Alex M. Johnson Jr., "Bid Whist, Tonk, and *United States v. Fordice:* Why Integrationism Fails African Americans Again," *California Law Review* 81, no. 6 (1993): 1401–1470; Robert Anthony Watts, "Shattered Dreams and Nagging Doubts: The Declining Support among Black Parents for School Desegregation," *Emory Law Journal* 42 (1993): 891–896; Michael W. Combs, "The Federal Judiciary and Northern School Desegregation: Law, Politics, and Judicial Management," *Publius* 16, no. 2 (1986): 33–52; Connecticut Advisory Committee to the US Commission on Civil Rights, *School Desegregation in Stamford, Connecticut* (Hartford: Connecticut State Advisory Committee, 1977).

8. Charles T. Clotfelter, "Milliken and the Prospects for Racial Diversity in U.S. Public Schools," in Kristi L. Bowman, ed., *The Pursuit of Racial and Ethnic Equality in American Public Schools: Mendez, Brown, and Beyond* (East Lansing: University of Michigan Press, 2015), 195–214; Gary Orfield, *Public School Desegregation in the United States, 1968–1980* (Washington, DC: Joint Center for Political Studies, 1983).

9. Derrick Bell, *And We Are Not Saved: The Elusive Quest for Racial Justice* (New York: Basic Books, 1987), chap. 4, 102–122; Gary Orfield, *Public School Desegregation in the United States, 1968–1980* (Washington, DC: Joint Center for Political Studies, 1983); Ronald D. Henderson, Mary von Euler, and Jeffrey M. Schneider, "Remedies for Segregation: Some

Lessons from Research," *Educational Evaluation and Policy Analysis* 3, no. 4 (1981): 67–76; Derrick Bell, *Shades of Brown: New Perspectives on School Integration* (New York: Teachers College Press, 1980).

10. Derrick Bell, "The Dialectics of School Desegregation," *Alabama Law Review* 32 (1981): 281–297, quote on p. 282.

11. Norman Cousins, "Busing Reconsidered," *Saturday Review*, January 24, 1976, 4. See also "Norman Cousins, 75, Dies; Edited the Saturday Review," *New York Times*, December 1, 1990, 31. Note that many scholars disagreed with his claims that busing did not work to improve the academic achievement of Black students and that it caused white flight. See, for example, *Public School Desegregation in the United States, 1968–1980; Fulfilling the Letter and Spirit of the Law.*

12. James S. Coleman, "Recent Trends in School Integration," *Educational Researcher* 4, no. 7 (1975): 3–12, quote on p. 12. This paper was originally presented at the American Education Research Association Meeting in Washington, DC, on April 2, 1975. It was picked up in the popular press immediately. See also Daryl Michael Scott, *Contempt and Pity: Social Policy and the Image of the Damaged Black Psyche, 1880–1996* (Chapel Hill: University of North Carolina Press, 1997); Christine H. Rossell, "School Desegregation and White Flight," *Political Science Quarterly* 90, no. 4 (1975–1976): 675–695; Paul Delaney, "Long Time Desegregation Proponent Attacks Busing as Harmful," *New York Times*, June 7, 1975, 25; Robert L. Green and Thomas F. Pettigrew, "Urban Desegregation and White Flight: A Response to Coleman," *Phi Delta Kappan* 57, no. 6 (1976): 399–402.

13. "Both Races Fight Integration Plan in Chicago," *New York Times*, September 20, 1981, A33; "Boston School Peace Believed Distant," *Hartford Courant*, September 26, 1976, 25; John Kifner, "On Paper, the Boston School Plan Functions," *New York Times*, February 8, 1976, E2. On patriotic elements of anti-busing protestors, see "7,000 Stage Anti-busing March as White Students Boycott South Boston School," *Los Angeles Times*, October 28, 1975, A5; "Stabbing Occurs in Boston during Third School Week," *Afro-American*, October 12, 1974, 3. On President Ford, see, editorial, "Mr. Ford's Opinions," *Crisis* 82, no. 9 (November 1975): 333; "President Shares Blame for Strife in Boston, Panel Says," *Los Angeles Times*, August 21, 1975, B1. On President Carter, see "Carter Recommends Atlanta Plan for Schools in Boston," *Atlanta Daily World*, January 13, 1976, 2. Scholars also noted that anti-Black racism remained a potent obstacle to northern school integration. See Stanfield, "Urban Public School Desegregation"; Christine H. Rossell, "School Desegregation and Community Social Change," *Law and Contemporary Problems* 42, no. 3 (1978): 133–183. On connections between anti-busing in the North and white supremacist activism in the South, see Elizabeth Gillespie McRae, *Mothers of Massive Resistance: White Women and the Politics of White Supremacy* (New York: Oxford University Press, 2018), 217–240.

14. For Gloria Joyner quote, see "Stephen Wermiel, "Boston Group Asks Ford to Lead School Integration," *Boston Globe*, April 9, 1975, 9. See also Michael Meyers, "In Defense of Court-Ordered Busing," *Crisis* 89, no. 8 (October 1982): 376–377; Vernon E. Jordan Jr., "The New Civil Rights Movement," *National Black Law Journal* 6 (1978): 174–178; Editorial, "Mr. Ford's Opinions," *Crisis* 82, no. 9 (November 1975): 333.

15. Paul Delaney, "Chicago to Attempt to Integrate Schools after Success in Other Cities," *New York Times*, September 4, 1977, 22; Paul Delaney, "Chicago Segregation Figures," *New York Times*, April 13, 1977, 14. See also Elizabeth Todd-Breland, *A Political Education: Black Politics and Education Reform in Chicago since the 1960s* (Chapel Hill: University of North Carolina Press, 2018).

16. "Those Who Stayed in Boston Schools," *Boston Globe*, June 22, 1984, 2; Derrick A. Bell Jr., "Serving Two Masters: Integration Ideals and Client Interests in School Desegregation," *Yale Law Journal*, 85 (1976): 470–516.

17. Susan E. Eaton, Joseph Feldman, and Edward Kirby, "Still Separate, Still Unequal: The Limits of Milliken II's Monetary Compensation to Segregated Schools," in Gary Orfield and Susan E. Eaton, *Dismantling Desegregation: The Quiet Reversal of Brown v. Board of Education* (New York: New Press, 1996), 143–178; *Milliken v. Bradley*, 433 U.S. 267 (1977); Derrick A. Bell Jr., "The Legacy of WEB DuBois: A Rational Model for Achieving Public School Equity for America's Black Children," *Creighton Law Review* 11 (1977): 409–431, quote on p. 425.

18. *Dayton Board of Education v. Brinkman*, 433 U.S. 526 (1979); Vernon E. Jordan Jr., "Civil Rights: Revolution and Counterrevolution," *Columbia Human Rights Law Review* 14 (1982): 1–13, quote on p. 3; Margo Evans, "From Denver to Dayton: The Evolution of Constitutional Doctrine in Northern School Desegregation Litigation," *University of Dayton Law Review* 3 (1978): 115–152, quote on p. 152; *Dayton Board of Education v. Brinkman*, 433 U.S. 406 (1977).

19. By 1980, nearly half (48.7%) of Black students in the northeast attended an almost all-minority school, compared to less than a quarter (23%) of Black students in the South. See Gary Orfield, *Public School Desegregation in the United States, 1968–1980* (Washington, DC: Joint Center for Political Studies, 1983), 1–3 and 8–12. See also Derrick A. Bell Jr., "*Brown v. Board of Education* and the Interest-Convergence Dilemma," *Harvard Law Review*, 93 (1980): 518–533, quote on p. 532. See also Lani Guinier, "From Racial Liberalism to Racial Literacy: *Brown v. Board of* Education and the Interest-Divergence Dilemma," *Journal of American History* 91, no. 1 (2004): 92–118.

20. James A. Banks, "Quality Education for Black Students," in Norene Harris, Nathaniel Jackson, and Carl E. Rydingswood, eds., *The Integration of American Schools: Problems, Experiences, Solutions* (Boston: Allyn and Bacon, 1975), 165–175, quote on p. 168.

21. Robert L. Carter, "A Reassessment of *Brown v. Board of Education*," in Derrick Bell, *Shades of Brown: New Perspectives on School Integration* (New York: Teachers College Press, 1980), 20–29, quotes on pp. 27–28. See also Jack M. Balkin, *What Brown v. Board of Education Should Have Said: The Nation's Top Legal Experts Rewrite America's Landmark Civil Rights Decision* (New York: New York University Press, 2002).

22. Kristi L. Bowman, "The Legal Legacy of *Missouri v. Jenkins*," in Kristi Bowman, ed., *The Pursuit of Racial and Ethnic Equality in American Public Schools*, 247–272; Kevin Fox Gotham, "Missed Opportunities, Enduring Legacies: School Segregation and Desegregation in Kansas City, Missouri," in Bowman, *The Pursuit of Racial and Ethnic Equality in American Public Schools*, 221–246; John R. Munich, "*Missouri v. Jenkins*: A Remedy without Objective Limitation," in Bowman, *The Pursuit of Racial and Ethnic Equality in American Public Schools*, 215–220; Douglass Bryant III, "A Failure to Act from *Brown v Board of Education* to *Sheff v. O'Neill*: The American Educational System Will Remain Segregated," *Thomas M. Cooley Law Review* 25 no. 1 (2008): 1–26, quote on p. 17. *State of Missouri, et al. v. Kalima Jenkins, et al.*, 515 U.S. 70 (1995); *Robert R. Freeman et al. v. Willie Eugene Pitts et al.*, 503 U.S. 467 (1992); *Board of Education of Oklahoma City v. Dowell*, 498 U.S. 237 (1991); *Riddick v. the School Board of the City of Norfolk*, 784 F. 2d 521 (1986).

23. *Parents Involved in Community Schools v. Seattle School District No. 1*, 551 U.S. 701 (2007). See also Erica Frankenberg, Jongyeon Ee, Jennifer B. Ayscue, and Gary Orfield, "Harming Our Common Future: America's Segregated Schools 65 Years after *Brown*," Report by the Civil Rights Project of the University of California, Los Angles, May 10, 2019, https://www.civilrightsproject.ucla.edu/research/k-12-education/integration-and-diversity/harming-our-common-future-americas-segregated-schools-65-years-after-brown; Sean F. Reardon, Elena Tej Grewal, Demetra Kalogrides, and Erica Greenberg, "*Brown* Fades: The End of Court-Ordered School Desegregation and the Resegregation of American Public Schools," *Journal of Policy Analysis and Management* 31, no. 4 (2012): 876–904.

24. Gloria Ladson-Billings, "Landing on the Wrong Note: The Price We Paid for Brown," *Educational Researcher* 33, no. 7 (2004): 3–13, quote on p. 11.

25. Marjorie Coeyman, "Black Pride Drives This Public School," *Christian Science Monitor*, October 6, 1998, B6.

26. Russell Rickford, *We Are an African People: Independent Education, Black Power, and the Radical Imagination* (New York: Oxford University Press, 2016); Amy J. Binder, *Contentious Curricula: Afrocentrism and Creationism in American Public Schools* (Princeton, NJ: Princeton University Press, 2002), 53–135; Jonathan Zimmerman, *Whose America: Culture Wars in the Public Schools* (Cambridge, MA: Harvard University Press, 2002), 107–134. On Afrocentric curriculum, see Geoffrey Jahwara Giddings, "Infusion of Afrocentric Content into the School Curriculum: Toward an Effective Movement," *Journal of Black Studies* 31, no. 4 (2001): 462–482; Tamara Henry, "Afrocentric Curriculum on Trial," *USA Today*, December 18, 1996, D06; Editorial Board, "Afrocentric Curriculum Would Segregate Schools," *Denver Post*, March 9,

1996, B7; Shaun Hill, "Schools Urged to Adopt Afro-Centric Curriculum," *Washington Post,* February 2, 1989, J07. On Afrocentric public schools, see Chastity Pratt Dawsey, "Afrocentric Schools Focus on Pride," *Detroit Free Press,* February 10, 2010, A1; Martha Woodall, "New Team Generates Optimism at Wakisha," *Philadelphia Inquirer,* April 13, 2005, B1; Coeyman, "Black Pride Drives This Public School"; Rick Van Sant, "Afrocentric School Draws Praise, Fire," *Cincinnati Post,* May 26, 1994, 1C; Winslow Mason Jr., "City Gets Its First Afrocentric School," *Philadelphia Tribune,* July 16, 1993, 1A; "Afrocentric School Nets White Anger," *Seattle Times,* September 30, 1992, A4; Lindsey Tanner, "Black Children Find Their Roots in Afro-Centric Chicago School," *Houston Chronicle,* September 15, 1991, 10; Chuck Taylor, "You Are Going to See Miracles," *Seattle Times,* February 26, 1991, A1.

27. Binder, *Contentious Curricula,* 54–57; Asa G. Hilliard III, "African American Baseline Essays, 1993," in Folder 83, Box 11–12, Asa G. Hilliard III Papers, Archive Research Center, Robert W. Woodruff Library at Atlanta University Center, Atlanta, GA; Molefi Kete Asante, "The Afrocentric Idea in Education," *Journal of Negro Education* 60, no. 2 (1991): 170–180, quote on p. 170; Asa G. Hilliard III, Lucretia Payton-Stewart, and Larry Obadele Williams, eds., *Infusion of African and African American Content in the School Curriculum: Proceedings of the First National Conference, October 1989* (Morristown, NJ: Aaron Press, 1990); Matthew W. Prophet, *Preface to the African/African American Baseline Essays* (Portland, OR: Portland Public Schools, 1987); Molefi Kete Asante, *Afrocentricity: The Theory of Social Change* (Buffalo, NY: Amulefi, 1980); Asa G. Hilliard III, "Equal Educational Opportunity and Quality Education," *Anthropology and Education Quarterly* 9, no. 2 (1978): 110–126.

28. Asante, "The Afrocentric Idea in Education," 171.

29. Jennifer G. Franklyn, "Why Afrocentric Is a Worthy Education," *Philadelphia Inquirer,* January 2, 1991, A11.

30. Mason, "City Gets Its First Afrocentric School"; Tanner, "Black Children Find Their Roots in Afro-Centric Chicago School"; Hill, "Schools Urged to Adopt Afro-Centric Curriculum." See also Molefi Kete Asante, *An Afrocentric Manifesto* (Malden, MA: Polity Press, 2007); Anne-Lise Halvorsen, "African-Centered Education in the Detroit Public Schools, 1968–2000," in Christin Woyshner and Chara Haeussler Bohan, eds., *Histories of Social Studies and Race* (New York: Palgrave Macmillan, 2012), 195–212; Cecil C. Gray, *Afrocentric Thought and Praxis: An Intellectual History* (Trenton, NJ: Africa World Press, 2001); Willy DeMarcell Smith and Eva Wells Chunn, eds., *Black Education: A Quest for Equity and Excellence* (New Brunswick, NJ: Transaction Publishers, 1989).

31. Sonia R. Jarvis, "*Brown* and the Afrocentric Curriculum," *Yale Law Journal* 101, no. 6 (1992): 1285–1304. See also Andrew Wiese, *Places of Their Own: African American Suburbanization in the Twentieth Century* (Chicago: University of Chicago Press, 2004); Douglas S. Massey and Nancy A. Denton, *American Apartheid: Segregation and the Making of the Underclass* (Cambridge, MA: Harvard University Press, 1993); Margaret Shapiro, "Black Middle Class Joins Mainstream," *Washington Post,* October 4, 1981, A1.

32. Kmt G. Shockley and Rona M. Frederick, "Constructs and Dimensions of Afrocentric Education," *Journal of Black Studies* 40, no. 6 (2010): 1212–1233; Charles C. Verharen, "Philosophy's Roles in Afrocentric Education," *Journal of Black Studies* 32, no. 3 (2002): 295–321; Eleanor Brown, "Black Like Me: Gangsta Culture, Clarence Thomas, and Afrocentric Academies," *New York University Law Review* 75, no. 2 (2000): 308–353; Subira Kifano, "Afrocentric Education in Supplementary Schools: Paradigms and Practice at Mary McLeod Bethune Institute," *Journal of Negro Education* 65, no. 2 (1996): 209–218; Jarvis, "*Brown* and the Afrocentric Curriculum"; Asa G. Hilliard III, "Straight Talk about School Desegregation Problems," *Theory Into Practice* 17, no. 2 (1978): 100–106.

33. Ameer Akinwale Ali, "Afrocentric Curriculum: A Paradigm for Healing and Education," PhD diss., University of Missouri, Saint Louis, 2016; Corey M. Sheffield, "The Efficacy of Students toward Learning within an Afrocentric Education Program," PhD diss., Argosy University, 2014; Martell Teasley and Edgar Tyson, "Cultural Wars and the Attack on Multiculturalism: An Afrocentric Critique," *Journal of Black Studies* 37, no. 3 (2007): 390–409, quote on p. 95; Chanda L. Pilgrim, "Afrocentric Education and the Prosocial Behavior of African American Children," PhD dissertation, Fordham University, 2006; Bernard Reese, "An Afrocentric Education in an Urban School: A Case Study," PhD diss., University of

Massachusetts, Amherst, 2004; David E. Neely, "Pedagogy of Culturally Biased Curriculum in Public Education: An Emancipatory Paradigm for Afrocentric Educational Initiatives," *Capital University Law Review* 23, no. 1 (1994): 131–150; "Afro-centric Suit Fails," *ABA Journal* 79, no. 12 (1993): 77–78; Drake D. Hill, "Afrocentric Movements in Education: Examining Equity, Culture, and Power Relations in the Public Schools," *Hastings Constitutional Law Quarterly* 20, no. 3 (1993): 681–724; Jarvis, "*Brown* and the Afrocentric Curriculum," 130.

34. Kmt Shockley, "African American Students: Profile of an Afrocentric Teacher," *Journal of Black Studies* 42, no. 7 (2011): 1027–1046, quote on p. 1037–1038.

35. Shockley, "African American Students," 1046. See also Kmt G. Shockley, *The Miseducation of Black Children* (Chicago Heights, IL: African American Images, 2008); Shawn A. Ginwright, *Black in School: Afrocentric Reform, Urban Youth, and the Promise of Hip-Hop Culture* (New York: Teachers College Press, 2004).

36. Stanley Crouch, "The Afrocentric Hustle," *Journal of Blacks in Higher Education* 10 (Winter 1995-1996): 77–82, quote on p. 77; Brian Cox, "Discord Mars Afrocentric Vote," *Chicago Tribune*, March 21, 2006, 3; Van Sant, "Afrocentric School Draws Praise, Fire."

37. For Todd quote, see Henry, "Afrocentric Curriculum on Trial." For Willie quote, see Coeyman, "Black Pride Drives This Public School."

38. A 2016 study located twenty-seven Afrocentric charter schools in 2016 in the United States, all in large urban school systems; see Martell Teasley et al., "School Choice and Afrocentric Charter Schools: A Review and Critique of Evaluation Outcomes," *Journal of African American Studies* 20, no. 1 (2016): 99–119. For quotes, see Rachel M. Cohen, "The Afrocentric Education Crisis," *American Prospect*, September 2, 2016, accessed August 16, 2018, http://prospect.org/article/afrocentric-education-crisis. See also Eliza Shapiro, "I Love My Skin! Why Black Parents Are Turning to Afrocentric Schools," *New York Times*, January 8, 2019, 1; Raven Moses, "Charter Schools and the Black Independent School Movement," *Black Perspectives: Blog by the African American Intellectual History Society* (blog), accessed August 16, 2018, https://www.aaihs.org/charter-schools-and-the-Black-independent-school-movement; Wilford Shamlin III, "Local Afrocentric Schools Face Challenges," *Philadelphia Tribune*, June 5, 2016, A4; John Eligon, "Poor Scores Leave Afrocentric Schools Vulnerable," *New York Times*, February 29, 2016, A9.

39. For "modern mecca" quote, see Michael Hill, "Beyond the Image of Harmony, Inequities in Montclair Remain," *NJTV News*, May 3, 2018, accessed August 21, 2018, https://www.njtvonline.org/news/video/beyond-image-harmony-inequities-montclair-remain; Kimberly J. McLarin, "Specter of Segregation Returns," *New York Times*, August 11, 1994, B1.

40. For William Farlie quote, see Lise Funderburg, "Integration Anxiety," *New York Times*, November 7, 1999, SM 83.

41. Patricia Hampson Eget, "Challenging Containment: African Americans and Racial Politics in New Jersey, 1920–1940," *New Jersey History* 126, no. 1 (2011): 1–17; Bernadette Anand, Michelle Fine, Tiffany Perkins, and David S. Surrey, *Keeping the Struggle Alive: Studying Desegregation in Our Town: A Guide to Doing Oral History* (New York: Teachers College Press, 2002), 18–21; Jane Manners, "Repackaging Segregation: The History of the Magnet School System in Montclair, NJ," *Race Traitor* 8 (1998): 51–97.

42. Elizabeth Shepard, "Desegregation of Montclair Public Schools, 1960–1975," 1, in Montclair Public Library, Local History Room, Montclair, NJ. "Parents Keep 50 Montclair Children Home, Charting Race Bias in School Transfer," *New York Times*, September 13, 1949, 31; Herbert Mitgang, "Created Equal?" *New York Times*, June 13, 1948, SM54; Austin Stevens, "Community Audit Aids Study of Bias," *New York Times*, December 12, 1947, 56.

43. Manners, "Repackaging Segregation," 58 59.

44. "Pickets Boycott School in Jersey," *New York Times*, September 8, 1961, 20 found in "School Desegregation Clippings File" at Montclair Public Library, Montclair, NJ (hereafter MPL Clippings File). The Cedar Street School was later renamed Nishuane.

45. *Morean et al. v. Board of Education on Montclair* 42, N.J. 237 (1964). See also Manners, "Repackaging Segregation," 60–67; "School Case Jurisdiction Still an Issue," *Montclair Times*, September 27, 1962, MPL Clippings File; "Jurisdiction Challenged by Parents," *Montclair Times*, June 26, 1962, MPL Clippings File; "Full Integration Urged by Council," *Montclair Times*, February 21, 1962, MPL Clippings File.

46. *Rice et al. v. Board of Education to the Town of Montclair* (1967). This decision was reprinted in the *Montclair Times* on November 21, 1967. See also Manners, "Repackaging Segregation," 72–74; Walter H. Waggoner, "School Imbalance Vexes Montclair," *New York Times*, May 29, 1966, in MPL Clippings File; "Segregation Hearing Set for May 26," *Montclair Times*, May 12, 1966, in MPL Clippings File.

47. Richard Lee, "Is School Plan Effective," *Montclair Times*, December 23, 1975, MPL Clippings File; "Montclair Board of Education Proposal for Implementation in September 1975, Grades K-4, Freedom of Choice," *Montclair Times*, August 22, 1974, MPL Clippings File; "Montclair's Busing Split Growing Bitter and May Intensify Black-White Division," *New York Times*, January 30, 1974, MPL Clippings File; "Board Approves Plan 'In Concept,'" *Montclair Times*, March 9, 1972, MPL Clippings File; "Integration Here to Stay," *Montclair Times*, June 24, 1971, MPL Clippings File; "Busing Question Opposed," *Montclair Times*, September 25, 1969, MPL Clippings File; "Racial Tension Hits Schools, Town," *Montclair Times*, October 3 1968, MPL Clippings File; "Firm Leadership Needed Now to Cope with Serious Situation at Montclair High School," *Montclair Times*, October 3, 1968, MPL Clippings File; "2 School Proposals Approved," *Montclair Times*, August 22, 1968, MPL Clippings File; "Educational Steps Urged for Town," *Montclair Times*, January 18, 1968, MPL Clippings File; "Citizens Respond to School Board Appeal for Views," *Montclair Times*, November 30, 1967, MPL Clippings File; "After a Brief Scare, Montclair Escaped Turmoil," *New York Times*, July 23, 1967, MPL Clippings File; "Committee Asks School Case Action," *Montclair Times*, April 20, 1967, MPL Clippings File. See also *Annual Report of the Superintendent, Montclair Public Schools, 1972–3* (Montclair: Montclair Board of Education, 1973), available in the Local History Room of the Montclair Public Library, Montclair, NJ.

48. Anand et al., *Keeping the Struggle Alive*, 47–49; Manners, "Repackaging Segregation," pp. 78–82.

49. Manners, "Repackaging Segregation," 78–90; Beatriz C. Clewell and Myra F. Joy, *Choice in Montclair, New Jersey: A Policy Information Paper* (Princeton, NJ: Educational Testing Service, 1990), 5; Howard Fields, "Different Paths to Education," *Washington Post*, October 17, 1987, in MPL Clippings File; Walter H. Waggoner, "Montclair School Plan for Racial Balance Challenged," *New York Times*, March 2, 1977, 48.

50. Manners, "Repackaging Segregation," 78–90; Montclair Board of Education, *Montclair's Magnets* (Montclair, NJ: Montclair Public Schools, 1993), 12–13; "Unanimity among School Board Members Critical," *Montclair Times*, June 6, 1979, in MPL Clippings File; "Montclair's 'Gifted Pupil' Integration Plan Praised," *New York Times*, May 29, 1978, in MPL Clippings File.

51. Manners, 52–54; Mary Lee Fitzgerald, "Application for Federal Assistance" (Montclair, NJ: Montclair Public Schools 1989), 13.

52. Walter Fields, "The Myth of Montclair: Is Tolerance the Best We Can Do?" *New Jersey Reporter* (November/December 1996): 17–21, MPL Clippings File; Craig Horowitz, "The Upper West Side of Suburbia," *New York*, November 18, 1996, 42–49, MPL Clippings File; "Hartford Considers Statewide School-Choice Plan," *New York Times*, October 8, 1992, B11; Amy Stuart Wells, "Once a Desegregation Tool, Magnet Schools Become Schools of Choice," *New York Times*, January 9, 1991, B6; Edward B. Fiske, "Wave of Future," *New York Times*, June 4, 1989, 32; Betty J. Veal, "A Comparison of Minority and Nonminority Parent Choice in School Selection in the Montclair, New Jersey Magnet Schools Program," EdD diss., University of Massachusetts, Amherst, 1989.

53. See the website for Imani, www.imaniprograms.org, accessed March 12, 2019. See also Catherine Baxter, "IAMNI: Improving Montclair," *Montclair Dispatch*, May 22, 2014, accessed March 12, 2019, https://montclairdispatch.com/imani-improving-montclair; Jessica Mazzola, "Russ Berrie Foundation Awards $150K to Jerseyans Who Make a Difference," *Patch*, May 10, 2012, accessed March 12, 2019, https://patch.com/new-jersey/mahwah/russ-berrie-foundation-awards-150k-to-jerseyans-who-m84df2cf78f.

54. Quote from Johnson, see Ricardo Kaulessar, "Montclair BOE Hears about Equity and Special Education," *Record*, April 29, 2017, accessed September 13, 2018, https://www.northjersey.com/story/news/essex/montclair/2017/04/29/montclair-boe-hears-equity-and-special-education/100940050. See also Amanda E. Lewis and John B. Diamond, *Despite the Best Intentions: How Racial Inequality Thrives in Good Schools* (New York: Oxford University Press,

2015); "Report of the Achievement Gap Advisory Panel, Montclair, New Jersey, June 2015," Montclair Public Schools District, accessed September 8, 2018, https://www.montclair.k12.nj.us/UserFiles/Servers/Server_889476/File/District/Equity,%20Curriculum%20&%20Instruction/Equity%20Commitment/ACHIEVEMENT%20GAP%20ADVISORY%20PANEL/agap-full.pdf. Dr. Kendra Johnson, email to author, September 7, 2018.

55. Jennifer Jellison Holme and Meredith P. Richards, "School Choice and Stratification in a Regional Context: Examining the Role of Inter-District Choice," *Peabody Journal of Education* 84, no. 2 (2009): 150–171; Cory Koedel, Julian R. Bettes, Lorien A. Rice, and Andrew C. Zau, "The Integrating and Segregating Effects of School Choice," *Peabody Journal of Education* 84, no. 2 (2009): 110–129; Jennifer Hochschild, "Is School Desegregation Still a Viable Option?" *PS: Political Science and Politics* 30, no. 3 (1997): 458–466.

56. Tonya Mosley, "Busing Blues: When Seattle Sent Black Kids to White North End," *KUOW*, October 29, 2013, accessed May 31, 2019, https://www.kuow.org/stories/busing-blues-when-seattle-sent-Black-kids-white-north-end. See also Quintard Taylor, *The Forging of a Black Community: Seattle's Central District from 1870 through the Civil Rights Era* (Seattle: University of Washington Press, 1994); Wallace Turner, "U.S. Shift on Busing Puts Seattle in the Spotlight," *New York Times*, September 21, 1981, A16.

57. Goodwin Liu, "Seattle and Louisville," *California Law Review* 95, no. 1 (2007): 277–317; Quintard Taylor, "The Civil Rights Movement in the American West: Black Political Protest in Seattle, 1960–1970," *Journal of Negro History* 80, no. 1 (1995): 1–14; Richard Weatherly, Betty Jane Narver, and Richard Elmore, "Managing the Politics of Decline: School Closures in Seattle," *Peabody Journal of Education* 60, no. 2 (1983): 10–24.

58. For NAACP quote, see Constantine Angelos, "Time to Tinker or Trash?" *Seattle Times*, March 2, 1986, B2. See also Sean Riley, "How Seattle Gave Up on Busing and Allowed Its Public Schools to Become Alarmingly Resegregated," *Stranger*, April 13, 2016, accessed online June 1, 2019, https://www.thestranger.com/features/2016/04/13/23945368/how-seattle-gave-up-on-busing-and-allowed-its-public-schools-to-become-alarmingly-resegregated; Constantine Angelos, "A Mixed Message on School Integration," *Seattle Times*, April 3, 1987, C2; Constantine Angelos, "School Busing—Right or Wrong," *Seattle Times*, February 22, 1987, H14; Constantine Angelos, "Desegregation Plan Faces Close Scrutiny," *Seattle Times*, October 31, 1986, C2; Editorial Board, "Improving Seattle Schools," *Seattle Times*, August 31, 1986, A18; Constantine Angelos, "NAACP Warns It Will Fight any Effort to Change Busing Plan," *Seattle Times*, February 6, 1986, B2; Constantine Angelos, "Suit Seeks to Stop Busing," *Seattle Times*, January 23, 1986, A1; Constantine Angelos, "School Busing Plan Draws Jeers, Cheers at Forum," *Seattle Times*, December 4, 1985, D1; Constantine Angelos, "Board to Study Busing, Black Achievement," *Seattle Times*, November 21, 1985, E1; Charles E. Brown, "Busing to Stay," *Seattle Times*, November 20, 1985, D1; Constantine Angelos, "Integration Plan Needs Revision Says Board Chief," *Seattle Times*, November 8, 1985, C1; Don Steele, "Seattle Did It," *Christian Science Monitor*, April 27, 1983; Luix Overbea, "Busing Still the Vortex of National Debate over School Desegregation," *Christian Science Monitor*, April 8, 1982.

59. *Parents Involved in Community Schools v. Seattle School District No. 1, 551 U.S. 701* (2007). For the purpose of racial balance, school administrators identified the Seattle public school population as 41 percent white and 59 percent nonwhite (all other racial groups). See also Dick Lilly, "Stanford Pushes Cluster System," *Seattle Times*, October 9, 1997, B1; Ruth Teichroeb, "Stanford Pitches His Plan for City Schools Primary Focus Now Academic Achievement," *Seattle Post-Intelligencer*, October 9, 1997, D1; Paul Shepard, "NAACP Head: Integration Always Was, Is Group's Goal," *Seattle Times*, July 3, 1997, A5; Dick Lilly, "Seattle to End Busing," *Seattle Times*, November 21, 1996, A1; Kathy George, "School Board Abolishes Controversial Forced Busing Plan," *Seattle Post-Intelligencer*, November 21, 1996, A1; Jerry Large, "Making Integration Work," *Seattle Times*, November 8, 1996, B1; Mike Barber, "School Board Reconsidering Busing," *Seattle Post-Intelligencer*, July 25, 1995, B2; Dick Lilly, "Move Grows to End Forced Busing," *Seattle Times*, July 24, 1995, A1; Editorial Board, "Forced Busing End Is in Sight," *Seattle Post-Intelligencer*, January 31, 1992, A10; Jonathan Tilove, "Many Prefer Top Education to Integration," *The Oregonian*, January 21, 1992, A3; Michelle Matassa Flores, "Hearing Set on Plans to Relax School Integration Rules," *Seattle Times*, June 20, 1990, H1;

Constantine Angelos, Jacqueline Ching, Don Duncan, Joe Haberstroth, and Blake Morrison, "School Plan Put to the Test," *Seattle Times*, September 6, 1989, A1; Constantine Angelos, "Controlled Choice," *Seattle Times*, April 10, 1988, D1; Timothy Egan, "Proposal to Curb Busing in Seattle Seeks to Attract Whites to Schools," *New York Times*, March 28, 1988. A17; Charles E. Brown, "Fewer Would Ride in New Busing Plan," *Seattle Times*, March 24, 1988, C3; Constantine Angelos, "Controlled Choice Busing Eyed," *Seattle Times*, June 7, 1987, B1; Jack Broom and Constantine Angelos, "School Busing: Stop or Go?" *Seattle Times*, May 17, 1987, A1.

60. Cara Sandberg, "Getting Parents Involved in Racially Integrated Schools," *Brigham Young University Education and Law* Journal 2012, no 2 (2012): 449–499, quote on p. 473, https://digitalcommons.law.byu.edu/elj/vol2012/iss2/8.

61. *Parents Involved in Community Schools v. Seattle School District No. 1.*

62. Erwin Chemerinsky, "Making Schools More Separate and Unequal: *Parents Involved in Community Schools v. Seattle School District No. 1*," in Bowman, *The Pursuit of Racial and Ethnic Equality in American Public Schools*, 279–290; Michael J. Dumas, "Contesting White Accumulation in Seattle: Toward a Materialist Antiracist Analysis of School Desegregation," in Bowman, *The Pursuit of Racial and Ethnic Equality in American Public Schools*, 291–314.

63. *Parents Involved in Community Schools v. Seattle School District No. 1.* See also Erwin Chemerinksy, "Making Schools More Separate and Unequal: Parents Involved in Community Schools v. Seattle School District No. 1," in Kristi L. Bowman, ed., *The Pursuit of Racial and Ethnic Equality in American Public Schools: Mendez, Brown, and Beyond* (East Lansing: Michigan State University Press, 2015): 279–290; Michael J. Dumas, "Contesting White Accumulations in Seattle: Toward a Materialist Antiracist Analysis of School Desegregation," in Bowman, *The Pursuit of Racial and Ethnic Equality in American Public*, 291–314; William J. Glenn, "School Segregation in Jefferson County and Seattle: The Impact of the Parents Involved Ruling and District Actions," *Cleveland State Law* Review 63, no. 2 (2015): 297–318; Erica Frankenberg, "Integration after Parents Involved: What Does Research Suggest about Available Options," in Erica Frankenberg and Elizabeth Debray, eds., *Integrating Schools in a Changing Society: New Policies and Legal Options for a Multiracial Generation* (Chapel Hill: University of North Carolina Press, 2011): 53–74.

64. In the late 1980s, educational activists from Hartford, Bridgeport, and New Haven founded a statewide organization called the Connecticut Coalition for Educational Equity. This group mobilized parents, students, religious leaders, and community activists to challenge high levels of segregation and inequality in the public schools. The organization's motto is "quality integrated education for all children." See website, "History of SMC," https://sheffmovement.org/history, accessed March 1, 2019. See also Elizabeth Todd-Breland, *A Political Education: Black Politics and Education Reform in Chicago since the 1960s* (Chapel Hill: University of North Carolina Press, 2018); Jack Dougherty, *More than One Struggle: The Evolution of Black School Reform in Milwaukee* (Chapel Hill: University of North Carolina Press, 2004), 167–202; Douglas S. Massey and Nancy A. Denton, *American Apartheid: Segregation and the Making of the Underclass* (Cambridge, MA: Harvard University Press, 1993).

65. *Milo Sheff et al. v. William A. O'Neill et al.,* 238 Conn. 1, 678 A.2d 1267 (1996). For Brittain comment, see Bill Daley, "Club Told School Lawsuit Would Curb Segregation," *Hartford Courant*, February 24, 1992, C7. For Sheff quote, see Robert A. Frahm, "Racial Balance Trial Nears," *Hartford Courant*, September 3, 1992, A1. See also Justin R. Long, "Enforcing Affirmative State Constitutional Obligations and Sheff v. O'Neill," *University of Pennsylvania Law Review* 151, no. 1 (2002): 277–310; John C. Brittain, "Why *Sheff v. O'Neill* Is a Landmark Decision," *Connecticut Law Review* 30, no. 1 (1997): 211–218; Preston Cary Green III, "Can State Constitutional Provisions Eliminate De Facto Segregation in the Public Schools?" *Journal of Negro Education* 68, no. 2 (1999): 138–153.

66. *Sheff v. O'Neill*, Complaint in the Superior Court of the Judicial District of Hartford/New Britain, filed April 26, 1989, https://sheffmovement.org/original-sheff-complaint, accessed online March 1, 2019. See also Robert A. Frahm, "Collapsed Ceilings and Dead Pigeons," *Hartford Courant*, December 18, 1992, A1; Robert A. Frahm and Rick Green, "School System Likened to Apartheid," *Hartford Courant*, December 17, 1992, A1; Robert A. Frahm, "City Students Trail Suburban Peers," *Hartford Courant*, October 17, 1992, A1. Some legal scholars

have challenged the evidence of educational inequality cited during the trial; see Michael Besso, "*Sheff v. O'Neill*: A Research Note," *Connecticut Law Review* 34, no. 2 (2002): 315–332.

67. For quote from Hernandez and Davis, see Rick Green, "Witnesses Describe Gaps Affecting Lives of City Students," *Hartford Courant*, December 22, 1992, D1. For quote from Sheff attorneys, see *Sheff v. O'Neill*, Complaint, filed April 26, 1989. See also Susan Eaton, *The Children in Room E4: American Education on Trial* (Chapel Hill, NC: Algonquin Books of Chapel Hill, 2007); Robert A. Frahm and Larry Williams, "Weicker Warns that State Must Desegregate Schools Quickly," *Hartford Courant*, March 27, 1992, B1.

68. For quote on sacred school district lines, see Robert A. Frahm, "State Education Chief Suggests Looking at Idea of School Choice," *Hartford Courant*, October 7, 1992, A1; for grumpy suburban school chairman quote, see Rich Green and Matthew Hay Brown, "We're Full, Suburban Schools Say," *Hartford Courant*, February 2, 1997, A1. See also Ann-Marie Adams, "The Origins of Sheff v. O'Neil: The Troubled Legacy of School Segregation in Connecticut," PhD diss., Howard University, 2010; Stan Simpson, "A Decade of Half Measures," *Hartford Courant*, July 23, 2006, 4. See also Christine H. Rossell, *The Carrot or the Stick for School Desegregation Policies: Magnet Schools or Forced Busing* (Philadelphia: Temple University Press, 1990).

69. Jodie Mozdzer, "They Persist," *Hartford Courant*, April 27, 2009, A1; Stan Simpson, "City Needs Diversity in Magnets," *Hartford Courant*, March 5, 2008, B1; Rachel Gottlieb Frank, "Desegregation by Order?" *Hartford Courant*, January 4, 2008, B1; Robert A. Frahm, "Missing Children," *Hartford Courant*, April 1, 2007, A1. See also Greater Hartford Regional School Choice Office (RSCO), *Explore the Possibilities: Regional School Choice Office 2019–2020 Catalog* (Hartford: Connecticut State Department of Education, 2019); Douglas Bryant III, "A Failure to Act from *Brown v. Board of Education* to *Sheff v. O'Neill*: The American Educational System Will Remain Segregated," *Thomas M. Cooley Law Review* 25, no. 1 (2008): 1–26.

70. Rachel M. Cohen, "Desegregated Differently," *American Prospect* 28, no. 4 (2017): 1–15; Simon Montlake, "Where Busing Works," *Christian Science Monitor*, February 25, 2017; Kimberly Quick, *Hartford Public Schools: Striving for Equity through Interdistirct Programs* (New York: Century Foundation, 2016), 1, 39. See also Rachel Martin and Cara McClellan, "Connecticut's Effort to Integrate Hartford Schools Is Working," *The Hill*, July 17, 2018, accessed January 21, 2019, https://thehill.com/opinion/education/397201-connecticuts-effort-to-integrate-hartford-schools-is-working. See also Genevieve Siegel-Hawley, "The Integration Report, Issue 12," *Sheff Movement*, July 9, 2008, https://sheffmovement.org/wp-content/uploads/2014/04/2008-Integration-Report_Spotlight-on-Sheff.pdf; American Civil Liberties Union (ACLU), "Sheff Plaintiffs Return to Court to Declare the State of Connecticut in Violation of Agreement to Reduce Racial, Ethnic and Economic Segregation in Harford Region Schools," August 3, 2004, accessed March 1, 2019, https://www.aclu.org/news/sheff-plaintiffs-return-court-declare-state-connecticut-violation-agreement-reduce-racial.

71. Matthew Kauffman and Vanessa De La Torre, "Integrated Magnet Schools Serving Fewer Hartford Students," *Hartford Courant*, November 28, 2017, accessed January 21, 2019, https://www.courant.com/news/connecticut/hc-news-sheff-magnet-school-enrollment-decline-20171126-story.html. See also Jack Dougherty, Jesse Wanzer, and Christina Ramsay, "*Sheff v. O'Neill*: Weak Desegregation Remedies and Strong Disincentives in Connecticut, 1996–2008" in Claire Smrekar and Ellen Goldring, eds., *From the Courtroom to the Classroom: The Shifting Landscape of School Desegregation* (Cambridge, MA: Harvard Education Press, 2009), 103–127. Available from the Trinity College Digital Repository, Hartford, CT. http://digitalrepository.trincoll.edu. See also Michael A. Rebell and Robert L. Hughes, "Efficacy and Engagement: The Remedies Problem Posed by *Sheff v. O'Neill*—and a Proposed Solution," *Connecticut Law Review* 29, no. 3 (1997): 115–186. For a point of comparison, scholars found a similar pattern in Chicago, where students living in wealthier neighborhoods of the city had far greater access to high-achieving magnet schools, while students living in the most marginalized Latino and very low income Black neighborhoods had the least access to these schools, which were designed to encourage integration. See Elaine M. Allensworth and Todd Rosenkranz, *Access to Magnet Schools in Chicago* (San Francisco: Mexican American Legal Defense and Educational Fund, Inc., US Department of Education, 2000).

72. Dave Collins, "Minority Parents Sue over Racial Quotas at Magnet Schools," *U.S. News & World Report*, February 15, 2018, accessed online July 19, 2018, https://www.usnews.com/news/best-states/connecticut/articles/2018-02-15/parents-sue-over-racial-quotas-at-magnet-schools; Matthew Kauffman, "Suit Challenges Sheff Magnet-School Lottery Process," *Hartford Courant*, February 15, 2018, accessed online July 18, 2018, http://www.courant.com/news/connecticut/hc-news-magnet-lottery-lawsuit-20180215-story.html. See also LaShawn Robinson, "Magnet School Limits Hurt Hartford Students," *Hartford Courant*, October 19, 2018, A15; Jacqueline Rabe, "Fate of Integration in Judge's Hands," *Hartford Courant*, October 17, 2018, B1; Matthew Kauffman, "Pacific Legal Foundation, Suit Targets Magnet School Process," *Hartford Courant*, May 9, 2018, B1.

73. Jacqueline Rabe Thomas, "Fate of Integration in Judge's Hands," *Hartford Courant*, October 17, 2018, B1; Matthew Kauffman, "School Desegregation," *Hartford Courant*, May 9, 2018, B1; Vanessa de la Torre, Hartford Schools: More Separate, Still Unequal," *Hartford Courant*, March 12, 2017, A1. The *Hartford Courant* produced a series of articles that investigated "the unintended consequences of the *Sheff* case" and tells the story of the "children left behind" in neighborhood schools. See "Hartford Schools: More Separate, Still Unequal," *Hartford Courant*, various dates from March 12, 2017, through November 28, 2017, accessed March 13, 2019, https://www.courant.com/education/hc-hartford-schools-more-separate-still-unequal-20170310-storygallery.html.

74. Matthew Kauffman and Kathleen Megan, "Busing, But: Not Forced," *Hartford Courant*, March 14, 2017, A1. See also Erica Frankenberg, *Project Choice Campaign: Improving and Expanding Hartford's Project Choice* (Washington, DC: Poverty & Race Research Action Council, 2007).

75. Kauffman and Megan, "Busing, But: Not Forced." See also Lucretia Anne Witte, "Can School Integration Increase Student Achievement? Evidence from Hartford Public Schools," PhD diss., Georgetown University, 2016; Janet P. Parlato, "The Perceptions of School Belonging, Identification, and Membership in Urban Students Who Attend a Suburban Connecticut High School," EdD diss., University of Pennsylvania, 2015; Kathryn A. McDermott, "Diversity of Desegregation? Implications of Arguments for Diversity in K–12 and Higher Education," *Educational Policy* 15, no. 3 (2001): 452–473. Scholars have found that majority white suburban school districts have mostly white teachers and administrators with little experience or training working with students of color. However, professional development programs can help prepare majority white school districts to work effectively with Black and Latino families and students. In other words, this is not an insurmountable problem—it just takes work to help majority white school districts learn to develop anti-racist practices and be deliberately welcoming to students of color. See Erica Frankenberg, Jongyeon Ee, Jennifer B. Ayscue, and Gary Orfield, "Harming Our Common Future: America's Segregated Schools 65 Years after *Brown*," report by the Civil Rights Project of the University of California, Los Angeles, May 10, 2019, 9; Erica Frankenberg and Gary Orfield, eds., *The Resegregation of Suburban Schools: A Hidden Crisis in American Education* (Cambridge, MA: Harvard Education Press, 2012).

76. Joan Richardson, "Charter Schools Don't Service Black Children Well: An Interview with Julian Vasquez Heilig," *Phi Delta Kappan* 98, no. 5 (2017): 41–44. The NAACP passed resolutions criticizing charter schools in 2010 and 2014, and a resolution calling for a moratorium on their expansion in 2016. See NAACP Press Release, "Statement Regarding the NAACP's Resolution on a Moratorium on Charter Schools," October 15, 2016, accessed March 13, 2019, https://www.naacp.org/latest/statement-regarding-naacps-resolution-moratorium-charter-schools.

77. Kauffman and Megan, "Busing, But: Not Forced."

78. Kathleen McWilliams, "Student Alleges Racism at School," *Hartford Courant*, March 11, 2016, A1; Parlato, "The Perceptions of School Belonging, Identification, and Membership in Urban Students Who Attend a Suburban Connecticut High School"; Mara Lee, "Changed Lives," *Hartford Courant*, June 30, 2014, A1.

79. Elizabeth Horton Sheff and Sandra Vermont-Hollis, "Lawsuit Threatens Sheff Desegregation Gains," *Hartford Courant*, October 16, 2018, A11; Vanessa De La Torre, "Sheff Warns of Growing Unease," *Hartford Courant*, August 18, 2016. See also Josh Kovner, "Milestone Agreement in Scheff vs. O'Neill School Desegregation Case Adds 1,000 Magnet School Seats to Ease Racial Isolation of Hartford Students," *Hartford Courant*, January 10, 2020, accessed online September 11, 2020, https://www.courant.com/news/

connecticut/hc-news-sheff-desegregation-expansion-hartford-magnet-20200110-7hpmkplwxjfxjedqu2r5bic44y-story.html; Jack Dougherty and contributors, *On the Line: How Schooling, Housing, and Civil Rights Shaped Hartford and Its Suburbs* (Trinity College, book-in-progress, 2018), http://ontheline.trincoll.edu.

Conclusion

1. For specific details on the rates of intensifying school segregation for US students, see Erica Frankenberg, Jongyeon Ee, Jennifer B. Ayscue, and Gary Orfield, "Harming Our Common Future: America's Segregated Schools 65 Years after *Brown*," report by the Civil Rights Project of the University of California, Los Angles, May 10, 2019. See also Rucker C. Johnson and Alexander Nazaryan, *Children of the Dream: Why School Integration Works* (New York: Basic Books, 2019); Eve L. Ewing, *Ghosts in the Schoolyard: Racism and School Closings on Chicago's South Side* (Chicago: University of Chicago Press, 2018); Kristi L. Bowman, ed., *The Pursuit of Racial and Ethnic Equality in American Public Schools: Mendez, Brown, and Beyond* (East Lansing: Michigan State University Press, 2015); Amanda E. Lewis and John B. Diamond, *Despite the Best Intentions: How Racial Inequality Thrives in Good Schools* (New York: Oxford University Press, 2015); R. L'Heureux Lewis-McCoy, *Inequality in the Promised Land: Race, Resources, and Suburban Schooling* (Stanford, CA: Stanford University Press, 2014); Erica Frankenberg and Gary Orfield, eds., *The Resegregation of Suburban Schools: A Hidden Crisis in American Education* (Cambridge, MA: Harvard Education Press, 2012); James E. Ryan, *Five Miles Away, a World Apart: One City, Two Schools, and the Story of Educational Opportunity in America* (New York: Oxford University Press, 2010).

2. Barack H. Obama, "Remarks by the President on Education: Benjamin Banneker Academic High School, Washington, D.C.," October 17, 2016, White House: Office of the Press Secretary, https://obamawhitehouse.archives.gov/the-press-office/2016/10/17/remarks-president-education; *Oliver Brown, et al. v. Board of Education of Topeka, et al.* 347 U.S. 483 (1954). See also Bettina L. Love, *Abolitionist Teaching the Pursuit of Educational Freedom* (Boston: Beacon Press, 2019); Christopher M. Span, *From Cotton Field to Schoolhouse: African American Education in Mississippi* (Chapel Hill: University of North Carolina Press, 2009); Charles M. Payne and Carol Sills Strickland, eds., *Teach Freedom: Education for Liberation in the African-American Tradition* (New York: Teachers College Press, 2008); James D. Anderson, *The Education of Blacks in the South, 1860–1935* (Chapel Hill: University of North Carolina Press, 1988).

3. Bureau of Labor Statistics, "Unemployment Rates and Earnings by Educational Attainment, 2018," March 27, 2018, https://www.bls.gov/emp/chart-unemployment-earnings-education.htm).

4. Gunnar Myrdal, *An American Dilemma: The Negro Problem and Modern Democracy* (New York: Harper & Row, [1944] 1962).

5. Grover J. Whitehurst, Nathan Joo, Richard V. Reeves, and Edward Rodrigue, "Balancing Act: Schools, Neighborhoods and Racial Imbalance," (Washington, DC: Brookings Institute, 2017); Jason Sokol, *All Eyes Are upon Us: Race and Politics from Boston to Brooklyn—The Conflicted Soul of the Northeast* (New York: Basic Books, 2014); Clarie E. Smrekar and Ellen B. Goldring, *From the Courtroom to the Classroom: The Shifting Landscape of School Desegregation* (Cambridge, MA: Harvard Education Press, 2009); Charles T. Clotfelter, *After Brown: The Rise and Retreat of School Desegregation* (Princeton, NJ: Princeton University Press, 2004).

6. Al Baker, "Law on Racial Diversity Stirs Greenwich Schools," *New York Times*, July 19, 2013, https://www.nytimes.com/2013/07/20/nyregion/law-on-racial-diversity-stirs-greenwich-schools.html, accessed online June 26, 2019.

7. John L. Rury, "Race, Schools and Opportunity Hoarding: Evidence from a Post-war American Metropolis," *History of Education Quarterly* 47, no. 1 (2017): 87–107; Paul Hanselman and Jeremy E. Fiel, "School Opportunity Hoarding? Racial Segregation and Access to High Growth Schools," *Social Forces* 95, no. 3 (2017): 1077–1104; Gary Orfield, John Kucsera, and Genevieve Siegel-Hawley, "E Pluribus . . . Separation: Deepening Double Segregation for More Students" (Los Angles: Civil Rights Project, 2019), https://escholarship.org/uc/item/8g58m2v9.

8. Johnson with Nazaryan, *Children of the Dream: Why School Integration* Works; . See also Century Foundation, "The Benefits of Socioeconomically and Racially Integrated Schools and Classrooms," April 29, 2019, Washington, DC, https://tcf.org/content/facts/the-benefits-of-socioeconomically-and-racially-integrated-schools-and-classrooms;   Raj Chetty, Nathaniel Hendren, Maggie R. Jones, and Sonya R. Porter, "Race and Economic Opportunity in the United States: An Intergenerational Perspective," March 2018, National Bureau of Economic Research; Eric A. Hanushek and Steven G. Rivkin, "Harming the Best: How Schools Affect the Black-White Achievement Gap," *Journal of Policy Analysis and Management*, 28, no. 3 (2009): 366–393; Robert L. Linn and Kevin G. Welner, eds., "Race Conscious Policies for Assigning Students to Schools: Social Science Research and the Supreme Court Cases" (Washington, DC: National Academy of Education, 2007); Richard D. Kahlenberg, *All Together Now: Creating Middle-Class Schools through Public School Choice* (Washington, DC: Brookings Institute Press, 2001); Christine H. Rossell, "Applied Social Science Research: What Does It Say about the Effectiveness of School Desegregation Plans?" *Journal of Legal Studies* 12, no. 1 (1983): 69–107; Frederick Mosteller and Daniel P. Moynihan, eds., *On Equal Educational Opportunity: Papers Deriving from the Harvard University Faculty Seminar on the Coleman Report* (New York: Random House, 1972); James S. Coleman et al., *Equality of Educational Opportunity* (Washington, DC: Government Printing Office, 1966).

9. Austin Dacey, "A Good School Is an Integrated School," *Psychology Today*, June 10, 2018, https://www.psychologytoday.com/us/blog/reasoning-together/201806/good-school-is-integrated-school, accessed online June 26, 2019; for quote from Nikole Hannah-Jones, see Dianna Douglas, "Are Private Schools Immoral? A Conversation with Nikole Hannah-Jones about Race, Education, and Hypocrisy," *The Atlantic*, December 14, 2017, https://www.theatlantic.com/education/archive/2017/12/progressives-are-undermining-public-schools/548084, accessed online June 5, 2019; Nikole Hannah-Jones, "Choosing a School for My Daughter in a Segregated City," *New York Times*, June 19, 2016, accessed online June 17, 2019, https://www.nytimes.com/2016/06/12/magazine/choosing-a-school-for-my-daughter-in-a-segregated-city.html. See also Alliance for School Integration and Desegregation (ASID) website, www.nycasid.com, accessed June 26, 2019. Policy Proposal: New York City ASID Policy Group, "Dare to Reimagine Integration for New York City's Public Schools," June 2018, published online: https://www.nycasid.com/learn-more, accessed June 26, 2019; "Our Statement on NYCDOE Adoption of School Diversity Advisory Group Recommendations," https://www.nycasid.com/news, accessed online June 26, 2019. A similar conception of "meaningful integration" can be found in: Paul Tractenberg, Allison Roda, Ryan Coughlan, and Deirdre Dougherty, *Making School Integration Work: Lessons from Morris* (New York: Teachers College Press, 2020).

10. Eliza Shapiro, "'I Love My Skin!' Why Black Parents Are Turning to Afrocentric Schools," *New York Times*, January 8, 2019, accessed online June 5, 2019, https://www.nytimes.com/2019/01/08/nyregion/afrocentric-schools-segregation-brooklyn.html; Rafiq R. Kalam Id-Din II, "Black Teachers Matter, School Integration Doesn't," *Education Week*, May 4, 2017, accessed online June 5, 2019, https://www.edweek.org/ew/articles/2017/05/04/Black-teachers-matter-school-integration-doesnt.html. For research that shows Black students have higher levels of academic achievement if they study with Black teachers, see Seth Gershenson, Cassandra M. D. Hart, Constance A. Lindsay, and Nicholas W. Papageorge, "The Long-Run Impacts of Same-Race Teachers," *IZA Institute of Labor Economics: Discussion Paper Series*, March 2017, IZA DP No. 10630, accessed online June 5, 2019, https://www.iza.org/publications/dp/10630.

11. Abolitionist Teaching Network, www.abolitionistteachingnetwork.org, accessed online September 27, 2020; Black Lives Matter at School, www.blacklivesmatteratschool.com, accessed online September 24, 2020. See also Syreeta McFadden, "Black Lives Matter Just Entered Its Next Phase," *The Atlantic*, September 3, 2020, accessed online September 24, 2020, https://www.theatlantic.com/culture/archive/2020/09/black-lives-matter-just-entered-its-next-phase/615952; Taylor Lorenz and Katherine Rosman, "High School Students and Alumni and Using Social Media to Expose Racism," *New York Times*, June 16, 2020, accessed

online September 27, 2020, https://www.nytimes.com/2020/06/16/style/blm-accounts-social-media-high-school.html; Georgia Chen, "Thousands Hear Montclair High School Students Share Experience with Racism at Unity Walk," *Baristanet*, June 8, 2020, accessed online September 24, 2020, https://baristanet.com/2020/06/thousands-hear-montclair-high-school-students-share-experience-with-racism-at-unity-walk.

INDEX

For the benefit of digital users, indexed terms that span two pages (e.g., 52–53) may, on occasion, appear on only one of those pages.

Note: Page numbers followed by *f* indicate a figure on the corresponding page.